Voices of the Indian Diaspora

VOICES OF
THE INDIAN DIASPORA

ANAND MULLOO

MOTILAL BANARSIDASS PUBLISHERS
PRIVATE LIMITED • DELHI

Dedication

To my late father, Jayram, who loved India

'Where the mind is without fear;
The head is held high...'
R. Tagore

First Indian Edition : Delhi **2007**
Earlier Published in Mauritius, 2004 by Imagepoint Publications

ISBN: 81-208-3197-7

MOTILAL BANARSIDASS
41 U.A. Bungalow Road, Jawahar Nagar, Delhi 110 007
8 Mahalaxmi Chamber, 22 Bhulabhai Desai Road, Mumbai 400 026
203 Royapettah High Road, Mylapore, Chennai 600 004
236, 9th Main III Block, Jayanagar, Bangalore 560 011
Sanas Plaza, 1302 Baji Rao Road, Pune 411 002
8 Camac Street, Kolkata 700 017
Ashok Rajpath, Patna 800 004
Chowk, Varanasi 221 001

Photo - Sew Chummun, Immigrant No. 356214, from village Boharee, Dhanapore, U.P. 1872.

PRINTED IN INDIA
BY JAINENDRA PRAKASH JAIN AT SHRI JAINENDRA PRESS.
A-45 NARAINA, PHASE-I, NEW DELHI 110 028
AND PUBLISHED BY NARENDRA PRAKASH JAIN FOR
MOTILAL BANARSIDASS PUBLISHERS PRIVATE LIMITED,
BUNGALOW ROAD, DELHI 110 007

CONTENTS

ACKNOWLEDGMENTS

I AM grateful to you, Bijaye Madhoo, who, on the occasion of the celebration of the First Pravasi Bharatiya Divas, P.B.D. 7 -9 January, 2003, New Delhi, suggested that I should write a book on the Indian Diaspora. This started the research process. I have referred to Indian press reports and reviews on the Conference and for which I would like to express my gratitude. I am grateful to Dr Bissoon Chummun, grand-son of immigrant Chummun, for supplying me the materials about his family background, around which the whole book has developed.

I was further encouraged in this venture by Dr Nandini Bhautoo Dewnarain, the University of Mauritius, who supplied me with a lot of materials and suggestions and also to N. Raya for his suggestions, and to Deven Maulloo for his assistance.

The writing of this book has been made easy thanks to the use of previous research materials I had made into the history of Mauritius since the early 1960's and the unpublished writings, including *Problems of Our Modern Society*, which I have updated for the purpose of this book.

I am particularly grateful to the wonderful Quad team including Mrs. Roshni Namah and Mr. Suhail Ahmadi in doing the page layout and to my son Sanjiv and my daughter Achala in seeing the book through. I would also like to thank Dr. Thomas Abraham, Chairman of GOPIO International for the foreword and its launching in Mumbai, P.B.D, Jan 2005.

My warm gratitude to my Mauritian friend residing in Sweden, Dr Jagdish Bhanpersad Jhowry, research scientist, Chalmers University of Technology, Götenberg, Sweden, for his deep insights into science, philosophy, Indian Culture and religion.

Email: elfbj@elmagn.chalmers.se.

Special acknowledgment is due to my friend, Dhaneshwar Sarjua of Conserverie Sarjua and particularly to the Hindu Entrepreneurs Association, Mauritius, for their valuable contributions.

FOREWORD

VOICES OF THE DIASPORA is a marvelous collection of the contemporary and historical experiences of the Indian Diaspora in different parts of the world. It reveals the accomplishments, the issues and problems faced by overseas Indians. The book also uncovers the potential of the 22 million People of Indian Origins for development in India as well as the countries with large Indian population. It indicates some of the reasons which have so far held back the NRIs and PIOs from actively pursuing investments and business opportunities in India.

Quoting several world leaders, Anand Mulloo shows what lies ahead of India on its way to becoming a world power. He maps out the need for leadership with vision, for social infrastructure, for work culture, education, individual and social responsibility.

Anand Mulloo has taken it upon himself to do an extensive research into the Diaspora by travelling around, collecting information and interviewing people. Very few people can do it. I want to compliment him on doing such a thorough job.

The author highlights the importance of networking the Indian Diaspora, based on the objectives and accomplishments of the Global Organization of People of Indian Origins (GOPIO) He shows how the tradition of openness of the global Indian family goes back to the Vedas, the mother of religions and philosophies.

In the wake of the Government of India's High Level Committee report, media accounts and other studies on the diaspora, Anand Mulloo has provided the best update on political situations and issues in countries such as Fiji, Trinidad and Tobago, Guyana and others. He talks about the implications and advantages concerning the PIO Card and Dual Citizenship.

The writer analyses the causes of success and failures of the Indian Diaspora in the countries of their adoption. He explains why Overseas Indians have been more successful in western countries than in certain developing countries. He advocates closer community relationships in order to ensure PIO success as a whole.

The book covers a detailed description of the migration of Indians overseas since ancient times and particularly during the last two centuries. It offers us a good comparison of the similarities and differences between the earlier Diaspora, termed (PIOs) and the newer immigrants (termed NRIs). The author describes in depth the history of Overseas Indians, their trials and tribulations in settling down, growing up in a new environment, their contributions as well as their relationships with other Diaspora communities, African, Anglo-Saxon, Chinese, French within the host countries.

Voices of the Diaspora is a must book for business entrepreneurs, students, academicians, historians, community activists, philanthropists, diplomats, both Indian and PIO political leaders and all those interested to know more about the 22 million PIO communities settled in more than 160 countries. It is a valuable contribution to the growing literature on Diaspora Studies.

Dr Thomas Abraham
Chairman, GOPIO International,
Stamford, Connecticut, USA,
12 November 2004.

INTRODUCTION

VOICES OF THE DIASPORA lends a voice to the 20 Million PIOs and NRIs spread in 125 countries speaking more than 20 languages, professing all the major religions of the world and reflecting the global society. For too long, the voices of the diaspora have gone unheard and their stories have remained unsung. The Indian Immigrants and their descendants have gone through a variety of historical experiences and sacrifices which need to be told so that we remember their sufferings and services, disappointments and hopes and draw the necessary lessons. We have to understand them and remain faithful to those lessons in order to ensure a better future for the diasporic children.

In a bid to articulate the voices of the repressed people, we have ventured across untrodden paths, left unexplored by many writers and historians. This book throws light on some of the controversies, failures and merits of the diaspora, including their social, cultural, religious, psychological, economic and political orientations, threats and aspirations.

Here, to give an insider's view of the Diaspora, we shall take up the story of an Immigrant family and follow up its journey across times. And while firmly grounded in real life situations, enlivened with stray biographical and historical details in chronological and thematic order, it outlines the diasporic similarities and differences in a comparative perspective. It addresses our broader diasporas - their social, cultural, religious and political organisations, their aspirations, their challenges, their shortcomings, their contributions and their achievements- with a few probing questions and insights thrown in.

It covers the historical movements which have shaped the diaspora, including the legacies of slavery, indenture, colonialism, assimilation, domination, subordination, marginalisation, resistance, decolonisation, Cold War, struggle against Apartheid and the new disaporic awarensess. Underlying it all is a deep spiritual message, the same that sustained the human spirit against all the overwhelming odds during the trying days of early immigration.

It maps out the diasporic space within which the issues of ethnicity, identity, racism, culture, class and power relations are played out in the daily lives of Indian immigrants scattered around the globe. It unfolds the context in which the Indian diaspora has collided, enmeshed with, resisted the British, French, Black and Chinese diasporas and how a transformed Indian diaspora is being constructed. The study of Indian diaspora in its relations to other diasporas enables us to take on board the burning issues of racial conflicts, religious wars, political strife, ethnicity, gender, sexuality, cultural, economic, social, political and psychological interconnections.

In the process, we shall adopt a multi-disciplinary approach, and spice the narrative with some of the concepts, data, findings. methods, theories and tools pouring from many disciplines, including anthropology, economics, history, geography, journalism, literature, politics, sociology and refer to the works of scholars in these fields. This book provides the intellectual framework for a deeper understanding of the diaspora.

We shall have to deal with the interrelationships of the dynamic forces of education, economic development, trade opportunities and networking and the past, the present and future of global Indian communities. Some of these issues have now been dragged from under the carpet so that we can see ourselves face to face, with our plus and minus points, in the social and historical mirror. The debate is now open. Our aim is not only to foster self-awarenesss and awareness of our inter-personal relations within our diasporas but also to provide the necessary tools for academicians, leaders, legislators, media people and all those concerned with PIOs and NRIs to reflect on these issues and take the necessary actions

This book is a rallying call to us all, the children of Mother India, to believe in ourselves, in our collective destiny and to draw inspiration from our glorious cultural and civilizational heritage. It demolishes the myths, the misunderstandings and prejudices which have held us back in the past. Its central message is to take a fresh look at the emerging new India, the awakening giant and superpower- seen from a self-critical, realistic but optimistic perspective. At the same time, it does not shy away from exposing our limitations which historically stemmed from the sub-continent. The idea is to face up to our waeknesses, take the necessary corrective measures and move forward. Briefly put, the book proposes a complete turn-around, a shift of emphasis from the traditional Euro-centric to a dynamic, self-confident Indo-centric approach.

This saga of the Indian diaspora and - in many respects a success story- spearheaded by the Global Organization of People of Indian Origins, GOPIO, has won global recognition. It is celebrated every 9th January during the Pravasi Bharatiya Divas, in India. It is now garnered as a precious part of the global Indian consciousness. In some way, this book tells us about our dynamic and fast changing Diaspora, what Mother India expects of her children overseas and what is expected of her.

By NRI is meant Non-Resident Indians who may happen to be first generation migrants in western or Gulf countries while PIO refers to Persons of Indian Origins, the descendants of the NRI or second, third and successive generations of Indian Immigrants. In other words, today's NRIs may become tomorrow's PIOs.

But first of all, we have to contextualise the diasporic issues. We need to know who the PIOs and NRIs are, where they come from, their diversity, something about their history, their geography, economics and politics, their cultural base and their relations both to their host countries, to other diasporas and to the homeland, India. Among other concerns, we shall look into the Immigration laws, the problems of the preservation of their culture, language, religion and ethnicity in the face of assimilation, domination and race relations.

We shall review their family life, their cultural, social and religious activities and their political participation and unearth any human rights problems. We shall also consider their main occupations, contributions, problems and achievements.

We shall also explore their internal relations with other sub-ethnic groups within the Indian community as well as with other ethnic or racial groups and see how they compare and contrast with other diasporas within their countries of adoption

What are their vast ramifications, their varied needs and expectations and their potential as well as the complex and diverse multi-cultural societies within which they operate? These and other issues are explored in Voices Of The Diaspora

Anand Mulloo

1

THE EMERGING GLOBAL INDIAN FAMILY

SPREAD GLOBALLY across 6 continents and 110 countries, the Indian Diaspora is 20 million strong with an annual income averaging $160 billion. They do not make a monolithic body as they diverged from different parts of India, speaking more than 22 different languages, left at different times, under different conditions for different reasons. The first group features the older diaspora in Sri Lanka, Malaysia, Nepal, Myanar, Malaysia and Singapore. The second group, starting from 1835 to 1920, moving in successive waves of indentured labourers, 1.5 million, poured into the plantation colonies of Mauritius (453,063), Reunion, Trinidad (143,934), Guyana (238,979), South Africa, Kenya, Suriname and Fiji (60,000). The result is that Indians formed majority only in Mauritius but minorities in Fiji, Guyana, Surinam, Trinidad and South Africa. The labour diaspora was generally followed by free Immigrants, mainly Sindhi and Gujarati traders and jewellers.

The third group, after World War II, mainly of individuals and families of professionals, doctors, engineers and technocrats heading towards industrial countries like Britain, Canada, Australia, European countries and USA, including the twice migrants from Mauritius, Trinidad, Tobago, Fiji, Guyana, Suriname and East Africa. Finally, we have another expatriate group of Gulf NRI's. The celebration of the Pravasi Bharatiya Divas every 9th January in India marks the confluence and the coming of age of a new, resurgent India recognising and embracing its children across the seas, all the People of Indian Origin, PIOs and the Non-Resident Indians, NRIs.

This is the privileged occasion to get to know one another,

keep the dialogue going, celebrate their achievements and build strong bridges to link the Diaspora into a powerful network. It is the forum where PIOs and NRIs :-

(i) circulate information,

(ii) ventilate their grievances ,

(iii) mobilise diaspora opinion in a bid to break the past isolation responsible for so much injustice and abuse of human rights on Indians,

(iv) solve problems and

(v) demonstrate greater India's concern for the welfare and security of Indians overseas- as has never been done before.

But equally important, the PIOs and NRIs have done India proud and cast a new aura .around the global Indian. The pravasis are also seen as channels to improve relations between India and their host countries. Briefly, the **event** strengthens the umbilical bond between the pravasis and India, the motherland of us all. It helps us to rediscover our common, inclusive Indianness-

THE SILICON Valley millionaires, IT, financial, professional, technocratic, business and academic NRIs have improved the image of India abroad. Initially, in the eighties, fingers were pointed at the emigrants towards UK and USA as deserting Bharat and pushing ahead for their own benefits after having benefited from subsidised education, thus bleeding their country of brain drain. But since the onset of economic liberalisation, globalisation, the IT boom, large incomes, easier facilities for foreign travels and investments as well as the inflow of foreign remittances which helped India through its difficult moments in the 1990's, the brain drain is now perceived as brain gain. It is now expected that more foreign direct investments could be brought in than the current $14 billion from their foreign remittances. It happens to be the single largest contributor to India's foreign exchange reserves. In a bid to attract their investments, the Indian government is now bringing the Diaspora together and is exploring new ways of shelving the restrictions and providing special facilities to PIOs and NRIs, including the grant of PIO cards.

The PIOs have brought new technologies and businesses by investing in core sectors of the economy, by contributing to India's foreign reserve, by helping in areas of education, health and charitable activities. The NRIs and PIOs have contributed to the building of a glittering image of India abroad and they feel bound to India by the umbilical cord of history, culture, tradition, social and economic ties.

(Dr Thomas Abraham, Chairman of GOPIO at GOPIO Convention, N.D.Jan.2004)

The beneficiaries of world class education from Indian pedigree institutes, the knowledge entrepreneurs have shown lots of guts, ideas and initiatives. They have made a whole world of difference to the thought process of India, giving it tremendous self-confidence and infusing it with a combative spirit. At first, they had thought that they could do it and - having done it- now they know -they have arrived! The story goes back to the Silicon Valley where, initially, the Indians worked in the American companies for some time when it dawned upon them that they could themselves set up their own business enterprises and earn much more. Soon, they brought over lots of other talented middle class Indians and after overcoming the initial obstacles of organisational hierarchies, they revealed great entrepreneurial and leadership skills. Sticking doggedly to their ideas, deploying strategies, they went on to reach great heights which they replicated back home. Side by side, they have set up a network of Business Process Outsourcing, BPO, operations in Bangalore, in Pune, Chennai, Hyderabad and New Delhi and in so doing they have conquered the world's imagination and are pushing New India ahead as a knowledge superpower.

It all adds up to prove that Indians have now realised that they are an intelligent and highly capable people. This means that they know their unique selling point, their constraints and they can bring their strengths to the fore. With every new success, their self-confidence has increased stemming from the knowledge that they are articulate, artistic, talented, creative, intuitive, practical and adaptable. They have proved their ability to depend on their own resources and to solve problems imaginatively. In overcoming problems, they never give up, they can go back, reverse the process and redo it. In the process of solving problems, the business leaders bring a unique combination of the heart, the mind and the soul. Indians have yet to make it to the top because of historical reasons but it is only a matter of time.

Gambling on Gulf

Besides, the 3.5 million NRIs in the Gulf countries, including its 5% professionals, 10% white collar workers and 85% skilled and semi-skilled workers, fetch an annual remittance averaging $7 billion. But these have to cope with different sets of restrictions- no family roots, no religious freedom, no human rights and no citizenship rights. Having no options, they have to send remittances back to India, mainly Kerala and Andra Pradesh, preferring to invest in properties, in the welfare of their children or in preparation for their retirement.

(*The Economic Times*. Mumbai, Feb, 2, 2003).

Driven by lack of job opportunities and low monthly income at home, compared to the alluring Rs. 25,000 in the Gulf, many Indians are tempted to sacrifice, beg, borrow- sell or mortgage their property and valuables, while some even run the risk of being swindled by their agents, in order to get to the Gulf Eldorado. Some are reported to have spent Rs.1.5 lakh for a job visa to the Gulf. Yet there are those who have spent one lakh and have been working in construction works in the torrid sun in the Gulf without having been paid for the past three months. According to the Centre for Development Studies census, 2003, 14 lakh migrant workers from Kerala, including 2.1 lakh women, are in the Gulf. These include 40% in Saudi Arabia while the Malappurram and Kozhidoke districts claim 49% Muslim migrants. The Gulf annnual remittances average Rs. 4,000 crore.

(C.Shamsher. *Sunday Times of India*. Pune. August 1, 2004)

The remittances sent by the South Indian work force go mainly into assisting their family members back home, in the construction of decent houses, in improving the quality of their lives and particularly in the education of the new generations. These are not really economically productive in the sense of pouring their savings into setting up new enterprises or into significant investments. The level of their wages, in most cases, is too low, averaging $200 per month for the hard construction labour they put up in the torrid sun. It shows tremendous sacrifices and determination to improve their lives and seek better opportunities abroad. Nevertheless, they go into the creation of future generations of educated middle class and from which the elite class of tomorrow may emerge.

The matter of human rights abuses, protecting expatriates and rescuing Indian women in distress caught in immoral trafficking racket is now being addressed by a helpline to be operated by the Consul General of India in Dubai, backed by New Delhi, according to *Gulf Today*, October 1, 2004.

Apart from the labour work force in the Gulf, the Indian business community, mainly Sindhis, are among the wealthiest and most successful NRI businessmen. This is to remind us that the Sindhis are the remote descendants of the trading community in the Indus Valley Civilization in Mohenjodaro and Harappa, excavated in 1924. The 1947 partition of India into Pakistan has dispersed the 600,000 Sindhi diaspora, then constituting 10% Hindus among the 90% Muslims. The refugees had to leave behind their billions dollars'worth of property and wealth, including schools, shops, the Karachi and Hyderabad airports developed by Sindhis, to spread into 100 countries. Having settled in the Gulf countries for generations, running their thriving commercial, business and professional enterprises, the Indians are also engaged in community service, in the preservation of their linguistic, cultural, social and religious heritage. Mr Vasu Shroff, the Sindhi philanthropist, has set up scores of Hindu temples, mainly in private places. The author was impressed with the close cultural and religious bonding, the satsangs and kirtans, celebrated among the north elitist Indian business communities, including Sindhis, Punjabis and Gujaratis, quite cut off from the majority working class South Indians.

Their major problem is political insecurity, the lack of citizenship rights and lack of permanent residence. They are at the mercy of the government. Unlike Singaporean Indians, they are unable to take serious business and investment decisions. They are forced to renew their visas every three years. This means that though some have erected large mansions and multi-storeyed business houses which they hold only on lease, the proprietary rights belong to the developers. Since they possess no free hold property, they are liable to lose their property on retirement. The unfortunate thing is that Abu Dabi is losing what it needs most, the highly skilled Dubai-born sons of Indian businessmen and professionals, educated in US, and who are driven to migrate to US and Canada in search of security.

Perhaps, this is understandable as the total UAE population averages 4 million, the locals constituting 25% or 300,000, Indians 40%, Pakistani and Philippines, 15% and the balance Europeans. The Gujaratis are mainly in jewellery and textile, while the Keralites form the bulk of the labour class., the Punjabis form an important business class. But under the pressure of globalisation, WTO and economic liberalisation, there are positive signs that the proprietary and citizenship issues may be addressed.

(Interview of Mr. Ramesh Lakhiani, October 2004)

Unlike what happens in the west, Indians feel very much at home in liberal places like Dubai where they have re-created another India, resonant with Hindi language, film songs, music, dances, food, products and entertainment. Hindi is a popular language in Dubai. The Arabs identify themselves with the Hindi language and Indian culture, as the Gulf Countries had long been maintaining close geographical, historical, commercial ties with the Peninsula.

Historically, the Arabs had been trading with India and China. After all, the Arabs had been acting as the intermediaries who had learnt from Indian civilization and passed on the learning to the west, including the numerals invented in India. The historical links were further reinforced under British colonialism when the British set up close India-Gulf links, strengthened by economic, commercial, cultural relations. Though India is further away than the 1200 miles distant Iran, it is Hindi which is the more popular and accepted and closer to Arabic than Irani language. This is reflected in the great popularity of Indian films and songs, an example of which is the song

April fool banaya to onko qussaya mera kya qussoor zamana see qussor yessni dastor banaya- of which April and fool are English, *banaya, qussaya, qussor, dastor, banaya* are Arabic while *onko, ya, mera, kya, see, yessni* are Hindi..

Indian films took the Middle East by storm since 1968 when they hit Cairo and the Egyptians began to hum and sing Indian songs, though they were foreign to Indian cultural background. The Indian songs had an instinctive appeal to the Arabs as well as to the Central Asians, in Tashkent. Films like *Around the World*, *Ganga Jamuna*, *An Evening in Paris* and songs like *buddha mil gaya* have haunted the Arab hemisphere. The cultural closeness makes the Arabs more Indo-centric than Euro-centric since they feel totally at home in India while they feel they are laughed at and rejected by the west.

Given the size and potential of the Indian and Chinese populations, they can overwhelm the world in the supply of cheap quality goods. Dr Al Shamsi believes that if India were to combine its immense natural and human resources with the Gulf countries, based on the historical, cultural, linguistic links, the synergy could be unbeatable in the creation of a strong nation. He says that labour is very expensive in the west and that it is more economical for a Briton to bring over a house painter from India to do the job than actually employing British labour. Further he finds the *lungi*, the *dhoti* as simple and convenient as the *kandura*, male Arab dress- both of which hide class and caste differences and are not subject to fashion fads. The simplicity of the traditional dress may hide the calibre and status of the wearer. He is looking forward to investing in Cochin, a green land of rivers, inhabited by sub-standard fishermen but which can emerge as a very rich land of opportunities once it is made a freeport. Another thing which strikes him is Indian food which has the quality, the taste, the flavour to conquer the world provided Indians improve its productivity and quality control and market it world-wide.

(Interview of Dr Mohamed Al Shamshi, Dubai, Oct. 2004).

But it was oil and transportation, the Dubai Creek, shipping, the international airport, free port, shopping and the transformation of Dubai into a sports city that lifted Dubai and gave it an upper hand on Bombay which once reigned as the star city of the East. As a matter of fact, it was the Soviet-style Regulation Raj, the Industrial Licensing Act of 1951, the Industrial Policy Resolution of 1956 under Nehru and Indira Gandhi which hounded and harassed entrepreneurs. Yet those very rare birds, with their 5000 years of experience and skills in trading and who generated the national wealth, large-scale employment and taxation felt they were not valued by the state which needed them most. When the socialist government persisted in favouring the over-protected, uncompetitive, nationalised as well as certain private industries, many of the Sindhis felt it was time to set up shops abroad, particularly in Dubai.

Until the 1990's, it was the bureaucracy which decided on the quantum of production, did the price fixing and judged on the quality of production when they themselves had not the least clue about business. Worse still, small scale industries, a major source of employment and consumer growth, was penalised because the government was prejudiced against the entrepreneurial class. Doing best elsewhere what they could not do in India, the Sindhi NRIs had helped turn Dubai into the shopping centre which lured other Indians who grabbed at the Japanese-made synthetic saris with Indian designs. Thus India, still stuck to its out-moded cotton saris, lost its edge over the textile business. The generous subsidies on export, heavy import duties and protection had smothered Indian industrial productivity. Instead of boosting production, employment and export, government's protectionist policies only served to encourage contraband, smuggling, corruption, bureaucracy and a thriving *hawala* business. While India had tied its own hands and feet in economic stagnation, it had helped in the creation of new potential competitors in Dubai, Singapore, Malaysia and Korea. Not satisfied with the second-rate, shoddy home-made industrial products, Indians had developed a craze for foreign products, particularly Japanese electronic goods. (Ram Buxani, *Taking the High Road*. Motivate Publishing. Dubai. 2003).

Taking a leaf from Dubai, Japan, Singapore, Mauritius or the

Scandinavian countries, India has yet to open its economy and set up free port in places like Cochin or Goa, and turn them into tourist havens, complete with attractive hotels, shopping arcades, waterfronts, water sports, airports and modern infrastructure. The peninsula is endowed by nature with a long, gorgeous, palm-fringed coastline, criss-crossed by rivers and forests, the envy of the world and of the desert people of Dubai and Oman who, on landing, fell on their feet and acclaimed *Kerala* as God's gift. The name is derived from Arabic, *ker*, meaning gift and *Allah*, God. Then the maritime Arabs got busy hacking the precious teak wood to develop a thriving boat building industry which still holds out vast scope for greater development. Little Mauritius, endowed with only a fraction of the Indian coastline but driven by visionary entrepreneurs, has turned itself into a tourist paradise, luring more tourists than the subcontinent itself.

Therefore, India has everything to make it a great maritime and fishing nation of the world and it cannot afford to throw away such opportunities. It cannot afford to go on sending millions of its citizens to toil in the Gulf when employment and economic opportunities are lying untapped in Kerala. It has to turn its gaze to the sea and its harvests. Overcoming its ignorance, prejudices and superstitions against crossing the black waters, the dreaded *kalapani*, the new knowledge-based India has yet to apply its best brains and urge its new breed of entrepreneurs to go out, develop fishing, tourism and a commercial free-port. The sub-standard, traditional coastal fishermen need to be trained into professional, well-equipped fishermen, backed by a strong fish canning and processing industry. India has tremendous potential to develop its fishing industry on modern lines and thereby transform the economy of the coastal belt into a milk cow for its people.

According to Sarah Leah Whitson, director of Human Rights Watch, July 2004, Saudi Arabia with its 17 million people and 8.8 million Asians, is guilty of many abuses where the overworked Asian women are confined to cramped, crowded dormitories. Many have been sexually harassed and raped while the perpetrators got away scot-free.

The judicial system is biased against them. The HRW calls upon the Saudi government to stop isolating the workers and to cease the practice of imposing excessive penalties on them and to compensate the victims of human rights abuses. (Le Mauricien. July 15. 2004)

Saudi Arabia has now taken the right step to offer naturalization rights to the 1 million NRIs, mainly the professionals, who have stayed and worked continuously over the past ten years. It is expected that other countries in the Gulf region will emulate Saudi Arabia in granting naturalization rights for Indian expatriates over ten years' stay.

We've Arrived!

Anyway, the Diaspora is no longer seen as constituting only of the older PIOs, the grand children of indentured labourers who were once told by Nehru to forget about old India and to integrate into their countries of adoption. It can no longer be dismissed as a bad memory that anybody would prefer to forget. It is alive and has assumed a global historical presence. We have to ensure that the sufferings and sacrifices of the diaspora are cherished in our loving memory and that we learn the lessons of history. New India must lend its ears to the voices of the diaspora. The ever-expanding and strengthening diaspora prides itself of the millionaire NRIs in UK, US. Canada and Australia. And the diaspora cannot but revert from time to time to Mother India in a bid to recharge its emotional and spiritual batteries. So, why is it that after years of neglect and abandon, New India wakes up and decides to remember her forgotten children overseas?
It is difficult to digest the fact that Mother India had not been particularly attentive to the woes, the injustices, the atrocities, the crimes and violence, the rapes and thefts perpetrated on its defenceless sons and daughters by criminals and thugs in the Caribbeans as well as in Fiji. The children of the victims have been deeply hurt and disillusioned with the indifference of the motherland which had failed them in their hour of need. They keep asking-where were the Indian

voices, official and otherwise, the UN, the Indian journalists, media people, writers, professors, academicians and the public? Recently, however, there has been a dramatic shift in new India's attitude and commitment towards its children overseas. This is marked by the post-GOPIO and post-Pravasi Bharatiya Divas events which seem to signal that NRIs and PIOs can count on a nuclear and resurgent India to stand up and defend Indians under assault overseas.

55 years ago things were different. India had just emerged from centuries of imperialism. Pandit Nehru was faced with more urgent tasks and could not afford to worry about the fate of overseas Indians. Yet he took a firm posture in standing up against Apartheid South Africa. However, India was then staggering on its own legs. Communications was than in its infancy when Indians moved on ox-carts and bicycles and travelled overseas by ships while poverty was rampant and everything had to be done to rebuild India and feed its starving millions living under poverty line.

August 15 is the birthday of free India. It marks for her the end of an old era, the beginning of a new age. But it has a significance not only for us, but for Asia and the whole world; for it signifies the entry into the comity of nations of a new power with untold potentialities and which has a great part to play in determining the political, social, cultural and spiritual future of mankind. (Sri Aurobindo)

But since then, much water has flowed under the bridge, *zamana badal gaya, zindagi badal gayi.* We are now living in the space age, in a global village. The Cold War years are behind us. We now face the challenge of globalisation, of the I.T revolution, of fast travels and tourism, of global competition and we have seen how China has been racing ahead thanks to the contributions made by the Chinese diaspora. How can India be left behind in the face of global competition?

And then, born in 1989 in USA, the Global Organisation of People of Indian Origin, GOPIO, has set itself the objective to network the Indian diaspora solidly behind India, through mutually beneficial linkages, including the flow of investments, remittances and technology into India.

GOPIO can play an important role in channelling the varied resources of Indian communities from abroad towards the development of the countries in which they live, as well as towards India, through mutually beneficial linkages

(H.D.Deve Gowda, former PM, India, 4th World Convention of GOPIO, Mauritius, 23.8.96)

GOPIO has had a direct hand in making the Divas come about. More important still, by 2003, nuclear India feels self-confident enough to assume her new responsibilities and to signal to the whole world a more positive brand image of India:-we've arrived!.

It is felt that New India is now a strong and powerful nation which has emerged on the world stage. In fact, the pace and intensity of diplomatic activity in India reflects her new status in the world.

The India bashing and favourite western media projection of snake-charmer-poverty-ridden image has now changed into the hi-tech superpower. This fact has been highlighted by American President, George W Bush, at the White House, during a news conference on Nov., 2001, in the presence of Shri Atal Bihari Vajpayee, the former Indian P.M.

India has a fantastic ability to grow, because her greatest export is intelligence and brainpower...We are grateful that the world's most skilled workers want to come to the United States. Our technology edge rests on the contributions of immigrants from places like India, or China, Russia, Iran and hundreds of other countries.

(NY Times, Nov. 10, 2000, as cited in Motwani's *America and India.*)

India has openly reciprocated to all the offers of solidarity from overseas Indians during this historic welcoming speech when its Prime Minister highlighted our common identity and our Indianness while recognising that diversity is the hall mark of our society. He offered an open-arm welcome, a homecoming, to all the sons and daughters of

India across the globe back home. *Bharat ma ke beton ka hai Bharat mein satkar, jab jab ji chahey tab aa jana sada khulen hai* (the children of Bharat are held in high honour in India, you may return any time, our doors are always open). (The Hindu, 10.1.03)

But has India really arrived? In that first flurry of excitement, we shouldn't forget that India is dragging its feet behind China and unless India proceeds with further economic reforms and attracts foreign direct investments, like China, the gap between these two Asian giants is likely to increase enormously to China's advantage. And economically the average Indian is miles behind the average westerner. Compare the $25,000 per capita income in USA or Singapore with the meagre $600 in India, the $4,000 in Mauritius and the road already covered by China. Measure the gap between the 1% super rich in India and the smallness of its 2% middle class (which is fast increasing though), 5% lower middle class with the 90 % + proletariat as compared with the Scandinavian countries with 1% super rich, 40%-50% middle class and the more balanced 50% working class. India could be said to have really arrived it if can raise its middle class bracket to a minimum of 20% and bring down its working class to a minimum of 70% and scale down or control the size of its population.

As it is, the process of economic growth is not reaching down to the 80% Indian peasant villagers who are largely deprived of the basic infrastructure of modern civilization-safe water, electricity, housing, roads, communications, education, health facilities.- though much effort is being made to reach this goal The villagers are still entrapped into the hands of extortionists and money-lenders. They have little spending capacity and are not really active economically and since they cannot afford to spend they do not generate economic activity. In return, there is little employment creation and less productivity and with less productivity there is less spending which goes on in a vicious circle of poverty. Rural backwardness has to be tackled immediately and simultaneously in a comprehensive manner, because India cannot afford to wait for wealth creation to trickle down at its own snail's pace into the villages.

However, unlike China which, at the very start, development in education and health happened before economic development, India has failed to deliver on both strategic counts. India should have democratised educational and health facilities- which should have been the real engines of overall growth within a comprehensive development programme. Had more emphasis been placed on education, there would have been a wider spectrum of talents, resources and opportunities available which would have expanded into the world and would have made India really shine from all sides. While avoiding the dogma, this is the lesson the other states can pick up from the successful experience of Kerala which primarily focused on education and which paid off handsomely as it transformed the nature of society itself from bottom-up. At least, this is also the little lesson which Mauritius could offer. From the early 1950's, Dr Seewoosagur Ramgoolam had focused on education and health as the twin pillars in the construction of his Welfare State and of economic development.

Economic development cannot be seen as a piecemeal approach. The reforms process cannot be allowed to touch specific sectors at the expense of other neglected sectors. The capital market should be broadened to allow more people to enter the market economy. The big challenge is to lift the rural population from poverty stagnation, raise their level of productivity and economic activity, open up fresh avenues for upward mobility and get them moving into an upward spiral. (Interview of Prof. Amartya Sen on NDTV, 26 July 2004)

Home and Away from Home

Earlier, on 6 Jan. 2001, in his inaugural speech on the occasion of the 6th GOPIO Convention, Vigyan Bhawan, New.Delhi, Shri Vajpayee had said:- :"*You are as much the inheritors of India's rich civilisational heritage as your brothers and sisters back home in India.*" This was an important statement as both the Indian nationals and the overseas Indians are put on the same level. The sense of strangeness, alienation and long separations has been wiped out in the age of globalisation, IT and instant communications. It's a recognition that all Indians - both from home and away from home- are equally embedded in the same rich civilisation. The time has come to forge new bonds of solidarity to link the global Indian family of one billion Indians and its 20 millions PIOs strongly behind their common identity and their Indianness.

India recalled their contributions in South Africa under Mahatma Gandhi, the Indian League in UK and the Gadar Movement in USA to India's struggle for independence, the support provided by PIOs and NRIs during the economic liberalisation and structural reforms. India is proud of the successful Indian entrepreneurs abroad, the I.T professionals of the Silicon Valley and all the PIOs and NRIs who have enriched the society, the economy and culture of their adopted countries.

"What we seek is a broader relationship- in fact, a partnership among all children of Mother India so that our country can emerge as a major global player. We value the role of People of Indian Origin as unofficial ambassadors providing a link between India, and the rest of the world"(Shri Vajpayee, GOPIO Magazine, 12 Jan.2003, N.D)

Under the long Nehru-Gandhi dynasty, India had entertained the wrong perception of the NRIs then considered as traitors, as foreigners and as outcastes. See what has happened to the Indians in South Africa who had been completely cut off from India due to Nehru's embargo on Apartheid. Deprived of academic and cultural contacts with the motherland, feeling uprooted, a large proportion of the young Indians in South Africa had strayed away from their cultural roots and had been assimilated into western and Christian civilization.

The Diaspora is important for India.

Besides, travelling or migrating abroad was officially banned and the Indian traveller was allowed the ridiculous $ 5/ as expenses. This restrictive measure- which fitted in with the traditional prejudice against travelling abroad- quite effectively clamped down on Indian emigration at a time when the Chinese, Japanese, Jews were pouring out across the globe, mainly in the US, Canada and Australia.. The position of the NRIs was further complicated by the indifference and ignorance of the insular and parochial Indian media.

The Indian image of the NRI, stoked by media and globs of misplaced envy and scorn, is seen as that of a traitor who has left home for greed and should be isolated rather than espoused.

(Ram Buxani, 2003).

Treated as unwanted, unwelcome, Not-Required Indians, fleeced at home and doubly taxed, the NRIs did not interact with India until after the 1980's. Nevertheless, a few visionary Indians like Swaraj Paul, Karan Billmoria, the CEO of Cobra Beers in UK, left India with nothing- except the precious Indian cultural values- and have worked their way up . "*Today they are millionaires, they give jobs to thousands of Europeans and pay huge amounts of taxes to these countries*", said GOPIO President, Inder Singh. This is apart from the 61 NRI millionaires in the US.

In this global competitive race, India is trailing far behind China which had the vision to open its doors far earlier to overseas Chinese so that today,

(i) overseas Chinese investments account for half the yearly $48 bn foreign investments flowing into China.:-

(ii) Chinese trade with the EU is six times that of India,

(iii) France is playing the Chinese card and is using China as a strategic economic alliance and as a counterweight against the US.

(iv) According to a recent study made by Goldman Sachs, by 2020, China's economy will have surpassed all of today's economic giants. By 2050, it will hit the $55 trillion mark, ahead of US, $33 trillion and India $22 trillion.

The Silicon Valley teems with Indian super-achievers. Yet it is the successful NRIs and PIOs who have brought credibility, respectability and a brand name to the image of New India today. Indian students in the west have contributed to the emancipation of India, to its economy through the inputs of high technology, the Green Revolution and the Information and Communications Technology.

Indians have distinguished themselves abroad in different fields, including politics. Seven Indian MP's are today sitting in the Canadian House of Commons while three Indian MP's are in the British House of Commons. Indians have been Prime Ministers and Presidents in Mauritius, Guyana and Trinidad. The Speaker in the South African Parliament has been a distinguished PIO. Dalipsing Saund was the first Asian to serve as a Congressman in the US for three terms, in the 1950's and 60's.

(Inder Singh, President GOPIO International in the Hindustan Times, 6th October 2004)

Today, recognizing their merits and contributions, the current Minister of Overseas Indians Affairs, Shri Jagdish Tytler has, during the 4th October Brussels Business Conference, called upon the NRIs and PIOs to contribute ideas in making Indian education world-class, in tourism, investments, financial services and infrastructure. Urged the Minister,

"let us work together to involve you in India's growth"

India has to be forward-looking. It has to give up its past third world mentality and start assuming the garb of the prospective super-power and all the responsibility that goes with this new status.

The Indian world has been changing dramatically in the wake of:- globalisation, IT technology, economic development and liberalisation, improved infrastructure, the emergence of an expanding and enterprising educated middle class, increasing foreign travels, Indian investments abroad, an enlarging diaspora overseas, a new PIO awareness, and particularly after the holding of the PBD. 7-9 Jan. 2003. Hopefully, the Indian mind sets have changed alongside towards a better understanding of the NRIs and PIOs, who are now seen as conferring credibility and respectability to the brand image of New India.

GOPIO
Global Organisation of People of Indian Origin

Providing a forum to foster fellowship and networking

But how did GOPIO come about? In January-March, 1989, Dr Jagat Motwani was deputed by the National Federation of Indian American Associations, NFIA, to visit 10 South East Asian countries and India to inform them of the NFIA's intention of launching GOPIO. Other NFIA officials, Dr Thomas Abraham, Sudha Acharya, Niraj Baxi, Ram Gadhvi, Ramesh Kalicharan, Sharad Metha, Inder Singh, Suresh Singh, Dhiraj Solanki and others covered other countries of North America, Europe and the Caribbean. The GOPIO pioneers were stunned by the similarities and differences in the life-styles of overseas Indians, -including their economic conditions, inter-ethnic relations, and political involvement. These visits gave rise to a rich crop of studies and publications on the PIO subject.

Subsequently, in September 1989, the First Global Convention of People of Indian Origin met in New York. Dr Thomas Abraham was the convener, assisted by five co-conveners, Mrs Sudha Acharya, Mr Ram Gadhavi, Dr Jagat Motwani, Mr Sureshwar Singh, and Mr Dhiraj Solanki. The Convention was attended by 26 countries, including Fiji, New Zealand, Trinidad and Tobago, Guyana, Suriname, Jamaica, Hong Kong, Philippines, Indonesia, Japan Malysia,, Singapore, Thailand, South Africa, Mauritius, Canada, United Kingdom, and other European countries. 23 major resolutions were adopted covering common issues in relation to India and human rights violations of PIOs in different countries, particularly of Indo-Fijians.

One of its major decisions was the setting up of GOPIO with the sole objective of bringing together the PIOs of the world and giving them a sense of oneness and togetherness. Dr Thomas Abraham was elected its first president, a post to which he was re-elected during the 2nd Convention in New Delhi in 1993 and in Zurich in 2000. GOPIO organized the Third Global Indian Entrepreneurs Conference in September 2002 along with the Indian and NRI/PIO Economic Summit in New York in September 2002. Since then, GOPIO has been setting up its chapters in major cities of different countries.

Since the Zurich Convention, Dr Motwani has been pressing for the creation of the following three entities,

1. Global Federation of Indian Chambers of Commerce and Industry
2. Global PIO Bank on a World Bank model to enable PIOs to lend money to other PIOs who need money for economic progress.
3. Global PIO Journal.

According to Motwani, Dr Thomas Abraham has made history by co-ordinating Indian ethnic organisations, at all levels- local, city, regional and international. He started with Columbia's University Indian Club to FIAs and then to NFIA to land finally in GOPIO. He has vision, dedication, commitment, organisational skills and untiring crusade.

(Dr Jagat K Motwani, *America and India in a Give & Take Relationship*, N.Y, 2003)

The GOPIO constitution was drafted and reviewed at several Steering Committee Meetings and further reviewed at the 2nd GOPIO Convention held in Paris in 1992. The GOPIO Charter and Constitution were adopted at the 3rd GOPIO Convention held in Montreal in 1994 by the General Assembly which authorised the then President to register GOPIO International in Montreal.

GOPIO is a non-partisan, not-for-profit, secular global organization promoting the well being of the PIOs. It enhances co-operation and communication among Indians living in different countries. It was born out of a desire to fight issues, among others, pertaining to human rights violations of PIOs.

GOPIO sets out, among other objectives:-

(I) To connect PIOs into a solid network through co-operation and communications.

(II) To promote the common Indian cultural heritage and thereby create a binding relationship.

(III) To mobilize financial, intellectual and professional resources of Indians abroad for their mutual development.

(IV) To provide a forum at periodical intervals to discuss, debate and decide on common problems and issues facing groups of Indians abroad and initiate measures to redress their grievances.

(V) To further the interaction between PIOs and other communities at global level in promoting world peace, progress and ecological harmony.

It is backed by its 20 country GOPIO chapters.

An example is GOPIO France, founded 8th March 1990. B.B. 215-75226 Paris Cedex 05. Ph: (33. 1) 45 91 20 63.

Its objectives:-

(1) To reinforce and develop the Franco-Indian ties in various fields: cultural, education, scientific, religion, social, political, commercial, tourism, investment, Human Rights, twinings of cities and in the economic sectors.

(2) To act as an umbrella organization with various associations both French & Indian in France & French Territories.

(3) To achieve these aims through exchanges, publications, conferences, seminars, meetings, religious activities, fashion shows, exhibitions, ceremonies and festivals, training courses, sports, club events, pilgrimages, film projections etc.

What can you do? You can mobilise the intellectual and material resources of the NRIs and PIO in order to :

(1) discuss and solve specific problem areas, interact with India, the governmental and NGOs in your country, and in India in order

(2) to promote better PIOs' conditions in the fields of education, sciences, culture, business; raise their social and economic status, the status of women and

(3) you can foster better understanding of PIOs about India both in your country and in various other countries.

Either join your existing GOPIO chapter or help in the setting up of a GOPIO chapter running on similar lines to those of Rotary International, instilling a culture of service among PIOs worldwide. To do so, contact and affiliate with GOPIO International.

It runs regular biennal GOPIO International Conventions, national conferences, publications, cultural exchanges, youth exchanges and conferences to network entrepreneurs. It has established six major GOPIO councils/ committees to promote specific objectives:- (1) Business Council, (2) Cultural Council, (3) Academic Council, (4) Philanthropic Council, (5) Human Rights Council and (6) GOPIO-GOI Liaison Committee. This is quite apart from the on-going dialogues, forums, held with senior government leaders and international organizations with a view to creating awareness of one global PIO community. It pursues a policy of unity in diversity designed to network the PIO community of diverse languages, above 20, and 7 religions and sub-ethnic identities spread over 125 countries through various means- electronic, publications, educational, business and an effective secretariat.

Let us join together to network the global NRI/PIO community to preserve and globalize Indian culture and heritage!

For further details, please contact:

GOPIO International
P.O.Box 1413, Stamford, CT 06904,USA
Tel: 818-708-3885
Email: GOPIO-INTL@sbcglobal.net
Website: www.gopio.net

Singhvi's HLC Report

Earlier, the report of the high level committee set up, in September 2000, by the Ministry of External Affairs, headed by L.M.Singhvi, former Indian high commissioner to the UK, had recommended that:- a three-day-annual-divas be celebrated in recognition of the outstanding economic, political, and philanthropic contributions made by the Indian Diaspora. In his report, Singhvi has listed 160 recommendations for a *"perfect partnership between India and the Indian diaspora"* The NRIs or Indian expatriates, having acquired wide-ranging expertise in education, health, science, technology could probably put their talents at work in India. The businessmen and traders could be attracted on terms which are not only sentimental or nostalgic but are solidly based on profits and safe returns on their investments. The report set out the 4 major objectives of the divas as

(a) to understand the sentiments of the NRIs and PIOs about India and create a policy framework for a sustained and productive interaction
(b) to acquaint the Indian people with the achievements of the Indian Diaspora and their expectations from India
(c) to create a network of the Indian Diaspora across 110 countries of the world
(d) to recognize the contributions made by the Indian Diaspora towards improving India's relationships with the host countries.

A Spoke-and Hub-Relationship

In his foreword to Motwani's book, *America and India in a Give & Take Relationship*, launched on the First Pravasi Bharatiya Divas, 9th Jan, 2003, Singhi describes the ties between India and the Diaspora as a spoke and hub relationship. It connects the diaspora globally with luminous and loving India at the heart of that relationship. Thanks to its Diaspora, the benefits of Indian civilization have reached all the corners of the world in a mutually enriching intellectual and cultural interaction within increasingly multi-cultural diversities.

Consequently, for the first time in history, in the wake of the Chinese, Greek, and Jewish Diasporas, in India, the 9th January is observed as Pravasi Bharatiya Divas. The first convention met on January 9-11, 2003 in New Delhi at the invitation of the Government of India in its desire to recognize their contributions and achievements in political and economic fields. India will celebrate every 9th day of January as Pravasi Bharatiya Divas. On the 9th January India's most famous Non-Resident Indian, Mahatma Gandhi, had returned to India from South Africa to lead our freedom struggle. Every year we hope to celebrate this day in a way that draws attention to our strong ties with People of Indian Origin and ensures their wide participation on this occasion

Ten Celebrated Global Indians

Ten of the outstanding overseas Indian achievers were awarded the Pravasi Bharatiya Pravasi Sammans, including:-

(i) Sir Anerood Jugnauth, P.M of Mauritius, 1982-95, 2000-2003, and guest of honour.

(ii) Sir Sridath Ramphal, former secretary general of the Commonwealth.

(iii) Prof. Fatima Meer from S. Africa and script writer of the film *The Making of the Mahatma* and one of the Top100 Women Who Shook South Africa, according to Femina, 1999.

(iv) Shri Rajat Gupta, managing director of Mckinsey world-wide since 1994.

(v) Mr Bob Naroomal Harilela, famous businessman of Hong Kong who started from scratch to head the Harilela Group of companies, including hotels, travel agencies, real estate, restaurants, seated in the stock exchange.

(vi) Lord Navnit Dholaka, of Waltham Brooks, West Sussex County and member of the House of Lords Appointments Commission.

(vii) Dato Seri S. Samy Velu, former president of the Malaysian Indian Congress and member of the House of Representatives of the Malaysian Parliament since 1974.

(viii) Mt Ujjal Dosanjh, the 33rd Prime Minister of British Columbia, Canada.
(ix) Dr Manu Chandaria, CEO of the Comcraft Group in Kenya involved in aluminium, computer hardware, plastics, software, and steel.
(x) Mr Kanakbhai Khemji of Oman.

The Ripple in the Pool

Shri L.K Advani, former Minister for Home Affairs, sees the Pravasi Divas celebration as signifying *the coming of age of India and also the coming of age of Indians outside India*. He urges the diaspora to achieve world class excellence in whatever field we are doing, as the more we use our talents and skills, the more we accomplish great heights, the greater is our service to India. The common endeavour is to make India a developed country by 2020. He adds that the convention is designed to help in building bridges across the Diaspora, strengthen PIO-NRI relations, international linkage, trade, cultural interaction and India's bilateral relations with their host countries. It takes up issues related to the Diaspora and widens their dimensions in a bid to keep the dialogue going on a permanent basis.

Sir V.S.Naipaul drops the little stone that will ripple in the pool of thought when he points out that India has failed to recognize the merits of its own people. He refers to the art historian Ananda K.Coomaraswamy who had spent his own family fortune travelling across India in the 1890's to collect rare Rajput paintings which he offered to but were turned down by the Benares Hindu University. Finally, he went to Boston University which gratefully accepted and preserved it. To this day, one can find Coomarasawmy's work in Boston, the work he had offered to India, but *India told him to go away*. However, the pravasi feels embarassed at the self-inflicted wounds caused by bureaucracy, casteism, corruption, inefficiency, and laziness still festering in modern India.

Taking a leaf from the Coomarasawmy's chapter, India could really *make its brand image shine across the world* if it sets out to encourage its vast pool of talented people in all fields:-- arts, writing, academic, sciences, technology, communications, business, sports to *reach world standards and radiate their talents and contributions globally*. Following what Japan did under the Meiji Restoration, and the Chinese example, India could link up with NRIs and PIOs and the many states where they are established in order to *develop and give recognition to* ***talents in various areas of excellence***. Apart from the NRIs in academic and technical fields doing India proud abroad, these great achievers in a wide variety of fields could be *India's real ambassadors,* provided they are given the scope and the necessary infrastructural facilities, back home. One example is sports and athletics which seem to have been neglected while top sportsmen could give India a new brand name. Despite entertaining privileged relations with Russia for over five decades, India has not profited in acquiring Russian skills and expertise in sports and athletics as China has done. Similarly, India will need to scan all leading countries in order to develop and diversify its basket of talents.

Take the example of Rajasthani-born Jaya Pachauri, kathak music teacher who has been adopted by Avignon Festival, in France. Popularly known as *la petite danseuse indienne d'Avignon*, Jaya is teaching kathak and giving performances on *Chintu la petite Indienne, Made in India*, *A dhoti for Bapu* (about Gandhi's life), *Meenakshi Trio* and enhancing the image of Indian arts and dances on various European stages. Jaya Pachauri is making ripples and - given the opportunity, why can't thousands of other Indians make it on the global stage? (Week-End, 5 Sept. 2004)

This brings out the relationship between the stay-at-home Indian, probably stuck in office work in India as compared to the more upwardly mobile NRI and PIO in other lands of opportunities. Preferably, it should be a relationship based on trust and mutual understanding. This becomes obvious when we compare the profiles of two friends, one Indian and the other a PIO, studying at the same Indian university and decades later we see the PIO graduate has scaled great heights in his career while his Indian counterpart has marked time in a frustrating environment. It is a reflection on India's query why the PIO is much more innovative, productive and successful abroad.

One of the thousands of the victims of red tapism is Dr Hari N. Harilela, recipient of the *Pravasi Bharatiya Samman* who narrated his experience to Hindustan Times of 10th January 2003. Starting from scratch after World War II, Harilela is now the business tycoon in China and Hong Kong where he owns a chain of Holiday Inn hotels. He said that he had made various attempts to expand into India but he had been debarred by red tapism:-

"I have been struggling to enter the Indian markets, but I have not been allowed to do so. The red tape has always posed a hitch. Today, if you want to do something in China, it can be done within a week. In India, it takes at least a couple of months, if not years". It looks like certain bureaucrats are still hugging to the hassle days of Regulation Raj.

Without going over the old sores of how the NRIs and PIOs have been mistreated by Indian nationals as undesirable, we expect the new Ministry of Overseas Indians Affairs to help repair old damages and make up for past mistakes. According to Ram Buxani, more than 2,000 NRIs applications for enterprises were stalled by short-sighted bureaucrats in a pillar-to-post runaround for licences and no-objection certificates.

This explains why India attracts a meagre $ 4 billion as foreign direct investments compared to the current $48 billion that flow into China, half of which flows from Chinese expatriates. In Europe, India accounts for just 1.6% of total EU imports of goods and 0.8% of import services while India attracts only 0.3% of EU world-wide investments. India stands in sharp contrast to the profiles of trade of other Asian countries with the EU, namely China, South Korea, Malaysia, Singapore etc. This shows vast scope for trade and investments.

However, it is now being realised that the Indian Diaspora, 20 million strong spread across 110 countries with an estimated combined income of $160 bn., is a huge asset in the creation of a global network and the building of economic bridges to assist both India and the host countries.

There has been no shortage of seminars and conferences about attracting FDIs from NRIs and multinationals over the last two decades. The latest of which, the NRI/PIO Business Networking for Trade and Investment and Contribution of Indian Diaspora in Europe, took place under GOPIO in Brussels, Belgium, 4 October 2004. What is required is a package of more economic reforms, infrastructure building, new legislation, changing mindsets and an openness to diasporic and global networking.

India - A Global Dynamo

In recognition of their achievements, the former Indian Prime Minister offered congratulations to:-

"The sons and daughters of India who have reached the pinnacle in so many fields of human endeavour overseas. The benchmarks for success which the Pravasi community have set are a challenge for us in India. They make us examine why the Indian is so much more innovative, productive and successful abroad than in his own country. They prod us to create a business, investment and economic climate which is conducive to success as anywhere else in the world. We are prepared to respond to your expectations from India. We would like to create an environment in India which will make you want to return, not just for sentimental or emotional reasons, but with the conviction that you can excel in this country as much as you can anywhere else in the world.

Indians who have chosen to settle abroad should be loyal to their country of adoption. The biggest challenge for every immigrant community is to integrate harmoniously into the political, economic and social life of the host society, while preserving and cherishing its civilizational heritage. Over the years, Indians have achieved the delicate balance virtually everywhere".

Backed by its rising foreign exchange reserve above $ 100 bn, the Indian government had promised to lift foreign currency restrictions. We are told that listed companies abroad and Indian corporations are permitted to acquire immovable property abroad. We are reminded that India-which has gone through a second great IT revolution- is the home of astrology, is set to be a health destination of the world. India is committed to growth and higher productivity, converting India's potential into a global dynamo and raise its share of foreign trade which is currently very low. The government had announced substantial imminent reforms to boost infrastructure, including ports, airports, and airlines, apart from the on-going highway projects.

The Divas is expected to chart out how the Diaspora can bring new technology and new investments into India, how to raise Indian productivity, Indian share of exports and the India brand and also what we should do to raise world perceptions of India.

But what is India? To Will Durant, the historian, it is *"India, the mother of us all"*. One cannot define India as simply a country since it has more inhabitants than Europe put together. It is a subcontinent which holds within itself a nucleus of the world- contrasting landscapes, the tallest Everest, snow-capped hills and icy cold mountains, rivers, fertile land, jungles, arid desert, torrid zones, people of diverse hues, customs, languages and religions. Prof. Asaratnam sees India not as Hindu, Moslem, Christian or Sikh India but as the continuity of its spiritual culture.

Former US President Bill Clinton added at India Today Conclave, March 2004:- *"The world cannot afford for India to be a pigmy. You have to be a giant, but you have to be the right kind of giant"*. Mindsets are fast changing. The shackling traditons of the past are being shed to make room for a new yearly elite of half a million engineers, a quarter million doctors pouring out at home and into the diaspora.

You have to be a Giant!

BILL CLINTON said it: India has to be a giant, that is, a right giant. It cannot be otherwise. If it fails to do so, it will be by its own fault. And all of us will feel let down. By all measurable standards, the sub-continent is a giant. It has a wide variety of climates, geographical and natural endowments, stretching from the Himalayan tops, across the flowing Ganges, fertile fields, desert, jungles, teeming cities, countless villages, gorgeous landscapes, flora and fauna and a long peninsular coastline. Its potential is limitless. It has a great culture and civilization. It has excelled in the art of religion, spirituality, philosophy, the arts, crafts, sculpture, decoration, music, songs, dances, theatre, movies, television, the media, advertising, fashion, modeling, jewellery, cuisine, languages, writing, science, mathematics, astronomy, astrology, medicine, pharmaceuticals, engineering, construction, manufacturing, space technology, nuclear armament. You name it and India has it. Its people are talented, creative, capable and, overcoming enormous difficulties, they have excelled wherever they have gone.

Where then is the problem? The only trouble is in the mind of many of its people who still think in Third World terms. These backward-looking people still hanker after a mythical and theological past and do little to overcome their limitations. In contrast, there are those who dare to be different. These are the leaders, the go-getters, the breed of creative, logical, rational, legal, scientific, entrepreneurial, risk-taking people They see the big picture, the emergence of the New India beckoning to them and the endless opportunities opening for business and development. They are the pioneers, the adventurers, opening new business frontiers. They are busy carving a niche for India, building national companies that are expanding and modernising on their way to becoming multinationals. They are the ones pushing forward into new sectors and working hard, training their managers, whipping up their workforce, investing in R&D, improving the quality of their products and services to build brand names and turning India into a developed nation.

These entrepreneurs have realised that they are not the ugly ducklings but the real and beautiful swans that can fly and do honour to their country. They have given up the Third World mentality that once held India back. They are hungry to push forward to conquer new products, new markets, to penetrate into the west, into the developing countries, to really go global. They are investing in the future. Tying up with the NRIs and PIOs overseas in the developing countries, in the west, they are learning about foreign markets. They are raiding cadres from foreign multinationals and putting them in charge of key sectors like product development, marketing, brand building. They are learning about foreign consumer needs and markets, how to reach them and how to beat the competition coming from China, Korea, Japan and western countries. To such business leaders, nothing is impossible. Great is their appetite and their vision. They know that the way ahead is long and hard, full of challenges. But that is what they like best- challenges and struggles which put them on their mettle, which is the life-blood of the entrepreneurs, the creators of wealth, employment, new markets and national pride. Some of them, in the electronics, car manufacturing, energy sectors, for example, are making huge investments in advertising and brand building to reach overseas markets. Inspired by the successful examples of Japan, Korea and China in building the new brands, they are learning fast in order to manufacture products that meet world standards and that can go global.

These are the heroes who are constructing a new self- image which allies Indian talents, creativity, capacity for hard work, managerial and leadership skills. Inspired by the ancient glory of Indian culture, civilization and commerce, these leaders are transforming the sub-continent forward into a giant. They are inspiring a whole breed of new entrepreneurs.

Why then can't the others believe in themselves, in their own ability, why? What prevents them from doing so, except their small mindedness, their lack of self-confidence, killed since their early childhood, mostly by over-protective parents. What is required is strong inspirational leadership from the state, from schools, from the homes, from society, from the media, leadership that can infuse fresh doses of self-confidence in the Indian psyche, since early childhood. Let the new generation grow as strong personalities, with strong independent characters, as capable, thinking people, as the new leaders of the world. (The author. *How Your Child Can Be a WINNER*. 2003).

The new *vyaparee* class has taken up the challenge given by inspirational leaders like Shri Vajapayee who saw *India shining* as a bright star among the firmaments of nations. They know that the world is looking up at India as an awakening giant, a super-power. Consequently, as entrepreneurs, as traders and as a productive people, they are going out with the killer instincts to bring out the best to face global competition. In outlook, they are far different from the past industrialists who used to hide behind protectionism, subsidies and the suffocating bureaucracy.

They are brimming with self-confidence and in their turn are bringing up a new breed of capable and performing Indian managers and future entrepreneurs who know how to turn the ordinary individuals into extraordinary achievers.

After all, this is the lesson which the Gita has taught us *-lift yourself by yourself*! Nobody else, but you can wake up to improve your self-image, create, experiment new areas that best suit the Indian genius like ayurvedic products, beauty care, Indian food, beverages, electronics. This involves having the competitive factors including cheap labour, low taxes, a package of incentives, modern infrastructure, a non-interfering bureaucracy and able managers. It means constantly raising the quality of your thinking, the quality of your products, of your education, your health care. It means experimenting and improving, investing in R&D to gain the competitive edge. So, why should we look at foreign-made products as being superior when we have all the potential of surpassing the rest of the world if only we put our mind to it?

Liberal, democratic India has now got over the restrictive practices of the unproductive, wasteful, amateurish pre-1990's Soviet-style Inspector Raj. New India is capable of taking foreign competition head-on. It is now aware of its enormous productive capacity. But it can only win the global race if **it changes its Third World mentality** and **shift to a developed mentality**, that is, from amateurism to professionalism, from craftsmanship to high technology, from the self-defeating *chalega* attitude to a cam-do management methods. This can only be achieved when India decides to improve the quality, the finish, the design, the package, the marketing of its wide range of products. Should India so decide, nobody on earth could hold it back from winning the race. It has five millennia old experience in agricultural products, leather products, garments, crafts. After realising the Agricultural Revolution, India can outperform many of its competitors in agri--industrial, food, fruit, flowers, pickles, sweets, snacks, beverages, leather, shoe products – provided it concentrates with single-minded purpose on upgrading its range of products to reach world class standards and put branded products on the world market.

The cradle of civilization must earn a brand name for itself. India, its people and the diaspora are fully awakened to take their place as the right kind of giant.

Breeding Success

In an interview to Times of India, N.D, 15 January, 2003, Prof.C.K.Prahalad is optimistic about New India's economic capability. He considers that in the field of Telecom, India has leap frogged and is deploying the most advanced technology, connecting both the urban rich and the rural population at incredibly low tariffs. What India has done in software, in telecom, in pharmacy, it can do in other sectors as well if it puts its head to it. He points at the miraculous success attained by Wipro, TCS, Satyam and Cognisant as well as the successes made by lots of small companies. *If India continues on the same trend of freedom to innovate, to experiment, and to remove barriers and restrictions, success will follow success.* Examples are plentiful: Barista, Jet Airways, Infosys, Ranbaxy, or Reliance. Indian achievements in manufacturing are no less outstanding when we consider success stories like Sundaram Fasteners, TVS Motors and

Kalyani Exports. He asks: *"The question is how do you enlarge this picture on a wider canvas?"*

He thinks that India can achieve a 10.15% growth rate and add 10-15 million jobs in a year. He senses *an emerging spirit of entrepreneurship bursting all around.* He sees resources trapped running to $ 1 trillion, market opportunities and emerging competence base while India holds the world's largest food stocks, despite the ghost of famines and mal-nourishment stalking the country. Given inspiring political leadership, and controlling vested interests, Prahalad forecasts that India can reach up to 15%. By using its vast domestic market as laboratories, India can well capture global export market if companies keep on being innovative, use new technology and keep costs very low.

Backed by its unmatched brainpower, its low-cost labour, vast internal market, its capacity to rise into a manufacturing base for the world, its well-developed financial markets, its independent judiciary, India is bracing to be tomorrow's giant.

(Aroon Purie, India Today Conclave, India Today 29.3.04).

Networking for a Purpose

Networking is viewed as highly desirable as a strategy to bind the global Indians umbilically to Indian culture, to provide them opportunities to share their varied and rich experiences, make necessary adjustments and alliances within their multicultural societies. Consequently, India could emulate these models, invite and exchange contributions in the fields of trade, investment, transfer of technology, health care and culture. (Hindustan Times. N.D. 9.1.03).

The networks building is taking place in different fields of activities:-

- Firstly, across the cyberspace on-line communications spearheaded by India.
- Secondly, social networks through access to educational, professional and social opportunities and to political empowerment.
- The formation of potentials and core competencies.

- The removal of traditional barriers.
- Coalition building among the social and political diaspora.
- This depends on how we ignite and synergise our shared values, family and social institutions, the NGOs, our enormous cultural, intellectual, religious and civilisational capital.
- Business networks are propelled by information and knowledge sharing, the circulation and pooling of resources, frequent Pravasis business meetings and global exchanges,
- During the October 2004 Brussels Business Meeting, it was realised that the Indian Diaspora could:- (i) enhance and strengthen the EU-India relations, (ii) attract FDIs and European multinationals, (iii) help build trade networks through the forging of strategic partnerships, backed by (iv) cross-cultural programmes, (v) scholarship schemes, (vi) broader media activities, (vii) interaction among business leaders, (viii) the new opportunities arising from the opening of the Indian economy and the economy of the PIO's host countries and finally (ix) the setting up of a Europe-India Chamber of Commerce and Industry, based in Brussels, in a bid to bring together the views and interests of EU-Indian companies, enterprises, missions and consulates of India in Europe. At the same time, India and its media should take more interest in European political and security issues.(GOPIO, Belgium, *Concept Paper on Europe-India Chamber of Commerce*, 4 Oct.2004).
- On the international level, networking means strengthening relations with neighbouring countries, including Pakistan,China,South East Asian Countries. This spirals forth to include the Non-Aligned countries, and the great powers, particularly forging India- US. collaboration on civilian nuclear co-operation and peaceful uses of space technology, in the fight against terrorism, the spread of infectious diseases, environmental degradation and drug trafficking. Both countries are building a strategic partnership based on their shared commitment to freedom, prosperity and security, added

Colin L.Powell. (India Today, 29 March, 2004).

- Another form of partnership has already taken shape where NRIs and PIOs have been actively engaged in supporting various social service activities in India, particularly in sponsoring their former schools and colleges, or in setting up new academic institutions, health and other environmental services in their native villages and towns. At a higher level, Indo-Caribbeans, Indo-South Africans or Indo-Malaysians can network with other PIO communities for the development of their adopted countries.
- GOPIO can forge linkages at two levels:- (i) the creation of economic opportunities by pooling NRIs / PIOs economic, professional and financial resources together, and (ii) among Indians and the PIOs host societies, including Indians with British, Indians with French,.Indians with Dutch, Indians with Americans, Indians with Canadians, Indians with Australians.
- The important thing is to build solid coalitions among the PIO communities to make our voices heard, to address important issues and human rights abuses affecting the emerging global Indian citizens wherever these occur- in Britain, USA, in the Caribbeans, in Fiji, the Middle East.(*PIOs - Emergence of a New Global Community* in The North East Age, 8 Jan. 2003)

"Among democracies, it is people that must engage. People in large and small organisations and institutions. People in great corporations, universities, health centres, hospitals, financial markets, cultural pursuits, agricultural co-operatives and certainly the media. The core is individuals-with individuals- such as Indian students in the US today, your sons and daughters on the campuses and in the towns of America.

Great national partnerships and alliances thrive when all elements of government, corporate and civil societies are engaged. If India is to build an Indian Century...it will be because India reaches out, opens up and engages to become a leader in today's globalised world".

(Dr David C. Mulford, US Ambassador to India. India Today, 29 March 2004).

The aim is to forge a common PIO-NRI diasporic unity firmly embedded in our cultural ties with Bharat- the homeland of our race, our civilisation, philosophy, our democracy, our Indianness and the Mother of us all. This is to remind ourselves that no matter who we are, where we are, you can take an Indian out of India but nobody can ever take India out of the Indian- *Phir bhi dil hai Hindustani!*

Openness - the Way to Greatness

Prof. Amartya Sen, the Nobel Laureate for Economics, 1998, and currently Master of Trinity College, Cambridge, UK, asked what is it that makes us proud of India? Is it its tradition, culture, civilization of openness, its inclusiveness, its dynamic interactive civilization, its Sanskrit heritage as vehicle of science and maths? He invited Indians not to adopt a frog-in-the-well attitude when they should *open up and interact with other countries in the outside world in different fields*. He referred to the greatness and contributions of Vedic civilization which had pioneered the great tradition in science, mathematics, medicine, technology, physics and astronomy. The dynamic Vedic civilization blossomed as a result of its tradition of openness and interaction with Arabic, Chinese and European scientists. He grants that we have reason to be proud of our tradition. He urges that Vedic Mathematics should be studied as it largely simplifies a lot of complex mathematical problems. Focusing on the value of openness, he referred to the Afghan-born Sanskrit grammarian, Panini, who pioneered the science of language and linguistics. He traced the word science from its Sanskrit origin when Aryabhatta named trigonometry *jiya artha* which later the Arabs adopted as *jeb*. The Latin translation became Sinoos for science in English.

As the earliest books of knowledge known to history, the Vedas poured out the divine revelations to guide the early steps of mankind and showed them the path of knowledge, wisdom and human civilization. After all, God did not have to wait tardily for millennia after to deliver His message through Abraham as the projenitor of Judaism, Christianity and Islam. Religion was born from seminal Vedic Hinduism, with the Vedas as the earliest book of God's knowledge which spread into Zoroastrianism, in neighbouring Iran which, in turn, descended into Judaism. Then came Buddhism, with its emphasis on love and compassion, as a reaction to the excesses of casteist Brahmanism. Taoism, largely inspired by the Vedas, came next to be followed by Christianity and Islam. It should be noted that Hinduism, Buddhism and Taoism focused on tolerance, on deep sense of respect for the others, on moderation, on the Middle Way and differed from Christianity and Islam in that they produced no fanatics, no religious wars and no proselytisation. From time to time, pockets of Hindu funadamentalism arose in self-defence and in reaction to the religious aggression of the proselytising religions.

The Vedas carry references to the astronomy, the sciences, to geography in which the whole planetary system revolves on the principles of gravitation and the knowledge that the earth is round. After all, is not it revealing that the Sanskrit word for geography itself is *bhugol shastra*, the science of the round earth? Indian knowledge about the law of gravitation and the shape of the earth had preceded the discovery of Galilleo and the Newton's law of motion by millennia.

Just refer to the *Gayatri Mantra* where the *Aum Bhu Bhuva Swa* encompasses cosmic consciousness. The congregational prayer, the *Shanti Paat* invokes peace among the celestial firmaments, peace in the intervening media of space, peace on earth, *shanti prithvi*, in the waters, *shanti apah*, medicinal plants, forest plants, whole nature, the forces of the universe, *vishwedeva*, among world leaders, learned people, *redhi* when *dhi* means the intellect, peace be unto all, to peace itself, to universal peace. (Swami Paramananda. *Prayer*. EOI. 2003)

These facts have yet to be apprehended by the west under its arrogant uni-polar homogeneity pushing dangerously towards a self-fullfilling clash of civilizations. It claims a monopoly over all scientific knowledge to itself with the erroneous belief that only western civilization is neutral, rational and universal while everything else from Chinese, Indian, Maya, Islamic, African civilizations are wished away as being ethnic, regional and trivial.

In 1924, the excavations in Mohenjodaro and Harappa in the Indus Valley, extending over 400,000 kilometres, 3000 B.C, had unearthed a thriving urban civilization complete with:- the art of writing, arts, crafts, elaborate architecture, a granary, seals of deities, drainage, sewerage system, private bathrooms, gold coins, utensils, toiletries, domesticated animals and the evidence of an open society of merchants who traded with the Gulf countries, Oman, Mesopotamia, Iraq, Greece, Egypt, Babylon. No caste distinctions had been found. It was a peaceful civilization.

Though the Aryan villages were made of wood, earth and leaf and no evidence has survived, the earliest evidence of Indian art and architecture goes back to Mohenjadaro which features the priest torse in terracotta, the bronze dancing girl, seals, Yaksi, 30 coins. Later sculptures and architecture include:- the Gandhar style Buddha, Kaniska, Buddha in Kandahar and Kabul, the Sun temple in Kashmir, Buddha in Mathura, Buddha, wearing Greek features and preaching the first sermon in Sarnath, Sanchi, the seat of Buddhist Sangha in 1st Century, B.C, the Asokan pillars, the Horse-shoe façade in Bodgaya, 4th century, B.C., the Amarvati stupa's decorative design, the wheel of Konarak, the Khajuraho showing the best erotic temple structure dating to 10th century A.D., Kailash temple, Ellora, rock-cut caves in Ajanta, on the hills of Mahabalipuram, the Trimurthi in Elephanta cave, the Apsaras, and Angkor Wat, the largest Hindu temple in the world and other masterpierces of the Nataraja in bronze and metal. (Benjamen Roland, Percy Brown).

"We owe a lot to the Indians, who taught us how to count, without which no worthwhile scientific discovery could have been made" (Albert Einstein).

India calls upon the NRIs to give back to her what they had received from her- including subsidised quality education, sometimes at Indian Institutes of Technology or medical colleges.

"In the morning I bathe my intellect in the stupendous and

cosmogonal philosophy of the Bhagavadgita since whose composition years of the gods have elapsed and in comparison with which our modern world and its literature seems puny and trivial".

(Henry David Thoreau, 1817-62).

The famous American travelogue who wrote that God made Mauritius first and then copied heaven on it, said of India:-

"India is the cradle of the human race, the birthplace of human speech, the mother of history, the grandmother of legend and great grandmother of tradition".

But prof. Amartya Sen forgot to mention the great achievements of Buddhist India. Buddhist teachings spread far and wide across the whole of Asia and South East Asia, by peaceful means, not through conquest or forced conversions at the point of the swords. These noble ideals, springing from the original Vedic source and enriched by Buddhism, have enhanced the culture and civilisation of these countries, which essentially share the same great Indian thoughts. Later, countless other prophets, seers, saints, teachers, spiritual masters, reformers would further interpret, re-interpret, explain, elaborate, illustrate the deep Vedantic thoughts across the ages.

According to Buddhist pedagogy, there are three methods of teaching which are valid for all time-debate and reflection, direct experience and meditation. Buddhist teachings were handed over through the *guru-shisya-parampara* tradition under the resident monks-yogis-scholars. The centres of learning for the whole civilized world were housed in universities and libraries, at Taxila, at the nine-storeyed Nalanda Library, the University and monastic schools and Vikramaditya till their destruction since 1200 by the Moghul vandals, which constituted an irreparable loss to learning and world cultural heritage. Fleeing the vandals, the Buddhist monks took refuge in Tibet where they were isolated but nevertheless part of the teachings was preserved.

The success of India as the largest democracy is firmly embedded on its cultural and civilizational heritage. Thus, according to Niraj Deva, Lord Buddha had preached democratic and liberal values of moderation and the via media policy in all matters, individualism and enterprise, profit making, savings and investments, entrepreneurship constrained by tolerance, mutual understanding and acceptance of other people's differences. Deva argues that the Hindu and Buddhist philosophy had created one of the oldest and the most tolerant civilisations which had spread to China, to Japan, Indonesia through the Sri Vijaya Empire to the Buddhist Borobudur to Bali. The values of democracy are articulated in the Vedantic philosophy and are firmly embedded in Indian culture- millennia before Bentham, Adam Smith, Hume, Berkeley, Voltaire or Tocqueville pronounced on the virtues of liberty, democracy, liberalism, market economy or a free open society.

(Niraj Deva, Member of European Parliament, *The Role of GOPIO in Global Security*, GOPIO Conference, Brussels, 4 Oct. 2004).

As India slipped behind into medieval Brahmanical obscurantism, holding the monopoly of Sanskrit learning into their hands, superstitions and ignorance descended upon the country. It banned foreign travels and pushed India back into the Dark Age and total isolation from other centres of civilization. It fell an easy prey to the Moghul invaders who decapitated its intellectual leadership. And there followed medieval India's rapid decadence. Hinduism would have spread across the globe if the Brahmanical priests had not barred the mass of the people from access to Vedas and Sanskrit scriptures. The strength of Sikhism rests precisely in the fact that it lay its emphasis on rendering the Guru Grant in an easily accessible language, the *Gurumukhi*. Secondly, it eradicated the caste system by the compulsory food serving after prayer meeting. It called upon all devotees to contribute, cook, serve and eat together on the floor in perfect fraternity. Similarly, in the nineteenth century, Indian nationalism owed its success to the contributions of the social reformers and the spread of Hindi as the rallying language.

Britain had surged ahead with the foundation of the universities of Cambridge and Oxford, fuelled by the grammar schools attached to the Church. During the Renaissance period, classical scholars had flooded Europe and spread classical learning, bringing forth successive generations of scholars, rulers and entrepreneurs which changed the course of history. India had to wait for the British to revive the academic traditions with the opening of Universities and schools which put up fresh generations of elites, spearheaded by reformers like Raja Ram Mohun Roy, Swami Viivekanand, Tilak and others.

History of Conflicts

THE NOBEL Laureate Trinidadian-born **Sir Vidia Sagar Naipaul**, UK, calls upon the PIOs to draw lessons from history and to reflect on important issues like:-

Why our civilization has collapsed and why we have failed in the past?

He urges Indians to remember that while *"the immigrant labourers were struggling the country did not give its people any kind of protection"*. He adds that the degradation within the country had incited thousands of Immigrants to take refuge abroad in British, French and Dutch plantation colonies. It appears that both India and the diaspora have a lot in their hands to salvage the scattered strands of diasporic history, to understand and pay tribute to the memory of our immigrant forefathers who suffered and sacrificed in order to hand over to future generations a better future.

Apart from some differences, throughout the former plantation colonies, the similarities seem to reproduce a set pattern. The economic and political situation of the Indian diaspora in the former colonies is still precarious and fluctuating, plagued by love-and hate-relationships between the Blacks and Indians, indigenous Fijians and Indo-Fijians, trailing enormous political consequences behind them. Since the abolition of slavery and indenture, the Black- and-Indian communities had been kept racially apart, with little social mingling, despising each other's culture- food, habits, customs, religion, dress and language. The pattern of Creolisation set by the French assimilationist policy had been so strong in Mauritius and Reunion and the peace-loving and tolerant Asiatic culture so predominant, that these multi-cultural islands have been able to preserve social harmony and peace.

In **Trinidad**, with its 600,000 Indians out of a population of 1.9 million dominated by Afro-Trinidadians, the Blacks, under the People's National Movement, PNM, had been in power since 1962 to 1995. Indians were marginalised, discriminated against in education, in bureaucratic jobs and cultural organisations until the charismatic Basdeo Panday, leader of the United National Congress, became Prime Minister for a second term.

In the Caribbeans, in Fiji, Mauritius, South Africa, East Africa, Madagascar, Malaysia and elsewhere, PIOs have to wrestle with serious economic, political and racial issues- to be further discussed in this book. In many of these places, the PIOs are still the underdogs. In their daily struggle, they look up to strong PIOs-NRIs networking and strategic alliances under India's aegis.

"I wish to encourage you to use this forum to address issues which are of paramount importance to all of us, such as racial conflicts, religious wars, political strife and economic deprivations".

(Basdeo Panday, PM, Trinidad & Tobago, 4th International GOPIO Convention, Mauritius, 23.8.96)

A Lesson in Caribbean Politics

FIJI HAS a 44% Indian population but Indians have no access and no proprietary right to land which they have to lease from the Melanesians, under traditional Chiefs. Indentured labour started in 1879 to work for the Australiam Colonial Sugar Refining Company, owning practically all the plantations and sugar mills in the Fiji islands. After their indenture period, Indians were allotted 10-12 acre plots as small holders. They were joined by free immigrants from Punjab, Gujarat, including teachers, lawyers. The racial problem and anti-Indianism was fostered by the white planters who set the Christianised native Fijians against the Indians, considered to be aliens, filthy, frugal and unassimilated, practising outlandish religion and strange culture Their children were kept in separate schools. Since the 1940's and 50's, Indians had to send their children abroad for higher studies and they migrated to towns to take up jobs in business, trade, commerce and the professions. The native Fijians languished in subsistence agriculture.

As in the Caribbeans, Mauritius and elsewhere, in Fiji the polarisation between the native Fijians and Indians stemmed from their different cultural backgrounds. While Indians worked hard to make a better life for themselves and their children, the Fijians stuck to their traditional communal lifestyle and few bothered to educate their children. By 1979, the lifestyle of Indians and of Fijians had clearly polarised, with Indians racing ahead educationally and economically leaving the Fijians lagging way behind. Inevitably, this socio-economic divergence replicated itself into the political system. Some Fijian politicians exploited the widening economic differences to fuel racial hostility between Fijians and Indians and they referred to Amin's expulsion of Indians from Uganda as a pretext to expel Indians from Fiji.

By 1980, in an effort to rally the two communities, some politicians founded the class-based Labour Party which competed with the two ethnic parties, the Alliance Party, backed by Fijians and the National Federation Party, backed by Indians. Consequently, the Labour Party allied with the National Federation Party and won the election. It formed an Alliance government featuring a majority Indian cabinet. The upshot was that in 1987, some members of the defeated Alliance Party staged a military coup and replaced the democratically elected Alliance government. Many Labour Party supporters, mainly Indians were beaten up and persecuted. This was followed by a second coup whereby Indians were prevented from holding political power anymore in Fiji.

(Cllr Satish Rai, London, *Fiji. Political Crisis in Fiji.* 2nd GOPIO Conference, Paris 1992)

This is how Indians had managed to elect a multi-racial government led by the Fijian, Timoci Bavadra, a non-racist. The latter was ousted by Sitiveni Rabuka in two military coups in May and November 1987 when he took office as Prime Minister. He violated human rights of the elected members and imposed a terrorist regime. Since then, Indians have been marginalised, leading to large Indian migration to Australia, New Zealand and Canada. Fiji is no more *"the little India"* it had been, though it still holds on firmly to Indian culture and to Hindi speaking. Under international pressure, in 1990, a revised constitution was adopted, resulting in the electoral defeat of Rabuka by Mahendra Pal Chaudhry's Labour Party in May 1999.

But on 19 May 2000, Prime Minister Chaudhry was ousted by George Speight, the coup leader, who, backed by a handful of gunmen, had stormed into Parliament in Suva to confiscate parliamerntary democracy at gunpoint. Later, he was condemned to life sentence for treason. The victim in all this had been the Indians who had come to power for the first time and had lost it over to the military which declared martial law while an interim government was appointed under indigenous Fijian Laisenia Qarase, who also won a new election. The indigenous Fijians have always resented the economic power of the Fijian Indians, just as it had happened to Indians in Guyana, when Prime Minister Chhedi Jagan was ousted in 1953 and Burhman ruled as a dictator from 1964 until 1992.

(Malakai Vetsamasam, L'Express, 6 Aug.2004).

In **Mauritius**, despite its mythical 70% PIOs, the transfer of power from Sir Anerood Jugnauth to Mr. Paul Berenger, a white man, followed in 2003, has sounded like restoring the country back into the hands of the colonialist and racist Oligarchy which had been ruling it for over three centuries. Indians do not feel secure in these countries and they consider that India has not stood by them in their hour of need. Indeed the middle class professional Indians from Guyana, Trinidad and Fiji feel deeply wounded by the past indifference of India when their families had been victimised, robbed, thrashed, raped by Black thugs and criminals, some wearing army boots in Guyana. This has driven 400, 000 Indo-Guyanese to migrate to Canada and the US. It's hard to accept that India had left them in the lurch. Overseas Indians have felt that could never have happened to British, French, American, German or Chinese citizens abroad. Therefore, India has to do a lot to repair past damages and win over its estranged PIOs. It has been made clear that India has a moral and diplomatic responsibility towards the PIOs and NRIs under assault.

(L.M.Singhvi. *Report of the High Level Committee on the Indian Diaspora)*

"India can and should do more to help people like us through the diplomatic channels. Being an Indian in Fiji means being politically marginalised, racially discriminated against and having basic rights violated everyday. In Fiji, there is State-sponsored, institutionalised discrimination," said ousted Prime Minister Chaudhry who added that the Indians do not own land and they are not represented in the army and have been victims of three coups.

(Indian Express, Pune, Jan. 8, 2003).

Guyana. According to Mr Ashook Ramsaran, Guyana-born and settled in USA, Indians got interested in education and politics since the 1950's. Dr Cheddi Jagan introduced schools and colleges and led the Indians forward. Both *education and politics lifted them up and showed them the way out of the trenches. They started thinking differently*. They built schools, canals, drainage and the floods suddenly stopped. The Indian population averages 46% of the 800,000 people. Apart from Mauritius which had a 70% Indian population, in the other plantation colonies, Fiji, the Caribbeans and Surinam, it was the colonial policy to keep Indian population well below 45%.

As a result of persecution and victimisation, 300,000 Indians have migrated to the US and Canada, leaving only 400,000 back in Guyana. Under the barbaric Burhman dictatorship, Guyanese Indians had been victims of human rights abuses, cultural, academic, economic, and political deprivations.

Since its inception, the GOPIO-GOI Liaison Committee, chaired by Ramsaran, has been actively monitoring human rights violations in the Caribbeans, including the kidnapping and murders of Indian children, outbreaks of racial unrest, in Fiji and in the Middle East. It uncovers discrimination and disparities like the recent distribution of awards in Trinidad whereby 6 Indians were awarded out of 70

Trinidadians. GOPIO acts and reacts to international issues and disasters affecting Indians, including the recent flood in Assam, the ousting of the Fijian Prime Minister, Chaudhry, the action of gangs of Black thugs in the Caribbeans. It creates global awareness, reports to governments, and get corrective action taken. It involves persons of local, regional and international levels, namely the UN Human Rights Agencies, the government of India, the Ministry of Overseas Indians Affairs. through the GOPIO website.

The leader of the People's Progressive Party, founded by Cheddy Jagan and strongly backed by Indians, is currently Mr Bharat Jagdeo, the President of Guyana. It is worth noting that the first non-Indian born President in a country inhabited by Indians had been Mrs Janet Jagan, wife of late President Dr Cheddy Jagan, thus forming a precedent to the ascendance of Mrs Sonia Gandhi.

(Ashook Ramsaran, Brussels, 4th Oct.2004)

Surinam. Originally inhabited by the indigenous Red Indian Caribs, the Surinamese Indians have to cope with different ethnic groups and their languages, namely English, Dutch, Portuguese, Lebanese, and Hindi. From 1873-1916, 40,000 Indian immigrants were brought into the plantation colony, populated by 40% Creoles, 40% Indians and 20% Javanese Indonesians.

In such a multi-cultural society, it has been difficult for Indians to preserve their identity. They have to assimilate into the mainstream culture of the host country. Seeing what had happened to the minority Indians in Guyana and fearing for their security, 180,000 Surinamese Indians migrated to the Netherlands, leaving only 160,000 Indians back in Surinam. To commemorate the arrival of Indian Immigrants into Surinam, 4th June 2005, an important international GOPIO Conference is being envisaged.

(Santa Debie Gurib, Brussels, Oct.2004)

Lord Parekh, UK, urges that the Diaspora- an open, outgoing and universal society- must be approached with great care and sensitivity. He adds that issues must be explored in the spirit of an on-going dialogue in a bid to pool our knowledge and ideas together and to use strategic negotiations to respond to multi-cultural diversity. *It is important to know what the world thinks about India.* Consequently, India will have to do a lot more to win back the sympathy of those alienated West Indian and Fijian PIOs who have felt let down and have shifted their loyalties to the industrial West where they have settled as the twice migrants. Another task is to continue helping Indian women to buttress family values and society and support them in rearing the young NRI-PIOs generation in our *sanskar*.

That's not all, the greatest challenge, according to GOPIO, is to ensure that the educated, westernised PIO Youth do not stray away from the path of Indianness and embrace western values, lock, stock and barrel. GOPIO is engaged in promoting scholarships, study and exchange tours for students and is pressing for the setting up of a PIO University. In these circumstances, the NRI's in the US and other industrial countries have a lot to do to overcome this alienation by transmitting their love and pride of India and an appreciation of Indian culture to their western educated children.

The PIO cards could be a double-edged weapon and are unwelcome to third, fourth, fifth or sixth PIO generations in African countries, Fiji, the Caribbeans, Mauritius or certain western countries. They could well have nefarious repercussions as occurred to the Indians who had been victimised in Myanmar in the wake of nationalisation, the wealthy Ugandan Indians who held British passports and were booted out by Idi Amin. But they are more useful to first generation NRIs, Indian passport holders, who have still to relate with Indian authorities on various regulatory matters. The special cards confer dual nationality. The facility to accede to dual citizenship, costing Rs 12,500, has been extended to PIOs in Canada, Finland, Greece, Ireland, US, Canada, Britain, Australia, New Zealand, Singapore, Israel, Portugal, Cyprus, Sweden, Switzerland and EU countries. The registration fees for an overseas Indian citizen amounts to $25. Though they are holders of an Indian passport, the holders of the special cards cannot be called citizens of India. The cards are designed to give them right of access to India but without political rights or full citizenship rights. However holders of dual nationality are entitled to live, work, invest, buy property and get education in India. *"Steps like dual nationality will reintegrate overseas Indians into Indian society"* said Lord Bhiku Parekh, expert on race relations, from UK. We need to remember that each one of the industrial countries has its own history, set of legislation and restrictions concerning the NRIs. In USA, the average income of the NRIs is twice the US average. In UK, the PIOs have risen from scratch in the retail and industrial sectors to emerge into one of the highest earning and the most educated minorities in the country.

(Indian Express, N.D, Jan 10, 2003).

But in **Guyana, Trinidad, in Fiji, in Malaysia**, Indians do not control political and economic power. They are not represented in State bureaucracy, in the army, in the police, occupied mainly by the Blacks. They are generally stuck in agriculture in the rural areas and are educationally backward and they have to cope with the deprivations underlined by Basdeo Pandey. In certain African countries where they are economically and professionally well-off, they have to face acute problems of insecurity. In the Caribbeans and in Fiji, the problem faced by the PIOs is their difficulty to hold power for long as the economic and bureaucratic infrastructure is not in their hands.

The setting up of the new **Ministry for Overseas Indians Affairs**, headed by Minister Jagdish Tytler, is a step forward. The new Ministry is expected to address and monitor the concerns of NRIs/PIOs, promote better NRI-PIO-India- networking, strategic alliances, interact and relate more fruitfully, provide greater awareness of available opportunities which can harness the enormous resources, potential, talents and expertise of NRIs/PIOs.

2

THE AWAKENING OF THE GIANT

IN THIS chapter we shall examine certain criteria reached by a handful of successful NRIs and identify what are the factors which have enabled them to get that far and what are some of the inhibiting factors they have hindered them to reach the very top. We shall round up with a comparative study of NRIs set against westerners, Chinese and see what's required to bridge the gap to reach collective Indian success.

Indianness Is the Best of Breed

MANAGEMENT GURU, Prof. C.K.Prahalad, US, urged that INDIANNESS IS THE BEST OF BREED. It's world class. It has excellence. Being the best of breed, even if he failed, with faith and perseverance, the Indian will succeed. This mantra, *hum howange kamyabh-* we shall overcome, is borne out by the world class talents and skills of 300, 000 Indian Americans in the California's Silicon Valley, many of whom are known to be involved in 700 companies, including 15 % of the high-tech companies. Not only this, the Diaspora has also made a breakthrough in the world of politics, featuring prime ministers and presidents. The list includes the late prime minister of Maurtiius and father of the nation, Sir Seewoosagur Ramgoolam, his successors, Sir Aneerood Jugnauth, Dr Navin Ramgoolam, the late Dr Chedi Jagan of Guyana, Basdeo Pandey of Trinidad, Mahendra Chaudhry of Fiji, backed by hundreds of ministers, MPs and councillors. The first Indian MP in UK was Keith Vors. Earlier, in the academic, professional and artistic fields, Indians have produced four Nobel Prize winners, namely Dr Har Gobind Khorana, 1968 in physiology and medicine, Dr Subramahmanyan Chandrasekhar, 1982, in physics, Dr Amartya Sen, 1998, economics and Sir V.S.Naipaul, 2002, literature.

Quite positively, Indianness is the best of breed- we repeat the mantra that Indians are the best with certain Conviction, Commitment, Concentration and Confidence and we need to believe in it and live up to it. It's our challenge and it's for our own good. If not, how else could we have produced a Gandhi, a Nehru, a Tagore- or a Sir Seewoosagur Ramgoolam, a V.S.Naipaul, Amartya Sen, and the host of world class brains and entrepreneurs throughout the globe.

According to a report issued by the NY State Department, April 2002, Asian Indians, numbering one-and -a half million, generally score better academically than any other ethnic groups. This comes as no surprise as the 1990 Census revealed that 58% of Asian Indians earned a minimum of a Bachelor's degree or higher as compared to white, 26%, Chinese 41%, Japanese and Koreans 35%, Filipino, 39%.. This accounts for the fact that two-thirds of all Indian professionals in the US possess advanced degrees, with 91% having college diplomas, almost twice the level attained by the others.(cited by Motwani.)

This explains why NRIs have reached the top in professional careers, in medicine, engineering, maths, computing, sciences, teaching and the health professions, earning an average income of $ 40, 625 outdistancing the native Americans by more than $ 4,000 a year. This trend is self-perpetuating as children of NRIs tend to outperform others academically and become professionals in their turn. Further, in the technological and professional fields, American Indians account for 12% of scientists, 38% of doctors, 36% of NASA scientists, 34% of Microsoft employees, 28% of IBM employees, 17% of INTEL 17% and 13% of XEROX. (Motwani)

But what explains the superiority of the NRIs and their children? The explanation is to be found in their Indian civilisational heritage which puts great emphasis on learning, strong family solidarity by which parents focus on the education of their children, and above all, the extraordinary passion of Indians to pursue learning and reach the highest levels of excellence. Since the beginnings of time, the Vedas, the book of knowledge, had placed great premium on the value of learning and the deep respect of the guru. It's not without significance that Indians had worshipped the two pre-eminent goddesses- Saraswati, goddess of learning and Luxmi, goddess of wealth , since they valued both, education and wealth equally.

After all, Indianness is embedded in the Vedantic philosophy of openness, truth-seeking, self-awareness, self-analysis, self-discipline, hard work and action (karma), and family values- which are the Indian recipes for success. But at the same time, Indians have a price to pay for their success. It turns out that on the average, it's all work and no play and which makes Jack a dull boy. They fail to lead a balanced life, materially and spiritually. It tends to become one-sided- work, work, work and more work unreleived by sports except for Indian music and entertainment.

Why Will Indians Rule Soon?

SON OF Dr Bissoon Chummun and great grand son of Immigrant Chummun, the Mauritian-born PIO, Dipak Chummun, a Regional Chief Financial Officer for Standard Chartered Bank for Middle East and South Asia, based in Dubai, is a UK trained Chartered Accountant, with significant Management Consultancy experience. As the emerging global Indian, Dipak has served in UK, Netherlands, Brazil, France, Singapore, Australia, Thailand, Hong Kong and is now in Dubai. He believes that NRIs will rule as the professional class globally before the end of this century. But how is this possible? Dipak explains that the current trend indicates that the sheer volume of professionals pouring out annually from Indian Universities is unbeatable. The Indian sub-continent boasts of the world's largest middle class which is growing at an impressive rate, displaying tremendous talents, confidence and ambition on many fronts. India has the five world class Indian Institutes of Management, IIM's. The yearly competition to get into any of these is so tough, 150,000 applicants for less than 1000 seats as compared to 10,000 applicants for 1000 seats at the top 5 US MBA Schools including Harvard University and Wharton. Some of those who fail to get into the IIM's somehow manage to go to Harvard or other prestigious American and western universities. Put together, out of its one billion population, the yearly output of Indian graduates and post-graduates will overwhelm the west.

The Indian job market can never absorb the totality of its graduate output. This spurs a constant brain drain-which ultimately turns into a brain gain. It works out as follows. The success of the professional NRIs inspires other Indians to emulate their trajectory and in its cyclical turn it pushes other Indians back home into the NRI's migration circuit. In other words, the successful NRIs provide inspiration and example to the Indian diaspora and resident Indians in a push-and pull-movement so that a larger quasi NRI community builds up and creates an international NRI network abroad. A classic example is the way NRIs have penetrated into the Citibank in Singapore over the last decade.

Already, NRIs overwhelm the IT sector, medicine, engineering and banking in the US. The Citibank, one of the largest banks in the world, is virtually run by NRIs at middle and senior levels, except for the top management. "*It's only a matter of time, though*" says Dipak. Standard Chartered Bank, an international and primarily emerging market bank, carries the same story. In Britain, for the first time in its history, the appointment of Rana Talwar in the 1990's as the first Indian born global CEO in a top 100 company has triggered a new wave of NRIs appointments at similar levels.

Since he started as a banker in 1996 in UK, Dipak has observed a significant transformation in the sheer volume of NRIs occupying senior management positions in international banks. *"You couldn't expect to see NRIs infiltrating into top positions into the British workforce but this penetration is now so deep and wide"*, says Dipak emphatically. Indians are fast acquiring the breadth and depth of international experience to enable them to compete globally. Owing to his wide geographical experience in UK, Asia-Pacific, Middle East, over the last 12 years, Dipak masters English, French, Hindi, and has a working knowledge of Spanish, German and Malay. His skills are in high demand. As a consultant, he has worked in a multitude of industries such as FMG, IT, Risk management strategy and finance.

Indians versus Westerners

In Britain, the top 5% of the population are graduates. representing 200,000 as compared to less than five times what India produces annually. The demand for professionals into the UK is rising in proportion to the increase in its ageing population. Relatively, fewer westerners are available to fuel their economies. Simultaneously, the search for a better life drives Indians to look for better jobs outside India. Besides, Indians are adaptable, hard-working, fairly honest, gentle and are deeply attached to family life values. Above all, they get on the job and are very enterprising, and persevering, their motto being- we shall overcome.

"India is now poised for her second tryst with destiny. Analysts predict that India will record the highest growth in the coming decades. It will surpass Italy, France, Germany, and Japan to be the third largest economy. They have put India's growth rate at 7.5% a year".

(Mukesh Ambani, India Today, 29 March 2004)

Westerners- in UK, US, Australia, Canada, South Africa- have had an historical edge over Indians in their ability to provide the right infrastructure, building of cities, roads, railways, legal institutions, banks, education, health facilities and providing the goods and services required by people in modern societies. In other words, they give top priority to top customer satisfaction and community living. Wherever they go, they are community-based and they build a solid infrastructure first. They built Australia, Canada and South Africa from scratch, just as they did Mauritius. In this, they are vastly superior to Indians who are not famous for infrastructure building. Indians care little to provide the essential urban amenities, nor for community-based living. Indians are primarily family-centred and they focus on the individual at the expense of community welfare. This is one of the reasons why Indians flock to western countries, in the UK, France, Australia, Canada and the US where it feels good to live.

Anand Mahindra, Vice-Chairman of Mahindra, suggests that the right environment to accommodate one hundred Indian multinationals will have to depend on the *Tropical Garden approach*. Accordingly, the gardener or the government, planner or developer, provides the right kind of conditions, enabling facilities and infrastructure for growth and then gets out of the way. The fittest will survive provided the soil is nourished and weeds constantly removed. The weeds, whatever they may be- infrastructure, roads, rail, airport facilities, bureaucracy, power shortage, red tape, must be identified and removed.

(India Today, 2004)

What Hampers the Growth Success of Indians?

This is the major failing of Indians. They do not add much to the basic infrastructure, particularly roads, rails, airports, as well as safe water, electricity, schools, health centres. On the other hand, Indians thrive best in the Tropical Garden approach, when government or developers have previously laid down all the infrastructure, the weeds or hurdles are idenitfied and constantly cleared. The Chinese and the Westeners have been focusing on this infrastructural approach. Consequently, where the westerners have built up the infrastucture, there the Indians tend to do very well in societies or corporations led by westerners.

It is unfortunate that historically, Indians have not proved to be good leaders so far. Some of them have risen to be great organisers and administrators but few have shone as great leaders. This is also the problem some of the Indian prime ministers have had to face in Fiji,

Trinidad, Mauritius and India. Similarly, in the army, the commanders and generals are the whites while the army and the infantry are Indians. In the Middle East, the top 5% people in corporations are westerners while the remaining 95% are Indians and Pakistanis. Similarly, Mauritius offers a picture of a chaotic structure under PIO administration. Dipak believes that Indians have to learn to be good disciplined rulers. Politics becomes an eternal power game. Therefore, Indians have yet to attain the global maturity before they can make a bid to rule major corporations.

Another strategic area where Indians have failed is in their total neglect to develop attractive inflow of foreign skills and investments into the motherland. This has been largely due to their weak social infrastructure. However, there are some isolated success stories starting to emerge as seen in Standard Chartered Bank which has had a large operational and IT hub in Chennai employing high calibre locals at low costs.

The story is different in Singapore which believes in a philosophy of growth and excellence according to planned phases.

Phase 1- Singapore attracts input of foreign leaders from the West in order to teach locals.

Phase 2- the Westerners develop higher calibre locals.

Phase 3- after 10-20 years, locals reach a level where they can take over the top job with confidence.

How about Mauritius? Mauritius will continue to struggle to improve because of its reluctance to acquire new skills from abroad. Once again, the culprit is in its defensive mindset and short-term vision and government's concern to protect local labour only and its nepotism in favouring its own boys. Thus, it is caught up in a vicious circle of mediocrity. The lesson we can learn here is that in order to progress collectively, Mauritius as a nation should become open to new ideas and people, even if as a temporary measure, in order to upscale and upskill.

The conclusion is that the success of the Indian diaspora takes place only in societies already developed by the West.

A Game of Numbers

The competitive edge held by India lies in the volume and quality of Indian graduates. India is set to conquer the world professional market. Its young people are the most educated, the most talented, they save the highest and invest the largest. They are the products of a great culture, civilization, religion and philosophy. It looks like an intellectual invasion by peaceful means. The Indian invasion is not aggressive, nor military. It's multilateral, multidimensional, multi-geographical and multi industry covering:- banking, financial services, insurance, marketing, advertising, media, shipping, trading, IT, pharmacy, medicine, engineering, publications, writing and journalism.

The output of Indian graduates accounts for less than 1% of the one billion population emerging from Indian universities. This trend will increase the more India becomes more sophisticated and the greater will be the volume of educated Indians. Can you imagine that every two weeks, the number of new-borns in India creates a new Mauritius? Every four months, India gives birth to a new Canada or Australia. Every year, it's a new UK and every 5 years a new United States.

You Need a Vision!

20 years, ago, Mauritius was ahead of India. Today, the calibre of the Indians is far superior while Mauritius has been receding far behind into a mediocre society. India is racing fast towards excellence. While Indians are aware of the journey and visualise the glittering destination ahead, Mauritians, and particularly Indo-Mauritians are basking in luxury, taking drinks and snacks watching the TV and wasting their time. People hardly realise that time is racing past and they simply can't afford to waste it. What matters is whether you have a vision and whether you are pursuing your dream. That's what gives a society its energy, its drive and dynamism. Indo-Mauritians will have to wake up and join the global competition. In Singapore, Indians are doing so

well academically and professionally that the Government has had to impose a quota on the number of seats for Indians opting for law studies at the University of Singapore in order to give the Chinese a 50% chance to catch up. With their 10% population, Indians in Singapore have captured 90% of University seats. *"The sheer quality of NRIs far outweighs what I 've seen anywhere else in the world"*, says Dipak.

"In Singapore, I hired a young Indian of 24 with a degree in engineering, a Chartered Accountant and an MBA! How can you beat this? I was 30 years then. Already he had been running a bank single-handedly at Coimbatore, with a population of 3 million, in South India. By the time he reached 30, he could be earning $20,000 monthly in Singapore. This man had been raised in the rural backwater and he studied humbly by candle light as his family could not afford electricity". In Singapore, Dipak has earlier worked with Pran, an Indian, 35 years old, who is now earning $30,000 a month. Yet when Pran started back in his native village he had not even a table to study. But he had a vision and the instinct to work hard, to persevere and never to give up.

In the United Arab Emirates, 80% of the 1.7 million foreigners are either Indians or Pakistanis. The top jobs in senior management, IT sector arc taken by the 100,000 Indians and Pakistanis while the skilled and semi-skilled jobs at the lower level are in the hands of Indians and Pakistanis. The 30,000 whites at the top are in commanding and top management positions. The local Arab population in UAE, Kuwait and Qatar are vastly unskilled. Living off the oil revenues, they do not bother to study and do not have the right mindset. The result is that only 2% of the local Arab people in Saudi Arabia are considered skilled labour while they depend upon Indian and Pakistani doctors, engineers, bankers, teachers leaving 98% Arabs as unskilled.

The majority of Indo-Mauritians has not the least clue that such job opportunities with such fat salaries ever exist. They cannot imagine that a bank director can earn Rs70 Million annually. But the young Indian has a vision and he looks forward to earning one million rupees a month before he reaches 50 years while the Indo-Mauritians would be earning a maximum of Rs.50, 000 a month. Mauritians simply don't realise that these jobs are there and they have to reach out for them.

The problem is that they don't have the mindset, and the confidence to aim high and how to get there. What we see is that people tend to lose a lot of their time doing little to improve their prospects and they do not realise that they are receding downhill while the world is racing fast ahead.

In Malaysia where the Malays, the Bhumi Putra, are generally complacent, the government has distorted and narrowed down tertiary education through imposing Malay as the medium of instruction. But the bulk of Malaysian Indians are not happy with a restricted sort of education. This situation has driven a number of Malaysian Indians to study abroad in British, Indian, Australian and US universities in order to be able to compete effectively for the global job market. Consequently, by adopting English as the language of education, Singapore has outclassed Malaysia more than ten times in the provision of higher professional skills.

Unfortunately, Mauritius has been facing a similar language problem in the neglect of English due to the adoption of Creole and the preference of French which narrow down their perspectives at the global level. The young Mauritian intellectuals offer a pathetic picture by world standard in their inability to handle English. After 15 years of schooling, they can hardly express themselves fluently in English, which underscores a disastrous waste of public funds. They lack the ability and the confidence to handle English with skills to such an extent that they feel crushed, intimidated and they crumble before you if you address them in good English and you can see their ego going down to the floor. 20 years ago, Mauritians used to laugh at Indian English, but in the meanwhile they have themselves been receding backward while Indians have been improving their language skills to meet world standard.

India as a World Power

WE SHALL now visualise India as a global player beyond 2025. **India has to start taking on the posture of a world power**. As the land of Gandhi and its unbeatable world reputation, India will radiate the values that infuse its own rich culture, civilization, philosophy and religion. It means that the emerging Indian elites have to assume the mantle of a great power and all the responsibilities, discipline, openness, coalition building that this involves.

To pursue this topic further, we shall set the Indians against their competitors, the Westerners and the Chinese, spell out their strengths and weaknesses according to the following six criteria:- (i)- leadership, (ii) vision, (iii) work culture, (iv) family (v) social and (vi) education'

Leadership. Indians are loose at the political level, held down by too much democracy which hampers progress. But all the same, India has a vibrant democracy, a multi-cultural society, an independent judiciary, and a vociferous free press, factors which slow down the pace of development, moving from bottom-up. The Chinese have strong leadership and discipline. The Westerners have the strongest demonstrable leadership, proven by history, at all levels- political, economic, literary, research and innovation. At the far lower of the scale are the Arabs still stuck in feudal autocracy where power is controlled by the oil magnates, leaving the power structure weak, bare and lacking in depth. What India needs is wise leadership, clever diplomacy and accelerated economic progress.

Vision. The Indian vision is manly focused on and around the family and on education. There is no-collective vision. This is blatant in the motherland where political success is purely generated on emotion and less on rationale. In fact even in the smaller countries where diasporas live, this relative lack of collective vision hampers unity. Indians must dare to dream and take risks and switch from the *chalega* attitude towards a *can do* economy. They must exhibit more confidence, creativity, determination and optimism and face up to global competition.

The Chinese focus is on emulating the western model on a larger scale, roping in the US as a major partner in technological fields. The Western vision has always been the strongest. It is nurtured on a pioneer culture full of explorers, innovators, inventors, artists, and musicians. They have been the pace- setters because of their strength in creativity, courage, ideation and strategic thinking.

Work Culture. To demonstrate this, let's use a scale of 1-10 to bring out the points, where a 1 is weak and a 10 is the absoluite strength. On this scale, Indians would score an 8 due to a work culture based on integrity, hard work and perseverence. We do not give them a perfect 10 because there is still some way to go in terms of creativity and efficiency. Chinese, on the same scale, would also score an 8 for the same reasons above. The westerner scores a 5 and the reason for this relatively lower score is because of the increasing complacency and reluctance to long hours of work, as witnessed by the numerous strikes for a 35 hour week in Europe.

"China seems to be ahead of India. This is explained by the fact that China kicked off its reforms in 1980. The brighter side is that India is ahead on entrepreneurship. Democracy fosters better entrepreneurship. I'll refer to a study by Messers Huang and Khanna from MIT and Harvard which points out that India seems to be doing better at creating world beating companies. They also say that our capital markets are more transparent and efficient and our legal system, although flawed, is apparently much more advanced than China's".

(B.J.Panda, member of the Rajya Sabha).

To Panda's statement, Tarun Khanna, prof. Harvard Business School, adds that *"in all creative spheres like advertising, publishing, filmmaking, non government organisations, India outperforms China".*

(India Today. March 2004).

Family. The NRI believes strongly in his family life values and therefore centres on his nuclear or extended family. The Chinese policy of one child per family has had a negative, knock-on effect as compared to the large Arab family lacking in skills, a major drawback. The westerner is less attached to his nuclear family than the Indian and sometimes leaves his children on their own after 15 or 16 so that they acquire some work experience at a part time level and learn to stand on their own feet and face life independently. That's how the western youth get an early start in education, develop their sense of creativity, initiative and independence. In contrast, the Indian family will go on supporting the children even beyond adult stage to the extent of causing unnecessary interference in their lives and by over-protecting them, parents stifle their sense of independence and creativity.

Social. The Indians are weak in creating community-based living and often disagree on strategic plans and a collective vision. They focus on the family, on the individuals and pay little to the needs of the commnunity and their environment. This means that the Indians just settle in the villages or anywhere where they have their agricultural land haphazardly without caring for the availability of the basic infrastructure like roads, transport, water, electricity, schools, health, lesirure and shopping facilities. Indians are reactive, they start looking or claiming these facilities much later and the development of the network of villages become chaotic and topsy- turvy. In contrast, since Roman times, the westerners have been pro-active planners, thinking in long-terms. They are builders of structured, organized, orderly civic environment, complete with well-laid out road networks, equipped with water, electricity, job and shopping facilities, hospitals, sports and other amenities that support community-based living and enjoyable and readily available facilities.

Another, fundamental weakness of the Indians is their inherent tendency to look inward at their personal interest, restricted to caste, linguistic or regional boundaries so that they fail to see the larger social or national interests. Further complications like caste, language and regional barriers shoot up like impenetrable walls which tend to separate the Indians from one another and prevent them from thinking in the interest of the group. Sometimes they find it difficult to work and get along together, bury their caste and personal differences in an effort to reach a common view. Unfortunately, this generates a lack of *consensus- reaching which is absolutely important for the success of the group and of the country*. This mutual suspicion is seen in the reluctance of one Indian from one province or one specific caste or language background to marry with another Indian from a different caste, language or province. They bleed themselves to death through self-inflicting wounds and tear themselves apart through their internal divisions. They treat one another as different and disunited people. Mahatma Gandhi who was acutely aware of this weakness since his struggle in South Africa had devoted all his energy to weld the Indian people into a strong nation.

"All religious antagonism, as that one is a Hindu or a Muslim, a Christian or a Parsi should be forgotten. Let there be no provincial distinctions such as Bengalis, Madrasis, Gujaratis, Punjabis etc. All ideas of high and low which divide men into Brahmins, Ksatriyas, Vaishyas and Shudras should be abandoned. Indians are all subject to the same laws, if so, how can we fight them disunited?"

(Gandhi's letter to Indians in South Africa. July 15, 1914, as cited in appendix to A.Sawant, ed. *India and South Africa. A Fresh Start.* Kalinga. N.D, 1994))

This problem does not arise among westerners who freely intermarry with other westerners from any language, region or religion. Set in a multi-racial society abroad, the Indians and the NRIs are tremendoulsy hampered by those divergent tendencies. Thus an English boy of Anglican faith does not have any problem to marry a Scottish, or French or Italian girl of Catholic faith, nor does the Moslem bother about the caste, or religion of the girl because he will simply convert the girl or the boy into Islam. It is a rare occurrence to see a Brahmin boy from North India marrying a girl from South India from a different caste, language or regional differences. The Chinese may choose their marriage partners from among their clans but they are emulating the west and are very fast learners.

The Chinese have raced a lot faster than the Indians and the distance seems to be increasing. They are building modern infrastructure on the western model which further attracts foreign investments. The westerners are the strongest social institutional builders so that it feels good to live in their countries.

Education. The Indian scores 8 out of 10 while the Chinese scores 7. But the education of the Indian is generally narrow, academic, bookish, abstract, parrot-learning, leaving little room for the acquisition of other social skills, like sports, the arts and the development of practical and entrepreneurial skills, self-development and independent living. His focus is on studying for a certificate. Finally, when he works and gets married he is focused on his family but has little to do to occupy his leisure creatively. He is not even able to help his partner in the home and thus in an open, western society, the foreign-born NRI girls would much prefer marrying a western boy who has broader interests and who is helpful in the home as compared to the demanding, unhelpful Indian husband. The Chinese are emulating the west and are brought up in business and entrepreneurial skills since early childhood. This explains why Chinese businesses and entrepreneurs control the Asia-Pacific Region- Hong Kong, Taiwan, Singapore, Indonesia, Malaysia and Thailand. The westerner scores 5 out of 10 while the Arabs come last with a score of 2.

(Interview of Dipak Chummun, June 2004)

3

ACROSS THE SEVEN SEAS

THIS IS the story of the 20 million strong Indian Diaspora, the NRIs and PIOs, spread across far-flung 110 countries in six continents and island states. But first of all, we will have to get to know who the PIOs and NRIs are, where they come from, their diversity, something about their history, their geography, economics and politics, their cultural base and their relations to India. What are their vast ramifications, their varied needs, expectations and their potential as well as the complex and diverse multicultural societies within which they operate? These issues will be addressed in this chapter and the remaining chapters.

The picture that emerges is of two kinds-the more prosperous NRIs established in western societies and the PIOs still having to struggle in their host countries against numerous odds. But the picture is not evenly sombre and, given proper leadership at the centre, from GOPIO, from India, and the building of a chain of strong strategic networks involving business, educational and cultural exchanges, the situation can improve dramatically.

THE MOVEMENTS that led to the emigration of Indians overseas dated to the Indus Valley Civilization and particularly since the 5th century B.C when Indians started spilling over the neighbouring countries, east and west. Indian traders reached to Thailand, Malaysia, Cambodia, Vietnam, Bali, Indonesia and Japan. The RgVeda alludes to *"voyages to distant lands, and galleys with a hundred oars"*. In Bali, for example, Buddhism and Brahmanism flourish until today.

(Emigrant, 1924).

This led to the creation of Indian kingdoms in South East Asia, the propagation of Sanskrit and Sanskritic Hinduism as remains of Hindu and Buddhist temples and structures, cultural heritage belonging to ancient India bear witness. An interesting landmark stands out in the Indian pilot who guided Vasco da Gama from east Africa to land on the Indian coast in 1498.

Indian Presence Overseas

It is no accident of history that Indian products had found their way abroad. The story of Indian products overseas went back to the age of ancient Indian trade with Rome, Java, Sumatra, Borneo, Cambodia when Indian traders exported spices and luxury goods, ivory products, textiles, jewels, peacock feathers had lured east and west. During the Renaissance period, western powers like Italy, Spain, Portugal, Britain vied with each other to capture the precious Indian spice trade. This competition to discover the sea route to India drove Spain finally to send out its navigators across the Atlantic until Christopher Columbus accidentally landed in the Americas in 1492. In his turn, the Portuguese Vasco Da Gama skirted rounded the Cape of Good Hope and, with the assistance of an Indian pilot in East Africa, cut across the Mozambique to reach Calicut in India, in 1498. Later, the British followed suit and the Pilgrim Fathers landed in Virginia to start settlements in the American colonies. The Portuguese and the Spaniards colonised South America. Much later still, the East India Company began to trade with India and the flag was to follow the trade.

Overtaken by the West

Historically, in ancient times, while India was a great empire under the Mauryas, Europe was still plunged in darkness. As late as the 16th century, under the Moghul Empire, India was already an unrivalled world power, an industrial country, boasting of a great civilization, culture and philosophy and therefore much ahead of the rest of the world. Europe was still split into a number of weak dukedoms and city states, the US was overrun by rival tribes. The factors that were to give the competitive edge to a few west European countries were firstly, their early interest in maritime explorations, spearheaded by the visionary Portuguese Henry the Navigator who launched a band of enterprising captains. The breaches had been made by the intellectual gains of the Renaissance and Reform movements, followed by the Age of Enlightenment, the growth of Parliamentary democracy in Britain and most particularly by scientific and technological advances leading to the Agricultural and Industrial Revolutions.

By 1750, Britain made a quantum jump ahead with the use of steam power and its steam ships dominated the seas. It had become a super-power which devastated the Indian textile industry and flooded the Indian market with British manufactured goods. It accounted for the expansion of British colonisation, into Australia and Africa, further economic transformations and consequently the transportation of the Indian immigrants into the plantation colonies. By that time, west Europe had caught up with and surpassed India which had remained frozen into splendid isolation, cut off from the excitement of new ideas, of exploration, the expansion of trade, intellectual, scientific and technological advances.

Emigration

The second emigration wave was marked by the Kangani system of contract labour to Burma, Sri Lanka, Malaysia and other SEA countries. Thirdly, from 1734, the first batch of Indian artisans, known as *esclaves à talents*, or Malbarş and Lascars, was imported from Pondicherry to Mauritius under Mahé de Labourdonnais. This was followed in 1816 with the arrival of hundreds of Indian convicts, who, for the next 20 years, worked incessantly to hew the stones and build the main roads connecting Port Louis to the south, while new arrivals replaced the dead ones. Governor Gomm gave freedom only to those above 65 years. The first experiment with the arrival of Indian engaged labourers took place in 1829 with the recruitment of Indian and Chinese coolies from Madras, Calcutta and Singapore. In 1833, after Earl Grey had abolished slavery through the Empire, between 1834-1837, 7000 immigrants, under the new **contract labour system**, a new liberal concept that arose in the Age of Enlightenment in France, were brought into Mauritius. The first consignment for Trinidad took place in 1844, Jamaica in 1845, British Guina in 1838. At first there was a vast disproportion between the male and the female recruits with 20, 332 men to 931 women in 1842, in Mauritius. The indentured labourers attracted free passengers, comprising mainly of Gujarati traders as well as English merchants, the intermediaries between England, India and the local planters.

Fourthly, the continuous waves of emigration followed the Second World War when Indians spilled overseas into UK, USA, Canada, Australia, joined by the twice migrants from the former colonies. The new 1965 legislation authorising the immigration of professional Asians, to be followed by their families, unleashed an unending river of brain drain, - now happily considered as brain gain to the US. The new immigrants were mainly professionals, technocrats, doctors, engineers, accountants, traders, businessmen. The NRIs include also the expatriates serving in multinationals and Indian companies overseas in various corners of the world, from Central Asia, China, Russia, Europe, Africa and across the globe. They have contributed to the Indian economy through their remittances from abroad, investments and transfer of skills, brainware and technology.

Fifthly, in the wake of the oil boom is the outflow of the 3.5 million Gulf NRIs. They differ from the other groups in the sense that they are mainly temporary male workers, professional, technocratic (doctors, engineers, accountants, architects, bankers), plus 70% semi-skilled labour- sending their remittances back home to their families, mainly from South India, half of whom is from Kerala. These have flowed as significant contributions to India's balance of payments.

It appears that the emigration of professionals, and of talented individuals followed by their families, will grow further in the wake of globalisation, Information Technology and economic expansion as India - fuelled by NRIs'investments and technology- flexes its economic muscles, liberalises its economy, and it pulls down barriers and restrictions. As its economy surges forward, its self-confidence grows, its core competences and technology improve, India will extend its trading and manufacturing activities with the establishment of Indian companies and corporations abroad backed by a plethora of state to state bilateral agreements, lines of credits, other trade treaties. In their turn, this will help expand and diversify its NRI diaspora and extend India's relationships with outside countries. At the moment, buoyed by a wave of self-confidence, India is poised on a global economic expansion and an unending increase of its diaspora.

Running across all the Indian emigration overseas are some common features, namely the strong family ethos which binds the NRIs and PIOs around their language, culture, arts, music, religion, philosophy, their customs and traditions - all wrapped around their Indianness or Indian culture and civilization. At first, the pioneering settlers or migrants have had to face numerous challenges, including:- geographical isolation, separation from their families, the pressures of inter-marriage, conversion and assimilation, race prejudices and misunderstandings, competition and discrimination in their efforts to settle in hostile conditions abroad. Nevertheless, they have struggled on to preserve Indian cultural traditions, to establish ties and networks of socio-cultural and religious organisations overseas. They kept organising cultural and spiritual events under different circumstances. They have retained their links with the homeland while adapting, reassessing, re-inventing their Hindu values and practices. All along, they have had to compete for jobs and for opportunities to improve their status and to educate their children.

Today, every capital of the world has its China Town. Similarly, the Indian trader has marked his global presence with the inevitable Bombay store, Bombay bazaar, its sari and textile shop, selling a variety of Indian goods, spices, groceries, Basmati rice, arts, crafts, carpets, furniture, jewellery, a wide range of Indian products, music, songs, Bollywood films, books, newspapers, magazines. The food stalls or hotels offer a variety of Indian foods, sweets, snacks, the inevitable *roti, thali, paapar, samoosa, kulfi, sherbet,* drinks. Other corners popularise yoga, meditation, marked by a temple here and there and when you look up you feel that India has arrived.

One cannot imagine the immense popularity of Indian music and films and the great respect and symbolism which an elegant woman in sari carries throughout the world. I felt this whenever I travelled with my wife in Europe, in central Asia, in African and South East Asian countries when I saw people looking at her with amazement and obvious admiration. Great was my surprise and delight when, in 1970, out of all places, when I was homesick, I was thrilled to hear Indian music pouring from a television featuring a Raj Kapoor film in a hotel in Tashkent, in the then Soviet Union. It clearly reflects the fascination and popularity of Indian entertainment, of music, songs, dances and of Bollywood to the outside world.

Following an initial period of assimilation and adjustment, the NRIs and PIOs have been quick to adapt themselves to foreign situations, aided as they have been by the open, adaptable, humanistic and universalistic nature of Vedic and Sanskritic Hinduism. During the early stages, overcoming tremendous odds, particularly in the plantation colonies, spurred by family support with every member pulling their efforts together, the PIOs focused on self-help activities thanks to their hard work ethics, sacrifice, strong determination and perseverance. In the process, the Indians broadened their religious and cultural concepts, integrated themselves with mainstream society and adapted their businesses and their new style of living on cosmopolitan lines. Finally, the dedication to learning and education, dating back to Vedic and Buddhist ages, has thrown up a spiralling and diversified technocratic and professional class who have spilled all over the world, particularly in medical, engineering, technological, economic and I.T disciplines. (GOPIO, Melaka, 1995).

After reviewing the situation in the diaspora, the Singhvi High Level Committee, in its desire to step up FDI and investment inflows from the diaspora, came up with 160 recommendations. These cover the need to invest heavily in infrastructure building, social, cultural in a bid to shake up the current mechanism and create a congenial environment for business development in the wake of further economic reforms and liberalisation. This package of recommendations is likely to release tremendous dynamism, a radical review of current procedures. It may trigger further reforms and some hard thinking within the Indian government, the mass media and involving Indian corporations which will have to embrace global possibilities ahead of them.

South East Asia

THE EARLIEST Indian emigration dated back to ancient time, well before the Christian era. This is evidenced in the cultural and re ligious relics and structures, the Sanskritic linguistic heritage, culture, art, customs, philosophy, religion across the whole of South East Asia starting from Burma, Indo-China and spreading across S.E.A countries. The ancient Indian civilization has interpenetrated into South East Asian way of life and still thrives in Hindu Bali with its ancient cults of Saivism, Vaishnavism, Buddhism, apart from the dance, music, theatre featuring works from the Ramayana, Mahabharata, the Puranas, and Sanskrit plays, spanning across Burma, Malaysia, Thailand. The temple architecture and sculpture of Angkor Vat in Cambodia and Borobudur in Java bear witness to the presence of Indian culture and remnants of Sanskrit language across South East Asia, reminding us of ancient Indian kingdoms.

But the Indian cultural influence was mainly courtly and political and did not penetrate deeply into the masses. It's true that Indian culture elevated them from tribalism to feudalism, from animism to Hinduism and Buddhism and left behind the cultural and moral values and concepts which went with the Sanskrit heritage. The feudalistic courtly manners inculcated absolute loyalty to the king and to the feudal authorities and discountenanced a rational, questioning, democratic outlook of the power holders- a tradition which had characterised Indian society everywhere, in India and across the diaspora.

Just as Europe owes its culture and civilization to the Graeco-

Roman civilization, similarly, it can be said that the whole belt of Asia-from China, Japan, Korea, to South East Asia, was influenced by ancient Indian culture, civilization, religious thought, philosophy, literature, political thinking, astrology, medicine, agriculture. For example, ancient Indian kingdoms transformed Malaysia politically from tribal chiefs to kings, the temple replaced ancient spirit houses, while the primitive hunters and food gatherers were elevated into peasants and farmers. In Malaysia, the Sanskrit influence has survived in the old words used for religious, moral and philosophical, astronomical, botanical and mathematical concepts.

(*Pioneers of Prosperity*, ed.by Sudarsan Kumar, ND, 2000)

According to Prof. Madya Noriah Mohamed, University of Kebangasan, Malaysia, South East Asia has witnessed distinct cultural persistance and civilizational continuity of ancient Sanskritic and Buddhist civilization. They have persisted and transformed themselves, not in a static mould, but through constant change and adaptation in a permanennt dialogue with indigenous culture. They provided the first layer and model of a dynamic, on-going civilizational pluralism in Malaysia in terms of Sanskrit language, literary forms, cultural, moral and political values.

Since the 4th century, the Sanskrit, Buddhist and Hindu influences had spread across SEA. The Hindu epics, Mahabharatta and the Ramayana are highly popular in Indonesia and Malaysia. The shadow play of Mahabharatta stories and Ramayana is quite popular even nowadays. The question is why have the Hindu epics retained their influence, including their value system both in Malaysia and Java?.Old Sanskrit language was adapted from Javanese into Malay version. But the epics were to be adapted to serve local purposes in a new setting of Javanese and Malay cultural ambience while undergoing local modifications, additions and changes under different names, different interpretations to the concepts and symbols of the original epics.

Thus, the *Hikayat Pandawa Lima*, the HPL, or The Story of the Five Pandawas, first written in old Javanese scripts, and later in Malay, *Bahasa Melayu*, at a time when Islam was pushing into Malay society, had its central theme revolving around the five Pandawas and the hundred Korawas in a new Islamic cultural setting. But the Malay version of the HPL omitted a number of episodes which converyed Hindu teachings and which clashed with Islam while the Javanese version, introduced since the fourth century, attached great importance to the Hindu moral virtues and teachings embodied by the Pandawas. The Hikayat is

an excellent exposition of humanity, encompassing life, thought, inter-personal relations as well as man's relations with the Almighty. The Mahabarata teaches that no single group has the monopoly over truth and there are many ways of reaching it if there is tolerance.

After all, the Mahabharatta has retained all its freshness as a tale of war between the Kauravas and the Pandavas. Krishna's role and relationship to Arjuna unfolds the song of life. His ideas of Dharma in the Bhagavadgita, on the battlefield of Kurukshetra, depict man's relation with God and express the basic tenets of Hinduism, with its emphasis on *dharma*, *karma* leading to *moksha*. Dharma is taken as the treasure house of dharmashastra. Arjuna emerges as the hero who opens up, who hankers after knowledge. He is a strong and powerful person who represents the Hindu moral world value as well as the ideal male, pious, caring and loving, a faithful and obedient student and a fearless warrior. The Ramayana also advocates the importance of dharma and karma while Rama is depicted as the good, if not the ideal person. Both the Mahabharatta and the Ramayana are taught at educational and University levels in Malaysia.

The story is performed on the stage and around those two epics have developed a whole crop of literature, publications, art forms, theatre, sculptures and moral values, spanning across Myanmar, Thailand, Malaysia, Indonesia and particularly Java. Since both epics, with their high literary and moral values had penetrated South East Asia in ancient times during the thirteen hundred years of Hindu kingdoms and are therefore firmly embedded in popular imagination, there is no reason why they should not be appreciated and preserved in Malaysia.

Malaysian culture and civilization is pluralistic, a mixture of Hindu, Buddhist, Islamic and western influences. Aspects of Indian culture, forms of salutations, the use of the banana tree before entering the house in Java, taking off one's shoes before entering the house, are adopted by all in Malaysia and Java, including Muslim Javanese. But this does not hinder the Malays to be Muslims, to speak Malay and practise Malay culture which is firmly embedded in Hindu culture, enriched with successive layers of Buddhist, Islamic and western influences.

(Prof. Madya. Noriah Mohamed, University Kebangasan, Malaysia, International Writers' Conference on *Beyond Borders: Regional Voices in the Global Market Place*, Mauritius, 23 Aug. 2004)

Malaysia

MALAYSIA BOASTS 1.8 Million PIOs or 8% out of a population of 23 million, made up of wealthy trading Chinese, and 6 sub-groups of Malays or the *Bhumis*. The Malay archipelago or Malay world covers Brunei, Indonesia, Malaysia, Singapore, Southern Thailand, Southern Philippines, and Southern Kampuchea with a total population of 250 million inhabitants. After independence from the British, Malaysia went through a turbulent period marked by Chinese/ Malay clashes in 1969, leaving thousands of victims. This led to a tremendous transformation and a policy of positive discrimination in favour of the Bhumis in 1970 with the passing of the National Economic Policy, designed to correct the economic imbalance, providing the Malays more privileges and opportunities to enable them to catch up with the Chinese.

The constitution itself discriminates against non-Muslims as it defines all Malays as Muslims and which put the Hindus and the Chinese Buddhists at a disadvantage though Article 3 provides for the principle of religious freedom. The Hindus have their Malaysian Hindu Sangam, the Batu cave and the Taipussam festival. Generally, only lip service is paid to the principle of tolerance, democratic consultation and justice. By 1979, Malaysia witnessed a period of Islamic resurgence, under the Islamic Party. After the 1990's economic crash and the 9/ 11 attack on New York, the Islamic Party has lost heavily.

(Dr. Ghazali Basri, Academy for Civilisational Studies, Malaysia, 25 August 2004)

Under the discriminatory legislation, the Indians are left with no choice but to cope with the disabilities imposed by the a racist policy of economic and political marginalisation in the wake of the New Economic Policy, NEP, designed to protect and favour the Malays. The NEP inflicts an iniquitous regime of economic domination and subordination which penalises the Indians and which finally holds back the development of the country itself. The Indians, considered as non-Bhumiputras, are discriminated everywhere in access to education, to jobs in the name of Malay nationalism that finally stifles meritocracy and social justice. Consequently, the Indians, despite their contributions, merits and talents, have been pushed down to the bottom of the economy. By 1990, their share stood at barely 1%, compared to the Malays at 20.7%.(against 2.5% in 1969) and the Chinese at 44.9% (22.8% in 1969).

Despite all the contributions made by the Indian labourers who cleared the jungles for plantations, built roads, bridges and public buildings and built the rubber and oil palm industries, one million of the 1.8 million Indians are still stuck in backward conditions in the plantations.

"*For every Indian labourer who succeeded in rising into the ranks of petty capitalists or professionals, there were many more who died or were left as destitute bags of bones. The great majority of Indians remained proletarians, many of them locked into a form of wage bondage on the plantations*".

(Prof. Michael Stenton, New Zealand economist, mid 1970's.)

Indians have not shared in the economic prosperity of Malaysia, starting in the 1960's. They have been deliberately pushed downward into a spiral of poverty providing them little relief for the future. They have been consistently discriminated against by the NEP which was designed to create an indigenous Malay entrepreneur community to own 30% of the corporate wealth of the country with a Malay workforce of 40% in all economic sectors. This is apart from the other benefits granted to the Malays like subsidies, direct assistance, discounts and handouts, access to government jobs. The NEP discriminates against Indians in access to human rights, to education, the professions, business, to employment in the civil service and to the enjoyment of their social, economic and political rights. Even in the urban areas, it is difficult for them to rise to the top in higher education or in business. The few Indians who manage to get admittance to the universities are denied opportunities to scholarships and study loans and are referred to non-professional science and art courses. After graduation, they are further discriminated against in access to jobs. Yet, the merits and defects of the NEP have never been openly debated in Parliament, within academic circles or in the media.

This contrasts sharply with the more numerous and wealthy trading Chinese community in Malaysia who have set up independent schools and colleges and who can afford to give their children expensive foreign education. Forced by a vicious system of social, legal and political inequalities, persistent poverty, parental illiteracy, an oppressive environment, Indian children tend to drop early out of schools to help their parents with supplementary income in the plantation works. Otherwise, they remain unemployed or they fall victims to drugs. Thus, they reproduce the proletarian class structure of social inequalities. It is no surprise that a recent survey has revealed a high rate of malnutrition and retarded growth among Indian children.

Being a minority and not forming a political force, the Indians are neglected and do not enjoy any official attention. And without central assistance, it is just impossible for them to break out from the cycle of poverty and achieve social mobility. To add to their distress, the Indians, considered as second-rate citizens and immigrants, have to contend with the constant flow of Indonesian immigrants who are preferred over them and who are quickly granted Malaysian citizenship

(Dr. S. Balakrishnan, *Country Report*. Malaysia. *An Overview of the Malaysian Indian Community*. 2nd GOPIO Convention Paris, France, 10- 14 July 1992)

While the Chinese, backed by their network, have prospered in business and trade, the bulk of the Indians have been stuck in agricultural work in the plantations where they have to compete for a living with imported cheap labour, mainly Bangladeshis and Indonesians. In 1938, addressing the Indian problem in Malaya, K.A.Neelkanda Aiyer described the exploited Indians as *sucked oranges.* This is despite the fact that the contributions of Indian workers to the development of the rubber industry, transportation (mostly run by Sikhs), and public works have been immense. Indian popular culture, both Hindi and Tamil, songs, music, cinema, cuisine, exotic trades, the typical Bombay shop, is widespread in Malaysia. Middle class girls are taught Indian classical dances. Taipussam festival draws huge crowds to the Batu Caves in Kuala Lumpur.

In the race for economic development, the Chinese are firmly entrenched in business, commanding the industrial and commercial sectors, hitching the Malays behind them, through Malay participation in their businesses, in line with the requirement of the New Economic Policy while the struggling Indians have been left miles behind. The few Indian businesses have had to struggle without any State support. Some Indian businesses which have managed to cultivate alliances with the Malays have survived and prospered while the struggling small businesses, hampered by State-sponsored racism, lack the critical ingredients of success, the starting capital, a strong business culture, equipment, technology and know-how. The only sector where they seem to make it is in the food industry ranging from little stalls, hotels and restaurants. (John Doraisamy, *Pioneers of Prosperity,* ed.by Sudarshan Kumar. Baleshwar Agarwal, N.D, 2000).

The restrictions and insecurity on business development imposed by the NEP have incited the Chinese traders and businessmen to invest in other countries, namely China, Taiwan, Indonesia, Australia and Canada. The only way the Malaysian PIOs can succeed in the face of the oppressive and stifling NEP policy is to build strategic business alliances, networking, exchanges, joint ventures and partnerships with Indian companies in India and the global Indian diaspora. The networking has a strategic role to play in order to supply the much needed capital and technology and capture the vast Malaysian and S.E.A market, particularly in agro-business and the food industry. (Prof. R.Ramsamy, National University of Malaysia, Bangi, in GOPIO, Melaka, 1995).

Singapore

INDIANS IN Singapore who have wider opportunities for self-development offer a sharp contrast to their Malaysian brothers and sisters having to face a regime of domination, suppression and subordination under the NEP. Indian settlements in Singapore started around 1819 as soldiers. Some Indian merchants accompanied Sir Stamford Raffles to Singapore. By 1824, there were 756 Indians from South India mainly engaged in trade, others were employed in *road building, railways and port facilities, in addition to Indian convict labour which built the infrastructure of canals, harbour, sea walls, jetties. They had been* ***responsible for building the whole road infrastructure of Singapore***. This is similar to what had happened in Mauritius when Mahe de Labourdonnais, around 1721, had recruited skilled Indian artisans to build the city of Port Louis.After 1815, chained Indian convicts had built all the principal network of Mauritian roads and bridges. The French and the British have thus built the necessary infrastructure, the civic institutions and all the basic facilities which have made life worth living in both Singapore and Mauritius. Both in Singapore and in Malaysia, the transport industry was largely in the hands of Indians.

More Indian traders and settlers poured in, including Sikhs, Punjabis, Gujaratis, Bengalis and Parsis. Most of the immigrants were single young men who had primarily thought of making money and returning. It so happened that the Muslim Indians married with the local Malay women while the Tamils mainly the Chettiars, from Tanjavur and Travancore, married local Malays and Chinese women while preserving their Hindu dharma. They lived and worked in the town and constructed temples, notably the Siva temple in Orchard Street in 1850, the Sri Mariamen temple in 1862 and the Subramanien temple on Tank Road in 1859.

Inevtiably, wherever the Indians lived in high concentrations they created Little Indias, noted for crowded buildings, temple domes and ornate structures, the sale of groceries, spices, Indian products and foods. The Indians lived in five main areas, namely:-

(I) Chulia Street and Market Street where they traded.

(II) The High Street was dominated by the cloth trading community of Sindhis, Gujaratis and Sikhs.

(III) Gujarati Muslim jewellers and cloth merchants occupied Arab Street.

(IV) Serangoon Road is almost synonymous with little India, dotted with Indian products and restaurants offering a wide variety of Indian foods from South, North and Central India.

(V) The docks and railways were lined with Tamil, Telegu and South Indian labourers.

After World War II, Indian immigrants from across Malaysia and North India, and Sikhs from Punjab poured into Singapore. The new arrivals set up textile shops giving rise to major business families. To these, could be added the immigration of small groups of wealthy merchants and professionals and their families,

As an achievement-oriented society, Singapore, somehow like UK, US, and to a lesser extent, Mauritius, offers the prospects that favour the progress of Indians overseas, namely

(I) Living in concentration and thus enabling them to preserve their Indianness.

(II) Entry into business, backed up by a 500 membership in the strong Singapore Indian Chamber of Commerce and Industry (SICCI), founded in 1924, and a co-founder member of Singapore Federation of Chambers of Commerce and Industry. (SFCCI).

(III) Active participation in trade union, philanthropic and political activities to consolidate their rights.

(IV) A keen interest in giving advanced education to their children who are increasingly taking to Information technology, social sciences, arts and languages, engineering, medicine, law, business and pure sciences.

(V) Unlike what takes place in neighbouring Malaysia, Singaporean Indians are amply represented in Parliament. Their civil and political rights are safeguarded. They hold key posts in important ministries including Finance, Defence, Law, Home Affairs.

(VI) Side by side, Indian women are pulling their full weight and are occupying major positions in both public and private sectors.

(George Abraham, *in Pioneers of Prosperity*)

Africa, Mauritius and Reunion Island

Mauritius

MAURITIUS WAS the first plantation colony to introduce Indian Indentured labour since 1834, after the abolition of slavery. Boasting a majority of 700,000 PIOs, forming 70% of the population, fragmented into sub-ethnic groups, Mauritius offers the spectacle of a harmonious multi-cultural society. Indians have preserved their cultural heritage, their languages, including the teaching of Hindi, Tamil, Telegu, Marathi, Urdu in the schools thanks to its nearness to India. The Indo-Mauritians had the great advantage of producing an important class of small planters from among whom had emerged an expanding educated middle class and the future leaders of the country. Another interesting feature is that, in the wake of the Arya Samaj movement in the 1920's, and their close relations with India, the Indians went through a period of religious and social reforms which deepened the Indian consciousness and united them in their demand for freedom and self-respect. It somehow resembled a period of cultural renaissance and religious Reformation and helped to set them on the path of Indianness, modernization and political socialisation.

Some of the Arya Samajist leaders, namely Pandit Cashinath Kistoe and Pandit Sahadeo who were intimately influenced by Mahatma Gandhi and the Indian nationalist movement, joined Dr

Maurice Curé and Emmanuel Anquetil in the founding of the Mauritius Labour Party. From the start, the MLP was broadly representative of the Indian and Creole population in their class struggle against the capitalist White. The Arya Samajist reformers and missionaries encouraged the Indians to focus on educating their children and to take part in trade union and political activities. This led to the early growth of an articulate middle class, across both urban and rural areas, spearheaded by a band of dedicated leaders, namely Basdeo Bissoondoyal and Sir Seewoosagur Ramgoolam who led the country to independence. After the first trial of strength whereby all the Indo-Mauritians had got together to wipe part of the humiliation and oppression suffered under indenture and after from the hands of the colonialist and racist white, they felt that the danger was over. Since the 1960's, a new trend towards fragmentation of the Indian community became visible. Somewhat corresponding to what had happened in India in the division into 14 language provinces, various sub-ethnic groups, Bhojpuri, Tamil, Telegu and Marathi sprang up to defend their own interest. The emergence of Hindu solidarity has taken place in almost every election held since independence which kept SSR and later Sir Anerood Jugnauth into power especially when Indo-Mauritians have felt the interest of the larger community under threat.

Another interesting feature which distinguished Mauritius from the Caribbean Indians was the massive entry of educated Indo-Mauritians into the civil service, army, police and teaching since the 1950's largely assisted by Dr S. Ramgoolam's far-sighted policy to foster their social mobility. In return, they were to be loyal to the Labour Party and they ensured its stability in power over three decades. Once firmly entrenched in public administration they were to dislodge the Coloureds who had hitherto monopolised white collar jobs and the latter, fearing the advent of independence in the mid 1960's and the threat of Indianisation, vacated their jobs and emigrated en masse to Australia. Freedom has been consolidated by a liberal democratic constitution which has ensured fundamental human rights and the rights of the minority classes. Unfortunately, in the Caribbean islands, the emergence of a Caribbean Indian middle class capable of entering the civil service, police and armed forces never took place.

Since independence in 1968, Mauritius has been ruled by PIO Prime Ministers, including Sir Seewoosagur Ramgoolam, the Father of the Nation, (1968-82), Sir Anerood Jugnauth (1982-95, 2000-2003), Dr Navin Ramgoolam, (1995-2000). This lasted until 2003 when Jugnauth transferred power over into the hands of the Oligarchy under the white Prime Minister, Paul Berenger, leader of MMM.

Reunion Island

IN Reunion Island, historically under the pressure of French assimilationist racist policy, the majority of PIOs, mainly of Tamil origins, had been assimilated into Frenchness and have lost their language, culture, religion and have thus been absorbed into French - speaking Creoles and Catholicism. The French-centred assimilationist policy has used every means at its disposal to suppress and kill the roots of Indianness which it treated as barbaric, uncivilized, superstitious. It held European civilization as the model civilization and whatever was Indian was rejected as inferior and subordinate. In the wake of its legacy of slavery, economic exploitation, the denial of democracy and human rights, backed by an intolerant Catholic Church, State racism and its racialist Euro-centric discourses, the French tried to root out Indian identity. Since 1920, the PIOs were granted full French citizenship, political rights and could therefore enjoy security and welfare.

Recently, the influence of Mauritius, travels, tourism, the mass media, communications and globalisation, the impact of Black Power and Civil Rights movement in the US, the struggle against Apartheid, awareness of democracy and Human Rights have triggered cultural resistance against the domination, subordination and suppression of Indian culture and civilization. A new questioning and spiritual search into the Indian identity has surfaced. This has led to the **decentering and deconstruction of whiteness and euro-centrism** imposed under colonialism and racism and the consequent **re-discovery of**

Indianness. It has inaugurated a revival of Hinduism and interest in Indian culture, classical dance, songs, music, celebration of festivals among the PIOs. The resurgence of Indian culture has sparked a new interest in cultural commodities- dress, fashion, entertainment, yoga, meditation, spiritual discourses and all the paraphernalia associated with the presence of Little India overseas. What has happened to Reunion Island has also occurred to the minority of Indians in Guadeloupe, Martinique, except that there they feel more insecure under Black domination. In their hour of cultural awakening, the Reunion PIOs - standing as the bridge between the Francophone world and India- look forward to closer relationships and exchanges with India.

South Africa

NUMBERING A million, the PIOs are mainly concentrated in Durban. In 1653, the first batch of Indian Immigrants was sold as slaves in the Dutch Cape Colony. Following the successful experiment of importing Indian Indentured labour in Mauritius, South Africa, particularly Natal followed suit in 1860 when the indentured system was introduced with Coolies from 10% Biharis, UP, and 50% Tamils, 10% Telegus, followed, as usual, by free passengers, 20% Gujarati traders. Sir J. Halett, former Prime Minister of Natal admitted that within 5 years *"Durban was absolutely built up by the Indian population"*

The Indians had their first taste of brutal treatment, flogging- they were not given their proper wages or were paid irregularly. The returnee immigrants made their complaints and immigration was stopped. It was resumed in 1874 after the Coolie Commission set up in 1872 confirmed the bad treatment, the lack of medical facilities, the fines. But soon the European planters began to clamp down upon the Indians and restricted their immigration. In 1893, an annual Poll Tax of three pounds, representing 6 months' wages was imposed on the Old Immigrants of male above 17 years, female above 13 years for permission to live in the Natal. The progress of the Indians was hampered through denial of education, lack of technical or secondary schools, lack of franchise, the closing of the civil service to Indians.

This is how in 1893, **Mohandas Karamchand Gandhi** landed in South Africa and started the long struggle against the poll tax, the stringent immigration laws, for the civil and political rights of the Indians. Soon after his arrival, Gandhi was brutally thrown out of a railway compartment at the Pietermaritzburg station, an event which changed the destiny of India and of South Africa. He founded and struggled under the National Indian Congress, in 1894, followed by the Transvaal Indian Congress, engaged in non-violence and Satyagraha until his departure in 1914, the precursors of the African National Congress in 1912.

Since the 1930's, the Indians had to struggle incessantly against a battery of **anti-Indian legislation**, including:-

(1) The Trading and Occupation of Land Restriction Bill of 1943.

(2) The Pegging Act (froze Indian holdings and bound them to their existing residences and business for 3 years and barred them from purchasing fixed property from whites, except in certain restricted areas).

(3) The Population Registration Act.

(4) The Group Areas Act.

(5) Prevention of Mixed Marriage Act - designed to restrict their freedom of movement, their civil, political and economic liberties under the repressive.

In the Dutch Republic of Transvaal, the discriminatory laws, including the Immigration Restriction Act, the Franchise Law and the Trade Licensing Act were particularly harsh. Indians were both hated and feared, treated as *"the squalid coolies with ruthless tongues, the parasites, semi-barbarous Asiatics"* who spread all sorts of epidemics of leprosy, syphilis, due to their filthy habits and immoral practices. All Indians were treated as coolies, coolie clerks, and coolie school masters.

The discrimination was designed to protect the poor whites against competition from Indians. Said the South African born Lord Delamere,

Governor of Kenya, *"if open competition is allowed the small white colonist must go to the wall"*

In fact the policy of apartheid was designed to protect the interest of European merchants, planters, mine owners and white workers against cheap non-White labour. It was backed by all kinds of repressive laws to restrict Indians from gaining access to land, jobs and commerce. Immigration restrictions prevented Indians from exercising free trade and mining.

Believing in the **Calvinist faith of predestination** that they were the chosen children of God, the Boers held that they alone were predestined to rule over others. Under the doctrine of White Supremacy - blending the power of government and of the Church, which then ruled the world, their Nationalist Party treated the Black and Asiatic races as born inferior and a threat to their faith. Their religious beliefs fuelled institutionalised racism, colour bar, the inequality of races, and the apartheid system or Apartness. Finally, the Verwoerd government converted racism into racialism by enforcing the doctrine of the separate development of ethnic groups. The native African population was pushed back into the restricted and arid homelands, surrounding the major industrial towns in order to supply cheap wage labourers. The implications of White supremacy were widespread throughout the colonies. In South Africa and elsewhere in modified forms, it justified the domination and oppression of the African and Asiatic races, the imposition of flogging, economic exploitation, use of slavery and racial discrimination. Under apartheid, and under the pretext of separate development, a system of racial segregation was imposed by which residences, schools, social institutions were kept separate for whites from non-whites.

The Apartheid system separated the population on racial lines. The 4.9 million white were separated from the 20 million Blacks, 3 million coloured and nearly one million Indians in order to give only the white absolute political and economic power. The effects of the apartheid policy meant that by the **Lands Act of 1913 and 1936**, 87% of the land went to the whites who made up only 15% of the population and who controlled 98% of productive land. This means that all the capital, economic power and large incomes remained in white hands as well as access to education, health, housing, roads and other infrastructural facilities. The average holding of a white farmer stood at 1700 hectares as compared to only 13 hectares for the black out of which only 0.9 hectares were arable. The average white worker earned 5 times more than the Black worker. The Mine and Workers Act of 1926 had barred Africans and Indians from entering lucrative employment in a large number of industries. The government invested all its attention in the building of modern infrastructure, the creation of modern cities only for the benefit of the white population while the Blacks were confined to squat in the underdeveloped townships of Bantustan

Since 1946, **Nehru** opposed the South African regime doggedly by condemning apartheid at the UN. He withdrew the Indian High Commission from the republic of South Africa, imposed a total embargo against South Africa, covering commercial, economic, cultural, political and sports. He recalled the tragedy of Africa at the Bandung Conference of Afro-Asian Countries, in 1955. India gave strong support to the liberation movement under the aegis of the ANC. In 1960, at the Commonwealth Conference in London, Nehru condemned apartheid and racial discrimination as immoral and he forced the Republic of South Africa to withdraw from the Commonwealth. The bloody massacre of peaceful demonstrators occurred on 21st March 1960 at Sharpeville, followed by Soweto in 1976 and WHAM, 1986.

Indians Under Threat

There was a price to pay for the 1946 unilateral imposition of the Nehru embargo on the Apartheid regime which effectively isolated the Indians of South Africa from India. Blinded by socialist ideology, India then showed complete disregard of their cultural, religious, social and political needs. The traffic between these two countries had been cut off for over four decades until South Africa won its independence under Nelson Mandela. In the meantime much damage has been done. .

Instead of coming to the help of Indians in South Africa, victims of Apartheid, of the iniquitous Group Areas Act, No 41 of 1950 and of

1970 which relocated and destabilised the 38,000 Indian families, India got carried away by its socialist ideology. India had little understanding of the reality of the Indians on the ground in South Africa. It is unfortunate that no serious studies, surveys, investigations had guided the official policy decisions. It ignored the intense pressure exerted to propagate evangelism and the Apartheid ideology of Christian National Education designed to convert Indian children in the schools whose curriculum was loaded with Christian propaganda and Bible stories. Inevitably, large-scale conversions of Indian children followed. The authorities disallowed the Indian schools from teaching religious knowledge. The deculturisation process was aggravated by the break-up of the joint or extended family system within which the elders used to pass on religious and cultural knowledge and practices to the young generations.

It is a shame that the real victims of the economic boycott happened to be Indians who were stranded, cut off completely from commercial, cultural, educational, religious and political ties with India. This exacerbated the conditions of the Indians who had suffered from a painful history of economic, social and political disabilities. Contrary to what Mahatma Gandhi had earlier fought for in South Africa, the Indian government imposed a ban on Indian academicians, religious and social leaders from visiting South Africa and even teaching in South African universities. India seemed to have targeted the Indians in South Africa while it kept trading with and sending academicians, visitors and artistic troupes to other countries with Indian populations, namely the UK, USA, Canada, Fiji, Mauritius and the Caribbeans.

Despite all these disadvantages, the Indians in South Africa have tried doggedly to hold on to Indian values. However, the casualties have been enormous. A high proportion of the young people, particularly of South Indian origins, taken off-guard, have fallen easy preys to western propaganda, to conversion, inter-mixing and inter-marriage, and to rapid deculturisation and the consequent loss of their Indian identity. This was aggravated by a dearth of cultural contact, including Indian food, films, music, entertainment, cultural influences and moral leadership. All these things happened despite South Africa's nearness to the peninsula. Fortunately, Mauritius had served as a bridge between India and South Africa and countless Indians who could afford it from South Africa found cultural and religious solace in the island, particularly during period of Hindu festivals, which were not celebrated or recognized in South Africa. Contemporary India has a debt to the people of South Africa and closer ties – commercial, cultural, social- must be made in real earnest in order to strengthen the broken historical links- left by Mahatma Gandhi. Now, after independence and under the pressure of Africanising the civil service and jobs in the private sector, the employment opportunities of Indians in South Africa have become further insecure.

According to the Pretoria-born Mrs Maneesha Chummun, the various Indian ethnic groups, Bhojpuris, Gujaratis, Punjabis, Sindhis, Tamils, Telegus have tried to preserve their cultural and religious traditions with the assistance of parents and grand-parents. But under the impact of Apartheid, the influence of westenisation and now Africanisation, coupled with the long absence of cultural support from mainland India, with each passing generation one notices a great change in the way Hinduism is practised. The influence of western culture and the lifting of Apartheid has been accompanied by a break-down of traditional racism, reinforced by a wave of inter-marriages between young Indians and White, Indians and Coloured, Indians and Black The younger generation seems to have lost their sense of identity and they do not know which way to turn.

In addition to the ethnic languages, Indians have to cope with Afrikaans, Zulu, Xhosa and English. Similarly, the ethnic costumes have been retained but again the younger generations seem to prefer western clothes and lifestyle. In the matter of food, the South African Indians are beef and pork eaters while cooking has evolved away from mainland India, the flavours being more enhanced.

The South African multi-cultural government promotes a mainstream culture based on a more liberal, secular, non-racial, non-sexist, democratic constitution which proclaims:-

Article 5.2:- *There shall be freedom of worship and tolerance of all religions, and no state or official religion shall be established.*

Art. 5.11 guarantees:-

Sporting, recreational and cultural activities shall be encouraged on a non-racial basis, drawing on the talents and creative capacities of all South Africans, and autonomous organisations may be established to achieve these objectives.

(Dr Anil Sooklal, University of Durban-Westville, South Africa. *The Future of Indian Religion and Culture in a Post-Apartheid South Africa.* 2nd GOPIO Conference, Paris 10-14 July, 1992)

While elsewhere, in the UK, USA. Holland, Calvinism had evolved into economic individualism and democratic political systems, in South Africa it codified into racialism. When de Klerk assumed power, South Africa was in a state of economic collapse under the weight of sanctions and economic boycott by European countries, US, Australia, Canada, New Zealand and neighbouring African countries. Hence, he started the process of liberalisation, lifted the emergency imposed in 1986 and the apartheid laws. He released the African political prisoners and started negotiations with Nelson Mandela and the ANC that were to lead to the post-Apartheid era and the election of Mandela as the new president.

The ANC had adopted a broad-based democratic and human right platform and the championship of freedom. India has been entertaining friendly relations with the ANC as witnessed by the warm welcome given to Nelson Mandela in 1990 in Delhi Enriched by their political experience, the South African Indians had been able to lend effective support to Nelson Mandela's African National Congress in their freedom struggle. Thus, the PIOs have been active political partners in the South African government under Mandela and Mbeki. The South African Indians are mainly English-speaking. Consequently, they have lost touch with Indian languages, not taught in the schools. Having shared the humiliation and deprivations under the Apartheid regime along with their Black neighbours, the majority Indians, though still proud of their Indianness, feel thoroughly assimilated in South Africa and identify themselves more as South Africans, though a handful of them are extremely rich. India had remained a steadfast supporter of freedom and human rights in South Africa. It is expected that the good relations between the two countries will be further strengthened at the political, economic and diplomatic levels leading to business and economic exchanges and partnerships in the fields of mining, industry, agriculture, education and health.

(Ankush B Sawant, ed. *India and South Africa. A Fresh Start. Kalinga.* N.D. 1994)

Other African Countries

UNDER BRITISH colonisation in Kenya, Tanzania, there followed batches of Indentured labourers engaged mainly in railway construction. Gujarati traders followed suit and expanded into Uganda. But since they isolated themselves from the political struggle of the Ugandans and concerned themselves exclusively with their economic activities, and maintained a superior attitude to the natives, the Ugandan Indians became easy targets of African opposition. This led Idi Amin to chase them out from Uganda when the majority migrated to Britain where they have been doing very well. In Kenya and Tanzania, they have tended to be more careful and wiser in following the example of PIOs in South Africa by participating in the civil, economic and political advancement of their countries of adoption. But due to their small size they cannot play any significant role and therefore are unable to safeguard their civil and political rights against the daily threats to their personal security.

PIOs have penetrated into various countries of Africa, namely Botswana, Namibia, Zambia, Zimbabwe, Mozambique, Angola, Ethiopia, Sudan, Ghana, Nigeria, Djibouti, Madagascar in comparatively small numbers. From 1970's, Indian professionals, traders and their companies have moved into the more prosperous Nigeria. This trend seems to continue and develop with the expansion of business in African countries and bilateral agreements

Mauritius and the Caribbean Islands, Fiji-

Similarities and Differences

BEFORE THEIR independence, Mauritius, the Caribbean islands and Fiji had been sugar producing islands under British colonialism. They had all been populated by descendants of African slaves and Indian Indentured labourers and native Caribs. Fiji had an indigenous population of Fijians besides Indian immigrants. Indian culture and Hindi had been widely accepted in Fiji. Mauritius had been populated by the French settlers in 1721, secondly by African and Malagassy slaves, thirdly, by 1729, a sprinkling of Indian skilled artisans from Pondicherry, known as Malbars and Lascars, followed, in 1834, after the abolition of slavery, by massive influx of Indian immigration from 1834 to 1922.

Life in Sugar Plantations

Life had been very hard under indenture. The racist white planters, ex-slave owners, exploited the labour of the Indians as if they were their slaves. Chief Justice Joseph Beaumont, (1863-68), in Guyana, described it as *"a monstrous, rotten system, rooted upon slavery"*

They imposed starving wages which remained fixed over a century, harsh laws which restricted the liberty and movement of the Indians who were subjected to fines, arrests, imprisonment against which they had no appeal so that Indians were maintained in a state of poverty, illiteracy, humiliation and terrorism.

'The enemies of progress had always regarded the workers as their livestocks to be disposed of as they wished.

(Dr. S.Ramgoolam. *Advance.* 25.12.1953)

In such moments of despondency, they were saved by their very Indianness which instilled in them a bundle of moral values, thrift, courage, resilience, hard work, attachment to their family values and the will to succeed.

Indian culture became the most lasting and *continuous form of resistance against the plantation system.*

(Dr Basdeo Mangru, *Indians in Guyana*, Adams Press, Chicago, 1999)

Mauritius has been the only country outside India to have had three successive Indo-Mauritian prime ministers, from 1968-2003. But in the other countries, despite their numerical strength, Indians have been thrown into political wilderness. In the Caribbeans and in Fiji, there is little mixing, little cultural interaction and inter-marriage between the Indians and the Blacks. In contrast, in Mauritius, since 1721, the tradition of French assimilationist policy which had imposed conversion and French supremacy had spawned a free flowing, mixing and Creolisation of the Indian population, though the majority of Hindus still cherish their Indianness. Here are some explanations.

Seek Thou the Political Kingdom First!

Unlike the other plantation colonies of the Caribbeans with minority Indian population in Trinidad, Guyana and Surinam, Mauritius claimed 70% PIO's. It was fortunate to produce an articulate middle class and great leadership which arose from among the small planters. Due to its nearness to India, it could preserve and cherish its Indian identity and the ancestral languages, particularly Hindi, which were fuelled by a vigorous social and cultural reform movement. It had enjoyed a powerful trade union and political movement in the wake of the Mauritius Labour Party, since 1936, which united and involved the working classes of Creoles and Indo-Mauritians, from the bottom-up against the white minority.

"A good society can only be built from the bottom up. No member can escape his responsibility. Civic consciousness, education must reach down to the village level. His own responsibility exercised as a trade unionist, co-operator, councillor, social worker or teacher."

(Dr S.Ramgoolam. Advance. 1949).

In contrast, the Caribbeans and Fiji islands had failed to bring the Blacks and the Indians on the same political platform under enlightened leadership, as supplied by SSR.

Ramgoolam had been a skilful politician who managed to establish social and political harmony through a system of political coalition and the respect of minority rights. Firmly grounded in Indian culture and committed to the British parliamentary system and to Fabian Socialism, he has led his country to independence and contributed largely to the establishment and consolidation of a sovereign democratic state, according to the constitution, leading to mature democracy and the Rule of Law. As a Gandhian and a man of peace, he set up the socio-economic and political conditions conducive to national solidarity and social harmony, the avoidance of racial conflicts and disorder, the triumph of the spirit of democracy, of tolerance, give-and take and of fair play. He guaranteed the political rights of the minorities and provided for their adequate parliamentary representation through the Best Loser System, unique in the world. It was enshrined in the liberal-democratic constitution, based on the respect of human rights. It provided for a fair and adequate representation of each community by means of seats reserved for the best losers in the Legislative Assembly.

He quietened the fears of the Whites and of the Afro-Creoles through setting up a sound government, fair system of taxation and finance, redistribution of wealth through a mixed economy, a generous Welfare State, a democratic constitution, backed by Fabian Socialism, and continued economic development.

But **Trinidad, Tobago**, Guyana and Fiji had failed to adopt the Ramgoolam style of democratic constitution based on coalition politics and the democratic representation of all minority ethnic groups into central government which could have ensured the continued triumph of democracy, social and political stability and economic development. Thus, by nurturing the smooth development of democracy, peace-loving Ramgoolam spared the country from ethnic bloodshed, coups d'etat, repression as have occurred elsewhere, particularly in Fiji and Guyana.

In contrast, the 1957, 1961, and 1964 General Elections, in **Guyana**, had been dominated by ethnic and not class cleavages, unlike what had happened in Mauritius. Guyana had been marked by extensive racial violence and African/ Indian riots which broke out on Black Friday; 16th Feb.1962, in Georgetown, countrywide in 1963, and 1964, again in Georgetown in 1992 and the Civil Disorders of 12 January, 1998. In Guyana, from 1964-92, the Blacks, under Burnham dictatorship had captured state power then considered as a prize from which to distribute the rewards of office in the civil service, police, armed forces exclusively to the Blacks. Indians have been totally excluded and discriminated.against. This repression lasted until 1992 when the first free and fair elections since 1964 were held under the supervision of US ex-president Jimmy Carter and which saw Dr Cheddi Jagan elected as the president.

Consequently, due to their lack of political stability, the latter two countries have remained relatively poor and backward. Theoretically, Trinidad and Tobago, with 40% Indians and 60% Blacks, had adopted the British parliamentary system of first past the post except that there is less evidence of coalition politics and the constitutional representation of minority groups in government which prevail in Mauritius. This fosters political ethnic polarisation. Thanks to their relative social and political stability, Mauritius, Trinidad and Tobago have made gigantic economic strides.

In Mauritius, the build-up to independence really got started after the 1963 general elections leading to the decisive elections on independence issue in 1967 which Ramgoolam won thanks to his LP-CAM-IFB alliance against the anti-independence PMSD, led by Gaetan Duval, strongly backed by the White and the Creoles. Independence was overshadowed by ethnic violence in 1967. In Guyana, the run-up to independence was marked by the 1961 election which saw an intensification of the racial/ ethnic cleavages. According to Ravi Dev, June 21, 1998, Guyana has never really moved forward from the mind set created since 1961 that a PPP led government would mean the liquidation of the Blacks. A similar propaganda was launched by the White-controlled PMSD in Mauritius that a Ramgoolam-led government would mean the Indianisation of Mauritius but the contrary has happened as the Indo-Mauritians have ensured stability all along in a fair, democratic, tolerant and power sharing spirit. Under the inspiring leadership of Sir Seewoosagur Ramgoolam, the unique Mauritian example can be held up as a clear demonstration of the political statesmanship of Indians in promoting harmonious social living and furthering economic development within a democratic coalition power-sharing government

Guyana. In a bid to throw Dr Jagan out of power, in 1964, the British and the Americans changed the electoral system from first-past- the- post to Proportional Representation. Consequently, L.F.S. Burnham, a Black lawyer and the former partner and chairman of Jagan's party, the People's Progressive Party, PPP, changed into the leader of the People's National Congress, PNC. In alliance with the Union Democratic Party (the League of Coloured People interests), and the backing of rural Blacks under Sydney King, Burnham ousted Dr Cheddi Jagan with British and American intervention. For the next 28 years, the Indians had been discarded from power sharing and Burnham stayed in power through dictatorship, brazen corruption, rigging the national elections, state terrorism and racial discrimination.

The PNC government practically unleashed a reign of terror on the opposition, particularly the PPP and the Working People Alliance, led by the eminent Black historian, Dr Walter Rodney Both Indians and Blacks suffered violent beatings by organized gangs of thugs. They targeted largely Indian homes, raping women and girls, robbing and killing other members of the family.

(Dr Basdeo Mangru, 1999)

Fiji has a system based on power sharing which set the tribal ethnic Fijians against the Indians. Therefore, in practically each of these countries, there is a polarisation of power holding, separating the Indians from the Creoles or ethnic Fijians. It is either the Indians in power for a very brief unstable period or the Blacks in power for long periods marked by racial conflicts and repression. The result of racial conflicts and political instability in Fiji and Guyana is that they have remained economically undeveloped. Guyana had suffered from chronic shortage of food, clean water, low productivity, low wages, high inflation, the looting and burning of homes and raping of Indian women. The Guyanese Indians had to flee to other parts of Guyana and live in squatter settlements, earn their living on rice farming, gold smithing, saw milling, petty retailing, and the professions of law and medicine. Therefore, Indians had learnt to lift themselves by their own efforts while the country was split into ethnic enclaves. A substantial number of Indians subsequently migrated to the United States.

Consequently, these four Caribbean countries differed entirely from Mauritius which had, under Sir Seewoosagur Ramgoolam, invented the new method of coalition government, ethnic co-habitation, peaceful co-existence in a bid to maintain social and political harmony. In contrast to the Caribbean islands, Trinidad, Guyana, where the Blacks control government jobs, the army and navy, in Mauritius, since the 1950's, such jobs had been filled by Indo-Mauritians who had edged out the Coloured, thanks to Ramgoolam's far-sighted policy. In return, they had ensured lasting political stability and economic development.

Cultural Relations with India

Due to their remoteness to India, the Caribbean countries had not benefited from the frequent comings and goings of Indian reformers who had earlier introduced the Arya Samaj and other social and cultural reforms which had modernized society considerably in Mauritius. The Arya Samaj had eradicated many of the obsolescent features and practices of feudal India. It had abolished the caste system, simplified rituals, revived Vedic and Sanskritic Hinduism, popularised the learning of Hindi and the importance of education. At the same time, the Indo-Mauritians had been inspired by the freedom struggle of the Indian National Congress under Gandhi and Nehru. It was an intense period of cultural renaissance, of social reforms and political consciousness, marked by the learning of Hindi and a unifying Indian consciousness which was being fuelled by reformist Indo-Mauritian leaders, in close touch with India. Besides, the Indian cinema and frequent visits and studies in India further consolidated the ties of Indianness, which, unfortunately, had not occurred in the Caribbeans. The social reforms had rejuvenated Indian culture and had given the Indo-Mauritians a sense of pride and self-confidence in their Indian heritage. Indian culture, and languages have been kept alive in Mauritius thanks to the close collaboration of the Indian government which kept sending, as far back as 1948 a free flow of cultural assistance, namely:- experts in the teaching of Hindi, of Indian culture, Indian languages, Indian music, dance, of Indian crafts, apart from books, library, musical instruments, cultural troupes, yearly scholarships for studies in India, the setting up of cultural institutions including the prestigious Mahatma Gandhi Institute, the Indira Gandhi Centre for Indian Culture, the Rajiv Gandhi Science Museum, a yearly cohort of Indian technical experts, the setting up of Indian corporations, including the Life Insurance Corporation of India, the Baroda Bank and various other private companies

Unfortunately, the geographically remote west Indian islands and Fiji which most needed closer cultural assistance from India were left in the lurch so that the Caribbean Indians did not have the same opportunity to upgrade their cultural level as happened to Indo-Mauritians. Worse, still, the Caribbean countries had been relatively culturally deprived. They had not experienced similar cultural movements which had initiated a pre-independence period of an enriching cultural renaissance, religious reformation and political revival. They had not known anything of the sort, no cultural and social reforms, no permanent contact with real India and no possibility of preserving Hindi as a link language. Hindi was never taught in the Caribbean schools and it vanished as a language while the Caribbean Indians spoke only an inferior pidgin English, which became more of a handicap than an asset whenever they migrated abroad, particularly to the United States. India existed only remotely in their imagination though the Caribbean Indians were initially able to fall back upon their Indianness to put up a strong resistance against the exploiting white planters. The saving grace has been the continuous flow of Indian music, songs and cinema.

Invasion of Americanism

But these reformist and modernizing movements had barely touched the Caribbean Indians who were left culturally stranded and in a vulnerable position. They were still stuck to their popular, obsolete rural traditions which had not evolved to a higher level of cultural development as had taken place in Mauritius. Therefore, being geographically remote from India and in close proximity to the United States, the Caribbean Indians inevitably feel less attracted to the many ugly features of the feudal Indian traditions in comparison to the more dynamic, glamorous, materialistic American culture, American songs, music, cinema and products. Inevitably, the more they fell under American cultural dominance, the more they drifted away from their Indian heritage about which they know little and which they associate with shame and social inferiority, just as the descendants of African slaves had embraced Americanism and had totally rejected their past African ancestry.

Consequently, the Caribbean Indians had lost touch with the binding and revitalizing effect of Indianness which had mobilised the Indo-Mauritians in their struggle for political power. Obviously, these factors have pushed the Caribbeans towards American cultural influence. They tend to be more attached to United States and they see themselves less as descendants of Indians or of Africans. This also explains how the Trinidadians are trying to forge a new mixed civilization, a blend of American and Indian values as reflected in the music, songs, food, customs and everyday life. The difference is that the Caribbeans revolve as the cultural sattelites of the United States particularly its technological, pragmatic and forward-looking culture while Mauritius is evenly poised between the Indian sub-continent and the West.

(Dr Kirk Meighoo, Trinidadian, interview, Week-end, 23 rd May,

2004)

Political Vulnerability

Unlike what had taken place in Mauritius, the Caribbean Indians were considerably hampered by the absence of a strong movement in favouir of cultural and social reforms, under inspired and dedicated leadership. Caribbean Indians, out of touch with political evolution in India, then convulsing under the Indian nationalist movement, lacked the political culture and the early political awareness which had awakened the Indo-Mauritians as early as the 1920's when they had elected two Indo-Mauritians into the Legislative Council. Further, Caribbean Indians always mistrusted the educational system dominated by Christian authorities. In the absence of an internal cultural renaissance and social reforms to counter the process of conversion, they did not feel motivated to embrace the value of education since they were put off by the Christian denominational schools which focused on converting the Indian children. The absence of a large educated forward-looking Indian middle class, as a driving force of political progress, condemned them to a state of permanent underdevelopment, a long way behind the more educated Blacks.

Another negative factor is that the Caribbean Indians, particularly in Guyana, had remained quartered in agriculture in the rural backwaters where they had little access to education and social mobility. Therefore, the Caribbean countries were polarised into a land of two nations, the Indians in the plantations and the Blacks in the urban centres. They had abandoned the towns with all their urban infrastructure of education, trade unions, employment and politics into the hands of the Blacks. In other words, they had, in the meanwhile, surrendered all the factors of modernization and development to the Blacks who had grabbed the opportunities conferred by education to gain strategic positions in government jobs, the army and police.

Too late, for over four decades, in the absence of a stable power-sharing system and ethnic co-habitation, since the capture of power by Burnham, the Indians came to realise that it was very difficult to dislodge the Blacks from the infrastructure of power. The Black government did not hesitate to use the power of coercion, the army, brutal force, organised crime to cling to power. Now, since the Blacks had secured the superstructure of government, they could keep Cheddi Jagan, who had earlier lacked the political far-sightedness and sagacity of a Sir Seewoosagur Ramgoolam, out of power for as long as they liked. It was only after the death of Burnham who had wrested power from Jagan and who had maintained Black power and domination until 1995 that Jagan could belatedly accede to power as the president of Guyana. But in the meantime, as in Trinidad and Guyana, the Indians had neglected education and had allowed the Blacks to monopolise the key sectors in the civil service, police and army.

It somehow resembled what had happened in Fiji, during the double coups d'etat in 1987 and the ousting of Chaudry in 2000. Despite their numerical strength, Indians were easily ousted from power for the simple reason that they could not support themselves in government due to their absence in the public administration. They were not backed by a strong politically motivated educated middle class and inspiring leadership to ensure their success in government. In most cases, the public administration has been run by a hostile civil service which could easily undermine any government spearheaded by Indian prime ministers or presidents- as had occurred frequently in the Caribbeans and in Fiji.

The United Kingdom

EMIGRATION FROM India and PIOs from the former colonies to the UK and to other European countries has picked up fast after World War II. In response to the demand for low paid, unskilled labour, vacated by the British in search of better paid jobs, South Asians, mostly males, were lured as migrant workers. At first they had to cope with the difficulty of housing, inadequate social services, little leisure hours and they had to face racial discrimination in jobs and were under attack as inferior beings, as aliens, dirty, smelling spices, practising strange religions, wearing funny clothes and crowded living as packed sardines. But their sense of exclusion and isolation ended in the 1950's and they could find their bearings when they were re-united with their families. Slowly the Asians threw up a business community. In contrast, Mauritians who migrated to France have felt more welcome, more at home and accepted as French citizens at par with other French citizens particularly as they were already accultured in French culture and language back home. Among the features that they cherish most are :-French democracy, republican values as liberty, equality and fraternity, freedom of speech, the liberty of the press and investigative journalism which daily uncovers abuses of power, corruption and injustice, based on factual evidence .

Immigration naturally brought in its trail not only people but their culture and cultural commodities. They began to recreate little Indias with Bombay style bazar shops, hotels, entertainment places, selling spices, Indian food, rice, sari, Indian music. Religious festivals, weddings and social and cultural events were being celebrated. Driven by the high rate of the rent, the main pre-occupation of both the men and the women was to work hard, put up with unsociable hours in the factories in order to save money to buy a house, pay the mortgage and educate their children. Due to the suffering and sacrifices of their parents, many of the younger generations have become graduates and risen into the professional class. In achieving this status, they have been aided by the new political consciousness and liberalism that has acknowledged the contributions made by the Asian community in Britain.

Britain is a multi-racial and multi-cultural society and all pupils must be enabled to understand what this means.

(Lord Swann in his report of the Committee of Inquiry into the Education of Children from Ethnic Minority Group set up by the Education Secretary to Parliament, in 1985)

But the problem with the second generation, as elsewhere in the US, is the problem of the disorientation of the **ABCD** (*American Babu and Confused Desi*), of wavering uncomfortably between two cultures. Fortunately, they are held firmly rooted to the culture thanks to the strong emotional bonds of family values, the sense of belonging to the Asian community and the racist attacks which give them the confidence and the strength to resist and protest against racial discrimination and violence.

(Avtar Brah. *Cartographies of Diaspora*, Routeledge, London. 1996)

The same story applies to the multiple journeys of PIOs into Britain from Mauritius, the Caribbean islands and African countries. Driven by difficult circumstances at home, most immigrants to Britain in the early 1960's had dreamt to get a good job, foster the education of their children, buy a house and improve the conditions of their lives and save money to return home. The PIOs form the largest minority of immigrants in the UK, including 75,000 Mauritians. In the early 1960's, the Mauritians who left for UK had comparatively low education and could only access to low paid jobs, mainly in nursing. But they were strongly motivated to improve their lives and the education of their children who, above 90%, became graduates and professionals - in teaching, medicine, law, engineering, accounting, finance, telecommunications, business, commerce, central and local government. This was to contrast with later immigration in the seventies when there were fewer graduates and professionals among the second generation who generally left after compulsory schooling to work in the factories, in the supermarkets, in the railways and transportation.

In general, children of Mauritian immigrants in France, Canada or Australia have done well in tertiary education and in the professions. According to Dr Mannick, 1987, 82% of Mauritians interviewed were home owners. One of the main findings of the Swann Committee Report, 1985, was that Asian children outperformed Afro-Carribbean children. Up to 98% of people interviewed said they were interested in British politics, with 79% pro-Labour, 14% pro Lib-Democrat, and 7% pro-Conservative. The conclusion is that Mauritians in UK have struggled hard to rise above the social pile in order to better themselves and secure better housing, better jobs and better educational qualifications. They have enhanced the living standards of their families. Coming from a multi-cultural society, Maurtians have settled down peacefully in their new British environment, except that they fear that their children are drifting away from their basic cultural values.

(A.R.Mannick, *Mauritians in London*. Dodo Books, Sussex, 1987).

However, not everybody has been able to adjust to a hostile and alien environment. Many have not been able to realise their ambitions and unrealistic dreams. There are those who, initially lured by inadequate information, western glamour and glitter, and having been uprooted and alienated from their traditional family values, and their essential Indianness, and feeling disoriented, have sunk into complacency, escapism, pleasure loving and social degradation. A few of them, unable to adapt themselves to the challenges of individualism, cut-throat competition and a heartless materialistic environment, and dogged by a sense of failure and powerlessness, have ended up as failures and drunks. Many have found emotional and psychological relief from total annihilation by networking with other Indian or Mauritian groups where they have re-created a Little India and a Little Mauritius that offers a more caring, more hospitable home community. It is unfortunate that many immigrants have been put off by the hostile reception of Britons who have treated them as racially inferior and as commodities and inanimate objects who could be replaced and disposed of with impunity.

It is not only the immigrantss' responsibility to try to settle down wherever they have emigrated, but it is also the duty of the receiving society to encourage them to do so.

(Dr Sam Lingayah, *Mauritian Immigrants in Britain*, London, 1987).

At Carlisle Road, Ealing, London, stands the prestigious Arya Samaj Sabha much frequented by PIOs from India and overseas while at Wembley the Hindu Sanatanists have put up the most splendid Swami Narayan temple. The Indian or Pakistani Muslims have set up a string of mosques which have generally helped them to close their ranks. The large number of Muslims in Britain and in France meet and interact in the mosques and this religious and social bonding has made it very easy for Indian Muslims from Mauritius to identify themselves with the wider Muslim and Arab society. Such fraternal relationships are strengthened by inter-marriage between Muslim girls from Mauritius and British or French Muslims. It has been widely observed that the Arabs or Pakistanis prefer to marry Mauritian Muslim girls, who, brought up in a multi-cultural society, are far more open, more liberal and more forward-looking than are Indian born Muslim or Arab girls. Briefly, the Franco-Mauritians, that is, Mauritians established in France, have made much headway in the education of their children who have become upwardly mobile.

Expelled by Idi Amin, the President of Uganda, in 1972, the **Ugandan Indians**, joined by other Indians from other African countries like Kenya, Tanzania due to uncertainties and security problems and also their failures to adapt to the mainstream society, migrated to Britain, Canada and India. They were generally of low education and were mostly small retailers, including a handful of very wealthy families. But by dint of hard work, sacrifices, high motivation, rising early in the morning distributing milk and newspapers from door to door, the small retailers have risen in business to comparatively prosperous businessess. Their main focus had been to invest in the education of their children who have branched out into various professions like law, medicine, engineering, trade, management etc. As they rise above in social class, the trend has been to sell off the small retail shops to new immigrants.

The NRIs/PIOs have not gone to UK empty-handed. Among other things, they have popularised Indian culture, Indian music, songs, the Bollywood films, Indian foods, Indian cuisine, Indian products, crafts, art objects, spices, in UK through numerous channels, including the Sunrise Radio in Southhall, television and cinemas, shops, hotels, groceries, books and publications. In most cases, by virtue of their simple living, their savings, their hard work ethics, their tenacity, their adherence to family values, their interest in education, and generally starting from scratch, mainly from small retail business and industrial sectors, many PIOs have climbed into the most profitable and professional sectors. Obviously, this remark does not apply to every single PIO family.

Success. But everywhere in the rich industrial countries, overcoming the challenges, the ambitious and serious minded PIOs, those who have got the fever of preserving their Indian values in their blood and who have assimilated the best from Britain, have shot up fast in different fields- education, teaching, professions, business. Within a short lapse of time, the PIOs include some of the most successful businessmen namely Lord Suraj Paul, Hinduja brothers, Lakshmi Mittal. PIO children are among the most educated in UK. The PIOs have excelled in different branches, including business, banking, the financial services, teaching, IT, the health sector, media and entertainment industries. PIOs are doing very well in the media, including the BBC, the Daily Telegraph, the Financial Times. They have also branched off into politics with 4 Members of Parliament, a number of Councillors. The chairman of the Liberal Democratic Party is Lord Dholakia, an eminent political position for an Indian. Other Lords of Indian origin are Lord Ahmed, Lord Parekh, Lord Paul, Lord Desai, Lord Flather, Lord Bathia, Lord Prashar, Lord Diljit Rana and Lord Sir Kumar Bhattacharyya.

Europe

IMMIGRATION INTO Europe has been checked by strict regulations. In France there is an important section of French-speaking PIOs from Pondicherry, from Reunion Island and from Mauritius and whose children are excelling in professional studies and jobs. Due to shortage of labour, Europe has been receiving a number of NRIs. The future generation is likely to be highly educated and highly paid just like the new professional Indians who are making their entry into Europe. As described above, the ambitious, hard-working, preserving their Indian family values have done far better than those who have blindly assimmilated Frenchness and have stagnated and many have ended their old age as lonely, unhappy individuals, abandoned by their French wife and their children.

In **Germany**, there are approximately 60,000 Indians engaged in hotels, restaurants, jewellery, textile business, I.T , research and software professions. They form an affluent and united community, celebrating Diwali together and other cultural, religious and social functions.

In **France**, Indians number 70,000 of whom 10,000 are NRIs. They are from French-speaking territories, Mauritius, Reunion, Martinique, Guadeloupe and principally from Pondicherry, India. They are well assimilated into French mainstream culture though they retain strong family ties with India. They are generally reckoned to be intelligent, hard-working and productive. During the early days of immigration, they have had to face many problems of adaptation and adjustment, particularly acute problems of isolation from their families back home in India or Mauritius. Those who have dedicated themselves to the promotion of their children's education and who have retained the basic Indian values of family life, savings, hard work, sacrifice, ambition and vision have vastly succeeded. Many of their children have distinguished themselves in the universities, in professions or in business. But generally, the second and succeeding generations see themselves more as French citizens and entertain little links with India.

It is obvious that the NRIs or PIOs who have strayed away from the path of Indian culture and have fallen easy preys to all the attractions, comforts and pleasures of the gay Parisian life have made little progress. Their families are often broken up, their children are caught up in working class occupations, some turning to alcohol while many of them who have been chasing a life of pleasures have fallen into ruins in their old age, their children remaining the eternal victims. Some of them have bought homes and business premises, others still rent small studios while some have preferred to show off their fortune by buying up property back home, in Mauritius.

This cycle of success and failure illustrates the fact that hardworking Indians, wherever they may be in the world, have had to struggle, bear sacrifices, have visions and sometimes they meet with triumphs

As in **Belgium**, the Netherlands, and Germany, Indians are in different occupations, trades and professions. Though it is a small community, it is quite active under the guidance of GOPIO Brussels which has organised trade fair, the Brussels Business Conference and is now heading the EU-India Chamber of Commerce. The majority of the Indians are Tamils 50% of the diamond business is in the hands of the Gujarati jewellers. The diamond polishers are among the most affluent society in Brussels. They are an independent community, self-employed, creating employment for Europeans and they supply the latest diamond technology to India. They have made Brussles one of the world's largest diamond centres, generating an income above $10 billion export from Brussles

In Brussels, alone, there are 40 Indian restaurants run by Gujarati Indians, 39 of which are owned by Gujarati Muslims who, for the most part, have migrated from Belgium Congo. They have retained close links with India and are the best exponents of Indian cuisine, arts, crafts, culture, music, and costumes. The restaurants owned and run by Bangladeshis, Nepalese or Pakistanis are equally known as Indian Restaurants.

The small Indian diaspora in Brussels, coming from Mauritius, Bangladesh, Nepal, Sri Lanka and India, is proud of its cultural and religious traditions. Indian festivals, including Divali, Durga and Saraswati puja are celebrated in common, leading as their Proggya booklet, 2003, says, to the " *establishment of better inter-community relationships, grounded in diversity and mutual respect*".

Selling New India's brand image in Europe

Side by side, New India should get out of the Third World mentality and take on the posture of an emerging super-power, urged Indersingh, GOPIO President. The Indian mass media should open itself to the wider world, give coverage to the 110 countries where live the 20 million PIOs and NRIs. Indian universities should have chairs of European studies. There should be more students of European languages and cultures and more Indian students studying in Europe. Indians should have a clearer idea of- what's Europe? What is happening in Europe? The European Union? The European Parliament? About the immigration laws?. How each European country is different from the other? .The NRIs in the west, particularly Europe, are hardly represented in the Indian press as it takes little account of what is going on in the 25 member European Union, European Parliament, European market, investments and business prospects. Apart from Britain, Europe, separated by the language and cultural barrier, is held as a world apart, little understood by the Indian public.

It is now recognized that there is **a lack of dialogue between India and Europe**, that neither India nor Europe has tried to understand each other's cultures, civilizations and commercial needs. The Indian media has yet to raise the profile of India as the world's largest democracy, as a profitable business destination and as an emerging super-power. It has to convince Europe of the full Indian potential. India needs to understand Europe and Europe needs to understand India.. And India has to start assuming the posture of a superpower. That's where the diaspora can be India's best ambassadors since they understand the European situation, European languages, European politics, trade, finance, needs, market and therefore they can provide the inputs in the fields of EU-India commercial and economic activities. They can offer capital, advanced technology, build joint ventures with Indian companies, promote import-export, credit provision and cultivate contacts with important segments of European industrial and financial institutions.

At the Brussels Conference, Ms. Neena Gill, British MP and Member of the European Parliament, has urged the NRIs and PIOs in Europe to engage with European society, with political and social life and all walks of life outside their economic and professional activities. While Dr Charles Tannock MEP has urged that the diaspora should not hide but make their voices and opinions heard. The message was – demonstrate, identify yourself, show your professional excellence and address the host country's agenda. Mr Karan Billimoria, CEO Cobra Beers, UK, urged the diaspora; "*integrate with the country you are living in but never forget your roots!*" It was also felt that a pro-India lobby should be built that can raise the profile of India in the 25 EU-member countries and not allow the negative Kashmir issue or Maoist threat in Nepal to dominate the news. Instead, urged Mr Barati from the FICI, India should sell its plus points:- its huge trading potential, its vast human capital made up of its yearly output of 3 million scientific manpower, one million engineers, half a million doctors and its monthly sale of two million mobile telephones, its expanding middle class. Recently, Dr Manmohan Singh has secured a strategic place for India among the five favoured nations trading with EU.

(GOPIO Brussels Conference 3-4 Oct. October, 2004)

The United States

THE NRI population in US stands around 1.7 million or 0.6% of the total 280 million people, plus an annual increase of 100,000. After the 1965 Immigration Act which opened the door to the immigration of professional Asians, to be joined by their families, the population of NRIs which had flowed into a trickle previously swelled into a tide towards the last quarter of the twentieth century. They are mostly professionals, IT experts, doctors, engineers, academicians and businessmen while their income tends to double the average US citizen. Being wealthy and successful, the first generation of NRIs have generally kept in close touch with India which they visit fairly frequently and have held on fast to their Indianness. As in Britain, they have brought a slice of India wherever they have gone, the Indian shops, groceries and hotels selling Indian products, foods, arts, crafts, songs, music, dress, newspapers, books etc.

In an age of coalition building, of One Europe, the American NRIs have built their political clout around their ethnic unity and their Indianness in order to strengthen their economic, cultural, ethnic and political visibility. While they have mainstreamed into the American cultural and political life, they have preserved and enhanced their Indianness through a network of powerful organisations in the metropolitan cities:- namely the Federations of Indian Associations,

FIA, leading to the apex body at the national level, the National Federation.of Indian American Associations, NFIA, the Asian American Voters Coalition, the AAVC, the Indian American Organization for Participation in Democracy, the Indian American Forum for Political Education, IAFPE, professional organisations like the American Association of Physicians of Indian Origin, the AAPI, the GOPIO- all of which help them to join in political fund raising for presidential and congressional candidates in order to articulate their collective political interests. These enable the NRIs leaders to act as the unofficial ambassadors of India in the US and they also secure them with an effective voice in Washington and at the Capitol Hill. In a highly competitive, open, achievement-oriented society where opportunities are boundless, where they are free from the restrictions of a mindless bureaucracy, their success stories have raised the brand image of India and of Indianness to world class levels.

(Dr Jagat Motwani, *America and India,* Center for Asian, African and Caribbean Studies, N.Y, 2003)

Canada

According to the *Keep Australia White Policy*, early Indian Immigrants were greeted with colour and race prejudices and discriminated against by the Immigration Restriction Act, 1901. This imposed tremendous pressure of assimilation, racial and religious prejudices. Australia relaxed its immigration policy concerning Indian migrants from different regions only after the 1970's. By 1996, there were 100,000 Indian settlers, pouring from mainland India, Fiji, the Caribbeans, Mauritius and UK.

Canada also followed a similar pattern of racist and sexist policy against non-white migrants, particularly Indian women. The first Indians to enter Canada were the Sikh soldiers in 1897, much later than the Chinese who had been there since the 1850's. By 1908, 2,623 Indians were admitted. The Asiatic newcomers met a cold, unfriendly welcome as they were greeted with *Keep Canada White* marchers. By a law passed in the Federal government in 1910 all Asians had to have $ 200 on their person on landing. Hindus were free to come straight from India knowing well that there were no such through ships. The result was that only 5 Indians were admitted in 1910, 37 in 1911 and 3 in 1912.

'*The Hindus will not assimilate but they will segregate in ill-ventilated and unsanitary surroundings, harboring disease and immorality'*, wrote H.H.Stevens in *Monetary Times* in 1912.

Racial prejudice hardened: "*To admit Orientals in large numbers would mean the end and the extinction of white people, and we always have in mind the necessity of keeping this a white man's country*". B.C. Premier, Sir Richard McBride, May 22, 1914. On 23 May, 1914, the *Komagata Maru* with 376 East Indians on board dropped anchor in Vancouver harbour. Led by Gurdit Singh who challenged the immigration laws, they were expelled by the Federal Government two months later.

Yet during the two world wars, the Sikh soldiers had fought in European,Turkish and African battlefronts, 14 had won Military Crosses. By 1951, an annual quota of 150 East Indians were admitted, rising to 300 in 1957. Then in 1962, immigrants were adopted on basis of education, work skills and language proficiency on a 50 out of 100 points basis. By 1967, Parliament allowed foreigners to apply for immigration status within the country.

(Ted Ferguson, *A White Man's Country, An Exercise in Canadian Prejudice*. Doubleday Canada Ltd. Toronto, 1975)

Said Cheddi Jagan, the late Prime Minister of Guyana, *Indians overseas are treated as second-class citizens*. Urged George Kurian, University of Calgary, Canada: "*We must become less tolerant of intolerance."*

Generally, Indians were less welcome than the Blacks or the Chinese and they had long been considered to be aliens, because of their Asian lifestyle. They were looked down upon because of the negative image of their country of origin, reckoned to be poor, under-developed and overpopulated. " *India, deeply-populated, plague-smitten, famine-stricken"*. Foreigners held all sorts of wrong ideas about India as the land of snake charmers with snakes and elephants moving about on the roads. With better communications and recent technological and economic advances, this image has been fast changing. This attitude is reflected in the type of Indian immigrants who have poured into Canada. At first, the early Indian immigrants were mainly Sikh soldiers, mostly low-skilled farmers and lumbermen, a fact which explains the overwhelming Punjabi presence among the Indo-Canadians, averaging 700,000, who have settled in Ontario, 55%, British Columbia, 25%, and Quebec, Alberta and Manitoba, 20%. The quality of Immigrants in the post- 1970's consisted mainly of professionals, earning an average income of $ 30,000, similar to what took place in the US.

Their large incomes enabled them to save more, send remittances at home to :- (i) enhance their status, (ii) invest in property, (iii) make religious and social donations, (iv) help the education of relatives, (v) fund the arrival of new immigrants and (vi) the transfer of much needed technology which speeded up the Green Revolution and gave it an edge in India. But in the 1980's, some of them have also funded terrorist activities in the wake of the Khalistan movement, a fact which put tremendous strain on Indo-Canadian diplomatic relations.

(Prakash Jain, *Indian Diaspora*, ed. Ajay Dubey, Kalinga. N.D.2003)

On the whole, the new NRIs have greatly enhanced the prestige and contributions of the Indians abroad, having diversified into a number of professions, trade and business, including:- the booming high tech industry, government service, trading and self-employment, owning shops, restaurants, software vending, entertainment industry, organising super-star events, television, radio and ethnic broadcasting, estate agency. Other examples are the Little India towns and Bombay bazaars of Toronto where Indian food, clothes, accessories, films, videos, music have been popularised. They are also active in teaching, research, publication, cultural, social, philanthropic and political activities, apart from holding Indian classical dance, music, yoga, language and meditation classes for those seeking internal peace.

(Kamlesh Gupta. *Pioneers of Prosperity*.Ed. S.Kumar.N.D. 2000).

4

WHY DIASPORAS SUCCEED

IN THIS section, we shall explore some of the reasons why diasporas- Chinese, Japanese, Indian- tend to do better abroad than in their homeland and also what happens when different diasporas meet in open competition. First of all, we need to be clear what we mean by diaspora. What is their relationship with their homeland and with their host countries, how they disperse in settlements abroad and how they compare with the nationals back at home, with other diasporas and what are the factors that explain their success or failure.

About Diaspora

BY DIASPORA, we mean dispersion of people who left their homeland through compulsion, through slavery, indentured labour, through expulsion or voluntary emigration in search of aslyum, or of better livelihood abroad. The diaspora may be part of a movement of population in the wake of colonization, leading both to migration and immigration. It could be mass migration or in trickles. It could also be motivated by national catastrophes, wars, geographical and political partition as happened in the partition of India in 1947, leading to **cleft and mobile diasporas** of Indians and Pakistanis.

What makes the study of our diaspora the more interesting is the way that diaposra has evolved through times, retaining its linkages with the mainland, its continuities, discontinuities through its civilizational encounter with the host country and its on-going transformation at the economic, cultural, social, political levels.

(N. Jayeram. Bangalore University. 1998)

Multi-cultural Mauritius can serve as a socio-historical laboratory in many instances. At the outset, the French East India Company induced French colons to settle in Isle de France and to constitute the ruling plantocracy, served by imported African and Indian slaves and later Indian Indentured immigrants who provided the menial labour. French settlements needed to be served by soldiers and sailors, missionaries who were sent on a temporary basis and many of whom set up relations with the slave women and thus founding Coloured and Creole families. The migrants tend to concentrate in certain specific geographical areas, develop ties of solidarity among themselves, sharing and preserving their cultural, linguistic and religious traditions and forming specific **ethnic** groups within a larger multi-ethnic society. These may still keep their contact with their homeland, through visits or send remittances back home. Another category is made up of the **expatriates**, soldiers, sailors, ambassadors, journalists, experts, businessmen and students who travel abroad on a temporary basis before they return to join the nationals who had stayed back home. In the wake of modernization, ease of travels, communications, the Internet and globalisation, people are crossing all geograhical boundaries, in all directions, shuttling back and forth from their countries into other countries, mainly into western industrialised countries. Thus, depending on their size, distribution, their organization, and relations both with the homeland and the host countries, the diasporas have to adjust themselves into mainstream culture, interact with other diasporas at different social, cultural, economic and political levels and are therefore ever evolving and dynamic and never static.

(Fred Riggs.*Diasporas and Ethnic Nations.* 10.10. 2003).

Diasporas link up the local with the global, the host country with the homeland, and are firmly embedded in social, cultural, religious meanings, political orientations and economic strategies. Socially, as a displaced people, the diaspora carry an idealised and fractured memory and also *a new consciousness of their homeland, its cultural, social, economic heritage* which they want to implant wherever they go into the reconstituted L□ittle India, China Town, etc. They might have left their homeland as victims of circumstances, which make them feel alienated, as happened to the Coolies. Their first instinct is to congregate together in certain geographical space in order to preserve their collective identity which they associate with the preservation of their language, culture, traditions and religion. It also indicates their concern to link up with their historic past, to revitalise and pass on their cultural heritage, without getting entirely assimilated into the host society.

From a religious perspective, the diaspora should start reflecting about itself in order to reconstruct its religious self-awareness, project and preserve its religious image, its faith, its symbols, its festivals in a bid to face up to the pressure of religious assimilation or proselytisation. The encounter with the west, with other cultures, with an aggressive, missionary Christianity may force the members of the diaspora to identify and cherish their religious heritage and core values. This prompts a desire to remodel, to reform and re-invent their religion in order to prune it of its irrelevancies, its taboos, its superstitions, its weaknesses and to give it more credibility in its core beliefs and practices in a new religiously competitive environment. The leading members of the diaspora may adopt shifting strategies in order to identify the core, universal values of their religion.

The objective is to forge a Cosmopolitan and universal Hinduism outside India, in the US, in UK and elsewhere and which can stand the test of rationality, linked up with the homeland under the umbrella of a new global organization like the Vishwa Hindu Parishad. This may involve creating new symbols like the Ganga Talao at Grand Bassin in Mauritius, the construction of shrines, temples, pilgrimage places and re-visiting pilgrimage places in the homeland.

The ultimate concern is to preserve and transmit the essential religious ideas, teachings, principles, rites and rituals while seeking to achieve a strategy to adjust and integrate within the host society within the context of a secular democracy. Politically, the migrants may have developed a diaspora consciousness and they want to retain links with the homeland. The members may feel more patriotic in the sense of investing their energy for the improvement of their collective well-being within the host country by strengthening relationships with the homeland. This is what urged Gandhi to put up the Satyagraha resistance against Apartheid domination in South Africa. It explains why Ramgoolam sought out the knowledge and the expertise from London in order to liberate his people from colonial domination. The immigrants were fully aware of their precarious political situation. Indians in the plantation colonies and in South Africa smarted under the feeling that they were being dominated by a superior power which had confiscated their legal and civic rights. It ignited a double consciousness, that of being a distinct entity and of being members of a new multi-ethnic society. One of the forms of protest and resistance against domination and outright assimilation into the Melting Pot or the Creolisation steamroller, the *ène sel lépep, ène sel nasyon* ideology, has been to reassert one's ethnic identity and loyalty to one's homeland.

Economically, they may adopt the strategy of asserting their economic survival and independence, of seeking their personal security in a bid to improve their livelihood. This may entail a series of activities:- strengthening the family ties, the collective network, the pooling of common resources, providing mutual assistance, developing their economic strength, mobilising capital, engaging in new economic activities, networking with other members of the diaspora across the globe, the provision of goods and services both to the ethnic group and to the outgroups.and revitalizing the PIO or NRI links with the homeland.

(Steven Vertovec. University of Oxford. *Three meanings of diaspora, exemplified among South Asian religions*. 1999)

Chinese Diaspora in Mauritius

Learning from the Indian experience, the Chinese Coolies, arriving in trickles since 1829, did not repeat the same mistake of sticking to the cane fields in the plantations. Though they came from agrarian background in Chinese villages, they were found unfit to undertake the hard agricultural jobs in the cane fields. The Cantonese emigrated from Kuan Tung or Canton, a province of South China, close to Macao and they were Cantonese-speaking. That's why the Chinese were popularly addressed as *Chinois Macao.* They came essentially as a trading diaspora in contrast to the Indians who came as a labour diaspora. They were destined to make rapid commercial, industrial progress and build strong trade relations with Hong Kong. The Chinese civilization threw up 400 clans, distinguished by the use of their patronyms and which facilitate networking.

(Mark Fok Cheung, Conference on *Les Cantonnais de l'Ile Maurice*, MGI, 1991)

Failing in agriculture, they were allowed to fulfil the important function of setting small shops, selling an assortment of food, groceries, liquor and other items of daily consumption, scattered near the sugar estate camps and branching into the villages and further into the towns. Thus, they were early spared the humiliation and hardship which met the Indian coolies in the plantations.

By a law passed in 1842, Chinese Coolies, not being British subjects, were treated as aliens and debarred from owning immovable property. Since they were mainly male, they had no option but to intermarry with propertied Creole women to enable them to set up shops. In the wake of the petit morcellement, after the abolition of slavery, the Chinese shopkeepers leased property from ex-apprentices, Indian and also from White land owners. A close ethnic solidarity started to grow when the shop keepers recruited new shop assistants through *chain migration* which enabled the new Hakka-speaking arrivals to acquire business experience until they set up their own shops through mutual help and sub-letting. Later, the majority of the Chinese who had been married to Creole women and had been naturalised sold or leased their shops to the new Hakka immigrants while they set up new shops into the interior or into the towns.

According to Tsang Mang Kin, the Hakka were a proud, educated people, steeped in Chinese laws. The Hakka settlers in Mauritius included members of the 60 clans originating from Han, Man Chu, Mongolian and Tibetan tribes based on joint families, extensive family kinship network and arranged marriages between clans. Thus, the clan name can be Li, the generational name is Min. The family system is based on respect of the elders, a factor which constitutes their social solidarity within which the individual is subordinate to the collective. It secures a place for each family member. Among the noted qualities of the Hakkas is his patience, the strong appetite for education, and support of the formidable and indefatigable *Hakka woman*.

(Tsang Mang Kin. *L'héritage Hakka à Maurice*, MGI, 1991)

From the start, the small Chinese traders had been keeping good relations with the other members of the Mauritian society, with the Muslim wholesalers in Port Louis who supplied them the groceries and textile products imported from India and from whom they obtained credit facilities.

Similarly, starting from home-made small production and manufacturing of a variety of products, the Chinese expanded into distillery and cigarette manufacturing with the collaboration of the Whites who supplied them the machinery and technology and the materials from Indian tobacco planters. The business of the Chinese as an ethnic group in commercial specialization was due to the *cummulative experience acquired on the ground, strengthened by a network of family, kin or clan-based business relationships*, backed by the support of other ethnic groups through leases, property sales and credit facilities.

(Mariner Carter & James Ng Foong Kwong, *Colouring the Rainbow*, 1998)

Being pragmatic and forward-looking, the Chinese climbed much further ahead. The secret lies in their strong family structure which gave a *central role to women*. The second success factor had been their trading culture, brought from mainland China. At first, not being British subjects, the Coolies were debarred from buying land and therefore they abandoned agriculture to concentrate on retail business. In the nineteenth century, when the immigrants were mainly male, they had little option but to inter-marry with the local Creole women as a strategy to establish themselves, acquire property and thereby got assimilated into Mauritian culture. But this did not help them to succeed in the business lines as many of their children integrated the

Creole working class culture.

However, just like the Gujarati retailers in the hinterland of Uganda, the great contribution of the Chinese shopkeepers had been to establish small shops near the estate camps, into the villages and later into the towns. The enabling factors seemed to stem from their Bhuddist and Confucian upbringing which instill qualities of hard work, pragmatism, blended with their aspiration, and their ability to cultivate good relations with the estate authorities, with the agricultural labourers as well as with their suppliers, the Gujarati merchants of Port Louis. Gradually, patiently, they built the necessary capital that was to help them expand into the towns, particularly after the Second World War. It also taught the later immigrants to merge with the mainstream French culture while retaining their basic Chineseness, attachment to traditional Buddhist or Taoist temple ceremonies ***while remaining firmly rooted in their family structure.***

"The extended Chinese family structure was ideal for the setting up of a support system which comprises among other advantages revolving credit, extensive linkage, kinship network and clan loyalties." (Ly Tio Fane Pineo, 1994).

The motto was simple- once a Chinese, always a Chinese. Like the Jews, the Marwari and Sindhi traders, the early Gujarati immigrants in Mauritius and in Africa, they always group together, help one another out, providing finance and setting their compatriots up in business to establish business networks. Though China did not produce any organised religion, they adapted many of the practices and Hindu deities into the Chinese religious system under Chinese names. Hence, in February 1843, they built a temple dedicated to Kwan Ti and had a Cantonese cemetery in 1861. Unlike the Hindus, Moslems or Christians, the Chinese were not attached to any religious dogma and they remained essentially a pragmatic people. However, they held on to the moral and social values of Confucianism, Buddhist philosophy of reincarnation, law of karma and the small wheel and from there the transition to Catholicism became easy. Confucianism taught the

Chinese how to respect the others in tune with the Bhuddist principles of **toleration, moderation, the Middle Way**, reinforced by the humanitarian, rational and universal philosophy of Buddhism, *may all beings be happy.* Taoism placed its belief in *The Way*, in a cosmic God, beyond time and space, and your life is between you and the Tao, somehow like the relation between the Soul and the Universal Soul, according to Vedantic philosophy.

They retained and improved upon the basic Asian culture of thrift, simple living, hard work, self-restraint, avoidance of extravagance, respect of elders and of ancestors, perseverance and re-investement in their business. They held on to their merchant and Confucian culture which prepared them to be very calm, patient and understanding in handling day-to-day problems with non-Chinese customers. Thus, armed by ancient Chinese wisdom, they became very pragmatic and developed sound business relations with their customers. The focus on customer satisfaction seemed to have been at the centre of their success.

Gradually, through serving and associating with the white and the Coloured customers, they learned to adopt the more aggressive western technology. Being a small minority, looking innocuous, and guided by their intellectual leaders, their strong clan system and their Chamber of Commerce networked across SEA and China, they were pragmatic and far-sighted enough to embrace Catholicism and merge into the General Population. In the White perspective, the Indians looked more threatening by virtue of their numbers and their desire to preserve their culture and religion and their reluctance to integrate into the General Population. Besides, within a strong racialist society, they found that their yellow complexion and their adoption of Catholicism and the all-powerful influence of the Catholic Church played heavily in their favour. This enabled them to take the influential Europeans as their protégés, their allies, as the godfathers and godmothers of their children and thus they secured privileged access to confessional schools and other trading facilities. While they had one foot in the European civilization and enjoyed all the benefits along with the white, whose association helped them in their business development, their aspiration had always been to go on improving themselves in order to **compete with and to outperform the white.** In this respect, in concentrating in their business, they have **accummulated strategic business experience and skills which have set them up as far more efficient and effective than other ethnic traders. In contrast, the ambition of the Indian has remained limited to getting a job, buying a plot of land and educating their children.**

Though the Indians have been in majority and have controlled political power for over four decades, they have lagged far behind in economic progress and the percentage of poor and marginalised Indians is shocking. Indians have neglected economic and business development and few have set their business vision as high as the Chinese. Except for the Gujarati Muslim traders and a few Sindhi families, the other Indian traders did not entertain business contact with their homeland with the same zeal as did the Chinese traders.

In course of time, the small shopkeepers, while retaining their ethnic identity, have graduated into large traders and have got firmly entrenched in trade and industry and have therefore acceeded to middle class positions. Joseph Tsang Mang Kin, writer, former Minister and diplomat, believes that the new bourgeois Chinese, heavily decultured by the Catholic Church, have stepped into the place of the Mullatos and have inherited all the vices of the Mullatos.

Historically, the ground had been prepared earlier thanks to the inspiration and guidance from mainland China. By 1912, the followers of the republican government of Koung Fou Tsen gave up their old feudal habits, cut short their pig tails, threw away their large straw hats, their traditional cotton and silken pyjamas and adopted the path of modernization and westernisation. By the Second World War, the new type of Chinese immigrants were ideologically motivated by the patriotic and political elite sent abroad by Dr Sun Yat Sen's nationalist government which indoctrinated them and tied them closely to mainland China to which they were expected to owe their loyalty and allegiance. The successive Chinese Communist government has pursued the far-sighted, open-door policy with the expanding Chinese diaspora. From then on, the progress of the Chinese has been meteoric.

In contrast, **India has been dragging its feet far behind China in the matter of promoting closer relations with its diaspora**. The Nehruvian policy of discouraging private enterprise, promoting the Regulation Raj and throwing cold water on the diaspora's search for closer relations with India has only been reversed lately. Concern with the PIO's and NRIs only took place in the year 2003 with the setting up of a special section in the Ministry of External Affairs and the organization of the Pravasi Bharatiya Divas. In the meantime, in Mauritius, despite their small number, currently averaging 3% of the population, the spirit of Chinese nationalism was fuelled by the publication of a Chinese weekly which appeared in 1923. This was followed, during the 1926-50, by six other newspapers in Chinese. The same period saw the founding of Chinese schools which gave a tremendous fillip to education. It reinforced Chinese nationalism, discouraged inter-marriage with local women and spurred **arranged marriage alliances with Chinese wives** locally and from the homeland.

Henceforth, their development was unstoppable. They diversified their activities, occupying renumerative positions in all fields-bureaucracy, the professions, business, trade and industry. Following on the trails of the Oligarchy, they have thrown up a few very powerful families, somehow like a Sino-Mauritian Oligarchy, capable of rivalling the Whites on their own ground. Consequently, the Sino-Mauritians have looked up to the Mullatos, the Whites and to the West and have become the new Mullato class, assimilating some of their ugly features of racial arrogance and prejudices. No wonder, compared to the South East Asian Chinese, in general, the contemporary Sino-Mauritians have tended to turn their backs on Buddhist culture, unlike what we see in Malaysia or Singapore. By collaborating with the Whites in business, they have naturally been fast distancing themselves from the Indo-Mauritians who have been trailing far behind on the economic path. By networking with the local White, the Catholic Church and the Chinese diaspora in South East Asia and in China, they have expanded into practically all areas of business, starting from the small production to large-scale production. In brief, the ethnic Chinese solidarity has enabled them to squeeze the Indians out of competition, in Mauritius, in Malaysia, Singapore and other countries where they are now reckoned to be the wealthiest traders and industrialists.

The Wider Chinese Diaspora

We have seen how the Chinese diaspora differs from other diasporas in that it is more closely knit with the homeland through the system of clan names. Thus the Chinese diaspora in Mauritius, in Philippines or Malaysia bearing certain specific clan surnames bring them closer together to the Chinese mainland and to network with other Chinese bearing the same clan associations across the world. The clan names association can serve to tie its members into a global mafia or secret society. Another example of Chinese global networking across boundaries is through the setting up of Chinese Chambers of Commerce in South East Asian Countries or in Mauritius. A Chinese Chamber of Commerce in Malaysia, Mauritius or Thailand may resemble each other in that it acts as a business organization to buttress the common business interests of its members, to serve as a mediator between the local government and Chinese government. It also networks with Chinese business chambers across the world and particularly with mainland China. It helps its members in various ways, including funding, settling down, advisory, educational, social, religious and political. (Fred Riggs, 2003)

In his study of why Diasporas succeed where others fail, Serge Berthier (*www. asian-affairs.com*) explains that the total economic output of the 50 million ethnic Chinese in Asia (including 23 million in South East Asia, 20 million in Hong Kong and Taiwan) averaged US $ 400 billion in 1991. It has been estimated that between 1978 and 1996, a total of US$120 billion has been invested in China, 80% of which has flowed from overseas Chinese. The fact that the Chinese have always been a fragile minority in most SEA countries where they are engaged in trade and industry as a wealthy community induced them to keep their assets in liquid so that they could diversify and readily invest in other countries whenever the opportunities occurred.

Now in response to Chinese invitation and a series of legislation under the 1990 Law of Protecting Rights and Interests of Overseas Chinese and their Relatives, overseas Chinese investments and technology started pouring thickly into China. By 1996, over 80% of Hong Kong labour-intensive industries had shifted to South China now completely transformed into industrial and trading sectors, known as the 5 **Special Economic Zones, SEZs**. Obviously, they were lured by the package of economic reforms, including modern infrastructural facilities, security measures, a vast pool of cheap labour and an increasing share of global market in light industry, electronics, textile and chemical industries.

The moral is that investments from NRIs or through them from big multinationals can take place smoothly only under appropriate conditions. *India must earn the trust of NRIs with consistent and bold policy reforms to ensure that the sub-continent is seen as a highly profitable investment destination- free from any bureaucratic hassle.* This should include decentralising decision making to empower local administrative authorities to attract investments in diverse Special Economic Zones and build freeports in places like Cochin or Goa so that the benefits of development could spread all over India.

Consequently, China has stolen a long march over India which has wok□en up tardily to realise the strategic importance of NRI- and PIO Communities. Since 1978, under Deng Xiao Ping's bold economic reforms, China opened its economy to welcome inputs from overseas Chinese entrepreneurs, their investments, technology by providing alluring incentives, knocking down all central regulations and bureaucratic controls, decentralising facilities. Consequently, *each Chinese province and region is busy competing with one another to lure Overseas Chinese, Japanese, Korean investors*. The emphasis is everywhere the **same-investments, trade and economic reforms** which help the whole of China to race ahead and to make gigantic strides. Thus, in 1997, 4 World Chinese Entrepreneurs' Conventions were held, followed by 21 World Chinese Traders' Conventions involving Chinese from all over the world, thereby highlighting ethnic identity as a means to strengthen business ties.

Japanese

SIMILARLY, THE Japan International Co-operation Agency, JICA, a state body, provides interest free loans, technical and vocational training and scholarships, including volunteers and experts to countries with a Japanese Diaspora. Annual conferences and conventions are held in Tokyo with the representatives of Japanese Diaspora. Eminent members of the Diaspora are invited over to Japan and in return, the *Diaspora acts like ambassadors to promote bilateral relations between Japan and the host countries*. Perhaps the Chinese and Japanese experience in caring for their Diasporas could be of some relevance to the government of India and to GOPIO.

(Empowering PIOs for Socio-Economic Development, GOPIO, 12.1.04, N.D).

We know that the indentured immigrants who were driven out of India by poverty had to overcome tremendous hardships so that their children could succeed in education, in business, in the professions and in politics wherever they had gone. But then why are the PIOs and NRIs wealthy and successful while resident Indians have remained comparatively poor?

Unlike what happened in India which clamped down on private enterprise for over four decades, Japan had a **clear vision** of what it wanted. At a time when India became independent, Japan was clambering back on its feet after the crushing defeat of World War II. Without the immense natural resources that have blessed the Peninsula, Japan took the right directions in reconstructing its economy. While in India it was the politicians and bureaucrats who arbitrarily set hurdles and deterrents on industrial production, in Japan, its *entrepreneurs were free to determine the location of their industries, their size, technology, products, costing*. They did not have to re-invent the wheel. Instead, they began to break down western machines and equipment, studying their parts and their technology in details through the process of **reverse engineering** in order to re-invent better models of cars, electronic goods. By focusing on *quality products, zero defects, Japan slowly conquered the world market while India stagnated under its system of subsidies and nationalised industries*.

The Japanese invested 7% of gross sales in Research and Development and set great value on quality production, world class goods, zero defects and best performance. Unlike India which granted subsidies to uncompetitive industries, on exports which never reached their destination, the Japanese government did not grant subsidies. Instead, *each manufacturing company was expected to export at least 20% of its products on the world market*, which meant that they had to produce quality goods at a competitive price. Nothing like this happened in India. The goods produced were so mediocre that Indians themselves were chasing foreign imported goods via contraband trade. Emulating Japan, other South East Asian Countries, including South Korea began developing some strong companies and world class products which built up the South Korean brand name – *Samsung, Gold Star, Daewoo, Hayundai*. Another good thing which Japan did and which India had neglected has been to focus on **primary education** first, which became the generator of secondary, vocational and tertiary education. Had focus been placed on primary education from the start the large undeveloped Hindi hinterland would have been developed and less populated. while the growth process would have started from bottom upward.

The PIOs

THE FEELING of every successful PIO on visiting India is one of cultural shock at the dire poverty that strikes him when he lands in his ancestral village. Then he falls on his knees and thanks his stars that his immigrant forefathers had the foresight to leave the gangetic plains or whatever to try their luck overseas though under trying conditions. To the Trinidadian born Nobel Laureate, Sir V.S.Naipaul, his

childhood memories of India were one of a "*vanished world, like trapdoors into a bottomless past*". Former president of Mauritius, Mr Cassam Uteem said that modernization had stopped short of his native village, still sunk in feudal backwardness while Sir Anerood Jugnauth, former Prime Minister of Mauritius confided that *" a trip to Bihar would make me sad. I know how poor they are, unlike us."*
(India Today, 13.1.03).

Having taken roots and spread like the banyan trees with their descendants dispersing across the globe, the PIOs have been inevitably tarred with the cultural brushes, the high living standards and plentiful opportunities of their respective countries. Though, somewhere, they have a soft spot for their Indianness - yet they are held back by a certain sense of alienation. Perhaps what is needed to heal the widening gap are closer relations between a caring and resurgent India and her diaspora. We suggest that the answer to this burning issue should be explored at different forums and this theme is dealt with in this book.

Once the ethnic Indians had stepped into the vessels to cross the seven seas, they had been jolted out of the complacency and comfort zone of joint family life. They saw themselves as adventurers and pioneers who had thrown overboard the baggage of taboos, restrictions and superstitions that had previously held them back into feudal fetters. This is how the PIO and NRIs have been magically transformed into new, independent, enterprising persons. All the pent-up potential, and energy arising from a great culture and civilization, enriched after encounter with the west, blossom forth to enable them to use their own enterprise to convert this cultural capital into wealth accumulation. This is why:

"each diaspora harnesses the individual quality of its members much more efficiently than the country of its origin harnesses its society". (Berthier).

"*If enterprise is afoot, wealth accumulates.*" (J.M.Keynes, Treatise on Money).

To Hernando de Soto, energy, like capital, is a dormant value. In other words, when the immigrant is put under hard circumstances, his tremendous capital- which has been otherwise lying dormant in his ancestral country- is unleashed. All the restrictive barriers blow up in one terrific blast. Under the new challenging environment, he comes to discover himself and his potential. It sounds like the giant Kimkaran who is at last awakened from his long sleep. This is one of the reasons why initially a migrant community has to struggle hard for survival in a threatening environment and finally they apply their determination, inventiveness and creativity to turn difficulties into opportunities. This is what happened to Gandhiji as an NRI when he drew from his cultural and spiritual resources to outwit Smuts in South Africa.

The Indian Muslims

HISTORICALLY, the bulk of the Indian Muslims were Hindus yesterday. Hinduism spanned across Afghanistan to Burma and the South East Asia to Hindu Bali while Buddhism became the main religion of China, Japan and of many SEA countries. Kashmir owes its name, *Kashyp-mar* (Kashyap's abode) to Sage Kashyap and it had been ruled ever since until independence by Hindu kings.

(S.L.Sharma, Denmark. Jammu and Kashmir in *Real Perspectives. Past, Present and Future.* 2nd GOPIO Conf. 1992)

But religious persecutions under the long Moghul rule forced the mass conversions of Hindus to Islam throughout the sub-continent. Under emperor Aurangazeb, Hindus were levied heavy taxes unless they converted to Islam until Shivajee rose against him and established the Maratha Empire.

It is a fact that the majority of Hindus got converted to Islam in protest and rebellion against the iniquities of the caste system which denied them self-respect and basic human rights. Despite its own shortcomings and unfair treatment of women, Islam had many features which were in advance of Hinduism, namely :- equality and brotherhood, religious discipline, absence of the caste system, a simpler religion based on a single Church and Koran as compared to the more unwieldy, unstructured and chaotic Hindu society.

Under the long Moghul rule, India plunged further into feudalism and isolation but emerged enriched with the wonderful mix of Indo-Islamic culture and civilization which is everywhere apparent in the Hindi language, literature, cinema, music, songs, dances, architecture, paintings, food, costumes, religion and the Oriental way of living. The Indo-Islamic culture is embedded on the precepts of Indian culture and philosophy, marked by tolerance, moderation, liberty, respect of the other person, individualism, enterprise, family ethos and investment in the future. Originating from Vedic and Buddhist sources, these are the very values that had evolved into democracy, private enterprise, the free market and liberalism.

It is almost impossible to go back to the pure Hindu culture so much has the Islamic inter-penetration run deep. The Indian Muslims are thoroughly soaked in the indigenous culture of tolerance, underscored by some of the Sufi Saints who did a lot to Indianise Islam and ground it on the local soil, preaching love of India, co-existence and patriotism.

(Kaleem Kawaja, Gen. Secretary, The Association of Indian Muslims of America, Washington. *India Belongs to Us All.* 2nd GOPIO Conf., Paris, 1992).

Embedded in Indian culture, the Indian Muslims, wherever they may have migrated, in Pakistan or elsewhere, have assimilated the Indian values of tolerance and moderation and are therefore foreign to the extremist concepts preached by the *Jihadists,* guilty of terrorism and cold-bloodedly beheading their hostages.

In the same context, present day Pakistan was part of India before the 1947 Partition. The Indians and the Pakistanis, the Afghans, the Bangladeshis, even the Malaysians and Indonesians share an unbroken history of common Indo-Islamic culture and civilization stretching westward across the Arab world through the links of language, religion, architecture, commerce, navigation, food habits and fondness of Indian music, songs, dances, Bollywood films and Indian television. Almost every big hotel in Dubai resounds with Indian music and the dance steps of attractive Indian female dancers to the applause of Arab sheiks who re-create the courtesan atmoshphere of yesteryears in India. Indian culture and civilization can be said to have dominated the whole of Asia, from north to the southern tip.

The Gujarati Muslim diaspora has kept the closest of contact with India and they are the best exponents throughout Europe and the world of Indian cuisine through the ownership of numerous hotels and restaurants enlivened with items of Indian culture, arts, crafts, sculpture, music, songs and entertainment. They have imported a little bit of elitist India, with all its royal splendour, its Maharajah style across the western capitals.

This is one of the reasons why Indians feel thoroughly at home working and living in the Gulf Countries. The peaceful dialogue between India and Pakistan may well point the way forward to better understanding and a continuation and flowering of the glorious Indian composite culture and civilization.

Earlier, Islamic expansion had been spearheaded by a small band of Turkish invaders who roamed over India and ruled over it for 800 years. Similarly, an ordinary man like Robert Clive showed his genius as he carved the British Empire in the teeth of the great Moghul Empire and the mass of inert Indian population, ruled by numerous pleasure-loving Maharajahs. This reminds us of the powerful Muslim diaspora which cuts across Indian diaspora. It has a long history of conquest and imperialism. It is powerfully bonded by Islamic brotherhood. It spawns an all-Islamic identity and a global Muslim brotherhood which cuts across national boundaries and threatens to overrun the western world. All Muslims would like to see themselves as brothers in the eyes of Allah. The Muslim tends to flout his identity in an open manner in the daily wear of ethnic dress and beard, the veil for women, beard and long robes for men, a custom which makes him or her an easy target of discrimination and controversy in western countries. Reacting to the racism, colonialism and imperialism of the West, Islam which is itself an intensely political and evangelical religion has thrown up a handful of fanatics and terrorists who constitute an embarassment to the vast majority of peaceful, liberal, moderate and rational Muslims across the world.

Otherwise, in its aggressive, nationalist and imperialist form, it erupts from time to time under different disguises, earlier as the Ottoman Empire, in Egypt under Nasser's rallying call for Pan-Arabism, Pan-Islamism which has brought together the 47 Muslim countries under the Islamic World Council. Democracy and tolerance are not its strong points. For a brief period, in Lybia, Khadafi posed as its champion and as a threat to the western world. Its passion is kept simmering by events in Kashmir, in the Gulf countries, in Iraq, the Middle East. Its influence is global as it embraces Central Asia, South East Asia, Pakistan and Afghanistan and spilling over the former Yougoslavia, split by war in Kosovo and the Serbian massacre of European Muslims. Now, compounded by the clash of civilizations and globalisation- it is threatening to engulf Europe, Russia and US (marked by the 11th September terrorist attack in New York), the March 2004 event in Madrid, and the unsettling Iraq war, compounded by Al Qaida network and all the rest. The hope for the future lies in democracy and liberalism as heralded by the democratic elections in Indonesia (September 2004) and Afghanistan (October 2004). In this venture, the Indian Muslims have been the great pioneers.

Anglo-Saxon

ANGLO-SAXON diaspora has been nurtured on colonialism. It all started with the 13 American colonies where the British settlers, forming a dynamic diaspora, were able to defeat the British army and navy in the War of American Independence, 1776, and they lay the foundation of the future United States of America. Thanks to the steam power and the industrial revolution, the British spilled all over the globe, in the north, the centre and the south, as colonialists, settlers and traders. The extraordinary thing is that, the ordinary Immigrant labourers, pitted against the hard, physical and political power of the mighty British Empire and the harsh French colonialism countered with the use of **soft power**, the power of their culture, civilization and philosophy. In other words, these formed the intangible cultural capital which helped them to survive, advance and prosper in the sugar plantations, retain their Indianness so that their children could adjust and rise as professionals, businessmen and politicians. And compared to the struggling Indentured labourers, the task of the NRIs, brought up on subsidised education in India, is far easier as they can shoot up in US and in other industrial countries.

The Success Stories

But what accounts for the success of Indian diaspora? The first observation to make is that *the strength of the diaspora reflects the strength of Indian culture, religion and civilization.* Wherever Indians have gone, particularly the Indentured labourers, they had carried with them their survival kit from India- comprising of their cultural and spiritual baggage, the close *Jahaji Bhais* in-group consciousness, a lot of sharing, solidarity and co-operation and the solid Indian family ethos. These *core values* helped them to stick together through thick and thin and overcome difficulties and provided them with a strong ethnic identity, mutual co-operation and the ability to share ideas, information and values. The individual held on to family and the community and felt accountable to them. He felt he had to share in the collective work, to pull his weight in making his personal contributions to the family welfare, the elder and the stronger members helping the weaker and younger ones in the common battle for the progress of the diaspora.

Cultural Capital. By dint of hard work, self-help, savings, sacrifice, simple living, perseverance, pooling their resources together, and the ability to adapt fast to changing circumstances, their passion for knowledge and education, their desire for progress, they managed to clear various roadblocks from their paths. In economic terms, these values are formidable cultural assets which have helped the Diaspora in the process of wealth accumulation- as we shall discuss in the following pages. This is evidence enough to prove that the diaspora system is indeed very effective. And the moral is, if you feel stuck, depressed, and you are stagnating in an economic quagmire at home, my friends, you'd better get out and join the Diaspora movement and seek your fortune overseas.

According to the Report of the High Level Committee on the Indian Diaspora, led by L.M.Singhvi, Government of India, 2002, almost all Diasporas- British, Chinese, Israeli, Italian, South Korean- make significant contributions to the host countries. It is instructive both for the Government of India and for GOPIO to make a comparative study of these diasporas and draw the necessary lessons so that appropriate policy decisions could be charted as regards Indian diaspora. This observation explains why the US, originally settled by British and followed by other diasporas, a nation of immigrants, is so successful as compared to other closed countries, like Africa, where immigration has been insignificant.

At first, after having been traumatised and wounded by their emigration experience, the Diaspora tends to idealise the memory of the ancestral home. They cling emotionally to the ancestral culture and core values and, after going through a persistent desire to return home, may finally settle down to carve out a creative and enriching life in the host countries. It is hardly surprising that, in Mauritius, the early Immigrants had re-created a Ganga Talao, in the memory of the ancestral Ganges, amidst a volcanic lake at Grand Bassin, into which a few barrels of *Gangajal* were ceremoniously poured. It is adopted as a sacred place of pilgrimage particularly during Shivratri festival, teaming with Indians from South Africa. This is in parallel with the number of Buddhist temples and sculptures in South East Asia, the remarkable Batu caves in Kuala Lumpur, another place of pilgrimage heavily frequented during Taipussum festival as well as other temples and mosques in the former plantation colonies.

The Diaspora has accepted the challenge which has brought out the personal contributions and the altruistic element in the individual members. Though they might not form a homogenous group, being split by language, caste or other sub-ethnic differences, in moments of crisis, given the right leadership, as Gandhi in India, Sir Seewoosagur Ramgoolam in Mauritius, they could stick together to foil the common enemy and win independence.

The extraordinary NRI's success in the US has been the more remarkable as it has been the achievements of individual talents and skills against stiff world competition, including multinationals. Unlike the Chinese immigrants in USA who had kinship networks to help them during the early period of immigration, the American NRIs were initially unsupported by family or group connections or historically accumulated private capital, which has generally been the case with other diasporas. It reminds us of C.K.Prahalad's theory of Indian diaspora being the best of breed-This is the message we must take home and apply in our daily life with conviction and commitment.

A look at comparative figures will bear this statement out.

PIO and NRI population	= 20 m.	Indian population	= 1bn.014
NRIs total income	= $160 bn.	India's national income	= $ 454bn
NRIs per capita income	= $8,000.	India's per capita income	= $ 448

(Cited from India Today, 13.1.03)

That's why Indian diaspora is known to be as dynamic as British, Chinese, French, Japanese or Jewish diasporas. It is widespread and far-flung all over the globe as compared with Chinese diaspora which is heavily concentrated in Hong Kong, Taiwan and South East Asia. With the exception of Mauritius, Malaysia, Burma since 1950 due to their nearness to India, politically, the diaspora was cut off from contact with and happenings in India. Since 1947, India had cut off diplomatic ties with South Africa, thus isolating the substantial South African Indian population from India. The consequence is that, all over the world, in West Indies, the Indian Ocean, the Pacific, the Indian Diaspora has been meandering and has evolved differently through loss of contact with and guidance from Mother India.

The Pains of Assimilation

One major aspect of diasporic studies has been left out by HLC, directed by Singhvi, concerning the behaviour, power and influence of French diaspora, compounded by a long history of settlement overseas, colonialism, slavery, racism, exploitation and a sustained policy of assimilation. French colonialism, aided by French diaspora in the former French colonies, spread over Africa, West Indies and the Pacific and outposts like Pondicherry, in India. From the beginning, it believed in its *mission civilisatrice*, that it alone was the carrier of culture and civilization and that Indians were barbarous, uncivilized heathens who had to be christianised and civilised. It reveals a history of assimilating, dominating, dislocating, inferiorising, stigmatising and subordinating the colonised people. It has destroyed the languages, cultures, religions, civilizations and entities of other diasporas, including African and Indian diasporas. If you look around to what has happened to Indians in Reunion Island, Guadeloupe, Martinique and in France, you will find that the bulk of the Indians have lost their Indianness, their dharma and their culture. They have been submerged under French culture which has suppressed their essential Indianness to the point that they have been made to believe that their ancestors were Gauls!

On attending the First Pravasi Bharatiya Divas, in New Delhi, January 2003, Mr Ernest Moutousamy, the Mayor of St Pierre and a Member of Parliament, Guadeloupe, exclained, with tears welling in his eyes, how France has robbed him of his ancestral heritage:

"La France m'a caché cette realité de mes racines que je découvre maintenant."

In countries like Mauritius where the Indians delivered a tough battle against the joint forces of British and French colonialism, the struggle for the preservation of Indian culture, languages and religion has not been easy.

The aggressive, predatory and assimilationist nature of French diaspora in conflict with other diasporas unleashes a perpetual clash of civilizations (Prof.Huntington of Harvard University, 1993). It is still going on as Indians are daily under pressure by the powerful Catholic Church which has been carrying on a relentless war of conversion even into our doorsteps, from street to street, and sweeeping across all towns and villages. What's more, the French diasporas are heavily and aggressively supported by France which has always had a special Ministry of Co-operation. It uses its francophonic umbrella to woo and assimilate the other diasporas through scholarships, awards, recognition, propaganda, publications, media support, entertainment and all sorts of inducements to increase its global influence. *France recoups its cultural investments by way of increased trade and diplomatic influence.*

The Mauritian experience has shown that successive generations of Indian immigrants and their children have tended to reproduce the pattern set by the early eighteenth century Tamil immigrants from Pondicherry and later the Indian convicts who, driven by shortage of Indian women, inter-married and merged with the Black African slave women to form the Creole community. This same Creolising phenomenon is being reproduced in contemporary western societies among NRIs children who are increasingly inter-marrying with western partners, thus forsaking their culture and religion. This is driving many overseas Indian parents crazy about the danger of losing their ethnic identity. They see their religion, their rich cultural capital, their core values, their dress and even their food going to the dogs. On the other hand, the author of *Global Migration of Indians* argues that the tendency of overseas Indians to preserve their cultural aloofness, their socio-economic isolation and their refusal to assist fellow Indians in distress exposes them further to the problem of racial discrimination against them.

GOPIO has been grappling with the central dilemma facing Indian immigrants in new societies. This relates to the problem of assimilation, compounded by identity crisis. The twice migrants, Indo-Fijians in Australia or Indo-Mauritians in Britain or in the USA, feel marginalised and they wonder who they are. Are they Fijians, Australians, Mauritians, Britons, Americans, Brit-Indians, Indo-Brits or what? Commented professor Jagdish Gundara, University of London, "*If the Scots and Welsh have not assimilated in Britain, if Blacks and native American Indians have not assimilated in America, why should the Indians assimilate?*"

As expected, this thorny problem is splitting many families, forging a wall of misunderstanding between the youths and their Indian-born parents who are sometimes mistaken to be old-fashioned by their progeny. Some NRIs girls are rebelling against parental control over dating with western boys. Many anxious PIOs' parents in western capitals are known to drive past midnight knocking from discotheque to discotheque in search of their stray daughters. This leads to the conclusion that, in western societies, the Indian family ethos, the pride of Indian culture, may be in tatters.

Gundara: added:- "*In Britain, the old patriarchal system is under threat. Young women do not accept it. They call for more flexibility*".

The break-up of Indian marriage traditions, including arranged marriages, erosion of parental consent and the increasing rate of mixed marriages spawning a whole host of problems shows how the overseas Indian community is under threat

(Brenda Angelo, *Mother India's Far-Flung Children.* Time Magazine. Sept. 11,1999)

The Sindhi Traders

THE SINDHI diaspora is a trade diaspora. It has spread into 100 countries where they generally hold the commanding positions as traders. In Malta, for example, the shops are run by Indian business community, made up mostly of the 50 resident Sindhi families who had originally migrated under the days of colonialism as free traders and who are well integrated into Maltese society. This explains one aspect of the Sindhi success- their uncanny ability to adapt to the situations:-, success or failure, even in the face of bankruptcy, they will bounce back to continue the fight in their trade which is also their religion, their way of life as if it runs into their blood and DNA. After all, Sindhis claim that they have inherited 5000 years of trading civilization going back to the period of Indus Valley Civilization in Mohenjodaro and Harappa. In Dubai and elsewhere they are after excellence of performance, seeking new processes, new production, better organization, eliminating waste and living a simple, practical life, avoiding all extravagance- which is often the cause of ruins among short-sighted businessmen. Like the Jews, the Sindhis group together, help-one another, preserve their language and culture and also compete with one another in order to achieve individual success. In one word, it's a very ambitious, highly motivated and achievement-oriented community.

The Gujarati Traders

WHEREVER THE Gujarati diaspora has spread, it has focused on trade, education, jewellery and the professions. Thus in Brussels, in Dubai, the Gujarati community has taken a hold on the diamond polishing and trade. Mr Vinod Gautam, founder of *Gautam Diamonds,* in Brussels, at Maison des Rois, a securely guarded historic place, has been in the diamond business for the past 25 years ever since he landed in Paris at the age of 18. He started from the shop floor, polishing, designing, trading in diamond, learning and improving continuously from day to day. The polisher has to be cool, calm, disciplined, patient and keep complete control over his feelings, have a sharp mind and deep concentration, a job in which only Indians excell due to their composure derived from meditation. 70% of the polishing is done by hands and the rest by machines.

To stay ahead in the business, Vinod Gautam has to go on creating new designs, keeping up with latest technology, participating in forums and exhibitions. Gautam accounts his success due to the blessings of his parents and of Lord Buddha. He says he has strong belief in God and he believes in philanthropy as he has started a school in his native village and helps 200 villagers apart from providing employment to thousands of Indians and Europeans.

In 1995, Vinod Gautam set up his first retailing at the Belgium airport and since then he has not looked back Gautam Diamonds has expanded to 70 different operations, in Europe, USA, Japan and he aims to set up 100 shops all over the world. He targets the upper middle class. All diamonds journey through Belgian Congo, Surat, Bombay, New York. The diamond business, mainly diamond polishing, in Antwerp, amounts to $ 23 bn, constituting one fourth of the Belgian economy. Surat which has taken over from Bombay boasts of 10,000 diamond factories, employing 500,000 polishers.

The story of diamond mining and polishing goes back to Golconda, and at Panra mining, 40 kilometres from Khajuharao, where diamond, sapphire and emeralds were mined. The Portuguese colonialists took the diamond business from Golconda to Lisbon and then to Europe, particularly Belgium, Switzerland and France. But from the very outset, the Gujaratis had taken a firm hold on the diamond business and on jewellery and Surat is emerging once more as a dominant diamond centre.

Mauritius. Among the Asian population, there was a small enterprising class of traders, mainly free Indian Immigrants from Gujarat, including those from Surat and Randher, known as the Surtee. (Goolam Mohamed Issac, the pioneer and cloth merchant at Corderie Street, Port Louis, played host to M.K.Gandhi in November 1901. He was the founder of Sunee Surtee Mussalman Society, decorated as Officier de Medijideah by the Sultan of Turkey in 1911, owner of four sugar estates at Grande Retraitrc, Rosalie, Masilia, Bon Air and two sugar mills, owner of 2 newspapers, including le Petit Journal, Journal de Maurice. He went bankrupt when he loaned the sum of Rs. 30 million on trust to a friend who went bankrupt the next day. Other names included:- G.D.M.Atchia, Port Louis Councillor, creator of Pleasure Ground, politician, philanthropist and manager of Sunee Surtee Mussulman Society, Major Atchia and brothers, who brought electricity to Beau Bassin, Rose Hill, Reduit and Quatre Bornes and founder of Muslim Girls' College, land donated by Kathrada in Port Louis, Ahmode Piberly, the first Municipal Councillor, Mamode

Ibrahim Atchia, Councillor for BB-RH, Mamode Ellam, Abdool Hamid Goolam, Mohamed Issac, journalist, writer and poet, manager of Tutorial College, Ranchordas Vaghjee, first Mauritian Speaker, Ahmad Jeewah, former mayor and current Minister of Civil Service Affairs, Abdool Carrim, Khader Bhayat, lawyer and former Minister of Commerce, former Chief Judge Sir Hamid Moollam, judge Maileck Ahmed, Ismael Limbada, the first engineer, Hajee Aboo Bakar Taher, the first president of the Sunee Surtee Mussalman Society, Mohamed Amin Timol, Bahemia, hardware traders, Toorawa, Yacoob Ghanty, the writer, Ariff Vawda, owner of India Boat trading between Mauritius and India , living both in Mauritius and in Surat. The Surtees used to live in big yards,equipped with a swing where husband and wife would talk to each other.and to their children. Their accountant was known as Mehtaji who kept accounts in Gujarati. They built the Jumah Mosque and their cemetery lay in Riche Terre.

From *Kutch,* known as the Kutchee Meiman (Ramtoola, Rajack Mohamed, Yusuf SaleMohamed, Abdoolah Ahmed trading mainly in rice and grains),

the *Borah*(Currimjee Jeewanjee also present in Kenya),

the *Khoja* , Shiite originating from Iran (Peerbhoy)and

the *Konkani*, (Marathi-speaking) (Ali Gafoor, hotel, the Nazir, cloth merchants, Dada Mallac, Mukadam, Meah, Mohideen Khan).

(Interview of Goolam Mohamed Issac, August 2004).

The Gujarati Muslim traders dealt mainly with import of food-stuffs, textiles and other commodities from India to cater largely for the Indian population. By 1870, there were 20 shops belonging to the Surtees. The Gujarati Moslem traders from Kutch monopolised the rice trade. Other traders came from Kathiawar, Cochin and Latna. The 1886 Almanach mentions the following traders:- Abdoola Noormohamode, Ajum Goolam Hossen, A. Essock, Ally Bhay Dawood, Hajee Haroon Tayeb. They were the representatives of wealthy Bombay merchants

Gradually, the Banias extended their trade to attract the more lucrative urban middle class and affluent Franco-Mauritians. Maintaining close links with India and holding on to Indian culture and their Gujarati connections, they formed a thriving middle class. They formed an elitist class entertaining limited political or social contact with the rural Indians. Through the bonding in the mosques, they were to provide an elitist leadership, successful role models and demonstration effects to the other Bhojpuri-speaking Moslems whom they pulled into the trade circuit. Consequently, they assumed early political leadership among the Indians, notably G.D.M.Atchia who later became the patron of Dr S.Ramgoolam.

Other Classes

All along, everything else has depended on the Whites. According to our pyramidical class structure, the narrow White ruling class, followed by the Coloured bourgeoisie, poised at the top, reproduced themselves in power and influence by barring all the escape routes of social promotion to their Black and Brown victims, pushed to the bottom of the social pyramid. In a purely agricultural country where opportunities were severely limited, the Afro-Asian races were pushed to the bottom from which they were to struggle hard in order to emerge and to threaten the power hold of the White elite. At the bottom of the social ladder, living precariously from hand to mouth were the passive, stagnant Creole proletariat, largely landless, manual workers, historical victims of economic and social exclusion who reproduced themselves from generations to generations in poverty, dependence and economic insecurity.

Echoes of the French Revolution and the hope of an egalitarian society had long been stiffled by the colonial-racist society, dominated at the top by those who had appropriated the principles of Liberty, Equality and Fraternity for their own purpose. All the gates to social mobility had been barred to the Ti Kreols. But the enterprising and frugal Indian Immigrants managed to squeeze their way slowly up through buying up land and poising as the forward-looking class of small planters, at one time-the hope of the nation and who bounced back into power from defeat and grinding poverty. In the meantime, the White owners of wealth and property had carved out an uncompromisingly inegalitarian society which has hurt the Ti Kreols most. Insecurely squeezed in the middle was a thin strip of the urban Coloured bourgeoisie and, heaped at the bottom of the social ladder lay the large masses of Indian labourers and Ti Kreols.

5

INDIAN IMMIGRANTS IN A MULTI-RACIAL SOCIETY

BACK IN 1936, my friend and neighbour, Bissoon, was born in the village of Les Mariannes, perched on the crest of Long Mountain, astride the Moka Range, almost at the foot of the imposing Pieter Both, overlooking a superb view of the sea towards Tombeau Bay. Spreading downhill and all around lay thick forests, fruit trees and undulating green cane fields, punctuated by small huts. Grand-son of an Indentured Indian Immigrant, Bissoon's life illustrates the journey of the average Indian across the diaspora who ascended from conditions of poverty, deprivations and underdevelopment to lift himself to social mobility by dint of his own efforts. It also shows some of the factors of change and personal development, including the cultural and social inputs.

Mauritian society has changed radically from what it was in 1936 to what it is now and will be in years to come. Mauritius was still a plantation colony, deeply entrenched in stagnant, traditional values. The plantation workers were stuck into a past agricultural economy where the few sugar barons wielded the power of life and death over them. But since then much water has flowed under the bridge

LES MARIANNES was populated with the children and grandchildren of Indian Indentured labourers who had migrated from neighbouring sugar estates from the north, mainly Pooliyar, making up a population nearing three hundred villagers. Though they were originally drawn from different parts of Bihar and Uttar Pradesh and belonged to different castes, they lived close together as one big family, in close co-operation and mutual respect. They addressed themselves in respectable terms, namely Mahaton, Sawji, Baboojee, and others. After having gone through the unique experience which had welded them together as Jahaji bhais during the long journey by ships across the black waters, they had learnt the first lesson of accommodating to one another. Since caste had no relevance, they shed their caste and regional differences in a bid to unite in a common front against the Whites, their exploiters. Secondly, they had come to value the importance of sticking together as one mutually reinforcing close knit community in the villages.

The Indian Immigrants

In Mauritius, the story of Indian Immigration goes back to the time of early French colonisation. Between 1724-28, 300 Indian male slaves were raided and captured from Bengal and Pondicherry and brought to Mauritius where they were forced into an un-Indian way of life. They were fed on African slave food, that is manioc, clad in coarse blue denim and prevented from practising Hinduism. Feeling dislocated, excluded, stranded, imprisoned, cut off from their families and their traditions, without any hope of returning, their identities suppressed, they found themselves in a state of absolute domination under racist French colons who treated them as barbarous, uncivilised and who had absolutely no understanding of their traditions. Meeting the same fate as the African slaves who had also lost all contact with their past traditions and culture, the uprooted Indian slaves had no choice but to adjust themselves to the situation and marry female African slaves. They were forcibly converted into Christianity and their children were christened as Antoine, Adolphe, Michel, Catherine,

Louise, Rosalie, Marceline and were classified as Creole slaves at the civil status registers.

From 1729, Mahé de Labourdonnais, brought more skilled Indian artisans as *esclaves à talents*, from Pondicherry along the Malabar coast, including masons, bricklayers, joiners, carpenters, lime burners, wheelwrights, blacksmiths, tailors, shoemakers, jewellers. They bore names like Jayamani, Savrimoutou, Chavry, Chavriraya, Arokium, Appavou, Mayepa. These are also familiar names in Pondicherry, in Reunion, in Martinique, in Guadeloupe. At home they spoke Tamil, used betel, coconut, banana leaves and they were quartered in Camp des Malbars, present day Plaine Verte. The term *Malabar* is derived from Arabic '*Male*' - full of, '*bur*' - land, meaning full of land. Many of the Indian slaves worked as household servants, the males were cooks, launderers, coachmen while the females were seamstresses, washerwomen, ironers. The Indian artisan slaves were engaged in construction works, in the building of the harbour, bridges, batteries, fortifications, public buildings, churches, shops, hospital and roads. By intermarrying with the African slaves they passed over their traditional crafts skills to their Creole children and thus they remained as the ancestors of our skilled workers who were the real builders of the infrastructure of Port Louis.

(Amédee Nagapen. *Indian Catholic Slaves in Overseas Indians-The Mauritian Experience.* MGI. 1984)

"The Malabars- a mild and gentle people from Pondicherry let themselves as servants for a few years for handicraft trade. Their features are as regular as European. They are sober, thrifty and much given to women. They wear turbans, muslim gowns, large golden earrings and silver bracelets. They let themselves as peons.

In short, the Blacks are sometimes unable to endure their hard lot, and give themselves to despair. Some hang or poison themselves."

(Bernardin de St Pierre, *Voyage to the Isle of France*, 1769)

Indian Convicts

Since 1815, the second batch of 835 Indian convicts brought in chains to Mauritius under British rule under Governor Robert Farquhar were engaged in road building and public works, a few of them were employed in de Chazal's silk factory. Of these there were six women, one from Bengal and five from Bombay. They were lodged at the Bagne. For 20 years, the 1500 dhoti-clad convicts, 55% Hindus, 32% Muslim, toiled and sweated. Their chains clanked as they bent double down, cleared the forests, hewed stones, did the quarrying, built and repaired the network of roads and bridges, including the old suspension bridges at Grand Rivière and Pont Coleville, linking the north to the south of Mauritius. Similarly, in Singapore, almost every street is a testimony of the forced labour and contribution of Indian convicts who were brought in chains for the purpose of road building. In like manner, *Mauritius owes its road network, transportation infrastructure thanks to the labour of Indian convicts. Yet no epitaph, no monument, no recognition or any tribute whatsoever has been paid to those forgotten people who lay their bones at the services of successive generations of Mauritian travellers.*

At first they were kept under strict segregation from the rest of the population. As early as 1823, some were reported to have had illicit intercourse with slave women. By 1832, discipline was relaxed, family life was more or less encouraged in order to foster their social stability. About 500 of them were dispersed and allowed to keep Creole or Indian concubines and even had children. The scarcity of women led to various scenes of domestic violence, including murders. There was clear evidence of conflict of cultures and traditions, Indian against African. The Black African women did not measure up to the strong Indian family ethos, the culture of wifely devotion and fidelity, the concept of honour, *izzat*, and men's proprietary claim over their women. The Indian convicts had a hard bargain to retain the loyalty of their wives who frequently changed partners, a tradition reminiscent of African polygamy and which has plagued Creole family life. After all, the Indians had little choice and had to make do with the dearth of Indian women. They managed to integrate within the Mauritian society through intermarriage, retaining their religious practices and engaging in economic activities. They must have passed on to their Creole children some of their values and their traditional crafts and skills for the good of Mauritian society.

New arrivals replaced those who dropped dead. In 1847, Governor Gomm freed the convicts who were above 65 years while the rest were freed in 1855.

(Clare Anderson in *Colouring the Rainbow*, ed. by Mariner Carter, CRIOS, 1998)

The Recruits

Fearing the approach of the abolition of slavery, the planters experimented with alternative sources of labour supply. In 1829, the first batch of Chinese and Indian immigrants landed in Mauritius. The conditions were not attractive. And the recruits proved to be unsuitable to cope with agricultural work and costly, due to transportation cost. In the Caribbean islands, planters tried immigrants from different parts of the world, including Portuguese from Madeira and the Azores, Malta, Blacks from southern United States, West Africa, from China and Europe. None of the immigrants proved to be satisfactory. But the story of Indian Immigration on a mass scale really started in 1835, after the abolition of slavery when the slaves refused to continue working in the cane plantations. Besides, the planters were not prepared to pay them higher wages. When the fields were abandoned, the cane left unharvested, the factories threatened with closure, the colonial governments, controlled largely by the While Oligarchy and a handful of British officials, in Mauritius, in the West Indies, in British Guiana, later in Fiji, turned to India in their hour of need. Henceforth, recruiting agents were sent to scour Indian villages of the north, mainly Bihar and the United Provinces (now UP, Uttar Pradesh). The gangetic plains were often subjected to vagaries of the seasons, marked by periods of famines, caused by drought or flood. Entire villages were deserted and people flocked to Calcutta where they were lured to the emigration depots, including 60% recruits to Mauritius. Another 33% sailed from Madras province while only 7% came from the Bombay Province to Mauritius in search of a better life.

From 1842 to 1872 the number of Immigrants to the colonies stood as follows:-

Mauritius	351, 401
British Guiana	79, 691
Trinidad	42, 519
Other West Indian islands	7,021
Natal	6,448
Reunion & French colonies	31, 346

(Huguette Ly Tio Fane Pineo, *Lured Away*. MGI, 1984)

Recruitment Made Easy

For ages, the people of the North as well as from the South had been used to migrating to other parts of India during time of hardships, marked by the annual uncertainty of the monsoons, exposing them to periods of droughts or floods. Under British colonialism, further changes had been taking place which had aggravated their livelihoods. The peasants and villagers were being rapidly impoverished. They were thrown out of their livelihood and had to roam about like the flotsam and jetsam, the cast-off victims of British colonisation. The British elite, poised from the top of the social pyramid as the fine products of British culture and civilization, were directing the fate of millions of Asians abroad. To them, the Indian villagers were available pools of Coolie recruits fit for the plantation colonies. These aliens were ssen as less than worthy wage-earners nor as workers but as Coolies and beasts of burden who needed to be made productive and to yield profits under the boots of European planters. The Coolies were to be brought under the harshest possible discipline, as if they were recalcitrant children without brains.

The villagers' traditional ways of life, their textile manufacturing base, their cottage industries were shut down to make room for the prosperity of Industrial Revolution in Britain and for import of British manufactured goods. In consequence, they were thrown out of their jobs and were turned into landless labourers in the bondage of the rising class of powerful and ruthless zamindars, money-lenders and tax collectors. But agriculture was seasonal, leaving a large number as unemployed or underemployed. So, it was in the British colonial interest to expedite them elsewhere in the sugar colonies in order to reduce the pressure on the overcrowded land and thus avoid the risk of trouble-makers on their hands.

Consequently, the Indian labour migrants were lured by the pull-push factor, mainly the push factor. On the one hand they were pulled by the dazzling promise of easy money in nearby *Mirsch desh* where they were told that they would turn stone and find gold. But the gold they found went into the pockets of the white planters. On the other hand, they were pushed by the widespread poverty, droughts, famines aggravated by British colonialism in its attempt to destroy the cottage industries and turn the Indians into consumers of British industrial goods.

In addition to their fixed monthly wages of Rs 5 for men, Rs 4 for women, each labourer was entitled to a daily ration of:- 2 lbs of rice for men, 3/4 kg for women, 1/2 pound of dholl, 2 0z. salt, some oil and tamarind, and an annual 4 dhotis, 1 sheet, 2 blankets, 1 jacket and 2 caps. As an inducement, on signing and registration at the police station, they received 6 months' advanced wages.

A vivid example narrated during the Pravasi Divas, in New Delhi, January, 2003, was told by a surviving immigrant to Trinidad, Nazir Mohamed, 93, himself.

I was only three then, the youngest in the family. All my three siblings had died. So my mother came to Trinidad as indentured labourers at a coconut plantation. Nazir left India in order to escape starvation and an outbreak of rat flea plague in his native village, in Basti district of Uttar Pradesh. Leaving his father behind and hoping to return after some time, Nazir and his mother joined other fellow immigrants sailing for Trinidad. After working for 6 years, when Nazir was 10 years old, they were given free passage but at their own cost back to India. They could not muster the $ 35 to pay for the return trip. So they stayed back as immigrants. (*Mid Day*, Delhi. 13.1.03)

453,063 Indian Immigrants from U.P, the Madras Province, including the Tamils and the Telegus and the Marathi-speaking people from Bombay, drawn mainly from the Konkan coast, crossed the black waters to Mauritius. Among them, thousands were fooled, cajoled, rounded up, kidnapped. Having signed the labour contract, the *girmit*, or agreement, they became known as the girmit people or *girmityas*. Thus they had become engaged as Indentured labourers, caught up in a system organised for maximum efficiency, in which they were mere commodities. They had bonded themselves by law to serve foreign white racist masters who were out to extract every ounce of their blood and sweat. Quite a large number of them, driven by the lure of adventures, or facing personal and family problems, had been brave enough to volunteer as Indentured labourers, many of whom had left their wives and children behind as they thought they might soon return with some savings to rebuild their lives.

"Les Coulies étaient amenés à conclure avec les agents des contrats. C'etait une veritable vente, déguisée sous le nom de transfert de contrats indiens, quoique le mot vente fut toujours soigneusement évité dans la conclusion de ces sortes de marchés."

(M.C. A. de Challaye. *Mémoire sur l'émigration des Indiens*, 1844)

They were brought to the Calcutta depot before being taken overseas in crowded, uncomfortable vessels. Sometimes, the voyage to reach Guyana or the West Indies or Fiji took them more than three months. It took them less than a month to reach Mauritius.

The long sea voyage was an ordeal for the one million Immigrants who left India for the plantation colonies between 1834- 1920. Packed, huddled together, without sanitation, without lavatories, exposed to the open sky, to gales and wind on the damp decks, the passengers were suffocated as they entered a nightmarish world. The mortality rate was excessively high. Aboard the Salsette, bound from Calcutta for Trinidad, the death rate climbed to 38%. The average mortality rate was 20% as compared to 1.2% for passengers bound for Australia and one tenth that figure for migrants to North America. The worst disaster occurred to the 500 Indians who were roasted alive in the Shah Alam, bound from Calcutta to Mauritius while the captain and the crews clambered safely aboard lifeboats. Dr Wiley reported that the sailors struck the boys while in other ships the doctors got drunk and raped the women with impunity and escaping only with a slight rebuke.

(Francis. C.Assisi. August 2004).

When they landed and stepped across the Immigration depot in Port Louis, Mauritius, they were barracked for some time until they were sorted out and distributed to the plantations. They looked travel worn, emaciated, sickly and terribly aged and shaken, as revealed by the pictures of the registered Indian Immigrants, minutely recorded and on display at the Mahatma Gandhi Institute museum, Moka.

"In most cases, I have observed that the Cooly had landed here a poor, sickly, emaciated creature..."

(The Brennen Memorandum, 1845)

The Plantation System

THOROUGHLY EXHAUSTED after a traumatic voyage, those poor, illiterate migrants found themselves captive in a hostile environment from which there was no escape but death. They were totally cut off for good from their ancestral homes. Nor did they have any say in the matter of choosing their employers. They had fallen like flies into the net of the fiercely intolerant and arrogant ex-slave masters who valued them as coolies or less than humans, only as beasts of burden. On realising that their whole world had crashed around them, they gave up all hope as they lay forever trapped into the small world of the plantation system, reeking of a new system of slavery.

Small wounds, slowly weeping
To the cruel rhythm of a whip
Those blows resound still
Healed by the sun and salt water
While the wind howled in the welts
A language of its own intensity.
In the shadows across the moon

My father saw his lonely country.

(Satendra Nandan, Fijian poet, *Lines Across Black Waters*, Academy Press, N.D, 1997)

Life in the plantations was a long nightmare. In West Indies, the indians were packed into the Nigger Yard. They were kept to work from before day break till after sunset. The penalties and punishments including beating, lashing and tormenting. Said a Manager in South Africa:

"*As long as the Coolie is working for you, you've the right to do what you like with him-short of killing.*"

The death rate, aggravaterd by lack of sanitation, lavatories and safe water, was alarming. It struck in the form of cholera, typhoid, small pox, malaria and depression and suicides. Driven to desperation, feeling nostalgic, unable to cope with such misery, many Indians preferred to die than live a living death. While in India the suicide rate stood at 50 per million, in South Africa it was ten times higher while in Fiji it rose to 20 times. Apart from this, the planters cleverly set the Black against the Indians, calling the Blacks as the sons of the soil and the Coolies as the dregs of Indian society, as low-born and criminal. Caught between the White oppressors and the Blacks, it was hard for the Indians to put up with the "*uncivilized ways*" of what they considered to be those Black "*savages*". (Francis Assisi, 2004).

Was it a New System of Slavery?

Suddenly, he found himself thrown into the vast multi-racial dek that would gradually mould his children into the colourful, complex and spicy Mauritian or Caribbean or Creolised melting pot. In every plantation colony, in the West Indies, the Indentured labourer met a similar situation, where he took over from the ex-slaves. Lying at the mercy of the white plantocracy, he had to bend low to the discipline of the plantation system and like the slave, he enjoyed no freedom whatsoever. On September 1834, Lord Glenelg, the Secretary of State for the Colonies, disallowed the ordinance which condemned the immigrant to compulsory labour for life on the plantations. Further, he added that the effect of it at least was to establish a new compulsory system scarcely less rigid, and in some material respects less equitable than that of slavery itself.

The high mortality and suicide rate in the estates, numbering 85 deaths out of 185 in Merven's estate at Pamplemousses in January 1838 was aggravated by the gross sex disproportion which put both the men and the women under tremendous stress and demoralisation. They had to work from 4 a.m to 8 p.m in the sugar house, including extra hours during crop season without compensation.

"The planters, long accustomed to a mentality of coercive control over slaves with great and unjust severity by overwork and personal chastisement, their lodgings either too confined or disgustingly filthy." (Justice Anderson's report, 1838)

Hugh Tinker likened the plantation system to a new system of slavery. The difference was that the slaves were rounded up, captured, embarked and brought overseas, sold on the slave market like chattels and they were entirely the property of their owners, just as a dog is its owner's property. Even the children of the slaves were slaves. As chattels, their masters exercised unrestrained power over them. They could be used and misused, ill-treated, thrashed and kicked around, their women or children taken away from them at the pleasure of the slave owners. They did not enjoy any form of human rights. They had absolutely no right to say anything or take their masters to court when they were abused. It was a permanent system from which they could not escape and, unlike the Indentured labourers, they had no guarantee of a return passage.

In that respect, the Indenture system was more or less voluntary, based on a legalised labour contractual system, the *girmit*. In practice, the Immigrant had no control and no say in the contract and to which, in the first place, he had put his thumb- print without understanding a thing about its implications. He had no idea of his destination either. But at least the indentured labourer could hope to earn some money, be fed, enjoy some human rights and be free at the end of the contract and hopefully return to India. In theory the Indentured labourer had the right to take his master to court for any breach of contract. But the magistracy courts were corrupt and controlled by the planters. As the Royal Commissioners noted, the fixed belief in Mauritius and enshrined in legislation was that Indians required to be protected against themselves.

"With a few exceptions, they were treated with a great severity, by overwork and by personal chastisement, their lodgings so confined and disgustingly filthy that they are generally pillaged of the six months' pay advanced to them in India."

(Justice Anderson to the Commission of Enquiry, 1838, cited in the 1875 Royal Commission)

Like the slaves, the Indians were exposed to lashes and harsh punishment in case of absenteeism, failure to complete the set tasks and other minor offences. Through various methods of manipulation and applying pressures, the Oligarchy, aided by the overseers or sirdars, their henchmen or *chamchas*, managed to cheat the labourers, under iniquitous laws, to reindenture, sometimes going up to 6 times, or 30 years under the contractual system.

Both, the slaves and the Indentured labourers, were subjected to laws which were unilaterally made by their masters, with the complicity of the colonial government. Indenture was based on a penal system, backed by harsh Labour Laws which regulated their hours of work, penalised them for absence at work, refusal to work, for failure to complete the set tasks, raised beyond their physical level. The penalties were harsh- jail, fines, extensions of indenture period. The courts were heavily stacked against them. They were simply commodities as the master owned their labour, controlling their time and movement within the estate camps.

Both were at the mercy of the plantation. Both knew that the plantation system was fixed, arbitrary, leaving them no hope of strikes, improvement or revision of their conditions. While slavery was forced labour, unpaid, indenture was paid labour- though the wages remained fixed for more than a century inspite of rising cost of living, higher production fetching higher prices of sugar and higher profits. The area under cultivation rose from 60,000 arpents in 1850 to 123,000 arpents in 1870. This was accompanied by the transfer of new technology, the use of railway transport from Riche en Eau to Beau Vallon in 1864. And as the capitalist system grew and developed in the plantation economy, the Indentured labourers were to profit from the system in the wake of the speedy centralisation of factories and the morcellement system.

"L'immigration est la clé de voûte de la prosperité de la colonie." (The President of the Chamber of Agriculture, 1859, Mauritius).

Unlike what took place in the civil service or private sector, the agricultural labourers did not benefit from any prospect of occupational mobility, pensions or any rise in the scale of their fixed wages. On the contrary, the more they aged, the weaker they became, the less was their income. Overcoming all their hardships in the plantations, the labourers and their families lived a simple, economical and productive life style. At the end of the day, some of them managed to save up to buy a portion of land and set up as a new class of independent labourers-planters in Mauritius. Hence they had access to landed property, over which the slave had cut himself off. Such facilities, as access to land, were not available to the Indians in Fiji where they were debarred by law from owning land. They were to remain a permanent landless class, leasing land from the Melanesians.

Despite their great contributions in raising agricultural productivity, in employment creation and petty trading, they remained anonymous in history. Their voices remained suppressed except in the pages of novels written by the Trinidadian-born V.S. Naipaul, particularly in *A House for Mr Biswas*, and a string of books on India, and one on Mauritius, *The Overcrowded Baracoon*, in 1972. Here, we have had a number of writers, including:- my own novel, *Watch Them Go Down*, 1967, Abhimanyu Unnuth, *Lal Pasina,* Deepchand Beeharry's *That Others Might Live*, followed by a rich crop of literary and historical writings, published in Malaysia, Mauritius, the Caribbeans, Fiji, India,

UK, US as well as a fast growing literature and studies on the Diaspora.

The other major difference was that since the slaves were taken from different areas and tribes and were foreign to one another, they lost track of their ancestral languages, customs and traditions. Besides, their ancestral languages were oral and they had no written scripts as literary support. Therefore, the African diaspora had no alternative but to assimilate the language, civilization and religion of their European masters, including their race prejudices. By assimilating them culturally through the process of acculturation and socialisation, the Europeans could dominate the mind of the slaves and of their descendants entirely. The Blacks and the Creoles became totally dependent upon the White race. They were to remain permanently helpless while the Indians struggled hard to stay self-reliant and independent. Further, the Immigrants had come in great numbers and sometimes they were uprooted from entire villages, so they struggled hard to preserve their Indian identity. The more the colonialists exerted hard physical power on them, the more they were persecuted, humiliated and ridiculed, the more they countered with a strategy of *soft power.* They took great pride in adhering to their cultural and religious heritage as a sign of their protest and resistance to White domination. In one word, they pushed back all attempts at assimilation by flouting their Indianness, forged across millennia of culture, civilization and philosophy.

"Our ancestors came in difficult circumstances. They let their bodies languish but they kept their heads high. They preserved their religion and culture with all their might."

(Dr. S.Ramgoolam. Leg. Council. 28th August 1976)

But the Indians had no chance in the French colonies, Reunion, Guadeloupe, Martinique and to a certain extent in Mauritius. Everywhere, the French settlers, holding on to their racial superiority, imposed their assimilationist policy of wiping out Indianness completely by banning Indian languages, customs, languages, Hinduism, or festivals in their bid to turn them into Christians. Their children were indoctrinated into the blind and uncritical acceptance of

French superiority- transmitted by the Oligarchy. In these Caribbean countries, and in Mauritius, the Indian Immigrants had to contend with a rival Black or Creole population which resented their presence as having taken a large share of the pie and were therefore seen as being responsible for their poverty. The diaspora hit against a wall of racial resentment from the Blacks and most acutely from the Mullatos and from the White minority ruling class.

"A stranger, on arriving at Port Louis, is struck by the variety of features, complexions and attire displayed in its streets - Europeans, Chinese, Malays, Hindoos, Africans, Arabs, mingling together."
(*Recollections of the Mauritius* by a Lady, 1830)

Who Were the Coolies?

COLONIALISM, RACISM capitalism and white domination went hand in hand. In their arrogance and ignorance, the Europeans, British, French and Germans and recently Serbians, came to regard themselves as the superior races and the Asians, the Blacks and non-Christians as inferior, subordinate and their subalterns. Wearing their Euro-centric blinkers, they viewed the non-white races as racially, culturally different and therefore as inferior and subordinate people. This is how they had justified the inhuman practice of slavery, followed by indentured labour and later apartheid in South Africa. Added to their imperial greed and their arrogance for power, the Europeans resorted to racialism to back up their imperialist claims. The ideology of racialism engendered the most destructive and blinding of prejudices. The German belief in their being a superior race had led to collective madness, the indiscriminate use of weapons of mass destruction, fratricidal, Fascist and anti-Semitist wars under Adolf Hitler. So, racialism has always formed an integral part of European culture and civilization. They have used racial violence to justify their colonial and capitalist domination over the non-white.

In this colonial-capitalist- and racist context, it was easy to give somebody a bad name and hang him as a consequence! Thus, the British colonialists could conveniently label the Indian Immigrants as Coolies as an offensive term just to downgrade them and then treat them as dirt and less than human. Now, they had got hold of the abusive term Coolies from the Gujarati word *Kuli* meaning belonging to the Kuli tribes of thieves, plunderers, vagrants, degenerate and inferior people, prejudices which they splashed over the Indentured labourers indiscriminately. The aim of the colons was to conquer, control, to subjugate the inferior Asiatic race. In the colonial perspective, every Indentured labourer was seen as a lazy, infantile, recalcitrant *"vagrant"* who needed to be domesticated, disciplined, exploited and sucked dry as an orange. The European viewed the Coolie as being socially and culturally different and therefore inferior. They were trapped in a system in which they were absolutely helpless, deprived of any organisation, any leadership, any rights. Unlike free labourers, they were not paid by the hour but by the tasks which were always measured beyond their physical limits. Their bosses, white, Coloured or Indian sirdars, were always arbitrary as they punished the trouble-makers savagely and rewarded their favourites and their mistresses. The sexual relationships and sexual violence, coercion and rapes perpetrated on the women by Europeans were part of the ordeal which forced many labourers to seek their independence and set up homes outside the estate camps.

It revealed the harshness of the capitalist system with its shameless exploitation of the proletariat. It was usual for contemporary literature and travelogues to depict the Indians as being docile creatures, the willing servants to the European masters. Like domesticated animals, the Indians were described as mild and gentle Coolies or beasts of burden. Sometimes, they were praised as the good, muscular, swarthy Malbards just as if they were some strange farm animals, relegated to live like primitives in barracks and to scrounge for their living in the wild by gathering *brède malbar, brède songe* and other greenery.

What emerged was the image of a demoralised, dehumanised, depersonalised, devalued Coolie. Having trapped the helpless, impoverished, insecure Indians into their immigration net, they found that the term Coolies fitted their captives marvellously. The Coolies were reduced into the victim class, servile, submissive and fatalistic. The indenture system was such in the plantations that the labourer developed a passive, fatalistic outlook on life which he had already carried over from his ancestral village. These attitudes induced a sense of acceptance, fatalism, helplessness, immobility and resignation. The irony was that, later, in the plantation colonies, by the application of their inequitous Labour Laws, the white planters were themselves turned into plunderers, thieves and criminals when they criminalised the Indentured labourers as vagrants whom they savagely incarcerated into vagrant depots.

"In Mauritius, the Indian is looked upon as fair game to be generally preyed upon."

(The Royal Commissioners, 1875). .

Unfortunately, the immigrants had been simple village artisans who had been pushed back into the land to make room for the industrial revolution in Britain.

"The Coolies who are ensared by those unprincipled intermediaries are often grossly deceived... Women are enticed away from their husbands and their families."

(The report of Beyts, the Protector of Immigrants, in 1861, cited by the Royal Commissioners).

The struggle against Coolitude was to be a long drawn battle against colonialism-capitalism-racism-white domination in order to recover one's identity, dignity, and personal freedom, thanks to the intervention of De Plevitz, Gandhi, Manilall Doctor, Basdeo Bissoondoyal, Dr S. Ramgoolam and a whole army of social and political reformers. Its use was a clear indication of the racial attitude of the white, the Coloured and the anti-Indian lobby. It was to be a battle for the assertion of human right and dignity and a total rejection of the white supremacy. Since the early 1930's, in the wake of the struggle for civil and political rights, the term Coolie was banned from circulation, just as people would not dare address others as Kreol Mozambique, Chinois Macao, Mulate Corbeau!

(John D. Kelly. *Coolie as a Labour Commodity*, MGI. 1985)

Why were Indians so Hated?

The reason why the Oligarchy hated and suppressed the Indians stemmed from their fear of the eventual loss of power to the Indians. As a reaction, the white tried to keep the Indians down by every means at their disposal, by repressive laws and excessive punishments for trifling offences:- low wages, unemployment, restrictions on their movement, limited access to education, insulting and humiliating them daily, keeping them under poverty. They were glad to see Indians shabily dressed, clad in the cast off clothes of the British army. Fully aware of such injustice, Governor Pope Hennessey tried to usher the Indians into the political system by appointing Gnandicarayan Arlanda as a nominated member into the Council in 1885.

(James Pope Hennessey. *Verandah*).

"Du jour ou l'indien venait massivement submerger la population générale, dans les deux îles, la société coloniale se sentit agréssée et avait peur de perdre son identité. Elle se sentait fondamentalement menacée par une main d'oeuvre qui n'était plus séparée d'elle par aucun fossé juridique. Le seul fossé qu'on pouvait créer entre les deux communautés, c'etait le fossé du mépris. Il fallait mépriser ces nouveaux immigrés si on ne voulait pas qu'ils deviennent un jour les maîtres."

(Hubert Gerbeau, Conférence à l'Université de Maurice, 2 mai, 1980)

Immigrant Chummun's Story

IN ORDER to illustrate the story of an Indian Immigrant, bound to Mauritius, we shall refer to the case of Immigrant Sew Chummun (seen on front cover). Aged 20, one metre 58 centimetres tall, bearing registration No 356214, Chummun left the village of Boharee, in the Zillah of Ghazeepore in the pergunah of Dhanapore, U.P. Like thousands of his compatriots leaving for the sugar plantations across the seven seas, Chummun was taken to the Calcutta Immigration depot where he journeyed by Nimrod No 1207 across a most uncomfortable journey to land at the Immigration depot, Port Louis, on 18 March 1872. He looked aged, emaciated, beaten, depressed as he was distributed as an Indentured labourer at Phooliyar, in the north of the island. From there, he married a local Mauritian teenage girl who gave him five sons, Beekharry, Sookharry, Dhanpal, Nanand and Mohabeer and daughter, Manon. After completing his Indentureship period, Sew Chummun was in a hurry to break away from sugar estate control in order to live independently in a village as many other Indian labourers had done.

The creation of a quasi independent and separate Indian family and communal life in Mauritius acted as a vehicle of resistance at the work-place, fostering an anti-employer socialisation, and providing an alternative cultural dimension, profoundly antipathetic to, and hidden from the world of the European planter.

(Mariner Carter. *Lakshmi's Legacy*. EOI. 1994)

It had been the dream of every Indian Immigrant to buy a plot of land and to build a house of their own to rear their family so that they could live in comparative freedom according to their customs and traditions. This dream had been made possible thanks to the system of morcellement which had started in 1865, triggered by the process of centralisation of sugar estates leading to the selling of the remote and inaccessible lands, mainly on hills and mountains, to labourers. The idea was to build up a vast pool of surplus labourers who could be availaible to the sugar estates as and when required on very low wages, not far from the plantations. At the same time, it saved the planters the cost of paying the return passage. In their turn, those casual labourers had to earn their living, work on their plots of land and cultivate every inch of that land, sharing and working collectively- father, mother and children on the family plot, the joint property, so that they could make both ends meet. On top of it, they had to save some money to pay off for the debts on the family property and possibly raise some more savings for the future to keep the wolf from the door.

"On all the estates of this district, the Immigrants are allowed to rear poultry in any quantity, and to keep as many cows, pigs, goats as they choose. The labourers employ their time in enlarging their gardens, in which I have found growing maize, potatoes, tobacco, onion, lettuce, radishes, sweet potatoes, turnips."

(T.M.Rennards. Stipendiary Magistrate. *Observations*. Stipendiary Court. Black River. 6 January 1865)

A House on the Hills

Now, due to their simple living, their habit of saving, of hard work and sticking together, Immigrant Chummun, his five sons and two daughters had realised the dream of every single immigrant. He had managed to do what he could not do in his native village in India. He had saved some money in order to buy a plot of land up on the hilly flanks of Les Mariannes, overlooking the Long Mountain village and which commanded a gorgeous view below and stretching to the radiant blue sea towards the west. Gradually, in their turn, each of his five sons bought some land on the brow of Les Mariannes mountain and pitched their modest huts amidst their gardens and cowsheds, forming a network of family units, close to one another. It should also be remembered that, like Long Mountain, all the other villages of Mauritius and in the plantation colonies were built by the poor labourers who tried to re-invent imaginary Indian villages, Little India overseas. They converted forests, mountains and bushes with some running stream or rivers into human habitations and gardens making do with civilised amenities like roads, safe water, schools or medical facilities. These were not their priorities. They took immense pride in constructing their own houses, cow sheds and living spaces by their own efforts. They were left behind by the colonial government which neglected them completely. And they paid dearly for the official neglect. They were devastated by diseases in those inaccessible, malarious and infectious places without the basic infrastructure system of civilised living- deprived of safe water, health, sanitation, school, road, transport, electricity services. The Asiatic villages were feudal Indian enclaves which were vastly outperformed by the western towns which enjoyed all the benefits of infrastructure system under municipal administration and central colonial government. At least, they were satisfied that they had found safe asylum from the white man's grips. They had to wait for the accession of the Labour Party, in the 1950's, under Dr S. Ramgoolam who, having himself been born in a village, at Belle Rive, identified himself thoroughly with the labouring classes. Ramgoolam was destined to transform the villages as viable places, equipped with modern infrastructure.

The little village of Les Mariannes, rooted in the ancestral past, ensuring social stability and a cultural identity of its own, formed part of a network of villages which sprang all around Mauritius. Similarly, in other plantation colonies, in the Caribbean, the Indian labourers were to found villages, as one of their great contributions to their countries of adoption. For his part, Bissoon's father, Sookharry, the second son of Immigrant Chummun, had bought one quarter of an acre and his family lived close to the other brothers in the same vicinity. As we shall see, the village, inhabited almost exclusively by Indians who planted their auspicious *jhandi* floating proudly outside their homes to proclaim they had arrived into this territory which was now theirs. It clearly symbolised their economic, cultural and social capital and signalled their Indian homogeneity in that it was free from the presence of the *Kirwal.* It became a nursery for social, human and economic development, based on the principle of self-help and co-operative living. The labourers created their own jobs and provided their own basic services, thanks to the existence of a pool of hereditary skills among them and which helped them earn their living as self-employed entrepreneurs. Starting as an isolated sector, completely agricultural and rural, Long Mountain was destined to change into a rural town under the impact of modernisation, urbanisation and rural development programme with the introduction of:- safe water, roads, electricity, radio, television, cars, buses, schools, a hospital, police stations, markets, shops, social centres and factories.

So Bissoon's family, his uncles, aunties and cousins lived close together, in intimate kinship relations, favouring daily contact, in peace and harmony and in a spirit of respect and tolerance, rooted in their ancestral traditions. They took pride in the preservation of their cultural heritage centred in a baitka, the seat of the panchayat of which Sookharry took a leading role as the president for a number of years.

"He elaborated in this alien land the system of village headman, the meeting hall baitka, arbitration and respectful acquiescence in periodical sittings and hymn singing, public recitations of the epics, grouping around a religious place. The balm of the great epics gave him the philosophical determination with which to strive for a footing".

(J.N.Roy. *Whither Indo-Mauritians?* 1937)

The family tradition was characterised by respect for one another, tolerance, sharing of everything- knowledge, skills and experience. It came as no surprise to anyone that the co-operative movement was to take its roots in Long Mountain as village life provided the cradle for democracy and decentralisation. This also explains why democracy has become so largely successful across the Indian diaspora.

There was a lot of sharing and close co-operation among the Chummun's relatives. As life was hard, it was not possible to purchase rare commodities like fish and meat every week. But whenever any of the uncles bought some fish, say once a fortnight or a month, he would make sure that it was in sufficient quantity so that the delicacy could be shared among all the relatives. At the same time, this indicates how life was hard, how the villagers were mal-nourished and how eating a thing like fish was considered a rare luxury. Similarly, at the end of the year, when a goat was ceremonially butchered, all the members of the Chummun's joint families as well as some close neighbours and other relatives would be invited to share in the feast.

Vegetable Selling

Similarly, on market days, Tuesdays, Thursdays and Saturdays, it was the practice of Bissoon's father who usually got up earlier to wake up his children and brothers. After brushing their teeth with guava twigs used as *datwạn* and a quick breakfast of tea and *farata*, they set out to the market to sell their products. By five o'clock, they would start their journey barefoot. Loaded with baskets of vegetable, pine apples or bananas on their heads, they would trek along the muddy, pebbly, slippery track winding downhill to the open market, close to the shivala of Long Mountain. It was a casual, seasonal job which added to the income of the large families. Many would save to invest in small business or in their children's education. Sometimes, the vendors squandered the income on gambling, drinks and friends at the village shop where they would gossip about their neighbours before returning home, drunk. The village marketplace was quite an animated scene. The petty vendors or *bazardiers*- mostly illiterate owner-cultivators, tenant cultivators or landless labourers, would display their vegetables in heaps outdoors, arranged, sorted out, on the ground, sometimes on carts or on low tables. They would rival one another by shouting in Bhojpuri. The buyers, mostly male, would haggle over the prices, and joke, in a spirit of warmth and rural exuberance.

After the sale, the Chummun brothers would buy the weekly food provisions at Saroop Jhowry's shop. Then, they would meet other friends to gulp down some pegs of rhum, taken with bread and fish or octopus curry or oily sardine and pickled chilly and spend some time in idle gossip before undertaking the journey uphill.

The Bissoon relatives were content to live an Indian way of life, the way it had been done for ages in India. Both in Les Mariannes and in Long Mountain, they used to live close together, speaking only Bhojpuri, - the link beween their ancestral homeland and their cultural heritage. They toiled in the cane fields, tending to their cultivations and cow sheds, worshipping their deities, Ram, Sita and Hanuman, as their ancestors had done along the Gangetic plains in India. Religion provided them with a set of ethical values, like hard work, honesty, self-discipline that regulated their daily lives. They would worship their deities every day and resort to prayers and rituals before undertaking any important functions, sowing, harvesting, as well as marking any events like birth, marriage, death or festivals.

Meeting daily in the local baitka, they would comfort each other and enjoy the simple pleasures of life. They cherished their cultural traditions as a sign of their collective strength, their identity, their Indian heritage which set them apart as a proud people impervious to assault from outside. At least they felt free from the daily humiliation of living under the shadow of the white master who had little understanding and no tolerance of them and whose only interest was to exploit their labour for cheap. Yet the labourers bore no ill-will and no hatred towards the planters. On the contrary, they were full of respect and loyalty to the *bara saheb* to whom they always showed gratitude. In return, their employers, the *gore log*, kept them firmly under their control in a paternalistic relationship, in the *mai bap*, *ou meme mama*, *ou meme papa* feudal tradition.

Indians in the Caribbeans

BACKED BY colonial power and his economic clout, the white planter, whether English or French, could impose his rule as the uncompromising exploiting class. The same policy enabled the racist Boers to practise their policy of racial segregation in South Africa. As was held in Victorian England that the sun would never set on the British Empire, the white man, sincerely believed in the superiority of the white race and its right to dominate over the brown and black races.

Thus colonialism went hand in glove with racism and capitalism. This is borne out by the colonial history of Mauritius, Trinidad, Guyana, South Africa marked by slavery, Indian Indentured labour controlled by a tiny white exploiting minority through a social order erected on racism, colonialism and savage capitalism.

Thus in **Trinidad**, society has been polarised on racial lines. The 520,000 Indians, 42% of the population, fragmented into groups and castes and class differences, and imbued with their ethnic and racial differences with the Black races, 44%, have tended to keep apart and were thus kept out of power for more than three decades. In Guyana, the divide- and- rule- policy on racial lines had enabled Burnham to knock the 400,00 Indians, 51%, out of power since 1966 until 1995 when Cheddi Jagan came to power as president until his death in 1997 when he was succeeded by Bharat Jagdeo of the PPP. Unfortunately, the upper and middle class educated Indo-Guyanese tend to be more western-oriented and to keep aloof from the working class Indians who are more attached to their Indianness.

The tragedy is that during the long period when Indians wandered into political wilderness, the key sectors like the executive, the judiciary, including the civil service, the police and the army had been filled by Afro-Trinidadians, Afro-Guyanese. Without a solid base of Indians within the superstructure of government, as technicians and bureaucrats, this weakness has rendered their hold on power very fragile and it has explained why, in Fiji, Indians had been easily ousted from power twice in 1987 and in 2002. As regards Jamaica with its tiny Indian population of 60,000 who have been submerged by the overwhelming Black population, the Indo-Jamaicans have been largely Creolised through inter-marriage and racial mixing with the Blacks.

(Ajay Dubey, GOPIO Magazine, 12.1.03, N.D)

In **Surinam**, the Indians, 35%, colonised by the Dutch have not been molested in maintaining their Indian way of living. They have evolved the Surnami language, a mixture of Bhojpuri and Urdu, and they are proud of their distinct chutney Indian culture. Like the other

Caribbean Indians, the Surinamese Indians, unlike Indo-Mauritians, preferred to focus on trade and on rice farming rather than on education. Consequently, they have produced a very tiny professional or technical class. As twice migrants, about 100,000 Indo-Surinamese, immigrated into the Netherlands, where, identifying themselves as *apanjhat* within Dutch society, are trying hard to retain their culture against the onslaught of westernisation which is sweeping across the uprooted younger generation. (Femmes des Iles.Jan. 1985)

The French Diaspora

BUT WHO were the French colons? Traditionally perched on top of the social ladder, the Franco-Mauritian could be graded in three categories:--the descendant of the old planters, aristocratic, living and spending lavishly as he had everything for free, land, slave or indentured labour and other privileges. A die-hard conservative, he might have belonged to the pre-French revolution era and in that respect he was agriculturist, despotic and backward-looking Otherwise, he might have escaped from the horrors of the French Revolution. In any case, he was the descendant of the European settlers who roamed the globe in search of greener pastures, open space, free labour which he exploited at will for his personal needs. He could have been an employee of the Compagnie des Indes:- a trader, a shopkeeper, or an adventurer, a soldier, sailor, skilled worker- that is, a *petit blanc.*

"La Compagnie des Indes recrutait des marins, pilotes, charpentiers, cochers, calfats, maçons, forgerons de 20-35 ans. Ces engagés, mal payés sont des mauvais colonisateurs laissant des descendants 'petits blancs' en concurrence avec des mulâtres. Les soldats libérés du service, y restèrent, les forbans amnistiés et des matelots sortis des navires de passage, des paysans, serviteurs de la Compagnie. Autour de Labourdonnais groupèrent les émigrants de familles bourgeoises, ses parents et compatriotes"

(*Les Bretons aux Iles de France et de Bourbon*)

Privileges Enlarged under Indirect Rule

Unlike the slaves and the Indians who had to toil hard in order to purchase a plot of land, the French colons were induced to come as settlers with the promise of generous 142 arpents of land per concession granted by the Compagnie des Indes, the French East India Company. Since they belonged to the bygone days of Royalist France, before the French Revolution, like all the other French settlers either in Quebec, Canada, or in Ile de France, they were steeped in racist and class prejudices. Thus, after their capture of Mauritius in 1810, the British- in their attempt to co-opt the settlers as agents in their policy of Indirect Rule- extended the same privileges to the French settlers as they had previously done to the French in Quebec. After the capture of Quebec from the French, sealed by the Treaty of Paris, 1763, the British had guaranteed the French settlers the preservation of French heritage- language, Catholicism, French civil law, and French customs. This arrangement had ensured the preservation of French language, their culture, their civilization and the dominance of French diaspora in Canadian politics.

After the capture of Mauritius, thanks to an army of 23,000 men largely consisting of Indian sepoys under British officers and a fleet of 70 sails led by General Sir John Abercromby, Mauritius became a Crown Colony. By the Treaty of Capitulation, 3rd December 1810, the French governor, Decaen demanded and obtained 4 other articles to guarantee the properties, the preservation of their religion, laws, customs and liberties. But Sir Robert Farquhar had already granted these demands in his proclamation to the Inhabitants of Ile Bourbon (Reunion) at St Denis on 29th July 1810. However the grant of these privileges was to have significant importance in the history of Mauritius, namely:- Article 7, *All private property shall be respected,* Article 8, *The inhabitants shall preserve their Religion, laws and customs".* In other words they were to retain control over:-

(1) the land, (earlier granted through the concessions)

(2) the French language,

(3) French customs and manners,

(4) French civil laws and
(5) the Catholic Church
(H.Ly Tio Fane Pineo, *In the Grips of the Eagle*, MGI, 1988)

This arrangement was in accordance with the British colonial policy of Indirect Rule which it pursued everywhere. It enabled the British to hold ultimate control over its colonies. In India, they used the Maharajahs, Nawabs and zamindars, the degenerate elites, as puppets and they skilfully played one against the other. They cleverly manipulated the caste system without having to interfere directly with Indian customs, languages, except by using English as an administrative and anglicising instrument while pushing steadily with Christianisation. They did the same in Africa, with Fiji via the indigenous chiefs and rulers. Consequently, starting with the privilege of free land ownership, control over the means of production, the French colons handled the leverages of power which sustained them throughout the history of Mauritius and rendered them impregnable.

The policy of Indirect Rule has worked wonderfully well both in Canada and in Mauritius. Originally, both the French Canadians and the Franco-Mauritians came from the old pre-French revolutionary, royalist stock. They were agriculturist, feudal, backward -looking and anti-commercial. They still believed in despotic rule- according to which they thought they were the lords of the earth. In Mauritius, under French rule, they had survived by sending their men as marauders at sea to harass British shipping and trade by corsair plunders. Ile de France had been stagnating until the coming of the British who rescued the French settlers from a state of permanent bankruptcy by persuading them to shift over to sugar production, backed by a guaranteed British market at par with West Indian sugar in 1825.

Besides, the tenor of the Capitulation Treaty suggests that the British were satisfied to keep the Indian Ocean free from French corsairs' attacks so long as they could focus their attention on the bigger prize, that was India. Secondly, it looked as if the British had given away possession of the island back to the French settlers who were free to maintain their proprietary rights over the land. Thus, the British restored and reinforced the French economic clouts and, what's more, they transformed the French settlers from economic insecurity and impoverishment into one of prosperity. They were now elevated into prospective sugar estate owners, with a guaranteed British market. Further, the British took the trouble of educating and apprenticing the backward French agriculturists as trading partners and gave them an understanding of the mechanism of trade and commerce. They were initiated into modern commerce, through British education at the Royal College, and British universities. They were offered learning opportunities in business by the establishment of Franco-British partnership in the setting up of commercial houses like Rogers, Ireland Frasers, Scott and other companies which they either took over or eventually held the majority of shares. This gave them a formidable competitive economic advantage over the population.

The Dominance of English and French

The continued use of French language, French culture and manners gave the French a tremendous cultural-social-economic and political edge over the rest of the population. Since language meant power, those who controlled the weapon of language also controlled the means of power. So, from the start, the French colons held the cultural and linguistic advantages which placed them at the top, leaving the aliens as their cultural beggars. The use of the French language gave them the great advantage of culture and civilization, apart from social prestige, control over communications, over the press and mass media, over education, daily conversation, over the institutions and daily commerce. It became the clarion call of a civilized society. The Indians and the Blacks who were unable to handle the French language were automatically relegated as backward and inferior classes. Since they stood as uncritical models to the Mullatos and the Black Creoles, the use of the French language, an appendage of the Whites, exercised a rare fascination which immediately marked out the social superiority of the French-speaking population over the Asians and the Ti Kreols.

Since 1814, the British administrators had been trying hard to push the English language into the forefront without much success. The renowned explorer and visitor, Charles Darwin, author of *The Origin of Species*, during his visit here in 1831, observed that :-

"Though the Island has been under the English government, the general character of the place is quite French. Englishmen speak to their servants in French and the shops are all French."

In 1847, Governor Gomm attempted to abolish French by decreeing Englsih as the language of the Supreme Court and timidly English began to make its way into the civil service, trade, the schools and public life. English was associated with the Anglican Church which was no match against the all-powerful Catholic Church which buttressed French language and French cultural dominance. Since 1839, in a bid to compete for converts, the Catholic Church reacted strongly against the threat of the Anglican Church and English education by establishing Roman Catholic aided schools.

Besides, the Creole language, itself a French dialect largely adopted by the majority of the people, was so close to French that it has acted as a transmission belt for the spread of French language, the same way as the learning of Hindi is helped by its nearness to Bhojpuri.

Similarly, in the Caribbean colonies, only English or pidgin English was recognized by the State and there was no encouragement for the learning of Indian languages, no educational provisions for their teaching. The result was that for some time Bhojpuri survived in the home and Hindi slowly disappeared though a lot of Hindi words have crept into Carribean English.

Mission Civilisatrice

As an important part of the French diaspora, the French colons could link up continually with France as the motherland, the source of their language, culture and civilization. Historically, France has been continually held out as the most civilized country on earth, committed to its mission civilisatrice. Paris was seen as the centre of culture and French as the most beautiful language on earth. While this propaganda has had the pull effect on the popular mind the other push effect has been the consistent running down of everything Indian as of inferior brand. In their self-defence, the children of Indian Immigrants held on to their culture, civilization and religion as their identity landmarks. To keep up the pressure, France has been injecting considerable investments in the promotion of French language and culture through generous grants, scholarships, incentives and an aggressive French cultural policy, unmatched by whatever Britain or India has done for their languages. This policy dated back to the 17th century when the French government had laid down its colonial policy to implant Christianity in order to consolidate its empire and trade:

"Implanter ou faire fleurir le christianisme dans les nouveaux établissements par l'évangelisation, car l'unité religieuse était considérée comme l'un des moyens sur de conserver à la France ses possessions acquises."

(Ly Tio Fane Pineo, *Ile de France*, 1715-1746, MGI, 1993)

Since the days of Mahé de Labourdonnais, French cultural and moral values have been firmly entrenched in Mauritius.

Power of the Church

More important still has been the visible power of the Catholic Church which has continually buttressed Franco-Mauritian **cultural racism**. French colonialism has been fiercely intolerant as reflected in its determination to establish Catholicism as the state religion as was the case in mainland France.

"Interdisons tout exercice d'une religion autre que la catholique, apostolique et romaine, voulons que les contravenans soient punis comme rebelles et désobeissants à nos commandements".
(Le Code Noir, 1723)

The Church's formidable power and influence has remained impregnable. It has acted as the long arm of the Oligarchy to keep the population under its heel and as a willing servant to subjugate the General Population, comprising the Franco-Mauritians, the Creoles, the Sino-Mauritians and the Indo-Christians under its tight control. The Catholic Church is so entrenched, so powerful that it almost constitutes a state within a state. It has consistently undermined the Labour Party under Sir Seewoosagur Ramgoolam and after. Through the process of assimilation into western civilization, mediated by Creolisation, it has exerted tremendous racial and political influence over the mass of the Catholics.

The power of the Catholic Church, of French-controlled judiciary and police was confirmed by the rebellion of the French colons under the leadership of Adrien D'Epinay who had staged a boycott of John Jeremie, appointed as the Attorney General in 1832. The British had to withdraw Jeremie and appoint Adrien's brother, Prosper D'Epinay, at the head of the judiciary, a period which had marked their quasi-military power, their permanent command of the law courts and the police. Once for all, it marked the capitulation and subservience of the British colonial government to the dictates of the French colons.

In his book, *The Hidden Priest*, 2003, Selva Appasawmy has revealed how the colons resorted to violence and crimes to get rid of their rivals and preserve their dominance in religion or in government. Reverend Charles Edward Clifford of Chudleigh had dedicated himself to improving the conditions of the unlettered, neglected, persecuted and suffering population of ex-slaves at Mahebourg, in south Mauritius. Since he was immensely popular and successful among the Blacks and fearing their consequent allegiance to the British administration, the French colons recruited a rival French priest, **Jacques Désiré Laval**, from Paris, as their agent to domesticate, *adoucir,* the Blackpushs and bring them back under the French-controlled Catholic Church. An agent of the Whites, Father Laval could conveniently pose as the Creole Messiah after he had ousted Father Clifford who had disappeared mysteriously. The same fate had overtaken the combative Coloured journalist, Remy Ollier, who had vanished at the young age of 29, at the hands of the anti-British cabal, described by Dr Collier as a *set of scoundrels*.

The Church keeps on reinforcing its power through a policy of conversion by any means and under many disguised forms, thus perpetually fragmenting and reducing the Hindu majority from the mythical 70% to its current 48%. During the long era of colonialism, entry into Catholic schools, government jobs, the private sector or promotion within the sugar estate hierarchy was open only to those who embraced Catholicism. Similarly, in Reunion Island, in French-controlled West Indian islands of Guadeloupe, Martinique, the French committed ethnocide on the slaves and the Indians who were completely assimilated into Frenchness. They had to embrace Catholicism, bear Christian names, bury their cultural heritage and proclaim France as la patrie.

Frenchness was stretched to the point of ridicule and caricature when children, originating from Central African jungle or Asian villages, were taught to repeat, parrot-like *nos ancêtres, les Gaulois*. The question is that what had the children of the African or Indian diasporas got to do with their ancestors, the Gauls. French colonialism was so strong, so well structured that it left the Indians with little chance to assert their identity. But recently there are clear signs that within the former French colonies, the Indian diaspora are coming back to Hinduism and Indian culture, thanks to the influence of Mauritius, the facilities of travels, communications and Indian films and the resilience of Indian culture.

Anglo-French Colonial Alliance

Ideologically, the French settlers belonged to the conservative, feudal, royalist school which subscribed to autocracy and despotic rule. They were completely foreign to the Anglo-Saxon concept of Parliamentary government, democracy, the Rule of Law, fair play and good governance. Since the take-over in 1810, the British tried to wean them away from despotism into adopting the more advanced British constitution of nomination within the Council of Government. Besides, they were also socialised in political and administrative government by their direct participation in British colonial administration, and in the maintenance of law and order. However, they continud to exercise French civil law which enabled them to dominate the law courts and the police. They utilised the law as an instrument of control and torture over the Indians and the Blacks.

This laid the basis for the establishment of close Anglo-French co-operation. It meant that they controlled everything, i.e, the legislature , the executive, the judiciary, the police, import-export, economy and finance, banking and commerce. They left the onerous job of vegetable growing, cow and goat keeping and other small- scale production to the Indians and pig rearing to the Creoles. But whenever they saw the Indians had already done the ground- work and that there were profits in any one of those ventures, they would quickly pounce on the business. In brief, the close Anglo- French alliance was consecrated by the constitution. Thus by the Letters Patent, dated 28 June 1831, regulating the First Constitution, the Governor, Sir Charles Coleville was empowered:-

"To establish and constitute a Council of Government composed of certain officers of the Crown and of an equal number of other persons to be taken from the chief landed proprietors and principal merchants of the colony, and to nominate and appoint the latter by commissions to be issued by him".(Government Notice of 18 January 1832)

Power Without Control

Given all those advantages, the French colons stood head over shoulders over the rest of the population. Since they held all the landed property of the island freely in their hands, plus other privileges, including free slave labour, they had a flying start which enabled them to accumulate wealth and impose their stamp on the island. French Governor, Mahé de Labourdonnais, a man of great vision, planning, long-term strategy and the real builder of the colony, had mapped out the essential social, cultural, economic and administrative structures. He spanned the Indian Ocean and understood the maritime and political implications of colonialism in India and therefore stood as a bridge between the East and the West. Having been hand picked by Labourdonnais, the colons had acquired considerable experience in the administration of agricultural, commercial, civil and political affairs. They evolved into a formidable Oligarchy of a few powerful families, strengthened through marriage alliances- which enabled them to concentrate all the wealth and power until today. As everything else depended upon landed property, upon money and employment which money commanded they benefited from all the strategic advantages wealth conferred, including - free labour, trade, employment, and investment capital and, briefly, the sinews of power. From the start they wielded the power of the sword, a quasi-military, socio-economic and political power first over the slaves, then over ex-slaves and the indentured labourers.

The racist colons had produced a powerful elite which was to provide leadership to match with the British colonial administrators, who buttressed the planters in tightening their economic, agricultural, commercial and political grips. The colonial administrators were content to give them leeway. They ceded meekly to their demands, as were first expressed by the influential **Comité Colonial**, set up by the leader, Adrien D'Epinay. In 1832, Adrien D'Epinay raised a rebellion against the political and economic emancipation of the slaves by forcing the expulsion of the British Attorney General, John Jeremie, in favour of his brother, Prosper D'Epinay. Further, they set up all manners of institutional, legal and psychological barriers to push the slaves and their descendants into poverty and marginalisation. Since 1826, the Comité Colonial, the Masonic Lodge, La Loge de la Triple Espérance and La Table Ovale kept working behind the scene to lobby consistently, here and in London, on behalf of the Oligarchy. Made up of white racist members, directors of the Chamber of Commerce, of the Mauritius Commercial Bank, of planters/politicians, the Comité Colonial represented the convergence of financial, agricultural, political and judicial interests

(Vijaya Teelock, *Bitter Sugar and Slavery in 19th Century Mauritius*, MGI, 1998)

Since 1825, by the Mauritius Trade Bill, the House of Commons opened the British sugar market to Mauritius on the same terms as West Indian sugar and thereby unleashed a sugar revolution which enriched the white planters considerably. The British fuelled the Oligarchy's wealth, power and influence by putting the privileges of the vast British empire at their disposal, both the access to sugar market and to Indian Immigration. Since they were firmly entrenched in all the rural districts, through the Stipendiary Magistrates, the Civil Commissioners and the plantations, the White agricultural bourgeoisie continued to poise as an aristocratic ruling class. They were buttressed by the power and prestige of money, the government, judiciary, the press and the Church, apart from the patronage of France in the background and the indomitable power of French language and culture. In one word, they enjoyed a long stretch of absolute, quasi-military and political power without control or opposition or any checks and balances. It was naked despotism. With the complicity of the British colonail officials, by 1 April 1839, they had dismissed the 50,000 ex-apprentices and chased them from the plantations into the wilderness and marginalisation.

Once the slaves were freed, the British officials washed their hands of all responsibility over their fate and, by 1838, applied the restrictive Vagrancy Laws which targetted both the ex-slaves and the Indentured labourers. They utilised *the Catholic Church as a weapon to keep the Blacks and the Asians under their cultural orbit*. Similarly, in other French-dominated islands like Reunion, Guadeloupe or Martinique both the Blacks and the minority Indians fell victims to a process of acculturation whereby their identities had been wiped, their language, culture, civilization, religion, customs and traditions savagely uprooted.

Power without control meant that the despots enjoyed all the material advantages you can think of and they could do anything they wanted. They could keep slaves, do whatever they liked with them. They held the power of life and death over them. They were free to thrash, torture them, rape their women, split their families and exploit them at will. The white dictators, nurtured in a long tradition of naked *despotism*, and of *lawlessness* exerted *barbaric* atrocities over the innocent victims and *nobody could take them to account*. They could shock them to the marrow by cheating them of their most precious heritage, their culture, their pride and dignity, their collective memory. And worse still, they filled their victims' minds with the poison of racism and fanned the germs of race hatred, born of the colonial superiority of the white race and of the Church, on their colonised consciousness to such an extent as to turn them into their mental slaves.

"*La démission de l'église Catholique perçue comme ayant été et étant toujours au service d'une oligarchie raciale et d'une élite de gens de couleur au mepris de la grosse majorité des mailles issus du milieu populaire créole.*"

(J.C.Chan Low, University of Mauritius. *Roots, Rasta and Riots*, MGI. 23 June 1999)

As in the Caribbean islands, the Europeans *deviated the class struggle into racialism, by targetting the Asians* as the scapegoats. It had been so easy for them to *set up the gullible Blacks against the Indians* who were blamed as the cause of their poverty. Accordingly, they pursued a clever strategy of divide-and-rule by blunting the class anger and rebellion of the ex-slaves against themselves as the oppressive capitalist class by pointing to the Indians as the culprits. That task was rendered easy as they discredited the Asian cultural differences, particularly Indian languages, customs and religion as marks of inferiority. Further. as a strategy to consolidate white hegemony, they exploited the influence of the church and western culture as baits to hook the Blacks into their net and thus drive a wedge with the Indian proletariat. By 1861, the Blacks were flattered to be lumped alongside what they thought were their half-brothers, the Coloured and their White masters into the category of the General Population with whom, however, they shared nothing in common except Catholicism. Targeted as aliens, the Indians were now isolated and vulnerable. As in South and East Africa, Trinidad, Guyana and elsewhere, the Oligarchy harassed the immigrants by a series of anti-Indian legislation, against which Gandhi and others had to wage a non-violent, civil disobedience campaign. This is what governor Pope Henessey had to say about these oppressive Forest Laws, Ordinance No 10 of 1881.

"I found that, for having in his possession a toothpick, being a piece of brushwood, a few inches long, an Indian had been fined Rs 5 and 10 days imprisonment. Another Indian complained that having a small bundle of such portions of things in his possession, the total value of which was under a shilling, he had been fined Rs 1000 or 200 days imprisonment. Other petitions were from Indians who had, in cutting grass to feed their cattle, unintentionally cut a little brushwood and who were condemned to pay for each twig a fine of Rs 50, though the twigs may not have worth one farthing.

I found that the legislation had come upon the Indian population like a sort of social hurricane, breaking up homes and families and sending men, women and children to prison who had been well conducted and industrious."

When slavery was abolished they appropriated the **two million pounds sterlings** granted as compensation into their pockets. Henceforth, they became financially impregnable by creating banks and erecting private fortunes. They could use the banks as private institutions to perpetuate their economic supremacy while keeping the Asians at ransom. Instead of going out to improve the economic conditions of the ex-slaves, the latter was left in the lurch to roam without food, without jobs, without land and without status. As a strategy to make them accept their poverty, divert their mind away from class war and from rebellion, they pushed the Creoles into alcoholism and self-destruction, just as they set up bars in every estate camps. But the cleverest thing they ever did was to import a missionary from France with the object of domesticating the ex-slaves under the sway of the powerful Catholic Church. Consequently, Père Laval was poised as the apostle of the Black Creoles. Pursuing the divide- and- rule- policy and the aim of suppressing class consciousness among the exploited working people, they converted the class war into race war by setting the descendants of slaves against the descendants of Indentured labourers.

All along, the Church, as the *permanent ally and agent* of the Oligarchy, made it a point always to target the Asians as aliens, barbarous, filthy, heathens who had betrayed the Blacks by slipping back into the role of the willing slaves. Fingers were pointed at them as being the real cause of Black misery. Since the Blacks had lost their African identity and their historical memory, they had descended into anonymity, into infantile dependents on the white race whom they revered as the masters, *a mentality which has survived until now.* Consequently, the ex-slave owners emerged into an all-powerful Oligarchy skilled at exploiting the divide-and-rule policy to their fullest advantages. Since historically they had been reared on despotism and slave ownership, they became the more dangerous as they controlled the key sectors of the government, the judiciary, the police, and the economy. Wielding these instruments of torture, they could get away with murder and arbitrary power.

"*While everyone admits that abuses exist, scarcely any one, except myself, ventures to denounce them; the planting interests, being paramount in the island, neither the press nor the public, dare to express an opinion opposed to these interests.*"

(William Walter Raleigh Kerr, Treasurer, in Council of Government on 15 November 1867 on behalf of Indian Immigrants)

The colonial government was only interested in perpetuating the convenient and less costly policy of indirect rule which the Franco-Mauritians gladly adopted to divide and rule over the Indians who were naturally fragmented into different castes and sub-ethnic groups, speaking different languages, Bhojpuri, Tamil, Telegu, Marathi. The Oligarchy became very skilled in handling the strategy of divide and rule which has enabled them to recover political power, in 2003, under the prime ministership of one of their own. Despite being a member of a tiny minority, Paul Berenger swung into power by skilfully fragmenting the Indo-Mauritians and playing off one sub-ethnic group against the other.

The Oligarchy Always in Control

Being firmly entrenched in power, backed by strong institutions like the Chamber of Agriculture, the successor of the Comité Colonial, the Oligarchy has developed a tremendous capacity of survival. It has never been defeated by any of the major political or economic revolutionary events. On the contrary, after each crisis, it has emerged stronger than ever before. Thus,:-

(a) During French colonisation, under governor Mahé de Labourdonnais, the importer of slaves, they were given liberal land concessions and slaves from Africa and from Pondicherry. He set up and handed over to them solid civil, economic, political, military structures.

(b) After 1810, they turned the British occupation into their favour, by preserving their Frenchness and increasing their political and economic power.

(c) After 1834, they profited largely from the abolition of slavery by pocketing the generous compensation, opening banks, commercial companies, founded the newspaper Le Cérneen, and nominated their members into the Council of Government.

(d) They replaced slaves by skilled and productive Indentured labour at little costs.

(e) From 1948-68, they opposed independence tooth and nail only to highjack its economic benefits and finally they got back into political power by placing one of their own as the Prime Minister.

(f) After the Lomé Convention, in 1973, when prices of sugar sky rocketed, they amassed considerable fortunes which they invested in tourism, factories, business, finance

(g) In the wake of industrialisation and economic development, thanks to their organisational and managerial skills, they have consolidated their economic grips. They have diversified from being mere planters and millers to becoming capitalists, owners of hotels, banks, factories, insurance companies, import-export and all large trading houses, in alliance with multinationals.

6

WHY HAVE WE FAILED HISTORICALLY?

IN THIS section, we shall deal with the sequel of colonisation, its impact on the Asian Immigrants, the problem of race relations and the myths, misconceptions based on ignorance concerning the Indians. We shall see how the colonialists held on to the euro-centric belief in their own race superiority through a systematic policy of domination, suppression subordination and domestication of the Indians and of the slaves. They were separated from the Immigrants by a wall of suspicion, mistrust and hatred. This situation deteriorated through a lack of dialogue between the two cultures, the East and the West. That it did not degenerate into a clash of civilizations was due to the spirit of tolerance inherent within Indian culture.

On the one hand, the British and French colonialists were keen to impose their culture and civilization on the Indians who, in their own self-defence, refused to embrace Christianity and stuck to their Indianness within the plantations and villages. Thus the plantation colonies became culturally and civilizationally polarised between two opposite camps- a Eurocentric and an Asiatic orientation. In between were the descendants of slaves who had been totally accultured and domesticated into the dominant culture and civilization of their slave masters. And all this had happened because India had rendered itself weak, vulnerable through its caste system, its disunity, its lack of a historical and political consciousness and national pride. The past degradation of India replicated itself in the degradation of the indentured immigrants. Hopefully, in future, a strong and developed India will restore pride and honour into the hearts of all Indians, at home and overseas.

A Sense of History

THE POLICY of the sugar barons was to flood the plantation islands with surplus agricultural labour in a bid to keep wages at starvation level and to maximise their profits and also to create a vast market for their industrial goods. In contrast, bound by their indenture contracts which they had signed without apprehending the contents, penned in English, the Indian Immigrants and their descendants were trapped largely in agricultural employment and they were held firmly into the grips of the racist planters, ex-slave owners. Because Indians had been meek, gentle and tolerant under the civilizing impact of their five millennia-old culture and civilization, the more aggressive and exploitative Europeans, rated them as weaklings. Everywhere in the colonies, Malaysia, South Africa, the Caribbeans, the early Indian Immigrants had played a low profile and had been stereotyped as *"docile, submissive, subservient, ignorant, guillible and easily governable."*

Lacking political knowledge, suffering from historical amnesia, reared in theological obscurantism, they easily submitted to whoever wielded the symbols of authority over their heads. They vowed feudal loyalty at the feet of the *gore log*. Unaware of the grandeur of their own culture, civilization and the Vedic dharma, they had earlier, at the national level, collapsed at the feet of the Moghul and the British imperialists in deep self-humiliation. At the local village level, the majority of Indians had fallen almost into bonded labour at the hands of the oppressive zamindars and blood-sucking money-lenders from whom no escape was possible except emigration. Thus, it is difficult to imagine how the Aryan descendants who had given birth to the rich

Vedic, Sanskritic and Buddhist civilization which had once spanned across the whole of Asia could be so totally deprived of a sense of history and to crumble into a race of weaklings.

The **Sanskrit** language had descended upon them as the gift of God. It had taken mankind thousands of years of culture and civilization to evolve a fully developed language like Sanskrit, the Mother of languages, three millennia before Christ and in which the Vedic, the Upanishadic and Mahabharata verses and Sanskrit plays had been penned. It articulated man's emotions, hopes, dreams and visions. Sanskrit had been the language of literature, philosophy, science, mathematics, astronomy and medicine. Its grammar had reached perfection in the hands of the Afghan-born Panini. Compared to Sanskrit, English and French were tribal dialects until they evolved in the fifteenth century. The only explanation can be given is their lack of a political culture and of a dynamic elite class and which had allowed the Sanskritic learning to slip into medieval oblivion and obscurantism under the control of selfish Brahmanical caste.

Having lost touch with Sanskrit, now monopolised by a hereditary caste, Indians had grown forgetful of their own past. They had no sense of community and civic living. They could not look beyond their immediate family interests into the nation state. It is also significant that the renaissance and reform movement in nineteenth century India was driven by the Arya Samaj's "*Back to the Vedas*" movement and the awareness of the Vedantic heritage which heralded immense political changes and the freedom struggle. With the discovery of their past history, the Indian revolution had taken place. Indians suddenly awakened from oblivion into self-recognition, that they, too, they had a glorious historical past and they were the custodians of a great civilization.

For millennia, having been cut off from their Sanskritic heritage, Indians had developed little sense of unity and nationhood. They suffered from a tortured memory,. a historical amnesia, *the absence of a critical collective memory, the lack of a questioning mind, the scientific spirit to help them get down to the bottom of the truth*. They placed uncritical trust in their rulers, the pleasure-loving Kings and

Rajahs preoccupied mostly with their wives and their hunting. They were obsessed with their internal caste divisions which had enabled the Moghuls and the Europeans to rule over them for centuries. Perhaps, they were too preoccupied with local gossips, with the affairs of their own families, castes and villages so that they failed to look beyond to the welfare of the wider community, the civil and political society. They were so blinded by the petty caste, family and local differences that they failed to take on board the wider *geographical, political, cultural, religious and civilizational commonalities that could bind them into a great nation.* They were more obsessed with differences than with commonalities which, for example, bound Islam into a political religion under a unique Koranic scripture and the ideology of Islamic brotherhood. Thus Hindus simply couldn't see the **interconnections** of economics-politics-religion-race-ethnicity and nationalism.

Caste and Class Divisions

Maybe also that Hinduism had failed to develop an over-all political ideology like the expansionist Christianity and Islam that imposed their will forcibly by proselytising and dominating the world. It could be that the political ideology of Hinduism was appropriated by the Brahmanical caste in maintaining and perpetuating the caste system for their personal class advantages. To maintain their privileged positions within the caste system, the upper castes had to push the lower castes and the Dalits forcibly at the bottom of the social ladder, condemned to serve their class interests. However, it turned out to be a short-sighted and *self-defeating ideology* which resulted in discriminating against, *inferiorising* and humiliating millions of low caste Hindus. Somehow like racism, it deprived them of their human rights, their self-respect and their self-confidence. By forcing them out of the social system, it left them with little alternative but to seek dignity and self-respect by embracing Islam, Christianity or lately into Buddhism. Fortunately for India, since the Arya Samaj and Mahatma Gandhi and the Indian Constitution had rejected the caste system, other cults have followed suit and have opened up to gather all Hindus irrespective of castes within their fold.

Caste divisions were bound to have immense political significance as they incited the converts to fight back with anger and vengeance at their tormentors. Under the democratic set up, it became easy for the Dalits and other caste groups to get together collectively to constitute massive electoral forces. The caste system codified and reproduced the class stratification. It clamped down on class mobility and suffocated the *circulation of ideas, knowledge, talents, entrepreneurship and creativity*. It deleted the potential of people who could otherwise have contributed to the march of progress and knowledge. It harked back to a feudal past and blocked the passage to an achievement-oriented future. It reproduced the dominant Brahmanical culture and the culture of subservience. It was designed to ascribe power and prestige to the upper castes while it marginalised and excluded the non-caste Hindus. It consisted of the self-perpetuating, so-called :--

(i) Brahmins, (traditionally the learned and priestly class),

(ii) Ksatriyas, (the warrior and administrative class),

(iii) Vaisyas (the trading caste) and

(iv) Sudras, (the working class) leaving out

(v) the non-castes outside the caste system as the Untouchables, called the Harijans, Children of God by Gandhi or currently the Dalits.

The caste system perpetuated a class structure which gave hereditary power and prestige to the two upper castes while it marginalised the low castes. Since it bore the stamp of Brahmanical religion on it, it became a fixed, stratified, hereditary system which reproduced itself from generation to generation without change. Thereby, it stiffled class mobility and class dynamism as people could not get out of the caste boxes and categories with which they were imprisoned and labelled from birth. During the dark feudal times, the caste system might have been accepted despite the enormous harm it had caused to the low caste who must have experienced a sense of lowness, of inferiority, of subservience to the upper castes.

While it had reproduced itself in Indian villages it lost all its relevance the moment the caste members had stepped into the ship as shipmates. They were compelled to stick together, welded by common bonds of language, history, religion, culture and traditions against the common enemy- the planters. They were bonded together with the strong *Jahaji Bhai* feelings when they had to share the same food, the same company and the same fate in the ships, in the immigration depots and in the plantations. Once liberated from the limitations of the stratified caste system, the different members of the Indentured immigrants could experience a level playing field which permitted their upward mobility, particularly after the Arya Samaj had come forward to abolish the system. It also explains why a large proportion of low caste Indians has embraced Christianity in the colonies as an escape route from caste humiliation. This is one of the basic reasons why Indians outside India have everywhere, despite tremendous odds, done done much better than casteist native Indians.

From an intellectual point of view, Indians had failed to transfer the mantal discipline of questioning and inquiry from the field of philosophy and spiritualism over into the material studies. Otherwise, they could have applied knowledge to decipher the social and scientific phenomena that governed their lives. They would have developed an awareness of the process of economic and political oppression to which they were subjected. They had to wait for the day that materialism and spiritualism were fused into the practical philosophy of Karma Yoga under the firebrands, Swami Dayanand and Mahatma Gandhi. That was the day when the Indian intellectual revolution had taken place. Once more, we must thank Apartheid South Africa, projecting in reverse the familiar caste and class stratification, which had compelled Gandhi to reject the caste system entirely. The defining moment in his life was the day he had been violently thrown him out of the train at Pietermaritsberg station.

Dayanand and Gandhi had found India stagnating in medievalism as it held on to the relics of an old, fatigued, crumbling civilization. All around, the Indian villages from which came the immigrant forefathers were entrapped by selfish, blood-sucking money-lenders and zamindars. For the most part, the feudal villages had been stagnant, traditional enclaves inhabited by generations of self-reproducing subsistence peasants immobilised in superstitions, Brahmanical obscurantism, fatalism, illiteracy and resignation- characteristics which they carried with them into the plantations. Betrayed by the archaic Brahmin caste, the villagers had been leaderless. Thus, they had to wait for the emergence of a dynamic western-educated Indian elite spearheaded by patriots and reformers like Ram Mohan Roy, Vivekanand, Gokhale, Gandhi before they were awakened from feudal lethargy to the shock of new ideas.

"To progress one must break up old constructions, buffet, demolish preconceived ideas.

Preconceived ideas are the habitual mental constructions in which one lives, and which are fixed, which become rigid fortresses and cannot progress because they are fixed.

Nothing that is fixed can progress. So the advice is to break down, that is, destroy all preconceived ideas, all fixed mental constructions. And this is the true way to give birth to new ideas or to thought- active thought- thought which is creative."

(The Mother. Sri Aurobindo)

In the colonies, the Indians, reduced to the level of dependent minors and infants, had conveniently shifted their subservience from the exploiting zamindaris over to the racist plantocracy. The problem with Indians was that they could never muster enough courage to rise and rebel against their oppressors, apart from the single example of Shivaji, the builder of the Maratha Empire. Indians had got stuck into a traditional, stagnant, backward-looking society that had lost the faculty of analysing, criticising and reforming itself.

In the meantime, taking over the relics from the Graeco-Roman civilization, Europe had broken with the shackles of feudalism. The universities of Oxford and Cambridge and grammar schools had sprung up from which had emerged an intellectual, political and entrepreneurial elite which took Britain further into the age of imperialism, mercantilism and modernization. Led by a succession of great leaders, freedom fighters and elites, Britain had leap-frogged into the future. It had emerged into a dynamic, open, rational- legal-scientific society. It had experienced a process of irreversible change triggered by intellectual movements, namely the Renaissance, the Reformation, the age of exploration, discovery and colonial expansion, the growth and expansion of entrepreneurship, Rationalism, the Enlightenment, the Scientific age, Agricultural and Industrial Revolutions and the advances of research and technology. Britain led the way because it had passed through a series of political revolutions starting with the Magna Carta, across the fire of the Cromwellian revolution to end with the evolution of parliamentary democracy, the Rule of Law. For its part, France was still stuck with autocratic despotism until the outbreak of the Revolution.

In this perspective, the Trinidadian-born Nobel Laureate, Sir V.S.Naipaul, was right in underlining that: *"the degradation in the plantation colonies matched the degradation which lay within the country of origin"* (India) and he added that it was time to: *"develop a true sense of history."* He urged Indians to search their souls and find out:- *"Why we have failed historically?"*

(First Pravasi Bharatiya Divas, 9 January 2003, New Delhi).

In 1856, two shiploads of 682 indentured labourers were quarantined on **Gabriel Island**, measuring 1200 metres by 700 metres, in the north of Mauritius without food, water or shelter in the sweltering month of January. Then on 13, a severe cyclone hit the island leaving 298 passengers dead. Their bones lay unceremoniously scorched on the rocks. The colonial authorities did nothing about it. Nivriti Sewtohul rightly suggests that a *monument* should be erected and the island should be put on the Slave and Coolie route,

Vagrancy Laws

THE COLONS indulged freely their anti-Indian passion by resorting to a harsh system of repression and exploitation to keep the labourers under their heels. This task was made easy under State racism when the Oligarchy wielded the power of the sword-government, the executive, the judiciary, the police, the economy and landed property against their victims who did not even have a shield to protect them. Labelled as coolies, as vagrants, Indians were now categorised as the lowest of classes, as savages, illiterates, barbarians, nomads, as bearers of diseases who were beneath the protection of the law and who needed to be disciplined and imprisoned for the least offence. The white racists used their power to dominate, domesticate, subordinate, oppress, suppress, marginalise, rob and punish the Indians at will. Generally, the colonial governor, himself having planting interests, stood as their ally in applying anti-Indian legislations. Unlike what had happened in South Africa, Apartheid laws were aimed at the Non-Whites, including Indians and the Blacks. In the plantation colonies, the repressive Labour Law targeted the Indians specifically and spared the rest of the population, Europeans, Chinese, Coloured and Creoles.

"Riche-en Eau & La Flora. Appendix B . 25.

The Creoles here, as on many estates, are not subject to the same rules as Indians."

(Royal Commission Report, 1875)

In Mauritius as in the Carribeans, they could pass any law, however harsh, inhuman, and repressive they liked that suited them. Thus in 1845, the Legislature resorted to the Merchant Shipping Act which became the dreaded Double-cut ordinance. By it:

"Every labourer engaged by the year or by the month, who, during the period of his engagement shall have absented himself. shall lose double the amount of his wages".

Further, the Ordinance No 7 of 1849 authorised the police to arrest without warrant deserters caught in any public place. They were to be brought to the nearest stipendiary magistrate. All the repressive laws were codified into the hated *Labour Law of 1867*, imposed by governor, Sir Henry Barkly, himself a planter in the West Indies where he had supported the sugar interests. He had been a former Member of Parliament and former governor of Jamaica, British Guina and Victoria. It provided for fines and imprisonment for failure to complete the onerous and demanding five tasks per week, for refusing to work, for absences. Absence by any person, including a woman even in an advanced stage of pregnancy was held as desertion and the offence was punishable by a fine of $ 24 or 6 months' wages or a month's imprisonment.

In all the plantation colonies, Indians were severely hit and impoverished by the Vagrancy Law, and the Pass Law. According to the Pass law, the Old Immigrants were compelled to carry a ticket worth one pound as proof of their status, plus a photograph costing 4/. To purchase the yearly licence he had to pay one pound. The effect of the Pass System was that, in 1868, 22,357 vagrants were arrested, 9, 804 of whom were convicted and 12, 553 discharged. As in the olden days of slave hunts whereby maroon slaves were caught, shot or maimed, the police force organised vagrant hunts to scour several districts and to arrest every Indian caught at home or at work whose papers were not in order. Once the Indians were targeted as vagrants, they were packaged as illiterate, as savages, brutes, uncivilized, barbarous, as nomads and unclean people who had been the bearers of diseases and epidemics. Therefore, any force was justified against them. Following Notice:

"1st June 1869.
To Inspector in Country Districts.
There will be a general vagrant hunt on Saturday next, 5th instant, time of starting, distribution of men will be left to the discretion of the inspectors themselves.
(sd) J.A. Spencer
As. Superintendent."
(Royal Commission Report, 1875)

The purpose of the Labour Law was to force the Old Immigrants to re-indenture and to send them back to the sugar estates and deprive them of their liberties. It denied them the right of citizenship. It enabled the planters to bleed the labourers, to resort to fraudulent pay-books, withold from paying their monthly wages and illegally exacting extra work during the 364 days in a year. Later, Sir Celincourt Antelme, planter and member of the Council of Government, in his testimony to the Commission of Inquiry, admitted that, in his sugar estate at Stanley, he had gained 7509 days of work for which he had not paid a cent.

The Vagrancy Law was intended to restrict their freedom of movement and thereby condemn them to a state of poverty, social degradation and loss of liberties. It took away their basic human rights. It denied them the means to explain and speak up against the unjustified accusations and penalties levelled at them before the police or law court. 6,000 of the Old Immigrants had to abandon their property and re-indenture.

"*An Old Immigrant's life is rendered so miserable that the vast majority of them are driven in despair to re-engage on the master's own terms.*" (The petition)

The planters justified their tyranny and oppression under the pretext that the Indians were like children who were incapable of taking care of themselves and therefore they required a strong paternal government using arbitrary authority and exercising it benevolently in their interest. (Royal Commission, 1875).

The law allowed the Oligarchy to intimidate and terrorise the Indians into a state of servility for the exploitation of their labour. Assaults on those malnourished, underpaid, overworked and mal-treated labourers were a daily occurrence. They were segregated into their respective estate camps and villages and they could not cross the boundaries without carrying a pass on their persons. No Indian could carry any vegetable or milk to market, visit any relatives, attend any wedding or funeral unless he reported himself first to the terrifying police station.

Rounded up like cattle by government, the law courts, the police and the planters, the Indians went through a reign of terror which drove them crazy, marked by a steep rise in suicide deaths. They were immobilised into an oppressive inertia aggravated by malnutrition, disease, poverty, ill-treatment, overwork, harassment, insecurity and imprisonment, their women raped and sexually harassed and coerced by the overseers, estate managers, their religion and customs under attack by the evangelicals. No one was spared. They were so demoralised that many committed suicides. Nowhere was the labourer as dependent on the planters for his daily bread as in the Caribbean islands where he was kept in a state of perpetual terror, rebellion against which incurred arbitrary terms of imprisonment. Thus, in Demerara, Chief Justice Beaumont was haunted by the daily spectacle of the:

"Creatures so worn by illness and starvation as to appear at first sight actual skeletons, every bone visible, perfectly fleshless, their legs appearing like long stilts, their very buttocks almost entirely exposed and worn to the bone, and the faces showing the terrible appearance of a skeleton's head, only lighted up in their great hollow orbits by eyes that yet reflected a dull glimmer."

(Cited in Carter and Torabully's *Coolitude*.Anthem Press. London 2002)

The Chamber of Agriculture-which practically ruled the country-deprived labourers'children under 10 years of their right to play and to education and forced them into the cane fields, on the pretext that they had to contribute to agriculture. All these depressive conditions induced a spirit of inertia, resignation and defeatism. All the attention of the laboureres was on how to keep body and soul together and live for the next day. Having lost the material battle, they stuck emotionally together under the jahaji bhai brotherhood, and resisted with all the forces at their command and retired into the last spiritual bastion which only the soothing Ramayana *chowpai* could afford.

"Culture defined as an area to which Indians, after the trials of the work place, could retreat to heal and bind the wounds, before sallying forth again. If there was derison and degradation on the outside, the safety of the cultural boundaries did allow scope for refreshment and for the infusion of self-esteem."

(Kusha Haraksingh, University of West Indies, Trinidad, Conference on Indian Immigration. MGI. Oct. 1984)

Then Came de Plevitz

At that time, not having produced any capable leaders of their own, Indians needed an outsider. A European soldier, Adolphe de Plevitz who understood the mechanism of economic exploitation and politics stood up for them. The German de Plevitz pleaded that children should be educated to get the benefits of western education and to improve themselves. No Indian girl attended school. Without freedom of movement, they lost their bargaining power and they could not know what wages and conditions were offered in other plantations.

Nor could the Indians complain to the police stations or the Protector of Immigrants who were *on terms of intimacy* with the planters. They mistrusted the police who exacted a percentage from the fines. The planters could take the labourers to court, get them fined and imprisoned for absenteeism, for not working, absence without leave, not finishing allotted work, malingering. Corruption ran through the judicial system when the magistrates were the agents of the planters. The Stipendiary magistrates themselves called for more stringent legislation on the labourers.

"*Indians attempting to seek justice in the district courts, staffed, as in this case, by men related to estate owners, or with a direct interest in plantations, were met with perjury, falsification, hasty judgments and clearly unequal treatment of witnesses, with evidence of white colonists almost always given greater credence than the testimonies of Indian witnesses.*"

(Mariner Carter. *Lakshmi's Legacy*. E.O.I. 1994)

In three years, the magistrates sentenced 63,000 Immigrants to goal for vagrancy. The only person in the Council of Government who dared to oppose the law was Kerr on the ground that the Indians were already being treated with hostility and being robbed by all including police officers and public servants. In vain did he appeal to the legislators, packed by planters/politicians, starting with the governor, to *calmly place ourselves in the position of the poor and humble against whom we legislate.* For his pain, Kerr was vilified.

(Loretta de Plevitz, *Restless Energy. Adolphe de Plevitz*, MGI, 1987)

In brief, the Vagrancy Law smacked of the White favourite sport of slave hunting. Indians were everywhere raided by the police and jailed into Vagrant depots, a ruined monument still stands at Grand River North West, in Port Louis. According to the Double Cut system, two days' wages were cut for each single day of absence, whatever the cause might be. This system lent itself to many abuses and the labourers were cheated of their wages and were subjected to arbitrary cuts by the robber barons. The double cut was stringently applied in Mauritius and the Carribean colonies.

"Dwellings of Indians were entered by the police, without warrant on the pretext of checking the passes, sometimes at dead of night and the Indians taken to the police station. It was impossible for Indian traders or hawkers to carry their business, gatemen at the railway station, an Indian servant to venture on the road on an errand, little children carrying their fathers' dinners to them at their work, without running the risk of being apprehended by the police and charged with vagrancy. The police raids were reminiscent of maroon hunts."

(Report of the Royal Commission of Inquiry, Williamson and Frere, 1875)

At last, in 1872, the Indians found a saviour in the person of a German-born planter of Nouvelle Decouverte, named **Adolphe de Plevitz**, a former soldier in the Prussian army, who, exacerbated by those inhuman abuses, drew up a petition listing the grievances signed by thousands of the Indian petitioners. Possessing the opportune qualities of *humanity, energy, impatience and defiance of authority, Plevitz wrote that the Indian was tracked and harassed by the police, all with the view of forcing him to re-engage*

Governor Sir **Arthur Hamilton Gordon**, son of a Prime Minister, former governor in Trinidad where he had helped the Indians, gave

Plevitz a helping hand and recommended it to the queen who despatched a Commission of Inquiry chaired by Williamson and Frere. **The Report of the Commissioners**, published in 1875, covering 37 chapters spanning across every aspect of the immigrant's life, is the most detailed and important document in the history of Indians in Mauritius and in the sugar colonies. It is highly revealing. It proved how right De Plevitz and the Indians had been and it elaborated on the injustices they suffered. Earl Carnavon, the Secretary of State, admitted that the *"system put such facilities for oppression and extortion in the hands of any police officer."*

It found the housing *"unfit for human habitation"*, the working conditions exploitative, the magistrates too eager to *satisfy the planters*, the Immigration Office *ill-treated and abused the Indians*, assaults upon Indians a daily occurrence, the hospital conditions in the sugar estates *"disgraceful"*, rum consumption on the estates *"excessive"*. Indians were being over-taxed at **12%**. It made 27 recommendations. And declared the oppressive legislation, *"illegal"*. By *1878*, the Labour Law was repealed and replaced by a *New Labour Law* which led to better industrial relations until 1922.

"It required a great deal of courage, I will say, a great deal of self-reliance, to stand up against the planters."

(Governor A. Hamilton Gordon, *Mauritius. Records of Private and Public Life*. Edinburgh. R.Clark, 1894.

A Wounded Civilization

During this Day of Remembrance on 9th January, on the occasion of Pravasi Bharatiya Divas, when we look back at this dark period of our history, we are haunted by the woes, wailing, agony, suicides, sufferings, sacrifices and humiliation of our Immigrant forefathers.

"Indians in Mauritius do not care about their public rights and privileges, which as citizens they can enjoy under the British government. They have lost all the noble qualities, such as bravery, patriotism, love of liberty, true ambition and self-respect. Their chief aim is to make money." (Nicholas Pike, 1873)

We cannot but wonder that- despite its great Vedic culture and civilization and its past glory- how India could have fallen so low and subjected itself to over 800 years of slavery under Moghul and British imperialism. What had happened to India? Had it lost its soul and its historical memory? Why had India inflicted so many wounds upon itself that it bled itself and its children to death under the weight of a feudal, crumbling system of castes, superstitions, political blindness, total absence of patriotism and isolation from world intellectual, cultural and historical movements, including:-the Renaissance, reformation, the age of exploration and colonialism, scientific and technological advances, agricultural and industrial revolutions, the age of Enlightenment, the growth of capitalism, entrepreneurship and modern management, the evolution of democracy, parliamentary government, among so many others. Had not the Indians learnt anything worthwhile from the lessons of history that they allowed their sons and daughters to roam over the seven seas and submit themselves to such unbelievable ill-treatment at the hands of those racist and rapacious Whites who robbed, looted, humiliated them with impunity? How long could Bharat go on sleeping?

South Africa

THE COLONY of Natal copied the Mauritian experience of utilising Indentured Indians in the cane fields when it imported a first batch of 310 Indians on board the Belvedere on 12 October 1860. More were to follow until 1866. They were followed by a batch of Indian traders hailing from Gujarat, including Muslims and Hindus from Surat, Kathiawar, the Kokanis and Khojas from Bombay. As in Mauritius and in the Caribbeans, the labourers were faced with a new system of slavery and racism. The Coolies were severely hit by a spate of anti-Indian legislation. In 1895, a poll tax of 3 pounds was imposed on the Indians and there started the political resistance under a young Indian lawyer, **Mohandas Karamchand Gandhi** who founded the Natal Indian Congress- the forerunner of the African National Congress. The *Coolies, Arabs and other Asiatic Act of 1885* confined the Indians to segregated areas. They were denied civil and political rights and the right to buy property.

The *Immigration Restriction Act of 1905* smacked of the earlier Pass Laws in Mauritius as it restricted the movement of Indians in South Africa within the Transvaal and Natal colonies against a fine of 3 pounds or 3 months imprisonment. The *Immigration Regulations Act of 1913* put a brake on immigration by Indians. In *1943*, the *Pegging Act* was passed to peg the penetration of Indians. Fearing the ability of Indians to work hard, save and purchase property, the Pegging Act was replaced by the more stringent *Asiatic Land Tenure and Indian Representation Act, 1946*, which severely applied a brake on their acquisition of fixed property. However, in *1950*, the notorious *Group Areas Act* enforced Apartheid or separate development. It severely restricted the commercial activities of the Indian community and it put their security into jeopardy. Both Indians and Black Africans joined their political forces together to oppose the Groups Areas Act.

The Seeds of Racism

AN AWARENESS of racism, its cause, symptoms and implications may throw some light on the complex web of factors which sustains the myth of whiteness. Racism goes deep into colonial, euro-centric history, built on slavery, indenture, savage capitalism, exploitation and human rights abuses. Like the banyan tree, it has anchored its roots into the unconscious so that it makes race relations such an explosive issue in our modern multi-cultural society, either situated in the industrial west, in the Gulf countries or in the former colonies. To Malcolm de Chazal, *Le pays cultive la canne à sucre et les préjugés* and to J. C. de l'Estrac: "*Le fondement de la colonisation en Ile de France est d'inspiation raciste." (Mauriciens Enfants de Mille Races,* 2004)

It is hoped that this debate may lift the lid of misunderstanding off this topic.

"The racial issue has to be apprehended not so much in terms of the epidermal colour as that of the preservation, purity and superiority of the French stock mainly."

(Dr Musleem Jumeer, Conference on Slavery. M.G.I. Feb. 1985)

Despite the reconciliation, the hand of friendship tended to the white in 1970, by Ramgoolam, after independence in March 1968, the Oligarchy, until today, do not seem to have given up on their residual racist, slave-owning and segregationist mentality. On the contrary, they have perpetuated themselves in power positions. They have only reproduced the dominant culture through their close association with the Catholic Church, their economic stranglehold and their cultural power and prestige. This is understandable.

Racism, somehow like the caste system, is *a mental conditioning,* it cannot be banned, nor outlawed. It's a mental factor, a chronic psychic problem, rooted in history and human memory. It has always been there and it's likely to be still there for ages to come. It has penetrated into the genetic make-up of the white. It is physical, it's the body, the skin colour, the texture of the hair that distinguish the white from the other non-white person. Racism runs skin deep. It's an ugly scar on Mauritian history.

"Il a marqué de façon inéffaçable les relations reciproques de la race noire vis-à-vis de la race blanche. De même, le prejugé de couleur, sous -produit de l'esclavage n'en subsiste pas moins à l'île maurice et empoisonne toutefois la vie sociale de ce pays."

(Karl Noel. *L'Esclavage à l'Isle de France.* Editions Two Cities. Paris. 1891, reviewed in L'express 6 Aug. 1991)

It's the shadow behind the substance, a ghost stalking our lives across the pages of the history of colonialism, of slavery, indenture and all the segregationist, racialist structures and institutions set up with the conspiracy of State racism and of a compliant Catholic Church. The Church has simply legitimised and perpetuated the power structure of the oligarchy, somehow representing as the elite caste and class- the Brahmin-Ksatriyas- and- Vaishyas castes bundled in one.

"Le clergé, sans exception, sera tenu de reconnaitre et de soutenir par le concours du pouvoir écclesiastique, l'autorité du Conseil Supérieur en tout ce qui touche l'ordre public et la police.

(Cited by Amedée Nagapen in Conference on Slavery MGI. 1985).

The racist white tend to think that *"the other"*, the non-white, is inferior and therefore subordinate to them. That's the rub! They see people always in strong black-and-white colours. In this game of power relationships, they feel they are the European elite. Just as the white in apartheid South Africa used to believe in the Calvinist doctrine of predestination, in the myth of their being the few chosen by God to rule over the non-white, so do the white carry the complex of superiority everywhere they go. They hide under their hard carapaces like tortoises. Every time they meet a non-white *the otherness* is constructed within a complex matrix of interconnected physical traits, culture, language, religion, traditions, inferior genes and social status. They read the other as belonging to the non-white ethnic group, the *them* as separate from the *us*. They rarely see the collective *We*. After all, racism is the product of history, the past legacy of colonialism, capitalism, slavery, indenture, class and cultural domination all wrapped together. Rarely is the non-white person seen objectively as standing on his own merits and ability. Though governments and laws might have changed, the colonial and racist structures of land ownership, sugar plantations and milling, economic inequalities, concentration of capital in the hands of a few families have remained unchanged. The gap between the white and non-white is almost unbridgeable.

(Avtar Brah. *Cartographies of Diaspora*. Routeledge. London. 1996)

The white still continue to live as a separate, apartheid race in distinct geographical boundaries, socially cut off from the 70% PIOs. Their children go to separate confessional or grammar schools, Ecole du Centre, Ecole du Nord, Lycee Labourdonnais, the Loretto Convents and practically none of the white would be seen as a workmate in any public office or travelling by public transport. Racial segregation goes back to white settlement in Ile de France, when the law, as under Apartheid South Africa, prohibited the white from marrying a Coloured woman and the child was not recognized by law and consequently he could not inherit the property of his father. As for the British, wherever they went, they lived apart from the natives and the greatest slap into their face has been the mass immigration of brown Asians into Britain.

In 18th century Ile de France, the white generally led an immoral life. The *Petits Blancs* had free unions and sex with the Black and Indian women whom they sexually abused as they wished and the aftermath was the birth to the Coloured population, "*enfants de mille races*" (Edouard Maunick). They carried the sexual exploitation into the plantations and harassed any women whom they envied. In certain villages of Mauritius, some children of labourers have blue eyes, fair complexion and blonde hair while some of the women are wine addicts- itself a comment on the sexual exploitation of the past. Ile de France was the site for the official propagation of westernisation, racial segregation and proselytisation of the non-white led by the

Congregation de St. Lazarre which was bent on turning this island into a Catholic sancturary. Side by side, the inter-racial marriages explained how the Blacks went through: *"a process of disafricanisation whereby the African blood was altered to a large extent by its Indian, Melanesian and European counterparts."*

(Musleem Jumeer, 1985)

"La ville était l'appanage des privilegiés; le cimetière était séparé en deux parties, l'une pour les morts de la population privilegiée, l'autre pour les morts de la population de couleur."

(E. Vanmeerbeck. Jean Lebrun, La Sentinelle, 1865).

Spatial Segregation

Accordingly, the centre of Port Louis, La Ville Blanche, was reserved as residential areas and business district for the whites The Indians lived in the Eastern suburb, known as *Camp des Lascards, Camp des Malbards*. The Western suburb was allocated to the *Camp des Noirs, Camp Yoloff* and the freed slaves, *Camp des Noirs Libres*. Mahebourg had its *La Ville Blanche*, *La Ville Noire*. The plantation colony was littered with its slave camps, sugar estate camps for the indentured labourers until the labourers liberated themselves to found their own specific little Indian-type villages, including their Camp Samy, Camp Bombaye. In other words, the segregation created a system of socio-spatial exclusion, dividing the people into clans and tribes. The subservient class was kept away at arms' length where they could not be a threat. They were well quartered within reasonable distance so that they could be available for menial jobs, including the villages, a source of labour supply, located fairly close to the sugar estates. It bore close resemblance with the caste system.

The ethnic and class segregation pattern reproduced itself in the slave camps which made way for the labourers' estate camps. It clearly defined the geographical space within which separate ethnic groups would cluster in villages as the Creoles separately from the Indians in the coastal villages of La Gaulette, Black River, Tranquebar, Roche Bois, Ste Croix, Cite Vallejee and other cites. Similarly, the Moslems have been clustering at Vallée Pitot and Plaine Verte. In a bid to escape the invasion of the non-white, the White who used to cluster in Curepipe have migrated to Tamarin where they are alluring the white settlers from South Africa and Zimbabwe to reproduce a new system of apartheid. Consequently, the pattern of such geographical disparities and stratification system has reproduced itself within our multi-ethnic society, creating artificial disparities and further reinforcing the ethnic and class stratification. It has hampered the constructive forces of national integration to take place. (N.Raya, 2004)

"We cannot encourage sugar estates or help them by subsidies or loans to build slave camps which they alone control."
(Dr S.Ramgoolam, Leg. Council. 20th Sept. 1955).

Colonialism, Racialism and Domination

The segregationist past is still with us. It is as alive today as it was in the eighteenth century. The white cling to the values of a bygone pre-French Revolutionary aristocracy which still hangs around their necks like a *dead albatross*. Racism is a psychic problem. It perpetuates itself from generation to generation almost unchanged. Over the decades, the victims of racism go on being excluded, exploited and humiliated. Growing up in a racial cocoon, they believe that they alone are the depositories of French or British culture and civilization cascading across ages, sourcing from the old, continuous aristocracy, grounded in the core of their personality. What they seem to forget was that India was far ahead of Europe in the sixteenth century. It could boast of a great civilization, a vast Moghul Empire, a flourishing textile industry except that it remained splendidly isolated from the mainstream of intellectual and maritime expansion which had given Europe the competitive edge.

We refuse to be a tool of colonialism and apartheid, stormed Prime

Minister, Sir Seewoosagur Ramgoolam, in his Independence speech on 12th March 1975, a point which he stressed again on 12th March 1977: *"There cannot be any compromise on the issues of colonialism, of racialism and of domination....People quickly discovered that the real issue was not race, religion or colour but freedom, opportunity for the common man and social justice."*

Nurtured since early childhood on a diet of racism, they look at the surrounding multi-cultural society from racist blinkers- never or rarely from a clear unbiased, objective perspective. The result is that they tend to see the non-white within the *grids of negativity*, exclusion, suppression, oppression, exploitation, subordination and inferiorisation. The Blacks are perceived as inferior stereotyped beings, a dominated, domesticated and subordinated race to be used, exploited and sucked dry and then thrown away, like sucked oranges. Despite their different political discourses, the white have placed the Blacks at the lowest scale of the social ladder, as their permanent subalterns. They look at the Indians subjectively as an inferior breed of humanity, superstitious, heathenish, barbarous, uncivilized while they see the Black Creoles in terms of domination-subordination-relationships, as the descendants of slaves, as genetically inferior, lazy, dishonest, smelly, subaltern and ugly beings. Both the Asians and the Blacks, whether here, in Britain, Europe, in the US, are stigmatised, inferiorised, discriminated against and excluded from the good things of life. They are kept well outside the white boundary- in jobs, in housing, the media, training, health services, as well as in their status, honour, dignity and upward mobility.

Historically, they have been conditioned to judge other people externally by their physical *looks*, the texture of the hair, the colour of their skin as well as by other social and ethnic signifiers like their class, race, ethnic, religious, cultural identities. Consequently, in their daily social relations with the non-white, they adopt a derogatory, patronizing posture. They are naturally pompous, arrogant persons, keeping the surrounding black and brown races at arm's length. By imposing an unofficial system of apartheid, set within prescribed boundaries, they feel compelled to adhere strictly to the norms and values of racism, colour consciousness and class superiority, inherited from the past and, as such, they nurture hostility to the Indians who had finally dislodged them from political power. In contrast to the PIOs who keep open house, inviting their neighbours or acquaintances home for a cup of tea, for a wedding or festival, the White does not entertain any social relations with the non-whites.

In practice, this racial segregation is expressed in three distinct ways. Firstly, they will never mix up socially with any member of the Asian or black population. To protect themselves from rubbing shoulders with the masses, the first two rows in the church are reserved exclusively for the White. Secondly, they will never invite any non-white home for a social cup of coffee, or to any family gathering as a birthday, a wedding. Thirdly, they are so invisible, secretive and exclusive that nobody knows anything about a birth, a wedding or a death among the white. The White children frequent exclusive schools like Ecole du Nord, Ecole du Centre, Lycée Labourdonnais where there is little mixing with non-white children. Though they are Mauritians like the rest of the population, their health expenses are exclusively subsidised by France at the Clinique Darnais. But the real Franco-Mauritians happen to be those non-white Mauritians inter-married to French and who hold French nationality.

(Interview of Tsang Mang Kin, August 2004)

According to prof. Mbulelo Mzamane, South Africa, under an apartheid system, no cross-fertilisation takes place, leading to an inclusive, degenerating society on its way to disappearance.

(3rd International Writers' Conference. P.Louis. 23-27 August. 2004)

Just as the British colonialist remained arrogant and aloof in India, as vividly depicted in Orwell's *A Passage to India*, so, even today, wherever the Oligarchy moves, he would wear two faces. First, as the employer who is seen in distant relations, impervious to the people while in private, his family life takes place in an ivory tower. In return, he has imposed a strict regime of sanctions and embargoes on Asian people, cutting off the economic grass from under their feet. From a recent survey revealed by *The Guardian*, 9 out of 10 White Britons entertain no friends among the Blacks, the Asians or Moslems. 94% of the native Britons interviewed by the Commission for racial equality state they relate only with people belonging only to the white race. On the other hand, 47% of the non-white claim to have friends among the white Britons. Trevor Phillips, president of the Commission, said that he was stunned at the extent to which the Britons ignore the minorities, a fact which fuels further racial discrimination and racial propaganda.

(*The Guardian,* cited in *Le Mauricien*, 19 July, 2004).

In many situations- even today- where PIOs have had to work under racist white or coloured management, they have been suppressed, discriminated against, persecuted just to make room for one of their own kith and kin at the top of the hierarchy, regardless of justice or meritocracy. Despite entry into the age of independence, human rights and Rule of Law, many Indian cadres have been cruelly dumped and have ended up, broken-hearted-in a sovereign democratic country where they are the majority.

There is no meeting and *no dialogue of cultures or civilizations*. Old habits die hard. It's all a matter of master-slave relationship. The minority White still dictates the social terms. They still control the superstructure of power, the Church, the economy, the power of language and the culture- that is, *their* culture. Europe lies at the centre of this euro-centric constellation keeping the periphery non-white circulating within its orbit. We are back at the old familiar domination-subordination-relationship. How can there be room for dialogue among unequals? How can we construct a positive inter-cultural communication, based on an understanding of the values of the majority? The door is kept hermetically sealed on a closed society. They send out an army of priests and their agents to assimilate the Asians into their religious values while they make no attempt to hold in respect the values of others. Theirs is a one-way-traffic hurtling through the barbed wires that spark the clash of civilisations blasting in the fires of the 11th September terrorist attack, in Middle East and in the Gulf countries. And they want you to bend your knees before their insolent might and to give up your religion, your culture, your ethnic identity and to embrace Christianity and euro-centricism- lock, stock and barrel.

Holding on to one's Asian values represented an affront to the white man. To him, nothing else mattered except the supremacy of his economic interest and his religion, his language, his laws and his authority. To counter this domination, the Indian felt driven to struggle hard to propagate and reproduce his values which alone would account for his success and upward mobility. The policy of the Oligarchy had always been to segregate the Indians, in Mauritius, in South Africa and the Caribbeans into deprived areas, with limited resources where they would stagnate within a vicious circle of poverty. The Vagrancy Law in Mauritius and in the Carribeans, the Group Areas Act, 1950, in South Africa, had the same objective to restrict the mobility of the Indians.and the Blacks within fixed boundaries. The immigration laws to keep Australia and Canada white restricted the entry of Asians. But in so doing, these discriminatory laws had the opposite effect of welding the heterogenous Indians into a homogenous group, prompting their ethnic resistance and *an awareness of their commonalties* - their shared ancestry, shared history, shared economic, social and political struggles attached to a shared homeland. In the final analysis, the behaviour of a person is conditioned by his religious precepts. If he behaves arrogantly it's because he is brought up on false religious premises, far removed from the deep universal Vedic principles of human brotherhood, tolerance, moderation and loving kindness - the pre-conditions for democracy and liberalism.

Vasudhaiva Kutumbakam- the whole world is one family

In an age of globalisation, our multi-racial society needs to function in a healthy spirit of give-and-take, mutual understanding and tolerance- according to the global Vedic principle and the democratic principles enshrined in our constitution. We cannot carry on and pass over to successive generations the burden of past prejudices and racial discrimination. At the same time, the upper and middle class, western-educated PIOs, wherever they may be, should not retaliate by turning a blind eye to their less fortunate working class brothers and sisters-who are deeply attached to their ancestral values. Having said this, it must be acknowledged that all over the world millions of white have liberated themselves from racialism and who are perfectly normal, sociable and wonderful human beings.

Economic Inequality Enforced by Law

Inequality of opportunity stems from the fact that the Compagnie des Indes had once granted the landed property of this country into the hands of the white minority by virtue of **permanent concessions** of 158 1/4 arpents, 312 1/2 for a double or 625 arpents for a quadruple concession. The same appropriation of colonial land took place in South Africa, Rhodesia where the best arable land had been grabbed by the Apartheid whites. Economic inequality contradicts all the precepts of democracy and equality of opportunity. It perpetuates a vicious state of social and economic injustice which has marred colonial history. The same injustice applies in Fiji where Indians are barred from owning land. Therefore, the whole history of South Africa, Zimbabwe, Mauritius and of Fiji is founded on injustice, on inequality, on the colonial and racist precept of the superiority of the white race or of control by the ethnic Fijians over the Indians who have no right to land ownership. Everywhere, Indians had been deprived of socio-economic opportunities and hampered by limited access to resources. The powers of the Oligarchy were to remain unchalleged for over two centuries because they had designed a social stratification system which only *reproduced itself* from generation to generation and into which both the Indians and the Blacks had fallen as the *casualties*.

"The powers of Government practically rest with a small Oligarchy of planters, who have so managed matters that, bit by bit, the laws have been rehandled till the poorest classes pay about twelve per cent of their income in taxes; the middle or professional classes,

large shopkeepers, doctors, lawyers, about six per cent; and the planters themselves only one per cent."

(Sir Arthur Hamilton Gordon. *Mauritius: Records of Private and Public Life*, 1871-1874. Vol.1.P.144.)

Mahatma Gandhi sent **Manilal Doctor** to defend the Indians in law courts against the arbitrary judgments meted out to them on flimsy charges as revealed by *Le Radical* of 3rd June 1908:

(i-ii) The magistrate of Rivière du Rempart jailed an Indian to three months for having pilfered four kilogs of manioc at Roches Noires and 4 other labourers of St Antoine to three months each for pilfering 30 cane stalks from a sugar estate.

(iii) An Indian woman was given the same sentence by the Flacq magistrate for pilfering 9 pounds of manioc from the Grande Retraite property.

(iv-vi) The magistrate of Grand Port jailed three Indian labourers for 3 months each, the first one for pilfering 3 kgs of manioc from Union Vale property, the second one for pilfering 10 kgs of tubers and the third labourer for the theft of a piglet.

(vii)The magistrate of la Savanne jailed a labourer of Trianon for 3 months for pilfering 2 kgs of manioc from the Savanne property.

(viii)The magistrate le Miliere sent an Indian to 3 months' imprisonment for having stolen 30 kgs of potatoes from the Indian Abdool of Eau Coulée.

(Pahlad Ramsurrun. *Manilal Doctor. Historic Court Cases in Mauritius.* Sterling Publishers. N.D. 2004).

In Mauritius, the Asian or Creole child is born an underdog when land ownership has been historically monopolised by a small group, though some politicians have been vainly pressing for democratising the economy, land ownership and for equal opportunity. In order to ensure their economic security, the immigrants starved themselves to save cent by cent in order to buy a plot of land during the petit and grand morcellement though they knew that those marginal lands could yield little economic returns in terms of capital reproduction. Earlier, the eviction of Indians had happened in certain African states, in the wake of the policy of africanisation- with the result that, in 1972, Idi Ami was applauded when he evicted 75,000 entrepreneurial Ugandan Indians just as the white farmers have been dispossessed in Zimbabwe under Mugabe. Yet those hard-working, frugal Indians, topped by a handful of wealthy traders, had started as railway labourers and had built up their fortune from scratch at great personal risks as retailers in isolated localities, just as the Sino-Mauritians have done. In Kenya, too, under the pressure of africanisation, Kenyan Indians have been under tremendous pressure. In **Madagascar**, the 25, 000 Indians live under permanent threat of insecurity and have been the objects of racial violence and robbery. Discrimination had struck as lightning at the Indian traders in Myanmar, former Burma, where the Indians have been largely dispossessed under the nationalisation policy.

In **Malaysia**, under State racism, the *Bhumi putra,* the majority Malays, have benefited from a policy of positive discrimination. The victims are the 1.8 million Indians marginalised and confined to agricultural labour with little opportunities for education and advancement into professional ranks and excluded from entry into government jobs, reserved to the Bhumi putra. While the Chinese traders have got around the NEP through their business organisation and networking by which they accommodate some Malays, the few Indian companies, unsupported by the State, have been hard hit due to their narrow base, shortage of capital and know-how. This is where GOPIO can intervene by forging alliances, transfer of technology and skills with other Indian business companies on a global scale in keeping with its objective of *"networking opportunities for business, trade, investment, tourism and education"*.

Racism, Colonialism and Casteism

Racism, colonialism and casteism are all evil, unjust, inhuman.

They are psychic problems which have reached into the bottom of the human consciousness. While racism and colonialism have united the white race collectively against the non-white, casteism has done the opposite. It splits from the interior. The house is fractured from inside and a divided house falls by itself. It has been a self-defeating weapon which pierced right into the heart of society itself to cause self-inflicted wounds. It had splintered Hindu society into conflicting groups on the basis of superstitions and injustice. Once the Indian immigrants stepped into the vessels taking them across the *kalapani*, they had to cast overboard their sacred threads and all the relics of an irrelevant and fictitious Brahmanical past as they had to mix with *Jihaji bhais*, shipmates, drawn from other places and castes. Outside the boundaries of the feudal, stagnant, casteist villages, casteism had lost its relevance in the cosmopolitan cities in India and overseas.

Outside the stagnant, backward-looking villages, casteism is an ugly word. It has been a source of deep embarassment and ridicule to all PIOs, NRIs and ABCDs in the eyes of the western countries. It has acted as a brake on the progress and unity of the Indian diaspora. Nurtured by Brahmanical Hinduism, casteism had cast a slur on all Hindus and it had given Hinduism a bad name, making it appear archaic, grotesque, irrelevant and stagnant. It stood as a barrier against human progress and against all the norms of a civil, decent, dynamic, open- minded, rational-legal-scientific society. To protect its caste purity, it banned travels overseas, condemned PIO's as outcastes and isolated India from the mainstream of global commerce and intellectual effervescence. It has crashed against the fundamental principles of democracy, human rights and social equality. Though it still survives in the minds of casteist Indians, it has been deleted from history and outlawed by the Indian constitution.

In the past, casteism used to fuel divisions, antagonism, misunderstanding and it alienated people of the same religion, culture, and civilization from one another on irrational grounds. It was totally evil. It created schism. It spawned a history and psychology of fragmentation within the global Hindu family and which has splintered the Indians outside India and kept them out of power- even where they are in majority. It has ripped the Indian diaspora right through. It stood against all the norms of sound democratic commonsense, of good politics as it split the Hindu majority into warring minorities which played dangerously into the hands of the white or black racist minorities. It bred a sense of fatalism, defeatism and frustration among the victimised low caste people. It ascribed social prestige and political power relationship arbitrarily into the hands of the upper castes, the very people who had historically failed to stand up for the honour, pride and dignity of their Motherland against Moghul and European invaders. But all that was yesterday. And today, India has shaken itself free from its past shackles to poise as the giant of tomorrow.

"In this changing and fast-moving world, we cannot afford to remain shackled by history. Today, India stands at a unique point in her ascendant movement in history. We must not let cynicism or negativity, despondency or disunity clog our veins and weaken our muscles."

(Former Indian Prime Minister, Shri Vajpayee, India Today 29 March 2004)

The awareness struck the young NRI, **Gandhi**, like lightning when he was brutally thrown out of the train at Pietermaritsburg in South Africa. It was out of such a shocking experience that Gandhi came to realise the evil of white racism and colonialism. The confrontation with racism made him aware of the gross irrelevance of casteism. This racial expulsion had carved a Mahatma out of him and had dragged him into the South African political turmoil. That was the defining moment in modern history. At one go, the giant had awakened and had thrown away the shackles of the past. Casteism had lasted for too long in India and it was now to be buried under the ashes of history. Under the new republican constitution, it was to be banished for good as the once low caste people could stand shoulder to shoulder with other Indians and claim equal citizenship rights and privileges at all levels. Of course, pockets of resistance erupted from time to time in feudal, backward-looking regions of India, yet untouched by economic development. But the historically suppressed people can hope to emerge. Opportunities are everywhere opening up and they no longer have to rush into the arms of Christianity or Islam in search of dignity and status, as they once did. Mindsets have been fast changing. The long battle for Indian independence had encapsulated the gains of many revolutions- cultural, intellectual, political, social, scientific, technological so that it has expunged the casteist evil from human consciousness. It has mentally embraced the revolutions which have taken place earlier in Britain, in America, in France, in Russia, in China. Fortunately, Gandhi and the founding fathers of the Indian constitution have liberated India from the shackles of history once for all and have cleared the way for the awakening of the giant.

Culture as Domination

THERE IS nothing strange about the fact that the European colonialists had used their culture, including language and religion, to justify their territorial, military, economic and political domination of the colonies. As a matter of fact, the ruling class had always used culture as an instrument of political and social control over the conquered or colonized people whom they had reduced into a culture of subjugation, a *culture of silence*, or *manze cou rester*. It had happened in ancient and medieval India when, in their bid to stay as the clerical class, the Brahmanical caste monopolised Sanskritic Vedic knowledge and deliberately kept the lower castes into spiritual darkness with a *debilitating effect on Hindu society* made vulnerable to foreign domination and conversion. During the sixteenth century, in South America, the Spanish Conquistadors committed cultural genocide and wiped off the great Incas civilization in order to implant Catholicism and Spanish language, culture and civilization. So did the British and the French in the colonies when they treated the African slaves as sub-humans whom they sold as chattels on the slave market.

The Indentured labourers fared no better as they were labelled as barbarous, primitive, backward, superstitious, filthy Coolies. Their religion and customs were reviled as outlandish, enclosed, fixed, ritualistic, structured and caste-stratified. Once the slaves had lost their ancestral languages, traditions and their identities and had been given new names, new religion, they felt they were no longer themselves but other people's commodities. Caught up in the grips of a heartless slave-owning system, they were deeply shaken by this traumatic and brutal experience that deprived them of the God-given gift of speech. Now, they felt they had been both physically and mentally crippled and that their descent to hell had been complete.

Colonial strategy depicted cultural differences as marks of inferiority. To be accepted into their society, one had to embrace their cultural standards and their religion and disown one's own as inferior. They believed that only their culture, their history, their civilization mattered. Asian and African knowledge and wisdom were discarded as marginal. It was unacceptable for them to accept Sanskrit and Buddhist learning. All this formed part of a colonial package of ethnicism, communalism, racism and xenophobia designed to divide the colonials in order to assimilate them.

"Without significant exception the universalising discourses of modern Europe and the United States assume the silence, willing or otherwise, of the non-European world. There is incorporation, there is inclusion; there is direct rule, there is coercion. But there is only infrequently an acknowledgement that the colonised people should be heard from, their ideas known".

(Eward Said, cited in Dr J.Gundara's paper, MGI, 8 Dec. 1998)

The de-Africanisation and deculturisation process went hand in hand, backed by the Euro-centric domination of knowledge. It reached the point of total ridicule when, in the very midst of the central African jungle, the school child had to digest, among other historical lies - *Nos ancestres, les Gaulois*! Naturally enough, the Euro-American societies kept devaluing non-western cultures as primitive and subordinate and the Afro-Asian races as being genetically inferior. They spared no effort in projecting the merits of their languages, their culture and civilization as the top of the world, as evolving, dynamic, rationalist, open-minded and even threatening to engulf the whole world in a clash of civilizations, in confrontation with Islamic terrorists.

(Bharat Gupt, http//www.indiastar.com/Gupt l .html).

From the very start, they used their language, culture and Catholicism as markers and clear-cut boundaries within which to assimilate and dominate the slaves and their descendants, later, for obvious political reason, loosely categorized as the General Population. As a result of emulating European standards, the Creoles were always left stranded way behind as they could never successfully whiten themselves and catch up with the arrogant white and Coloured in a fiercely racialist society in which their social importance depended on the degree of their white complexion. It was an unequal competition in which the Blacks and the Coloured failed from start to finish.

All along, what the Blacks had failed to appreciate was that by meekly submitting to White superiority they were only playing on the white man's territory and were therefore engaged in a losing battle. It was only after realising this mistake and shifting their strategy into embracing their Black identity and Africanity and by staking a bid for Black Power politics that the Black Americans could succeed. But such a Black identity movement, a re-assertion of one's ancestral past, both African and Indian, has yet to take place among the Blacks in the Mascarene and Caribbean Islands, in the wake of **Walter Rodney's** strategy. The Caribbean historian and politician, Walter Rodney, suggests that the way forward is to forge a Black and Indian alliance to resist the White cultural and political onslaught. People ought to remember and examine the way the Oligarchy had manipulated economic and social relations, separating these two groups on residential and cultural lines in order to wield power over them.

(Prof. Edward Alpers. MGI. June 1999).

Unfortunately, both the Blacks and the Asians had been unable to see through the Oligarchy's political game according to which they exploited cultural differences to separate Creoles from Indians, both in Mauritius and in the Caribbean. Yet, as descendants of slaves and of Indentured labourers, these two struggling groups had shared a common history of colonial domination. The white employers had shamelessly exploited both working class groups. The white had dangled the carrot of French culture and Catholicism in order to entice the Blacks away from their natural allies, the Indians. It was left to political strategist, like Manilal Doctor who forged a Creole-Indian alliance with Edouard Laurent's Action Liberale to foil the Oligarchy. Later, the same Creole-Indian alliance was revived under Dr Maurice Curé, Rozemont and Ramgoolam which led to the overthrow of the white under the Labour Party.

Culture cannot be divorced from political control. Thus, by the year 2000, the Oligarchy bounced back to power by devious means under Berenger's own policy of *scientific communalism*, by which he manipulated the mathematics of ethnic segregation to suit his own political calculations. He had tried to fragment the majority Hindu community into conflicting minority sub-ethnies which he segregated by various means: through a policy of political nominations, the setting up of conflicting cultural centres for the profit of a handful of political agents according to the tried divide-and-rule policy, inspired by NMU. Instead of consolidating the existing democratically elected Hindu federations, he has undermined their position by adding further confusion and misunderstanding by funding those controversial cultural power blocs as political structures. In accordance with the colonial tradition of using cultural racism as an instrument for political organization and power hierarchies, historically the Oligarchy had occupied the top power structure, backed by a compliant Church and other cultural power structures.

Towards A New Indo-Centric Approach

The success of a propaganda rests largely in the repetition of a lie a hundred times especially if it emanates from above until it is uncritically accepted as true. This is how the slave masters had dominated the slaves and their descendants and had instilled all sorts of complexes and prejudices into their psyche and their DNA. Consequently, the descendants of slaves tend to internalise an inferiority complex vis-à-vis the descendants of slave owners. Similarly, Indians who still harbour the Coolie and the peasant mentality keep on belittling themselves in the eyes of others. Some of them give a hand to those who discredit India and Indians like themselves. These are people, particularly the youth, who have assimilated large doses of anti-Indianism from western sources. Then they tend to pass on such prejudices to others, to their children who in turn pass on such self-inflicted humiliation on to their children's children.

There are those who accept everything from the west, who look down upon their own customs, traditions, religions, language as inferior. They are unaware of the great world-wide Indian ethos, India's unique cultural and civilizational heritage, its achievements in science, knowledge, information and communications technology. They go on absorbing the poison of anti-Indian propaganda from newspapers owned by the anti-Indian lobby. They will incur enormous debts to ape the white, mortgage and borrow heavily in order to buy a BMW, send their children to study in Britain, live beyond their means and adopt expensive habits just to keep up with the Jones. In so doing, they stray away from the path of simple living and high thinking that underscored the sufferings, sacrifices, contributions and visions of their immigrant ancestors.

The result is that they go on throwing mud on themselves, their kith and kin by wearing the bad names and labels which the white had applied on them. They go on reproducing the same old pattern of anti-Indianism, the same old wine in new bottle, in their daily thinking and behaviour. Despite their immense majority, the PIOs divide themselves up into fragments and conflicting sub-ethnic groups and then ally piecemeal with their traditional enemy to whom they have handed over power on a platter. They have sold their social and political conscience away to their traditional enemies and have become the willing slaves and agents to *perpetuate their self-degradation*. They have ended up making fools of themselves by joining in the campaign of their historical detractors for their own self-destruction. This is what happens to people who yearn to go back to the days of Coolitude. How else could you explain that in a country where Indians form 68% majority, both political and economic power rest in the hands of a tiny minority?

It is time that overseas Indians woke up to stop playing second fiddle, to assert their honour, their dignity, their unity and realise their individual and collective worth as a reflection of the great cultural and civilizational heritage of India. Stop backing those who are only out to exploit and use you for their own interest. Know your individual and collective worth and stop bickering over small things and unite for a higher purpose so that you can call off the game of those who are out to divide you piecemeal in order to destroy you. Know yourself and *get connected with the powerful diaspora* where your true interests lie. Shun the company of your detractors. Be forward-looking and take pride in your identity. Be aware of the achievements and potentialities of the emerging New India. Don't let anybody take away your pride in your undying core values and the most precious thing about you- your eternal Indianness.

7

VOICES OUTSIDE THE WEST

THERE IS gross ignorance and imbalance between material and spiritual knowledge. People have the most fanciful ideas about Indian culture and Hinduism and it is the purpose of this chapter to clarify some misconceptions to foster a better understanding of some core Indian values. The central problem faced by overseas Indians has been how to make Hinduism credible in the eyes of westerners.

At the same time, we shall deal with some of the values of Eastern cultures, civilizations, religions and philosophies which are unheard of in the West and some of their great qualities which can save the world heading towards an inevitable clash of civilizations and terrorism, stemming from a lack of understanding.

WHEN DIFFERENT cultures and civilizations meet they enrich each other. In this inter-cultural dialogue, everyone is a winner, none is superior or inferior. It is wrong and dangerous for any self-righteous world power, on the threat of terrorism, to go out on pre-emptive war in order to impose its ideology on other cultures and civilizations which it does not understand and respect. The value of *multi-culturalism* comes precisely from the open dialogue of cultures and languages from which emerges this cultural creolisation, hybridity and syncretism. Multiculturalism is born from the contact and clash of colonials with the colonised world, countered later by the migration of slaves, indentured and other peoples who have brought their *"other"* languages, cultures and civilizations and their *"elsewhere"* into the former colonies and later into western countries. Thereby, they have created the mixed global space which enables individuals to understand and respect the *"other"*.

Despite the onslaught of other cultures, the colonised people have had to struggle hard to preserve their identity based on shared culture, civilization, religion, history, ancestry, motherland, customs and traditions. Looking back in nostalgia to the motherland, to reconstruct imaginary homelands, in towns and villages, in Little Indias or new China Towns becomes an urge, a habit and a compulsion, a *"homeward journey"*, with its imaginative geography and history, its politics, memory and desire.

The ancestral culture did not remain static. Through the colonial encounter, the Immigrants have gone out of their way to embrace Western civilization and thereby they got transmuted by this pluralistic experience into *becoming* and continue becoming- But the cultural give-and-take never took place. They found themselves being cold-shouldered by the West which, lost in its arrogance, self-importance and fearing for its hegemony, never reciprocated. It has remained a one-way traffic, buttressed by assimilation, proselytisation and the Melting Pot theory. But lying somewhere between those two cultures, the hybrid culture has given birth to a third space charged with *"other cultural meanings and identities, the contact zone of multicultural experience"*.

The NRIs from Asian cities are already familiar with the West and do not meet with the same cultural shock that once greeted their predecessors, the Indentured immigrants transported from feudal villages. However, they might still feel a certain nostalgia, *"disorientation, longing, romanticism, shock , revulsion and sadness"*. The new émigrés, torn between divided loyalties, are eager to adapt and settle down in the new society. Though still longing for the homeward journey, the few who dare return feel pulled back to the new adopted home closer to their children in the west. (B.Fraser, 2004)

In this age of globalisation, Western academics need to pull down their Euro-American blinkers and open up their perspective to survey the third reality of the non-Western world. For a while, the West will have to give up its colonial, neo-colonial, capitalistic unipolar domination over world economy, backed by the US media machine and military power.

"For God's sake, open the universe a little more! And look beyond the United States or Europe for something that can spice our palate, colour our dress, add new textures and patterns and bring new rhythms of bhangra, jazz, the blues, karioki, haiku, corroborrec, calypso, rap and raga, enriching life's pace and making it more exciting and invigorating."

(B.Fraser)

Euro-centric Blinkers

"Multiculturalism in Britain is a liberal notion which accepts or recognises the presence of "other", "exotic" cultures existing in spite of or within or alongside the mainstream dominant culture. It recognizes and acknowledges the cultural diversity with its range of separate and distinct systems of behaviour, attitudes and values."

(Dr Bashabi Fraser, 2004)

HISTORY REPEATS itself. It is the same old story. In the UK the British have held Indian civilisation as *what has once been* and its scientific achievements as anachronistic against western rationality and technology. Similarly, in Europe and in the colonies, western education was limited only to Euro-centric knowledge, shutting out the vast field of the history of civilizations, of Sanskrit, Chinese, Egyptian, Phoenician fields of learning. They had come to believe in their own discourses of the superiority of the western world. It was unacceptable for the culturally enclaved planters to accept the knowledge content in the Asian languages, culture and the glorious Indian civilization. Knowledge was never truly a search for the truth but a vehicle of western propaganda. The Apartheid white continued to live in a cultural ghetto, a dogmatic Calvinist world, a frog- in- the- well civilisation. The planters naively believed that the world began and ended in Europe, that Paris was the world cultural centre and that French was the most beautiful language on earth. Beyond that, nothing else mattered to them. In their ignorance, they believed that the rest of the world was mere barbarism, that Africa was the *Dark Continent*..In treating the Asians or Africans as savages, the Immigrant labourers as *Malbars Coolies*, what the racist Britons would call *Paki*, they did not differ much from how the ancient Hindus mistrusted all foreigners as *mlecchas* or primitives or the way the ancient Greeks treated them as *barbaroi*. Poised at the top of the social hierarchy, they have exerted an evil, narrow-minded hegemony, particularly on the Blacks, throughout colonial and post-colonial history. Having been nurtured on prejudices, they have splashed racism across society and the Blacks are helplessly tarred with colour prejudices.

In their naiveté, they believed that paradise was created only for their consumption and that the worshippers of many gods and goddesses would roast in hell. That's why the Church, as the political arm of the state, had been sent to scour from door to door to convert the pagans in order to admit them into the kingdom of heaven to which they alone held the key. Apart from Bible knowledge, their level of spirituality ran shallow because there never was anything as deep as Vedic, Upanishadic, Vedantic or Buddhist learning and spirituality to satisfy one's deep philosophical and spiritual yearning. This is where India and Hinduism lead the world. The concept of religious tolerance, of human brotherhood, the whole world as one family, and choosing one's own path to godhead, according to the principle of *many ways to God*, lay beyond their comprehension. What only mattered to them was their belief in the superiority of their Christian God. Steeped in ritualism and in spiritual ignorance, they could not envision the breadth and universalism of Indian culture based on:- the concept of tolerance and openness, inter-penetration of cultures and learning, the acceptance and respect of other faiths as mere pathways to the same God, called by different names and attributes.

Despite all the cruelties that our forefathers had gone through, the PIOs have remained tolerant and forgiving to the extent of accepting a descendant of a slave owning white as Prime Minister, in 2003, a new version of Adrien D'Epinay, the champion of the Oligarchy. The Hindus have a great soul and a large heart. The Labour Government under Sir Seewoosagur Ramgoolam had never dreamt of retaliation, of persecuting or hounding the White minority- despite their fears which despatched thousands of the Coloureds into emigration. In Guyana, not far from the United States, the despotic Burnham ripped apart the Indians from the Blacks and unleashed a reign of terror and horrendous Black racism which saw thousands of Indians looted, beaten, killed, their houses burnt, their women and daughters raped. All these occurred- despite the American concern for human rights and democracy, while Mother India had watched these events with folded arms

Luckily for them, towards the end of the century, in South Africa, President Nelson Mandela offered a hand of friendship and reconciliation to the former White persecutors. In Mauritius, while Ramgoolam pursued a policy of reconciliation, peace and social harmony for the purpose of nation building and in keeping with the highest principles of Indian culture, the Catholic Church has consistently undermined the Labour Party by whipping up ethnic Creole opposition to it. It's never easy to maintain peace and security in an explosive multi-racial society unless you have broad-minded, tolerant, forgiving and peace-loving PIOs in power.

Cultural Racism

Throughout this volume, we have demonstrated how culture, including language and religion, had been employed by a ruling class or colonial power as a strategy of class, political or territorial domination. It happened in ancient India when the upper Brahminical castes had devised the caste system as a handy instrument to subjugate and rule over the mass of the people. Similarly, the European colonialists imposed their political and economic domination through the supposed superiority of western culture. We have seen how the French exaggerated their own culture, civilization and language as the best in the world, Paris as the European capital. They treated the African slaves as sub-human and the Indian Coolies as primitive, barbarous, superstitious, filthy *ethnics*. They devalued Afro-Asian culture and suppressed their identities, their names and their outlandish religions. Accordingly, non-western cultures were projected as inward-looking, communalist, ethnic, tribalistic, traditional, static, backward, ritualistic and self-enclosed. Thus, they manipulated culture as a strategy to create power structures, in which political power and the ruling hierarchy were ascribed to European culture.

In implementing the divide and rule strategy and fomenting ethnic cultural divisions between the Blacks and the Asians, the planters were backed up by the powerful Catholic Church and the Lazarist missionaries. They have proved prof. Samuel Huntington's theory of the clash of civilizations and have accelerated the dangers of cultural conflicts, which, however, are now flairing up in the hands of Islamic terrorists. In the plantation colonies, the white had consistently held out a Euro-centric culture and western hegemony, projected as rationalist, legal, open-minded in order to fend off the imaginary threat of invading Indianisation. In every case, they stressed on the cultural differeces, even forging a cultural no-man's land, the hysterical *Malbar nou pas oulé* warcry, separating the Blacks and the Asians on the basis of cultural differences, a game which they had successfully played out in the Caribbean.

"My contention is that the case for the dominant role of racial division in the historical sphere has accepted without scrutiny the proposition that Indians and Africans existed in mutually exclusive cultural compartments.. This division was aggravated by the residential separation of the two main groups, the mutual unintelligibility of some aspects of the non-material culture, the slow

rate of diversification of the economy, and the conscious manipulation of the society by those who had state power".

(Walter Rodney, cited in Prof. Edward Alpers, MGI, June 23, 1999)

There was nothing strange about it as in ancient and medieval India, the native Indians treated all the invaders and foreigners as *mlecchas*, while the Greeks scorned foreigners as *barbaroi*. Even in the US, the Melting Pot policy has been devised as a clear strategy of assimmilating and brewing all other foreign cultures and languages into the huge Americanisation cauldron. The MMM adopted a strategy of nationalism as a cover to press everybody else under the Creolisation steamrollers. Concurrently, they tried to hack the Hindu majority into conflicting sub-ethnic fragments and cultural centres, on the basis of regional languages to fit their strategy of divide and rule, fuelled by a lot of confusion, misunderstanding, misconception and mischief. Elsewhere, these divisive strategies have borne serious political repercussions spawning ethnic claim of a separate homeland for the Sikhs or the Tamils in Sri Lanka, as a province of Tamil Nadu. All these are happening in the backdrop of a consolidated European Union of twenty five states.

What they Never Hear In the West

Steeped in their own arrogance and self-importance, their materialistic knowledge gathered and codified by scholars, the white could not grasp the idea that Indian culture is derived from:- man's highest thinking, flowing into the Vedas, mankind's most ancient book of divinely inspired knowledge, expanded and interpreted in the Upanishads and summarised in the Bhagavadgita, itself a part of the Mahabarata epic. This is quite apart from the other grand epic Ramayana and the teachings of Buddhism, Jainism, Islam distilled, discussed and continuously renewed by great saints, sages and scholars in different countries and throughout the ages. Among other books calling for academic studies are the works of Ibn Al Arabi, Al Ghazzali, the 13th century poet and mystic, Jalauddin Rumi. Briefly, the cultural voices from outside the Euro-American zone are not given a fair hearing. Humanity stands the poorer for limiting its intellectual horizons to the West. Yet Vedic knowledge, the fountain head of all knowledge, addressed to mankind, as adapted, expanded and re-interpreted from age to age is hardly known outside a small circle of scholars. The broad cultural divide encompassing Asia and the Middle East against Euro-Americanism fuels a modern day problemof clash of civilizations and anti-Americanism.

"But comparatively little is known about these cultures among Western universities. Courses of study make it a point to dismiss them as irrelevant and exclude them from their standard curricula. Thus, while students in the West are raised on Shakespeare, Corneille, Milton, Goethe, Molière, the classics and the modern authors, they are seldom exposed to the incomparable civilization of early Chinese dynasties or the glorious era of the Ramayana and the Mahabarata.

Had western leaders been introduced to the East through a selection of its vast literature and monumental philosophical debates, they would have learnt a great deal in:- education, science and etiquettes, social norms, honour, pride of birth, duties of royalty, leadership, state craft and many arts which were highly developed and taught in China, India and Japan to an elite that has little to learn from our world but a lot to impart to us."

(Mohamad Vayid, 2004)

While it is profoundly Vedic in its essence, the Sanatan Vedic dharma remains eternal. It has no beginning and no end. It is ever dynamic, evolving and open-minded. It is profound and that's why it needs gurus, spiritual masters to explain its tenets. Nor is it based on any fixed scripture or church or just one prophet. Being the mother of religions, it reveres all great prophets from all religions. Vivekananda says that Hindus not only tolerate but also accept other faiths. This is the secular concept of unity in diversity, inter-religious harmony, of many ways to God.

"There is in Hinduism room enough for Jesus, as there is for Mohammed, Zoroaster and Moses." (Mahatma Gandhi)

The Hindu dharma is not dogmatic. It does not preach extremism or any form of fundamentalism. It's not evangelistic. It's not domineering and stultifying. On the contrary, it's broad like the cosmos. It's ever open, eclectic, accepting the truth wherever it comes from, from any direction. It is just the stairway that leads the individual to God as it holds that each individual is but a Soul, a spark of the Supersoul. Even though you may be a busy NRI, settled in Europe, America, Canada, Australia and having little time to attend to the temple, you are still firmly embedded in Hinduism. You can just *lock in to Hinduism* by simply recalling one mantra or just invoke the name of God by any name, AUM, Krishna, Ram, Shiva or Ganessa, or just say Hari Aum! or hare Krishna, hare Rama!.

"By whatsoever way men worship Me, even so do I accept them; for in all ways, oh Arjuna, men walk in My path." (The Gita, IV.11)

Hinduism is erected on the pillar of tolerance. It opens itself to perpetual questioning, debates and scrutiny and the individual quest of the Soul to unite with the Supersoul. Throughout the ages, great saints, seers, scholars and philosophers belonging to different schools of thought have tested its broad principles. It re-invents itself and keeps on embracing new spiritual experience in a bid to stay young, energetic, humanistic and universalistic. The very depth and breadth of Indian culture, its flexibility and the plethora of cults, scriptures, divinities, saints, spiritual masters, philosophies and counter-philosophies, elaborate rites and rituals- all flow like diverse tributaries into the broad ocean of the dharma, marked by the concept of many ways to God:-

Ekam sad Viprah bahuda Vadanti- Truth is One, the wise call it by various names.

(This stresses the principles of tolerance and moderation).

But the ever expanding and evolving Hindu dharma whose spiritual depth is unmatched by any other religion baffles the individual. It leaves room for spiritual masters, gurus, learned pundits or missionaries to go about interpreting its tenets and to keep it as a living dynamic faith. But then, this often leads to further confusion as each master may go about selling only one particular brand, or sect. So to make sure that Gandhi's precept: of inter-religious harmony prevails- *Ishwar/Allah Tera Naam*, somewhere along the line, there is room for a global Hindu institution or federation at the top which has to take the bull by the horns. It has to streamline the disparate teachings and sects, focus on the essential Vedantic content under the Sanatan Vedic Dharma, in a bid to build India as the global spiritual fountainhead. At the same time, it has to re-invent the dharma on the Gandhian path of inter-religious harmony as a presentable package to future generations of Indians, NRIs and PIOs and the outside world.

That organization, call it by whatever name- the Vishwa Hindu Parishad or whatever- has to provide world spiritual leadership and see to it that the universal Vedantic teachings are shifted, distilled, safeguarded and handed over in a meaningful dynamic form to future generations and to the entire human family.

Krinvanto Vishwamaryam, Let us make the whole world righteous.

It has to foster inter-religious harmony while protecting Hindus from both the threats of Moslem funtamentalism and evangelisation.

But what applies to Hinduism also applies to Malay civilization which emerged from indigenous animism to civilization across thirteen hundred years of Hindu kingdoms and Hinduism, Buddhism, succeeded by Islam and overlaid by British colonialism and the current age of globalisation. Thus in 671 A.D when the Chinese pilgrim Yiping landed in Srivijaya he discovered a community of 1000 Buddhist monks in a thriving centre of learning. The different civilizational encounters were not without their tensions, their conflicts and their excitement. Nevertheless, it is the *dialectics that make a civilization vibrant and worth experiencing.*

The Clash of Civilizations

In contrast, the average Christian or Moslem or Jew holds on to only one prophet and one scripture, channelled under a centrally organised church in the hands of a Pope or intolerant clerics. Therefore, the three intolerant religions, born in Jerusalem, daily clash over the relative superiority of the Jewish God, the Christian God or the Moslem God. They are locked in a state of perpetual war, called by prof. Hutingdon as the **clash of civilizations**. This dangerouus theory can turn into a self-fulfilling prophecy unless the encounter of cultures and civilization is transformed into a dialogue of civilizations.

Despite the unity of the Christian Church and the Islamic World Council, their inherent intolerance breeds aggression, fundamentalism which erupt into terrorism and violence in a world rendered unsafe with access to Weapons of Mass Destruction. Western imperialism is still obsessed with its own superiority conveyed in the theory of the *'divine dispensation'*, and *the white man's burden,* the *mission civilisatrice*. The West should stop its aggression and learn to appreciate the merits of non-Western cultures Unfortunately, as part of their ideology of Euro-centric political domination, Christian missionaries are let loose around the world to proselytize the Coloured and destabilise society. Somewhere, in between, is the all encompassing, peace-loving, non-violent, universalistic principles of Indian culture- as represented by Mahatma Gandhi, the apostle of non-violence.

Throughout recorded history, with its focus on spirituality, Hinduism has never been aggressive or threatening to other faiths or nations. In its pure Vedantic form, universal Hinduism shows the road ahead to world peace and understanding.

On the negative side, the ordinary Hindu is baffled by a barrage of rituals, superstitions, taboos, legends and mythologies and incomprehensible Sanskrit prayers. Historically, the Brahmanic clerics had utilised their positions to impose rituals as a weapon to befuddle the simple folks with Sanskrit jargon which nobody understood. In the process, the universal, humanistic Vedic philosophy- which is clear, simple, logical, scientific and divine- has been submerged under a tidal wave of superstitions and ritualism.

The truth is that though the NRIs and their children, in the UK, in USA, Canada and Europe may have attained some professional, technocratic and economic levels on the acquisition of material knowledge, their spiritual knowledge has not evolved correspondingly. And this spiritual vacuum is getting worse day by day with the onslaught of western and American popular materialistic culture overpowering the younger generation. It's a matter of great concern for every Hindu family. There is the permanent need to get back to the spiritual spring of the Sanatan Vedic Dharma.and to find out why such a great Vedantic culture which has so much to offer to restore world peace and harmony is so little known and understood throughout the world. Somehow, we have to answer why we have failed historically and spiritually?

Imprisoned to geographical and cultural isolation by the Brahmanical ban on maritime travels, Indian scolarship missed the great historical movements of modern western classical learning during Renaissance, Reformation, Enlightenment and the age of Reason. What followed was a Dark Age in India until the advent of British colonial education.

Modern Knowledge

Nevertheless, the coming of the Europeans into Asia signalled the entry of new modes of thought and knowledge formation. The British brought in their trail a new pedagogy of learning and construction of reality based on investigation, research, enquiries, surveys, fact finding and recording on the ground by patient scholarships and their diffusion. The new methodology is based on investigation, verification and validation of knowledge, on statistical surveys, imperical evidence, criticism, academic scrutiny, debates which pour into books, publications, newspapers, journals, encyclopaedias, legislation and legitimised as knowledge and information, circulated in schools and colleges, and broadcast in a knowledge-society. This passion for the discovery of knowledge has sent thousands of scholars, explorers, scientists, researchers to collect and evaluate data, gather evidence, classify, categorise, map out the discovery into many branches of knowledge, history, the arts, the sciences, social sciences, botany, medicine, economics, sociology, political science, Management studies. It makes for an intensely creative and inventive society which keeps spawning new technology and changes. And there is no doubt that this is the direction into which our diaspora will have to move.

The business of information gathering, development and dissemination of education must bear the stamp of respectability and academic authority. Once published, discussed and disseminated in public debates and conferences, the new knowledge goes a long way towards questioning and amending old knowledge. It adds to the stock of new knowledge and finally it fuels new debates and pours into new development channels prompting new personal and social improvements in an unending spiral:- into the mass media and adopted as the new guidelines for personal improvements. Thus, every research-based society can adapt this methodology to frame its own particular field of knowledge, namely Mauritian studies, African studies, Chinese, Indian or Malay studies bearing their own specificities, based on scrupulous research on the ground. The adoption of this methodology can only thrive in a democratic, knowledge-based society in an atmosphere of experimentation, free-thinking, free press and Parliamentary democracy.

(Shamsul A.B & Supyan Hussin, Malaysia. 2004)

Stop the Aggression!

Historically, since 1721, under the Code Noir, the Catholic Church had believed in its *mission civilisatrice* and its right to convert the colonised pagans for their own good. This is precisely what they had tried to do in Pondicherry, in the Mascarenes, in the West Indies, in Guyana. Under the governorship of Mahé de Labourdonnais, they had assimilated and Creolised the Tamil craftsmen and artisans and absorbed them into the General Population. They thought that it would be only a matter of time before the successive waves of Indian Immigrants, emerging from an inferior culture and religion, fragmented into castes and language groups, would be christianised and creolised and brought under their control. In this calculation, they have been both right and wrong.

Elsewhere, in Reunion Island, in Guadeloupe, in Martinique and other French colonies, they had obliterated Indian culture, deprived the Indian of his name, his religion, his identity, his language, his pride and why couldn't they do the same in Mauritius, so they thought? Assimilation, conversions, ethnocide and cultural genocide have been a historic crime perpetrated against humanity- against which the PIO victims have asked no compensation. Perhaps it is time that PIOs addressed this issue.

The colonists pushed forward with their cultural aggression and put the immigrants under tremendous pressure of deculturisation as they had previously done with the slaves. Due to their Euro-centrism and anti-Indian prejudices, they used every means at their disposal, the colonial government, the Church, the schools, the police, the control of job opportunities to impose their rules and to proselytize and uproot the Indians. In Surinam and in French colonies, Indians had to bear European first names. At home, someone would be addressed as Dharam but outdoors as Daniel, the surname Gannesh becomes Gamess, preceded by Jean Pierre, Robert, Patrick or Marie, Suzanne,

Simone, Lucienne or whatever.

"L'Asiatique ne devrait pas figurer dans la police; pour cette raison que l'Asiatique est aussi facile à se laisser séduire. Nettoyons nous de l'Asiatique!"

(L'Eoville l'Homme, L'Express, 4 August 1896)

This proselytisation campaign has continued unabated throughout our history and it attacks us relentlessly from all sides. It's foreign-funded, and it descends upon us under different disguises and Christian sects, with the political objective of annihilating the Hindu community completely and installing the Oligarchy perpetually in power.

In reply to foreign religious aggression, Overseas Indian need to fight back, publish and distribute religious leaflets and booklets about the greatness of Hinduism from door to door.

On the other hand, Hinduism is broad, *comprehensive and universalistic*. It does not lay claim to holding any monopoly of wisdom. It does not denounce other religions as false or evil. It does not impose its concept of God on anybody. Hence it is *tolerant* and is all-inclusive. Unlike other religions, it abhors violent propaganda and forcible conversions. It *accepts all faiths* and all deities as *manifestations of the same* God called variously by different names.

(D.S.Sharma,. *A Primer of Hinduism* .1981)

The Wonder That Was India

The White colons, the erstwhile slave-owners were steeped in conservatism, crass ignorance and uncompromising racism. After all, colonialism went hand in glove with racism. Blinded by their arrogance and hegemony of power- economic, political, administrative, legislative, executive, judiciary- they had no idea that the oppressed labourers were the heirs to a glorious, ancient civilisation. Because of their ignorance of history, they little suspected that the Indian diaspora held tremendous potential and, given the opportunity, could well bounce back into world leaders, just as was the case in ancient India. But at the back of their mind, the South African Whites were scared stiff of the genius of the Indians as Smutts once confessed to Gandhi. They were afraid of the Indians who were hard-working, adaptable, persevering, tenacious and capable.

They had just a vague idea of the ancient Vedic civilization namely:

The great Vedic philosophy and learning which had preceeded Graeco-Roman civilization by millennia and which had subsequently come down to humanity through various religions. They did not know that mathematics, the decimal system, zero, algebra, trigonometry and calculus had been formulated by ancient Indians well before the Christian era. Nor had they heard about the development of science, surgery, Ayurvedic medicine, associated with the name of Sushruta, 2600 years ago.

After all, the mass of literature and information from the Mohenjodaro and Harrappa civilizations and the wealth of Sanskritic Hinduism and the glorious Buddhist heritage in thoughts, arts and civilization still lay buried in the East. These waited to be translated and disseminated through the globe and channelled through the process of education.

None of them had ever heard of Gautama Buddha, the Light of Asia, whose teachings had spread across the whole of Asia 500 years before Christ. They had not heard of Taxila, the Buddhist seat of learning and of Nalanda University, in Patna, Bihar- unfortunately razed to the ground by the Moghul vandals. Even in Mauritius, ignorant people commonly assume that Buddha was a Chinese God!

What did they know about the glory of the Upanishads, the Gita, the Mahabharrata and the Ramayana? They did not know that Sanskritic Hinduism had survived while the old civilizations- Babylonian, Syrian, Persian, Egyptian, Graeco-Roman, Aztec- had long vanished.

They did not realise that the great values of Indian culture and Buddhism had once spanned across the whole of Asia as testified by the Buddhist temples, shrines and monuments, in China, Hong Kong,

Japan, Afghanistan (recently destroyed at Khandahar by Al Kaida) and South East Asia. In this respect, GOPIO has a gigantic task of explaining to do on a global scale. (Dr Jagat Motwani, *America and India*, New York, jagatmotwani@yahoo.com, 2003)

Unity of Creation

Wherever the Indians went they have played a low profile. In contrast to the aggressive, intolerant and racist Whites, they have remained vegetarian, non-violent, moderate and tolerant. Their humility springs from their belief in the essential unity of mankind, that all life is sacred as it emanates from One Universal Source which permeates through everything. This profound idea of the unity of creation, the reverence for nature goes beyond the comprehension of the Church which described Hinduism as polytheistic. The Immigrants believed in the Vedantic principle that every man is an incarnation of God who resides in each one of us. Our soul carries the divine spark within us and binds us to our Maker. God lives and acts in us when we consciously live with the Eternal presence within us.

Mamaivamso jivaloke jivabhutah sanatanah
(Every individual soul is a part of the Supreme Brahman)
(The Gita).

Every part is thus endowed with the same divine qualities as the Whole. So, every individual, without exception, is a spark of the Divine. They also held that God is everywhere,eeencapsulated within his creation and He is within each one of us. Everything is God-pervaded and God-protected. Everything is sacred and therefore He does not reside in special pilgrimage places or only in churches or mosques or temples, in specific direction or somewhere up in the sky. While those great Vedantic ideas were embedded in the people's daily life practices they were not grasped and spelt out intellectually or sufficiently communicated to the rest of mankind as world cultural and spiritual heritage.

It is generally accepted that Vedic and Buddhist philosophy had reached very great spiritual heights, far above what could be conceived in Christianity and Islam. But in practice, very few of the Hindu priests are educated enough to explain the depth and significance of the Sanskrit mantras which they simply mumble during the performance of rites and rituals. They are far from being scholars in Indian philosophy, in the Gita, the Vedas and other scriptures as compared to the qualified and well-paid Catholic or Protestant priests. Can they explain what they repeat parrot-like:

Om Purnamada Purnamidam Purnaat
Purnamudashyate Poorashya
Poornamaadaaya Purtna Meva Vashiyate

(Om, That is Whole; this is whole; from the whole, the whole becomes manifest. From the whole when the whole is negated, what remains is again the whole.)

Or how about a single line from the Upanishad;
Asato Maa Sad Gamaya
(Lead me from untruth to Truth)

"The world has great respect for India and its spiritual vedantic vision, which has the potential to resurrect a world drowning in materialism."

(Fatima Meer, South African freedom fighter and whose family emigrated from Gujarat in 1890, *Times of India*, Pune, 8 Jan,2003)

Vedanta had reached the highest flights beyond human intellect. In contrast, certain religions or cultures are boiled down into just what their scriptures say and which the clerics, fanatics and fundamentalists learn by heart and believe in everything, without questioning, without contextualising, interpreting, re-interpreting and re-evaluating-what these sacred books once said. .

The Whites have also failed historically. They are steeped in ignorance of the wisdom and civilization of the East lying at their very doorsteps. They hardly knew anything or cared about Sanskrit, the mother of languages, and the depth and range of Sanskrit literature and Sanskritic Hinduism. They knew next to nothing about the great Indian arts, paintings, literature, philosophy, sciences, crafts, architecture and sculpture. In their naivete, they thought that only the West held the monopoly of knowledge. They thought that only the West had a history. It could be only appalling ignorance on their part to lump all the rest as Dark Continent. They knew not that the highest and deepest thoughts of men, divinely inspired, had poured into Sanskrit verses. How naïve and chauvinistic were they! In their ignorance, they just drew a curtain over all the learning and wisdom that rose like the morning sun from the East.

"The philosophy of the Vedas, their wide appeal, their high literary value, the message they contain for the whole world and not for a chosen people, the eternal truths they teach, their scientific outlook, their high ethical value, their importance for all ages - have earned for them the admiration of European scholars, scientists, metaphysicians and rationalists. Vedic culture has a great future. The Hindu religion is of all time".

(Prof. Basdeo Bissoondoyal. *Life in Greater India.* Bharatiya Vidya Bhavan. B.B,.1984)

How could they appreciate the wonder of the impregnable 300 Maratha forts strengthened under the Maratha Empire, perched on mountain tops along the Deccan and from where erupted the hardy Marathi-speaking Immigrants? They had never heard of the great empire of the Mauryas which once prevailed in North India from whence poured the majority of the Bhojpuri-speaking immigrants. They knew next to nothing about the vast and wealthy Vijaynagar kingdom and the Dravidian civilization from which poured the South Indian Immigrants. The Moghul Empire, under the great Akbar, remained a closed book to them. Retreating behind a wall of cultural ignorance erected by the Church, they revealed an attitude of deep-rooted distrust, dogmatic opposition to Oriental languages and civilization which they tried to stamp out in the West Indies, Guyana, Fiji, Mauritius, Canada, Australia but against which they have been powerless.

The conclusion is that, in this age of globalisation, if mankind is to avoid the impending clash of civilizations, it has to look beyond Euro-merican centricism. It needs to draw inspiration and wisdom from the broad, all-inclusive, global Vedic civilization which holds out the prospect of human brotherhood, the concept of the family of mankind and the philosophy of universal love, non-violence and tolerance.

In conclusion, the study of cultures and civilizations, of the East and of the West, teaches us one important lesson:- that of blending material knowledge gathered on the gound and codified by scholars and media people and spiritual knowledge pouring from the yearnings of the soul in its relation with the Supreme Soul.- gushing down to humanity in scriptures and philosophies and transmitted by spiritual masters and writers.

8

THE CLASH OF CIVILIZATIONS

THE CLASH of civilizations has long occurred with the meeting between Indian culture and civilization and western culture and civilization in the colonies, in Mauritius, South Africa, the Caribbeans, US, Canada and UK. It has produced a fine harmony of cultures which is taking place and some of its distinguishing features are here noted.

OUR IMMIGRANT forefathers were shocked by their daily experience in the plantations, the tortures, the heat, the hunger and the hourly struggle to keep body and soul together. They were so overawed by all the mysterious powers wielded over their heads, including the unjust laws, the spiteful faces of their employers controlling a biased, colonial government that they felt that they needed time to adapt themselves to the changes. Though they were the carriers of the core Indian values, the Immigrants themselves felt trapped in an alien system which would take them a considerable amount of time to grasp. Being simple village folks, totally unaware of the intricacies of politics, exclusively concerned with earning a living, they had yet to learn about the sophistication of politics, about the working of western economics, the value of western education and the inexorable march of technology.

The Two Civilizations

In 1882, in a despatch to governor, Pope Henessey, the Secretary of State, the Earl of Derby requested him to appoint one Indian representative *"whose presence in the Council would secure a full expression of the views of some considerable section of the people"*.

In reply, Pope Henessey stated that *" After much inquiry, I was compelled to give up the idea, as I could not discover that there was one Indian among the 250,000 in the colony who was qualified for a seat in the Council."*

(Papers respecting the Constitutional reform, 1884)

Indians were entirely strangers to the complexity of western politics and the capitalist economy which had been dominating their lives ever since the day they had stepped into the vessels to journey across the black waters. By the end of the nineteenth century, the immigrants were still grappling with the mystery of colonialism, racism, capitalism and western politics.

"The class of Indians who come to Mauritius have no political aspirations... They are foreign to our style of politics; they have certain customs and usages of their own, in some respects perhaps more rational than ours; but at all events, they are not in our political system."

(Governor **Sir John Pope Hennessey**. Council of Government. 5 June 1885).

The meeting of the Indian Immigrants with the British and French diasporas represented the clash of two civilizations, the East and the West, and it took some time before each could understand and appreciate the other. In a way it was a clash of cultures. But the West had won the historic race and it had sharpened its weapon through the fires of Renaissance, Reformation, navigation and geographical discoveries, scientific learning, the age of enlightenment, Agricultural and Industrial Revolutions, mercantilism, colonialism, capitalism and, most important of all, Parliamentary government. England and France had been free countries and colonial powers and had developed tremendous experience in all fields while India had been part of the British Empire and had been staggering under the weight of an ancient, feudal, crumbling civilization, marked by casteism, division and widespread poverty. India was far from being a match against the all-mighty British Empire or its immediate representatives, the Oligarchy.

There is no doubt that European civilization was solidly organised around its church, its colonial system, its code of legislation, its constitution, its army, its navy, its educational system and its social organisations. It has been a well-lubricated and powerful machine. The colonialists could resort to their rich heritage of culture, language, literature, arts, recorded history, wars of conquest, economic power and evolving technology. After the Renaissance and Reformation movements in Europe, the evolution of philosphical and political ideas, Europe was racing far ahead of decadent Asia. India, stagnating under an old crumbling civilization, was lagging way behind the dynamic and aggressive west. Exhausted by caste divisions, betrayed by pleasure-seeking and decadent Maharajahs, Nawabs and zamindars, steeped in medievalism, India had expelled its immigrant children who transported slices of decadent India wherever they landed.

The civilisational and technological advantages gave the planters a tremendous edge over the Immigrant labourers, hands and feet bound and delivered at the mercy of the White planters in the plantation colonies. Backed by their wealth and colonial privileges, enriched by contact with the British administrators, the planters could easily throw out an elite, educated in western universities and which justified and perpetuate their rule. The simple, ignorant, superstitious and dispossessed immigrants.were no match against the western-educated elite. They needed time and opportunity to produce their own elite who could outmatch and outperform the traditional elite.

In the meantime, the Oligarchy had already produced a succession of brilliant politicians, artists, writers, builders, businessmen, professionals and administrators who perpetuated the myth of white superiority. They took immense pride in the achievements of Mahe de Labourdonnais who had brought many of his compatriots from St Malo, in France, and who had built the city of Port Louis from scratch-of course with Indian technical assistance. His successor, Governor David, left behind the chateau du Reduit while Pierre Poivre developed the Pamplemousses garden. Robert Surcouf, the Corsair, is regarded as a hero for having harassed English shipping and maritime trade in the Indian Ocean. They could also cite the unique maritime conquest over the British at the Battle of Grand Port at Ile de la Passe. Therefore, the planters poised as the ruling class. They were the more aggressive, the more articulate as they controlled political power, the public and private sectors, the mass media, the church and public opinion. They enjoyed the prestige of forming a closed aristocracy of wealth and influence.

The Best Breed

In that confrontation, the Indian Immigrants had suffered many casualties and needed plenty of time to learn and to fight their masters with their own weapons and on their own linguistic and intellectual grounds. Being the heirs to a great culture and civilization, they had the potential and the resources to outperform the white on a level playing field. Instinctively, when they looked back at ancient Sanskritic Hinduism, the revelations in the Vedas, the Gita, Ramayana and so on, they knew that somehow they belonged to the best breed of mankind. But they sorely needed time and resources to muster their strength before grappling with their opponents. Somehow, they knew that once they had ignited their rich culture and civilization with a spark of western education and professionalism, they could turn the table on their oppressors.

Had not a simple, half-naked fakir, named Mohandas Karanchand Gandhi- without any hard physical resources, any army or navy- toppled the mighty British empire from its lofty heights by the mere use of soft spiritual power? Does this not prove that Indians, as the *holders of soft power, were made of a stronger metal*? Now take a look into history and think of figures like the ancient vedic sages and philosophers, Buddha, Ashoka, and their global vision and influence across Asia at a time when India was the unrivalled superpower proud of the unbeatable power of its culture, Sanskrit language, civilization, religion and philosophy. Where were Europe and the rest of the world then? In darkness.

Eighteenth century India had its Shivajee, followed two centuries later by Swami Vivekanand and the list goes on, endlessly. You can see what children of immigrants, the PIO's and NRI's are doing in UK, USA, Canada, Australia and why not, in little Mauritius. It all shows that the Indians, heirs to a great civilization, have all the potential to awaken the giant in them. What they need is awareness of their own strength and to rise up to the challenge of being a great people, a superpower in the making. While surveying the progress made by NRI's in USA and the fast economic development of India, during the Pravasi Bharatiya Divas, January 2003, Management guru, C.K.Prahalad, urged that Indians are the *best breed of men.*

Anyway, during the nineteenth century, the combined English and French alliance on the Mauritian soil was to produce a vigorous brand of western civilization marked by French culture and language, topped by British administration, justice, business, trade, communication, health, education and political systems. These marked the core values of western civilization and modern technology to which the Indian Immigrants were complete foreigners and they obviously were taking some *time to complete their learning curve.* Under Mahe de Labourdonnais, the French could boast that they had laid down the beginning of colonial development by founding the city of Port Louis. The subsequent British colonial administration gave the country all the infrastructure of development, the schools, roads, public buildings, law courts, hospitals, trading houses, a boost to the sugar industry, and above all, the English language.

But the Oligarchy had never been concerned about the welfare of the underdogs. The good thing about the British is that it had made outstanding contributions to the civilizational heritage of the former colonies, of which the PIOs have been equal inheritors. They have established the essentials of good government, law and order, public administration, the education and health systems and, above all, the priceless gift of the Englsh language, English culture and a sense of fair play.

Indian Culture is One and Indivisible

In contrast, the Indian Immigrant, though heir to a great historic civilization, culture and a comprehensive religion, had emerged from a backward, feudal, casteist India. But he had not come empty-handed. He had brought his culture wrapped up in his heart, mind and soul along with him. This culture comprised a whole complex of distinctive material, intellectual, emotional and spiritual features and value systems and beliefs. (Unesco definition, 1992).

The rudimentary Indian culture brought by the Immigrants was made up of a full package of cultural traits enriched by millennia of evolution, including:-

(I) Material and social values-
Pots and pans, food habits, forms of respect, customs and traditions, festivals, costumes, occupational skills, emotionally charged family values.

(2) Spiritual-
Religion, philosophy, beliefs, values, rites and rituals, prayers, symbols, icons, divinities.

(3) Artistic-
Performing arts-, music, songs,dances, drama, languages, literature,crafts, oral traditions, folklores, entertainment, myths and legends.

Indian culture, in its artistic and spiritual expressions, remains one and indivisible. The regional specificities should not be mistaken for separate cultures. There is one India with a diversity of its people, languages, religions, Indian Culture, just as Hinduism, is one composite whole, and pluralistic in nature. It cannot be fragmented nor balkanised into Bhojpuri culture, Tamil culture, Telegu culture or Marathi culture- Indian culture is Indian culture just as Indian civilization is Indian civilization. Most emphatically, there is one Sanatan Vedic dharma, comprising many sects or cults.

"Indian culture is not seen in a segmented way either in terms of language, region, or religion. We do not hear of a Hindu or Muslim or Christian view of Indian Culture nor do we hear of it as Assamese or Bengali, or Punjabi or Tamil Culture".

(P.S.Sahai, former High Commissioner of India to Malaysia, GOPIO Magazine, 12. 1. 03, N.D).

It was given to the Indian Immigrant to be the custodian of his culture- the components of which we have outlined above. Even if he had brought nothing material, he was proud of his cultural and spiritual legacy as he felt hc was reliving what once upon a time, Lord Rama had to endure when he had been exiled from Ayodhya into *banwas*. Now, he found himself confronted with an aggressive alien culture, buttressed by the Oligarchy and the Catholic Church, to which he had to adjust himself while he was determined to preserve his cultural integrity. And he happened to be perfectly right as his rich culture contained within it the seeds of all learning, logics, wisdom that would enable his children and grandchildren to shine in UK, USA, Canada and all over the world- through interaction with western scholarship and technology. The impact of culture on human mind has been greater than science, technology or materialism.

"Culture has greater influence over minds than science or technology or industrial growth and if there is that cultural bond that brings minds together, that is the more lasting bond than any other."

(M.C. Chagla, President of ICCR, 1966, cited in GOPIO Mag. 12.1.03).

Hybrid Culture

The initial contact with western civilization was a period of **cultural shock**, of instability, of unlearning, self-questioning, relearning, acculturation, assimilation and adaptation. On the one hand, Indian culture and civilization had been more philosophical and

and theological than rational. Western civilization. had been soaked in materialism, on a pragmatic and scholarly research for truth on the ground.

The same efforts of assimilation have confronted many subsequent PIOs or NRIs having to adjust themselves to mainstream culture in South Africa, UK, USA, Canada, Australia, Germany. So, the Immigrants decided that their first task would be to accommodate themselves to the mainstream culture and civilisation. They preferred to play it safe, cope with the initial difficulties until they could be firmly grounded in the new cultural environment. What generally emerged within the first and next generations was a *hybrid* or a *creolised* culture.

The NRIs who land in an aggressive industrial city and forming a minority community need to be adaptable. Facing economic, social, cultural and political pressures, they may drop the outward signs of their culture, like the *sari, salwaz kameez,* the *bindi,* the *sindoor*, the ancestral language in order to adopt western dress and European language. After a period of assimilation into the mainstream culture, as in Reunion Island, in France and elsewhere, the PIOs may come out from hiding to throw off the cultural blackmail and humiliation, to reassert their cultural identity and reconstitute the Indian institutions. By this time they have well mastered the foreign medium. We have seen this phenomenon in Reunion Island where the PIOs have recently been going back to Indian culture, language, rites, rituals and festivals. In Mauritius and in Canada, for example, Indians have come up with a literature of their own in Hindi, Gujarati, Punjabi and Urdu.

(Harish Narang, JNU, paper presented during the VI Gopio International Convention, Mauritius, 6 December, 2003)

The Indian Immigrant needed time to purge himself of the burden of the past. He emerged as a transformed individual from the experience of indenture or historical contact with the west. It was more so with the indentured labourers who were mostly illiterate villagers unused to the demand of the west to which the modern NRI's are used as they have migrated from westernied cities in India. However, the process of hybridisation or new identity formation was the result of the inevitable transformation, blending, adaptation, adjustment, interchange that formed part of a dynamic multi-cultural cultural life and that produced a new diasporic identity, distinct from the original Indian identity. The Immigrants had to evolve according to mainstream culture, itself the result of a distinct social structure and history, which further marked them off from native Hindus but with whom they shared a common Indianness, however transformed they might have been by their diasporic experience. Having blended the various cultural experiences, they became the bearers of multiple creolised identities. In their turn, the Indian immigrants, being the custodians of a rich culture and civilization, wherever they have gone, in whatever historical or social conditions, have also deeply transformed their host societies. Wherever Indians have gone, they have planted the flags of little Indias across the world, complete with their ethnic cuisine, dress, music, entertainment, festivals, family ethos and an attachment to Indian culture, civilization and philosophy. Finally, despite a tough cultural resistance, in the end, everybody is swept over by the strong waves of interculturalism and creolisation. Everybody gets creolised.

The early Indian immigrant had to go through a period of renaissance, reformation and enlightenment before he could properly cope with the challenges pressing around him. It was a difficult period of adaptation and self- renewal. In that battle, he had weakened himself through the divisions and ravages caused by the caste system and a number of taboos and superstitions. But the movement leading to the renaissance, reformation and rejuvenation had just started in contemporary India with the birth of the Arya Samaj, the creation of the Indian National Congress. It only awaited inspiring leadership, the birth of an avatar, incarnated by Mahatma Gandhi who could alleviate his suffering, bring righteousness and punish evil.

Ethnicity

FORMERLY, IN the colonial and racist days, without a proper understanding of their social and cultural organisations, Europeans used to lump the Asians and the Africans as if they were barbarians, savages, primitive or tribals, hence terms like Coolies, Malbars, Negroes were thrown at them. Later, the term ethnic or ethnicity, from Greek *ethnos* or Sanskrit, *jati*, and also, *apanjhat*, and *khoon ka khoon,* or *communalism* became fashionable to signify ethnic groups, bearing specific physical features, culture and religion, both western and others, living within certain geographical boundaries. The sense of xenophobia, of regarding foreigners with suspicion was carried over by the colonials who dubbed natives as inferior. This psychology of mistrust and suspicion goes back to ancient India when foreigners were addressed as *mlecchas*, or *barbaroi* by the Greeks. Later, the growth of European nationalism and colonial expansion found their legitimacy in the ideology of racism, fuelled by slavery and Indentured labour.

To Max Weber, 1961, ethnicity is defined *as the sense of community and political belonging, the sharing of common customs, traditions, languages, moral values as distinct markers from other groups*. On the negative and restrictive sense, it has been viewed as ghetto formation, ghettoising, inward-looking, groupish, traditional, ritualistic and self-enclosed. From the insular point of view, it has been translated into the *splendid isolation* perspective. It was also considered to be a fixed, static, enclosed, unchanging identity in contrast to western society which was seen as dynamic, changing, evolving, rational-legal and technological. Ethnic categorization can also feed ethnic separatism in the wake of Sikh and Tamil separatism, fuelled by the demand of a separate Sikh state and the Tamil Tigers in Sri Lanka, and the erroneous claim that Tamils are not Hindus.

(Bharat Gupt. http://www.indiastar.com.Guptl.html)

In Europe, national sovereignty and nationalism had grown around the distinctions of language, culture, customs, religion, geographical boundaries, the sense of their uniqueness and homogeneity and the formation of political organisations. Spread to the rest of the world, it was to ignite different forms of nationalism in the colonies and elsewhere. Henceforth, culture and religion formed the rallying point for political organisation. In order to justify colonialism and their military and political superiority, the Europeans resorted to the ideology of Eurocentricism and intolerance by which the west held itself up as the model of culture and civilization. It was seen as part of the white man's burden to attempt to civilize and Christianise the backward Afro-Asian races.

The new western-educated colonial elites, in India and elsewhere, were awakened to their ethnic identity in response to the ideology of European nationalism and Euro-centricism. They were inspired by the latent energies and merits of Asian cultures, religions, customs, traditions and political consciousness-which had earlier been quashed under feudal backwardness and imperialism. It saw the emergence of a tidal wave of political and national consciousness around cultural and religious revival. Asian nationalism evolved into a wider form of national identity. It generated nationalist effervescence and ethnic consciousness.

The first signs of nationalist conflagration flared up in Japan under the Meiji Restoration. In India, it sparked the Indian Mutiny of 1857 and which later prompted the formation of the Indian National Congress in 1875 and thereafter the rise of Indian nationalism. Sun Yat Sen spread the gospel of Chinese nationalism. This is how the new forms of nationalism, consensus building and ethnicity were generated in the colonies. In brief, ethnicity arose in response to the spread of Euro-Americanism, a consolidated Europe and to all forms of imperialism, spiralling into the clash of civilizations, the rise of Islamic fundamentalism, September 11 and terrorism, fed by globalisation and the ammunition business.

Ethnicity has evolved as a way of fighting back, of asserting one's ethnic identity, wrapped around one's religion, culture, civilization, language, customs and traditions associated with one's homeland.

To F. Barth, 1969, an ethnic group comprises four elements, namely biological transmission, sharing cultural values, languages and communications, and it identifies itself as distinct and is seen as distinct by other groups. At that time, the term communalism was used by the white to describe the political behaviour of the Asians who were struggling to organise themselves and to articulate their collective and group interests in the political marketplace. Other sociologists have stressed on the fluid and dynamic aspects of ethnic political, social and economic organisations within the larger competitive multi-ethnic contexts. Each ethnic group tends to hold on to its customs, languages, religion and cultural values while interacting with other rival ethnic groups in the public arena.

Ethnicity is always in flux. It is ever evolving. It is driven by a number of socio-cultural and political organizations. It keeps interacting with other ethnic groups and mainstream culture which triggers a dynamic process of cultural exchanges, give-and-take, adjustment, hybridisation, acculturation and deculturisation face-to-face with the aggressive forces of western capitalism, modernization, Creolisation and Euro-Americanism. In all these negotiations, religion can play a stabilising role as well as a latent and determining factor in ethnic politics in its resistance against the invading forces of Creolisation.

The pre-independence period was a time of intense political changes. It was marked by a politics of bargaining, negotiation and accommodation leading to the founding of a new democratic, multi-ethnic society, the march towards independence and its aftermath, nation-building. It also witnessed a shift of ethnic alliances whereby the white manipulated Catholicism and Euro-centrism as political baits in a bid to mobilise the Black electorate under a fabricated King Creole and the PMSD against the Asian electorate, now perceived as distinct and hostile ethnic groups, labelled as communalism. It led to tensions and sometimes violent clashes, in India between Hindus and Moslems, in Mauritius and in the Caribbeans between the Asians and the Blacks, in Fiji between the Indians and indigenous Fijians, generally instigated by the white sugar oligarchy.

A democratic government has to accommodate various ethnic demands through a process of negotiation and give and take among various ethnic groups as components within the multi-ethnic society. Thus politics becomes a matter of negotiation, bargaining and out-bidding between competing political parties during election times, each party bidding for the favour of the electorate in the formation of government or opposition. All these activities take place on the public arena between the constituents and the politicians, marked by *a politics of clientism* by which the state values and satisfies the demands and expectations of its constituents in the political market place just as a business corporation would deal with its clients.

The Enemy Strikes Again

One should never under-estimate the strategy and subterfuges of the oligarchy in their bid to take back political control. After enjoying political power for over four decades, the majority Indians had sunk back into a state of complacency and they were soon taken off-guard when their own group split up and allied with the Oligarchy. By resorting to a strategy of *scientific communalism*, Paul Berenger, leader of the Oligarchy, has split the majority ethnic group into rival sub-ethnic groups in order to negotiate with each of them separately as *different market segments in the allocation of state resources, political nominations, offices and rewards.* Consequently, the local Oligarchy has managed to climb back into political and economic power by manipulating the mechanism of internal caste and sub-ethnic linguistic divisions and thus deliberately fragmenting the majority Indian community into splinter groups within a secular state.

In the USA, multi-culturalism and the Cultural Mosaic theory arose in response to the imposition of Americanism under the general Melting Pot theory for the purpose of propagating uniformity. The MMM was to borrow part of the Melting Pot theory to suit its own purposes. Since the 1970's, according to its strategy to capture power by revolutionary and undemocratic means and by general strikes, the MMM had pushed the country on the brink of disaster. While, on the one hand, it stepped up Creolisation as a political weapon, it went on *fragmenting, submerging and undermining the Hindu majority* on the other hand- all in the holy name of fighting *communalism.*

"The MMM has tried every undemocratic means to overthrow the government: general insurrectionary strikes, 1971, Sheik Hossen scandal, 1978, insurrectionary strike, 1979 with violence, burning of sugar crops, destroying of public property, terrorism, an unholy and ridiculous hunger strike, letting off prison criminals loose on the defenceless public. The MMM, we must agree, is really a dangerous enemy." (The author. *A Dangerous Enemy*, Advance. August 1979)

It targetted the State Bourgeoisie or Establishment which it described, in Marxist terms, as constituting of one section of the Hindu community. To attain this goal, it used caste and linguistic divisions in a clever game to set up rival sub-ethnic groups at one another's throats. The cummulative result of this underhand anti-Hindu State bourgeoisie campaign erupted in the February 1999 anti Hindu and anti-State riot at Roche Bois. In adopting the Creolisation Melting Pot theory, the MMM had provoked a general ethnic backlash and its consequent loss of power in 1983. Since 1983 until 1995, under Sir Aneerood Jugnauth's Prime Ministership, Mauritius pursued the policy of Rainbow Culture and multi-culturalism. However, by 2000, the MMM bounced back to power on the strength of its cultural policy of Scientific Communalism, divide-and-rule, aggressive Creolisation and breaking up the ethnic Hindu majority into rival sub-ethnic groups. It backed up its cultural policy by funding the creation of Cultural Centres to rival and weaken the established cultural and religious federations.

Throughout its short history, the MMM has reflected the hypocrisy and inconsistencies of its leader, enmeshed in ideological contradictions and political bluffs. In Guyana, the Indians had remained stranded as peasants in the rural areas with little access to education and personal development. In contrast, after abolition of slavery, the Blacks had flocked to the towns, benefiting from access to education and more lucrative jobs in government, police and the army and the private sector. The consequence was that, deprived of a solid Indian educated bourgeoisie in the bureaucracy, police and army, as in Mauritius, the Guyanese Indians, though in majority, could not hold power under Cheddi Jagan. Having seized power, Burnham had combined brute force and Black ethnic violence and had exploited division among the Indians in order to stay in power for three decades.

But in *Trinidad*, during the period of 1911 to 1946, a large number of Trinidadian Hindus had got converted to Christianity, thus their majority had depleted from 77% to 65%. During that time, the Moslems, adhering more strictly to their religion, saw their proportion increasing from 14% to 17%. Following the introduction of universal suffrage, the Hindus began to mobilise as an ethnic majority behind their religion and their *Apanjhat* solidarity as a strategy to face Black Creolisation. Realising the dangers of inter-caste and internal Hindu divisions, the leaders, generally belonging to the high caste, submerged their caste and linguistic differences and mobilised their socio-cultural organizations and Hindu Apanjhat consensus for their political survival against the Blacks. They also reduced the religious and ethnic cleavages between the Hindus and the Moslems and forged a cultural unity in order to back up their 52% majority against the 31% Blacks.

Unlike in Mauritius and in the Caribbeans, in **Fiji** the 50% Indian majority were torn by ethnic and caste divisions, particularly between North and South Indians, Hindus and Moslems cleavages, and they failed to *develop an ethnic political consciousness* and leadership to face a common threat from indigenous Fijians. After indenture, they had simply hired the land from the Melanesians which they planted in extended family unit without developing cultural, social and political institutions ahead of the advent of independence. Consequently, *political power slipped away from their hands*. Though, in majority, they continued to remain like pockets of scattered, conservative agricultural planters, without evolving any ethnic cohesion for political purposes. Hence, in that loose structure, they were politically vulnerable and they twice lost power in 1987 by Colonel Rabuka and in the May 2000 coup forcing the ousting of Prime Minister Mahendra Chaudhry, replaced since then by the indigenous Fijian Laisenia Qarase

(Ameenah Jahangeer, MGI, 1994).

Gujarati Traders

Since they had the means, the Gujarati traders had been keeping close links with India and they had been some of the proudest Indians abroad. It was the Gujarati businessman, Dada Abdullah, who hosted Gandhi's 21 years' stay in Durban where he led the struggle for their political and civil rights. His descendants, Yusuf Cachiala and his wife Amina have been the closest associates of Nelson Mandela from the earliest days of struggle against Apartheid. At the same time, Gandhi's political struggle in South Africa had inspired Nelson Mandela in leading the African National Congress towards the freedom of South Africa. It had served as a political bridge between the Indians and the Africans in their common struggle for independence.

(*Indian Express,* January 10, 2003)

Coping with the demand of the West would involve a long, painful and patient educational process. In the meantime, the Immigrants had not the least inkling how to defend themselves. In Mauritius, there was nobody in the Council of Government, in the government or the press to raise a single finger in their favour. Except for Kerr, the precursor, one lone voice dared:

"to express an opinion opposed to these interests."

(**William Walter Raleigh Kerr**, Treasurer, Council of Government, 15 11 1867)

But Kerr himself was severely reprimanded for his pains. Otherwise, they would never have been caught unawares into the hands of their masters. But once ashore and having stepped into the Immigration Depot in Port Louis, battered and fatigued, the shock was to come when they were distributed to various plantations across the Island. Soon, they found themselves tucked into the ex-slaves barracoons. Most of them had to make their makeshift shelters, without safe water or any hygienic provisions. They had to endure the treatment and shame previously meted out to slaves, except that there was less flogging. They had to put up humbly with the harsh, racist, slave-owning mentality of their backward-looking white masters who treated them as sub-humans. But this time the planters were dealing with people who had come in large numbers and who were proud of their Indianness. The masters, backed by formidable material powers, were soon to find themselves up against the unconquerable spirit of simple people who were armed with spiritual qualities. In brief, they were pitted against *the invisible force of Indian culture* which had once prevailed across the whole of Asia where it had incorporated into the very essence of Asian culture. Yes, it was the same spiritual force that Gandhiji had mobilised to topple the might British Empire.

Carrot and Stick

These Immigrants had carried their cultural past deep into their consciousness and into the very fabrics of their daily lives. Their religion differed from the Sunday Church going religion. It was a way of life, a system of belief and thinking which governed the very lives and dreams of those humble folks. So the French colons had not found any material weapon against the divine forces. They fell back upon the authority of the Church to break their spirit and proselytize them by dangling the carrots of employment and the stick of coercion, backed by the weapon of ridicule and racism.

The Church used the modern jargon of rationality to distort Hindu theology. It criticized Hinduism, scrutinised and listed its faults, ridiculing its deities as elephant-headed, monkey-shaped, addressed the non-christians as pagans in a way that displayed their total ignorance of Hinduism and their inability to see it from the Hindu perspective. Unlike the Chinese and the Blacks who had unconditionally assimilated western culture and Christianity and emulated the West, the Indians held on stubbornly to their cultural and civilizational heritage despite tremendous pressure from the colonialists until they established Indian culture as the mainstream culture.

The white ignored the great Hindu concept of God and of creation by which All is One. Nature, plants, animals and humans are all part of divine creation. This concept of the unity of creation, unity in diversity, is symbolised in the personality of God Himself aș being half human and half animal and surrounded by the forces of nature:- water, the planets. This does not mean that Hindus are polytheistic. Far from it, this idea is repeatedly carried into various stories and mythologies in order to instill a respect of nature and the spatial environment.

God is visualised as *Cosmic Consciousness*-as being the energetic force in the cosmos. Westerners had no idea that the Hindus believe in the central concept of many ways to God, that the One Supreme Brahman manifests himself differently under different names, forms and attributes, variously addressed as deities. After all the prophet, Ibrahim, in Mesopotamia, (Iraq), not far from the Indus Valley, and his wife, Sarah, 600 B.C, were modelled on Brahma and Saraswati.

The Indians were ridiculed as Malbars Coolies, as *Ti Malbars*. In Britain, Indians are sometimes addressed as Paki. In the initial period of adjustment, the Indian would play low profile, adopt a strategy of submissiveness. He would appear to be docile but in the end his hard work, his productive labour, his personal sacrifices, his humility, his tolerance, his honesty, his sweat and his toil, his cultured manners-which were spiritual qualities culled from Vedic scriptures coming down the ages- would win the day. Those who had jeered at the Indians learned to cheer:-

"Après les grains dont ils sont les seuls détenteurs, après les sucres qu'ils sont, pour ainsi dire, les seuls à acheter, après les plus beaux de là grande partie de l'immeuble de Port Louis qu'ils ont acquis, les voilà qui se lancent maintenant dans les propriétés sucrières... Nous ne pouvons lutter contre l'Asiatique: la prise qu'il a sur nous est trop forte. Pendant qu'il thésaurise, nous dépensons. Il devient fort et nous nous affaiblissons. C'est nous qui l'avons voulu, c'est nous qui en sommes cause, reconnaissons le, disons le même et laissons l'Asiatique en paix!"

(F.L.Maurel.L'Express, 21 July 1896)

Many Pathways

His detractors would see his usefulness as providing cheap labour and as a market for western goods. The Indian Immigrant did not have any mass media or structure which could enable him to put across his point of view. Unable to speak English or French, and not having yet produced an articulate elite class, he was practically dumb and passive. Thus in his silence, he submitted to ridicule. Profiting from this gap of communication, the Europeans entertained fanciful ideas about a polytheistic Hinduism. They ridiculed the daily practices and beliefs of the simple labourer who prayed to the sun, venerated plants, animals and rivers, which they saw as manifestations of divinity. All those beliefs were interpreted by the west as polytheistic and superstitious. Since the Indians had no one to stand for them; in their silence lay their main weakness. They lost the battle of communication and of information. They had to wait for Shri Ramakrishna and for Swami Vivekanand to project a more coherent, holistic view of their dharma in order to explain the vedantic truth of many pathways to reach the same godhead. Somehow, being simple folks and not learned scholars, they had a vague notion of the depth of their philosophy. They were fully aware of some grand divine purpose which governs the universe, the planets and everything that moves on it and which they could not explain. They could not fully explain their beliefs in the theory of karma, in reincarnation, in dharmic principles and the conviction that everything is created by the same God who pervades through all His creation.

"That by which one sees one imperishable entity in all beings, undivided among the divided, know that knowledge to be of the nature of goodness."
(The Gita, XVIII)

Knowing that the *whole creation is sacred*, they regarded the forces of nature, man and everything as manifestations and projections of divinity- a belief which was mistaken for polytheism. Everything is the property of God. But they also knew that in that divine hierarchy of things, man was the superior creature in that he alone could think, could talk and relate to his God. They felt that it was up to man to protect and revere the other creatures of God-inert nature, plants and animals. This explains why they treated the cow as mother cow, why they remained non-violent, why they preferred to be vegetarians and why they worshipped the sun, why they linked their own destinies to the planets and considered the Ganges or the local Ganga Talao as sacred.

In their simplicity, they showed the virtues of yogic discipline, that is, of mental and psychological discipline, of moral control over their desires and over their body in the teeth of so much provocation, confusion, hatred, violence and terrorism. They did not worship the physical body but they went beyond to reach out to the divine consciousness and grasp at the higher level of supramental consciousness. In other words, they saw God everywhere:- *All is Om. All is Allah. All is God* and the concept of a common humanity And Gandhi has said it: *Ishwar/ Allah, Tera Nam*! In their own way, the simple labourers were profoundly spiritual. They worshipped the divine attributes associated with their deities, forming part of the divine scheme of things.

"Everything in this whole round of the Universe is God-made, God-protected and God-pervaded. Enjoy what He gives thee sharing it with thy fellow creatures and without attachment; for, whose is all this wealth? It is God's and God's alone. Be not proud, be not greedy."
(Y. Veda.40. Translated by Basdeo Bissoondoyal)

Man is ordained to enjoy what is given to him and what he honestly earns by the sweat of his brows, without stealing or coveting other people's property or encroaching upon their rights. Lest you forget that whatever is given to you, health, beauty, youth, strength, wealth, power is only for a short time and will be taken away at any time, man is subject to the ups and downs of life. Man carries within himself the seeds of his destruction. Lord Buddha had said that the body is but a nest of disease. Remembering all this, the Indian Immigrant bowed down with humility and gratitude to his employers who mistook this simple Oriental gesture as a sign of servility. Since he owned the land, controlled the government and the economy, the planter thought that he owned everything he surveyed and that he could bend the Immigrant into his compliant slave.

The Deities Walking out of the Stones

But, in whatever directions the Immigrant turns, pointing like the Swastika towards the four cardinal points, he sees himself in the presence of God's beautiful creation, the bountiful earth and everything that it provides, the sun, the moon, the stars, the vast limitless oceans and all that live in it. He sees the Great Spirit in the sparkle of the stars, in the whisper of the breeze, in the brilliance of the sun, in the juice of the sugar cane, in the sweetness of the cow's milk, the flow of Ganges and his greatness in the majesty of the Himalayas. He feels strongly protected by a host of divinities. If he needs art, inspiration and learning, he turns to Lord Ganesh and Saraswati. If he needs physical protection and strength, he invokes Shri Hanuman, the god of strength and of the wind. When he seeks wisdom, he turns to Lord Krishna. When he asks for wealth, Lakshmi is there to shower her blessings on him. If he wants righteousness, he calls upon Sri Rama. If he needs security or strength to face his enemies, he invokes Kali. Over and above all, he knows that creation is the work of Brahma, preservation of Vishnu while Mahesh takes charge of destruction and renewal. But in his heart, he knows that he is praying to the same God in his different attributes and manifestations. The divinities make sense to his simple mind and when he addresses them, he can visualise Krishna, Ram or Hanuman walking out of the pictures or out of the stones to come to his silent rescue.

In gratitude to God for the gift of life, he invokes Agni, Indra and

Varuna and fondly calls the Creator by so many loving names and sees Him in different forms and shapes, man, half man-and-half woman, elephant-headed, monkey-tailed- as an expression of the unity of the universe. What wrong is there in it? If all the paths lead to the same Creator, call him Brahman, Allah, Aum, Jesus, Khoodah, Bon Dieu, God, Ram, Rahim, Shiva, Ganesh or Hanuman or by any other name, the rose will smell as sweet.

In contrast, the Moslem immigrant feels more secure and comfortable in his mosque, his Quran and his clergy which give him a simple answer and a straightforward guide to Allah. Despite the divisions between the Gujarati and Calcutteea Muslims, between the Sunee Surtee, the Bhorah, Kutchee Maiman, the Muslims generally close their ranks. Some of them have been known to go out of their way to help one another, not only here but also in France where they have stood up for another Muslims or Arabs, providing them shelter and food in times of difficulties. After all, the Muslim is less hampered by caste divisions or the other taboos and superstitions that block the Hindu society. Like the Hindu, his ancestral brother, the Muslim shares the same basic values of Indian culture, family and social ethics derived from the epics. As in Malaysia where they have imbibed Indian culture and Hinduism, including the epics which they have modified by replacing Hindu values by Islamic values, the Indian Muslims have cherished the universal Indian values that have accounted for their general progress. They also share Indian cuisine, Indian arts,crafts, customs, traditions, folklore, the diluted Vedic principles, the Hindustani language (except for the scripts), the same music, songs, dress, food habits, family ethos, art as well as the same long Indian history. These have enabled them to emerge stronger and better off from the trial of strength with the European master.

We're All Hindus!

At the everyday, practical, mass level, there is tremendous ignorance and confusion about who we are. One would be surprised to find out that the western-educated Hindu, professional or otherwise, equipped with deep academic or technical knowledge, which is not balanced by spiritual knowledge. Their average understanding of Hindu culture and philosophy is shockingly superficial and sometimes erroneous. Hindus do not know that they are Hindus since they mistakenly identify themselves with various cults, sects and languages and claim that they are not Hindus but Tamils, Telegus, Marathis, Bhojpuris, Hare Krïshna or Sai Baba! They confuse language, the Tamil language and its Dravidian scripts as indiçating a different religion. Otherwise they mistake the Kovil as indicating something different.

Language or place of birth does not always determine one's religion. Just as the Portuguese, the French, the Australian, the Danes can claim to be equally Christians, so the Indian from whatever part of India or the diaspora are simply Hindus. It's somewhat like the story of the three blind men who get hold of the elephant tail, its trunk, its ears and each affirms that the tail, or the trunk or the ears is the elephant. They fail to see the big picture. This is one of the reasons why evangelicals go around and profit from this general confusion and ignorance of the dharma to win converts from the gullible Hindus. But what all Hindus should know is that *Hinduism is the broad, all-embracing, all-inclusive, all-comprehensive, universalistic Eternal Sanskritic Religion based on Vedic sources and its various derivatives.*

Hinduism is fathomless and is as broad as the ocean. It's not static. It's an experiential relgion. One has to soak oneself into it, experience it through and through, medidate upon it. After all, every Hindu is also a seeker in his journey to attain salvation. It's not a matter of externals, of wearing a beard, a cap or long flowing robes or attending temples or mosques or church. This is mere ritualism. It's not religion. It's not spiritualism. Many people confuse between ritualism with spiritualism.

What then is religion about? According to prof. Ghazali-Basri, Malaysia, a religion has five fundamental features:-

(i) It has rituals, including temple, church or mosque worship, offerings, puja, yaj, prayers.

(ii) It has a fundamental code of ethics, family, social md moral values, commandments, principles.
(iii) It has a social system, a body of sanskar, ceremonies, marriage, birth, death.
(iv) It has a core of spirituality that relates the individual to his Maker.
(v) It has a core doctrine based on scriptures and prophets.

As the oldest of religions, Hinduism is a way of life. It keeps growing, developing and re-inventing itself all the time. It's never shallow, never superficial as it contains layers upon layers of meanings, symbols and thoughts. It goes ever deeper and deeper and is incomprehensible to the western mind which is so baffled with its complexities that it regards it as outlandish. It is so rich, so varied, so deep that, from time to time, it requires spiritual masters, sages, philosophers, scholars, reformers, saints, godmen, gurus, maha gurus, sat gurus to reveal the path to others. Some would put more emphasis on certain aspects in an attempt to infuse new life and vitality into mankind's oldest religion. In the meantime, Hinduism keeps growing, adpating itself to the times, the different places and situations.

In the final analysis, whatever cults or dogmas they might profess, all Hindus subscribe to *the core beliefs* in:- reincarnation, the theory of karma, dharma, the paths of devotion, of action and of knowledge, the values of truth, honesty, non-violence, living the good life, the unity and sanctity of creation, the union of the Soul with the Supersoul, the efficacy of prayer and the observance of certain rites and rituals, centered on the personal or impersonal God. As a result, different cults or sects or schools of thought crop up within the Hindu family. These sages and spiritual masters form an integral part of the Hindu system and they are always welcome as revealers of truth. They will keep coming to spread their teachings because Hinduism is not a fixed, rigid religion, bound by one prophet, one scripture or one church.

This is why we have a plethora of temples, religious places, social halls each propagating its particular creed and cults which have spread throughout the world, the East, the West, the North and the South, on the trails of the Hindus. They keep Hinduism alive and take it into the global society where traditional, ritualistic Hinduism could not penetrate. They bring new people and new converts with a fresh understanding and perspective of Hinduism. They may be called by whatever name, they are all one. They may be:- Hindu Sanatanist, Arya Samajist, Vaishnav, Saivite, Vedantic, RamaKrishna Mission, Auroville Association, Bharatiya Vidya Bhavan, Arsha Vidya Gurukulam, Brahma Kumaris, Brahmo Samaj, Buddhist temples, Chinmayananda Ashrams, Hare Krishna temples, Sai Baba centres, Sikh dwaras, Kabir Pant, Seva Shivir, Krishnamurthi Foundation, Mahatma Gandhi Memorial Foundation, Swami Narayan temples and the list is endless. The negative side to it is that some of the fanatics or crazy people from these cults tend to wear blinkers and enclose themselves within narrow domestic walls. This forments a permanent tendency towards division and schism. They may fail to get together to face the common enemy- the Christian missionary, the racist white who are out for their blood.

On the positive side, the Hindu is a *free, democratic, liberal individual* and he can dip into any of these cults or sects, interact freely with and borrow certain teachings from Islam, Christianity, without feeling that he is less of a Hindu. He may choose freely from any of the scriptures, the Vedas, the Upanishads, the Ramayana, Mahabharata, the Gita or the Puranas. They all preach and elaborate on the same essential Vedic truths. They all take you along different pathways to God as they see divinity residing in God's creations. That's what makes the Hindu so peace-loving, so gentle, so cultured and so tolerant, so democratic and liberal. Moderation is in his DNA. .

The common Vedic thread runs through each one of these sects as they engender a vigorous spiritual life centred on *satsangs*, socio-cultural-religious events, preaching. In turn, these spawn a large circulation of publications, pictures, pilgrimages, spiritual retreats, worship places, video, radio and television programmes, music, dances, songs, charitable, social and missionary activities. That's why we say that Hinduism is *broad, universalistic because it contains within itself everything else that exists in other religions* though it does not believe that any single religion holds a monopoly of truth.

Westerners Fearful of Indians

Therefore, instead of helping such noble people, animated by divine, universal thoughts to be better Hindus, to continue as a peaceful, tolerant, hard-working, honest, productive workers who earned their living by the sweat of their brows, the White did the opposite. They tried to destroy their faith and their soul. They put all sorts of pressures to convert them so that they might remain for-ever dependent on them as they had earlier crushed the soul of the slaves. To be a Christian meant to be entirely dependent upon their sway. Afraid of their numbers, the westerners fought back by suppressing them, denying their children educational opportunities.

At the age of 10, **Mauritian children** were put to work. Thus, out of 39,112 Indian boys and girls, only 829 attended schools according to census of 1871. While Ordinance No 21 of 1857 made primary education obligatory on children from 6 to 12, this ordinance was made optional to Indian children. The same educational discrepancy occurred in British Guina where Indian children remained illiterate in the agricultural backwaters while Black children had access to western education in the towns followed by access to government jobs. The reasons for the backwardness of Indian children were attributed to the indifference of their parents, secondly the hostility of the planters, thirdly children could earn some money by doing some light work for which they received full rations, fourthly, the medium of instruction was in foreign languages and the teachers were hardly sympathetic and the more they were illiterate the more they were victimised.. The fundamental reason was the unwillingness of Indian parents to send their children to euro-centric, Catholic or Anglican schools which entrapped their children into the conversion net.

As we saw earlier, unlike the slaves, the Indians had come with their developed languages, Bhojpuri, Gujarati, Hindi, Marathi, Tamil, Telegu, their scriptures, customs and traditions which they valued above material possessions. Through wielding these languages and traditions which ensured them a broad general culture, they possessed the wherewithal of learning, thinking and reasoning and the linguistic structure which they could apply and transfer into the school curriculum with astonishing ease.

Besides, they had inherited five millennia of civilization and history. They had other comparative advantages. They were a versatile people who had once been building forts on top of the Deccan ghats and whose ancestors had toppled down the mighty Moghul Empire. Others possessed a multiplicity of occupational skills and talents gathered in ancestral villages bordering the Gangetic plains or the hills of the Karnataka. Quite apart from agriculture, they were skilled in a number of crafts. They had a special aptitude for abstract thinking and the poetry of life.

Despite the meagre wages, Rs. 5 per month, including weekly ration of rice, dhall, salt fish, oil, two pairs of clothes per year, the Indentured Immigrants worked day and night and managed to save some money from the sale of their market produce, eggs, goats and milk. Soon after the expiry of their five year contract, many of them managed to buy a little plot of land nearby to the sugar estate in order to live independently and with some dignity in the villages which they created all over the island. Throughout all the plantation colonies, the White and the Creoles saw those rare qualities of sacrifice, self-reliance and productuve labour as a threat for which Indians were persecuted.

"The very quality of Indians counts for their defect in South Africa. The Indians are disliked in South Africa for their simplicity, patience, perseverance, frugality and other wordliness. Westerners are therefore afraid that if thousands of Orientals settle in South Africa the westerners must go to the wall."

(Smuts, Prime Minister of South Africa, addressed to Gandhi, 1913, cited by Hassim Seedat in India Perspective, Jan. 2003)

Now compare this sentiment with the following:-

"Si l'on considère que les Asiatiques sont industrieux, économes et vivent de presque rien, on peut prévoir dès à présent que le nombre des électeurs de leur race augmentera d'année en année dans les

proportions écrasantes pour les créoles.

Le sol, l'argent, le commerce, tout tend à passer entre leurs mains."

(Sir Celincourt Antelme, *Papers relating to Alteration of the Constitution*, 1883)

Yet by their very industriousness, their hard work, they had made great contributions to the countries of their adoption. They had everywhere saved the sugar industry from ruin and had brought great fortune to the planters who rarely showed any gratitude:

"The condition of the colony before importation of Indian labour was one of gloom; now the coast has been turned into one of the most prosperous parts of South Africa."

(Sir Liege Hulett, a sugar baron, Natal, 1908)

Proud Legacy of Industriousness

The first one is about their examplary conduct and their patriotism:-

"Pendant que les Asiatiques se faisaient remarquer par leur conduite digne, noble même, dirai-je, que voyons-nous? Des bandes de Créoles se livrer au pillage des demeures abattues ou abandonnées. Non contents de piller, ils ont aussi violé. Oui! Des femmes, des jeunes égarées dans la tourmente mises à nu par le vent, ont été ignomineusement violées par des brutes de Créoles! Vous ne l'ignorez pas? Ils ne sont pas si méchants et à craindre que vous le dites, ces gens là. Plaise à Dieu que toutes les classes qui vivent chez nous, soient aussi laborieuses et aussi tranquilles que les Indiens, et tout ira bien."

(F.L.Maurel., L'Express. 24 July 1896, on the memorable 1892 cyclone)

The second statement testifies to their dignity, their self-reliance and their independence:

"As regards the great disproportion pointed out by the Royal Commissioners in parag. 236 of their report, in the number of cases relieved among the General Population. I can report the Indians, as compared with the total population of each category, it is owing to the fact that the Indians being a more industrious and more thrifty people, they are in general in more easy circumstances and therefore do not have recourse to Poor Law Relief."

(D.P.Garrioch, Poor Law Commissioner. 20 March 1911 in *Despatches relating to the Recommendations of the Mauritius Royal Commission*, 1909)

And finally, how about their industriousness and their contribution to the cause of independence of South Africa?

"The Indian community of today is the final depositary of that call for freedom and final social redemption, which call has been passed down to generations. I respect and salute the Indian communities because I know that the level of prosperity they had achieved in South Africa is the direct result of their industriousness and hard work of many generations, by what is proven to be one of the most self-reliant people of Africa. South Africa is proud of this legacy."

(Dr Buthelezi, Home Affairs Minister and President of the Inkatha Freedom Party, 9 Nov. 2002, S.Africa).

9
DIASPORAS IN CONFLICT

THE COLONIAL system, regulated by the White, set up a fixed racial and social stratification and prescribed the rules of the cultural, economic, social and political game within which our diasporas, from Europe, Africa and Asia, had no choice but to meet, collide, conflict and coalese in the plantation colonies.

This chapter uncovers the hidden psychological and sociological reasons which lie at the roots of the tensions and challenges facing the Indian diaspora in its relations with other ethnic groups, particularly Black and Fijian. It shows how the White minority has cleverly used cultural and racial differences as a weapon to polarise these two ethnic groups into opposite camps, marked by coup d etat, violence and human rights abuses.

In Macmillan's *Mauritius Illustrated*, 1914, Albert Pitot, graded and classified the social hierarchy from the traditional oligarchical perspective thus:

A - White population.

B - White elites.

C - Coloured middle class, professors, accountants, railway employees.

D - Working classes. artisans, tailors, joiners, -elastic- Creoles intermarried with Indians and Chinese.

E - The Afro-Malagassy Creoles, fishermen, woodcutters, porters, cooks, masons.

F - Indian agricultural labourers.

At that time, he ignored that the Gujarati traders had stepped into the middle class, soon to be followed and outperformed by the Chinese traders, particularly after World War II. He failed to read the signs of the time, the awakening of the Hindus, under the impact of Manilall Doctor and the Arya Samaj reforms, spearheaded by an upwardly mobile class of small planters and their educated children, destined to rise to middle and ruling class positions. Since we have dealt earlier with the White ruling and elite class, the Chinese and Gujarati traders, in this chapter, we shall focus on the Coloureds, Creoles and Indians.

The Coloureds

AS IN many French colonies in the West Indies, namely San Domingo, the French settlers in the Mascarene kept mistresses and this gave rise to the rapid growth of a mulatto class. Professor Chenba André Julien refers to the *doudous*, mainly Indian women, employed by the French colons as free sex objects, since their childhood and who won *"leur affranchissement et firent souche d'hommes de couleur"*.

O.Bijoux's comment on Prentout's statement in his book, *"L'Ile de France sous Decaen"* is quite revealing:-

"Par noirs libres, Prentout entend tous les membres de la population de couleur- noirs libres proprement dits, mulatres, métis, créoles, indiens, ou les descendants de ces divers types d'espèce humaine."

In the West Indies, the French absentee landlords left the *petits blancs* in charge of their land while they spent their time in France. Inspite of their numbers, their wealth, their culture and command of the French language, the mulattos were allowed no voice in government and they enjoyed no civil liberties. Though they were proud of the fact that the blood of some of the oldest aristocratic families ran in their veins, they were barred from occupying official positions and had no voice in the government of the colony. Very conscious of their grievances, many of the mullatos were rich, educated, well--bred and handsome. They were assaulted, harassed and humiliated by the incompetent, and dissolute class of *petits blancs* against whom they could get no justice. The Protestant missionary, Rev. Jean Lebrun, and later the combative Remy Ollier who professed to be an admirer of English and of British liberalism and institutions, campaigned hard to secure their civil rights. Ollier's paper, *La Sentinelle*, was at loggerheads with *Le Cernéen* which championed French laws, the French language and French supremacy.

The Mullatos were mostly illegitimate offsprings of White males and Indian or African slave women and were treated favourably by their fathers and given their freedom. They were a schizophrenic group, defined as Mixed, rebuffed by White society but holding themselves above the Africans. *"The Mullatos generally despised the black blood in themselves and made sure Africans knew it. The hybrid culture formed, where everything was evaluated with the White and his culture deemed to be the standard, the only culture that mattered."*

(Ravi Dev, *Aetiology of an Ethnic Riot*, Guyana, Jan. 12,1998.)

Similarly, in Mauritius, the Coloured or the *gens de couleur* of mixed African- Asian -and- European blood, being French-speaking and urban-living, belonged to an intermediate class; which, by birth, were stigmatised as being racially subordinates. Though they gravitated towards the white race, pulled by the twin forces of desire and envy, they were rebuffed as being socially inferior and therefore were generally victims of an *acute identity crisis*. They insisted on distinguishing themselves from the Black Creol□es by seeking to identify themselves with their white father. But this desire was never requited. Hence the ambivalence, the anguish, the disappointment, the craze, the madness of it all in a brutal social environment poisoned with prejudices. It was a problem which sprang from the deep affective, emotional needs of men, the desire to belong to a collectivity. (Dr R. Moss. MGI. 1999).

There is nothing which a coloured could do about it since he was born into that racial group. The problem was that, not being of pure white blood, they felt caught between Scylla and Charybdis. Here's the ambivalence. While they naturally hankered after the myth of their European ascendancy they emphatically rejected their Asian or African origins. They self-consciously recognized themselves as being socially inferior to the white but superior to the Blacks and to the Indians pushed to the bottom of the social ladder. Side by side with the acceptance of the idea of white superiority went the denigration of African culture. Mistrusted by the White, the Blacks and the Asians, they ended up as a frustrated, complex-ridden community which projected its hostility on the Indians, their eternal scapegoat.

"Le plus grand malheur des hommes de couleur à Maurice, c'est leur désir absurde de cesser d'être soi; de vouloir se faire passer pour blanc. C'est de s'oublier et de se renier en public ses frères, ses soeurs, ses amis, et chose incroyable, sa mère, quand cette mère, qui devrait être adorée, porte le cachet de son origine sur son front."

(Evenor Hitié. *Histoire de Maurice.* Bucktowansingh. Valonville Street. Port Louis)

Hitié also condemned the Coloured for their servility and self-humiliation to the white whom he castigated for their selfishness and arrogance in monopolising all the immunities and privileges *attachées à la caste blanche*. They met with the full blast of racial segregation at the civil status office where there were separate registers, mixed marriages were prohibited by law. They were discriminated against in coffee bars, in government offices, in law courts, at the Royal College. It was thanks to Lebrun who founded free primary schools that allowed the emergence of a Coloured elite. Lebrun was severely persecuted by the Catholic clergy.

"Les plus dures persécutions qu'avaient endurées le Révérend, furent en conséquences dirigés par le clergé."

(E.Vanmeerbeck.*Lebrun*. Sentinelle. 1965)

This involved a period of *seasoning* of the slaves, of domesticating them so that they would not dare to rebel against white authority. From the start, French colonisers had depended on the compliant Catholic Church to do precisely this job of subordinating the Blacks under the magical authority of the Church. Therefore, this task of *adoucir* the slaves had been left into the hands of the Catholic Church. Hence their socialisation into European culture hegemonised the Blacks and the Coloured who *begged for and treasured their mental chains* under the white. (Ravi Dev). Thus, according to differences in race, colour of their skin, religion, culture, the different ethnic groups had to occupy unequal positions in economic, social or political hierarchy.

The lady writer of *Recollections of the Mauritius*, 1830, wrote that the Coloured and free Black slave masters far surpassed the White in atrocities towards the slaves, not stopping short of murders. She added that *those who were once slaves are always the most cruel masters.* This dichotomy sparked tremendous ambiguity, confusion and pain. It is human urge to strive upwards towards social mobility and seek to identify with one's imaginary European paternal identity. Likewise, those who had climbed to the middle stage tended to kick those at the bottom off the social ladder, particularly the Ti Creoles of Afro-Asian ancestry. As they were co-opted into the French-speaking bourgeoisie, they rejected both the Kreol language and Kreol culture and refused to identify themselves with the Ti Kreols The Coloured, insisting on the purity of blood, constituted themselves into an exclusive class, hermetically closed to the Black Kreols.

"The natives of India. The breed between their women and European produces a singularly handsome and graceful race, very beautiful, though very black, with regular features, expressive black eyes and long, straight fine hair."

(*A Transport Voyage to Mauritius*, by the Author of Padima, 1831)

Unfortunately, in a colonial society dominated by racial discrimination, the Coloured people became the direct products and victims of race prejudices. Therefore, one felt driven to reject one's black or brown maternal identity and culture. One is caught up in a deeply racist groove where one's importance is measured by the colour of one's skin. How frustrating could it be to be patronised by the White master, but into whose society one is never admitted as equal! And as a reaction, one would sink deeper into colour, class and race prejudices and smear others with such racism. Aye, there's the rub!

But in compensation, by the end of the nineteenth century, being somehow related to the Whites by blood, and envying the same Frenchness in culture and language, the Coloureds were employed as the trusted staffs in the sugar estates, in white-owned private companies, in the civil service and teaching. They secured some seats in the Council of Government. They threw up a powerful urban bourgeosie, deeply anti-Indian in their psychology. Indians who happened to work under Coloured bosses came under their violent and pathological hatred.

"Encore une fois et mieux qu'ailleurs je ressens le pathétique du complexe de couleur, plus sensible dans une île ou tout mûlatre est assuré d'être de la parenté des Blancs qu'il cotoie chaque jour et dont il n'a jamais ni l'amitié ni même la sympathie."
(*Tropiques Noirs*, Maurice Bedel)

Forming the tiny middle class, the average Coloured was generally upwardly mobile, looking up to the Whites as role models and therefore taking to education, French culture and manners as ladders of social promotion. The early adoption of French language and culture, the weapons of power, helped him to reach upward in the clerical or professional occupations. This enabled him to claim all the civilizational, economic, political and technological advantages pertaining to the White supremacy. To say the least, it conferred upon him tremendous comparative advantages over the descendants of slaves, the Ti Kreols who were marginalised and excluded from such privileges and social mobility. Consequently, the white master would very conveniently co-opt him as his preferred employee and close subordinate, closer to him by the colour of his skin, language and religion. Further, his adoption of French language, manners and culture stood firmly as badges of class superiority and also as separate identity from the brown and black races within our complex multi-racial society. In other words, he stood mid-way between the white on top of the social pyramid and the Blacks and Asians at the bottom of the pyramid.

It's all right for the poet to cry in the wilderness about negritude, about Black Power and Black is Beautiful, but daily reality is far otherwise.

Moi cet enfant de mille races
Pétri d'Europe et des Indes
Taillé plus profondément
Dans le cri du Mozambique
(Edouard Maunick, *Les Manèges de la mer.* Presence Africaine. Paris)

Anti-Indianism

The European planters had been the first to propagate anti-Indianism and coolitude as *a racialist ideology* which first they infected the coloureds. In their turn, the coloureds were to contaminate the Kreols with anti-Indian racialism in their resistance against freedom and independence. It is ironical that, in reaction to their being derided by the Oligarchy, the Coloureds of B.B- Rose Hill, though of *predominantly Indian descent* (J. C. de l'Estrac,2004) turned out to be a notoriously complex-ridden community, which disgorged anti-Indian venom. They did not think twice before heaping abuses upon the latter as Malbars Coolies, as pagans, as superstitious or as an inferior breed of humanity, *smelling spices, filthy, oily and barbarous*. They embraced and championed the anti-Indian ethnic politics of the white and became its most vociferous supporters. Hark, their hysterical war cry banging down our ears and reverberating across the corridor of history!

Malbars nou pas oulé!
Enveloppé nou pas oulé! (P.L.Nov. 1963)

While we understand that the Coloured have been the sad victims of White superiority complex, there was no excuse to discredit PIOs. The Whites had conditioned people in narrow, twisted euro-centrism and stuffed their minds with misconceptions and prejudices against everything Indian.

Self-evaluation

In a multi-racial society, *self-positioning* and self-evaluation is a *continuous process* which drives the lower classes on a course to catch up with their betters. The agenda of the evaluative process with its structural demarcations, as set from above by the white, produced a social status system which ran through the whole of the colonial and post-colonial society. At first it overpowered the subordinate classes, the descendants of slaves and of indentured labourers. But after the 1930's, with the flowering of social and political consciousness, it began to generate a new social dynamism and a competitive spirit- at every level, political, economic, social and educational. The self-evaluation is powerfully charged with intense emotion and passion, hence the anti-Indian hysterial war cry. There are times when collective emotions break out in paroxysm of hatred. The stage is set for violence. The contrary happens when a majority community gets trapped into the comfort zone. Then they tend to be complacent and uncompetitive and gradually they slip behind in the race for progress. This has happened to Indo-Mauritians under Paul Berenger's administration.

Since the onset of cultural and social reforms which had been shaking the Hindu community to its foundation and had instilled a new self-worth and purpose, the Hindus were stepping ahead with bold new confidence. In their onward march, they were to hit against the Coloured rearguards. The trouble is that the Coloureds had always compared themselves with the white and in their self-evaluation, they perceived themselves as being far superior to the barbarous Indians, who however, were seen as transgressing on their territory in the civil service and in teaching.

It's no wonder that the BB-RH Coloureds were known to exceed the white in their colour pretensions and arrogance. It was an uneasy relationship. The outcome was that the more the Indo-Mauritians felt hated and threatened the more determined they became to prove themselves in the eyes of their competitors. Wherever the Coloureds were employed in government, the private sector, and the banks, they did little to hide their feelings and they generally victimised the Indo-Mauritian subordinates or public. Now all this hatred flared up in a country where the White and the Coloured have been in minority up against a 70% Indo-Mauritian majority! Just imagine what would have happened if Indo-Mauritians had not seized the political kingdom. We must thank *the father of the nation* for having ensured everybody a climate of peaceful co-existence, justice and fairness according to Vedic-inspired humanitarian principles that has done honour to Mauritius as a lighthouse of democracy and multi-racial co-existence in this region- *a perfect blending* of the Eastern and Western civilizations.

The hysterical fear of Indianisation, of their being swamped and subordinated under a demographic wave of the hated Asiatic hordes, raised by the white-funded PMSD, which drove thousands of them packing to Australia never really materialised in the post-independence period. SSR maintained social harmony, guaranteed by a liberal democratic constitution, sustained by an undercurrent of the broad tolerant Indian culture. Mauritius would surely have plunged into a blood bath if its majority population were White or coloured, or Blacks or even Muslims. On the contrary, by the end of the twentieth century, the white were to recapture power by devious means.

And the more they hated the Indo-Mauritians the more they fuelled the Indian sentiment and drove the victims into the lap of Indian nationalism under Sookdeo Bissoondoyal's Independent Forward Bloc, inspired by Subash Chandra Bose nationalist militancy. But the bulk of the Indo-Mauritian voters rallied behind the Fabian, moderate, democratic Chacha Ramgoolam who took the country to independence and ensured peace, security and social harmony within the island.

Now, put yourself into the shoes of those descendants of Indian Immigrants who had to put up with the arrogance and intolerance of Coloured and White bosses. They believed that the rewards of office naturally came to them as they perceived themselves situated a step below the white. And there came those marauders, the Indians who were claiming their share of the pie. As an ethnic goup, they felt their position and privileges threatened by the outsiders. The Coloured saw it as a psychological and an economic struggle for the survival of their ethnic group against the social ambition of the upwardly mobile Indians. This rivalry for the limited job opportunities which they considered were their preserves and which were now being snatched by the outsiders naturally generated intense ethnic conflicts. You must admit that it can be a very harrowing experience requiring tremendous courage, patience and tolerance for any conscientious Indo-Mauritian having to work in such a stressful and threatening environment. Just imagine how harassed and victimised he could get whenever any incompetent and inexperienced junior members of the Coloured or white community got promoted over his head. The Indian whose parents had suffered and sacrificed to educate him and who had helped him to reach this class position by dint of hard work and merit had now to face the brunt of racial discrimination from his colleagues. This situation applies to thousands of people who have had to work under white administration in racist countries of the industrial west. Many PIO's have had to cry in silence over such abuses which flared up in a country with a 70% Indo-Mauritian majority!

After all, despite the big talk about meritocracy and democracy, very few Indo-Mauritians could scrape through the net and secure employment, especially at the higher level, within the big private sector companies. Consequently, one can hardly envisage the possibility of seeing an Indo-Mauritian heading any of these white-owned companies, including Rogers, IBL, or MCB or whatever while Indo-Mauritians, who form the majority population, had placed a white man as Prime Minister in 2003.

Coloureds, Creoles and Indians

AT THE very approach of independence and fearing reprisals from and competition with Hindu majority, the bulk of the Coloured people emigrated elsewhere to France, Australia, Britain, France and

Canada. But times have proved that the Hindus have remained forgiving, broadly tolerant and accommodating while the under-current of anti-Indiannism has gone unabated within the private sector. All the gloomy predictions about the bug-bear of Indianisation, the *envahisseurs Asiatiques,* the decline of westernisation, the loss of French hegemony raised by NMU since 1950 were proved wrong. Due to their subservience to the Catholic Church, controlled as a political arm by the Oligarchy, the Creoles had been lured away from the Labour Party into the arms of the white-controlled PMSD in order to defend French hegemony and French language, to oppose independence. They were even dragged into violent conflicts with Hindus and Muslims against the scare of Indianisation.

These same feelings had motivated hysterical anti-Indian persecution by the minority Black government under Burnham dictatorship in Guyana. Quite the contrary happened in Mauritius which became firmly entrenched as a mature democracy. The Black and other minorities had never had it so good as under constitutional government under tolerant and forward-looking Hindu Prime Ministers.

One can imagine the tension which such a negative attitude generates from successful professionals and businessmen from the Asian society who resent being looked down upon by both the White and Coloured bourgeoisie. Unfortunately, this social sickness has also contaminated many Indo-Christians to such an extent that, in Mauritius, unlike in India, the Church has banished the *tika*, the *mangulsutra*, the sari and all signs and symbols reminiscent of Indianness as a sign of barbarism and inferiority. Thus have they imbibed mouthfuls of those race prejudices and vices without being able to retain the core Asian virtues. In this strange *plus royaliste que le roi* self-defeating attitude, they have closely resembled the Coloured and free Black slave owners who, forgetting that once they had been slaves, were the worst persecutors of their slaves.

Perhaps, now, you can imagine the daily insults heaped on Indian minorities overseas in Britain, in the Caribbeans. Wherever descendants of Indian Immigrants are, they tend to do well as a result of their innate qualities, hard work and their culture. Instead of welcoming these as added values to their countries of adoption, the contrary happens. Lacking those virtues of honesty, hard work and a planned life, the racist Coloured or Black people resent the PIOs success. We all know how in 1972, Idi Amin Dada hounded out the 75,000 enterprising, self-reliant Indians from Uganda at the expense of ruining his country's economy. Apartheid South Africa imposed a series of anti-Indian legislation to quarter them in restricted areas, deprive them of access to education, job and trade opportunities and acess to buy landed properties. Other gruesome stories took place in Guyana when Cheddi Jagan was booted out of office to make room for Burnham.

The **Guyanese** planters had cleverly exploited cultural differences with the Indians. They diverted the common class struggle of the Indians and the blacks against them by deviating it into racial hatred. This strategy has been uncovered by the Guyanese historian and leader of the non-racial Working People's Alliance, **Walter Rodney** who argued how the Afro-Guyanese and Indian indentured labourers were made to submerge their common class struggle in order to confront each other as racial competitors. This came as the planters' response designed to neutralise the joint Black-and Indian class struggle against European capitalist-colonial and racial domination'

In Guyana, Burnham ignited the anti-Indian Black racism which deteriorated into the worst form of racism imaginable, compounded by discrimination, injustice, brutality, rapes, looting, home burning, insults, persecution, Human Rights abuses and all that. The same thing happened to the ousted former Prime Minister, Chaudhry, in Fiji, where anti-Indiannism is almost a daily occurrence. GOPIO is the only international institution to speak out against these abuses.

No, we don't mean that the Coloured are uniformly a bad lot. There were hundreds of shining examples of cultured, progressive and talented personalities, model teachers, professionals and administrators who have done yeoman service to their country. Side by side, there have been others who took their anti-Indian obsession too far and who could not help pretending to be what they were not. There is nothing like being at peace with oneself and trying to live at peace with others just to make this world a better and happier place for everybody concerned.

In other places, like Fiji, Indians are not allowed to own property and are not represented militarily. They have been victims of three coups. Similarly, in Guyana, Indians have been barred from entry into the police and the army which are reserved for Blacks.

"Though Fiji has ratified the UN Convention against all forms of racial discrimination. and yet there is State-sponsored, institutionalised discrimination.

Being an Indian in Fiji means being politically marginalised, racially discriminated against and having basic rights violated. India can and should do more to help people like us through the diplomatic channel."

(Mahindra Chaudhry, former Fiji Prime Minister, New Delhi, January 8, 2003, *Indian Express*, Pune).

The Old Enemy

In Mauritius, the white planters have consistently followed the same strategy of divide and rule by weakening the working class forces. They started by luring the Coloureds as their natural allies to their side. Next, they deviated the Kreols away from class struggle into anti-Indian racism, under the cover of the Catholic religion and the mythical identity of the General Population. At first they resorted to repressing the Labour leaders, Curé and Anquetil, followed by buying off the successive Labour trade unionists, until they blackmailed the Kreols under an emotional anti-Indian, anti- independence campaign under their manufactured King Creole, Gaetan Duval. Having made use of the Black Kreols, after independence, the white dumped them to join the LP-PMSD Coalition government to secure their economic interests under the Ramgoolam-Duval administration. Having got what they wanted, they hankered to secure power back into their hands and they found in one of their own, Paul Berenger, the likely candidate to wrench power away from the Labour Party. Then, by devious means, Berenger lured the Kreol electorate and tried to divide the Hindus into minority splinter groups as a strategy to capture power by revolutionary means, as had happened in Seychelles and Madagascar under Ratsirak. It's old wine in new bottle. In 1972, Paul Berenger confided to V.S.Naipaul:-

"I doubt whether we'll go past this year without the government crumbling or an uprising or general elections."

Having witnessed the coup d'etat in the West Indies, the journalist-novelist V.S.Naipaul warned that the White could muster the South Africans to stage a coup d'etat and wrench power from the Indians. Aware of the alliance of the old enemy with the new enemy, Sir Seewoosagur Ramgoolam told the writer that

"I think this new movement, the MMM, is a devious approach by these same people to revive themselves. I think they want their own back on me especially and my party".

(V. S. Naipaul. *The Overcrowded Baracoon*, Penguin Books. 1972)

The African Diaspora

BEING DAILY humiliated, oppressed and treated as objects and chattels in the slave market, the African slaves and their descendants assimilated a load of inferiority complex, compounded by race prejudices from a distorted colonial, post-colonial and racist background. Having been de-Africanized, uprooted from their ancestral and tribal kinships, the slaves were cast into an alien environment. Since they were mixed up with people from different tribes, customs and languages, they lost touch with their original languages, traditions and their ethnic identity that gave a meaning to life. As they mixed and inter-married with other tribes, drawn from

West Africa, East Africa, the Mozambiquans, the Malagassy and a sprinkling of the Indian slaves, they had diluted their African blood. The writer, Charles Baissac, 1831-92, attributed the loss of the Black Africanness to the westernisation of the Black Creoles, the increasing mixing of races, the emergence of the Coloured and inter-marriage with the Indian slaves.

"The Black Creole population first modified by European intercourse, and in a far greater measure, by inter-mixing with the Indian races. The original type of Creole is fast disappearing."

(Albert Pitot, A.Macmillan, ed. *Mauritius Illustrated*, 1914).

Under the pressure of colour and race prejudices, Catholicism and the demonstration effect of the Coloured, whom they saw as their half-brothers, the Blacks forged a new Creole identity, oriented towards westernisation, which they strongly desired and envied. It is obvious that when they had lost their languages, they had lost their memory, their voices, their articulation and their Africanness. They were *silenced into static, stagnant non-beings, enjoying no self-importance, no self-esteem, no self-confidence, nothing*! They had lost their vitality. They felt absolutely vulnerable and powerless. They had to submit to daily abuses, flogging and violence and were reduced into infantile level. They ceased to exist as persons but only as other people's property, as chattels. They had no land, no privileges and no status. They simply lost their dignity as they were compelled to bow down to their masters all the time. They became thoroughly dependent on their masters and lost all faculties to stand on their own legs, to think for themselves or rely on themselves.

(Interview of Prof. Joseph.E.Harris, Howard University, Washington D.C. *Femmes des Iles*. June 1985)

And since the Slaves and the Black Creoles acquisced and qiuetly submitted to white supremacy and they never dared to rise in revolt against and shake off White racism, they never made any serious bid to assert their independence and identity. Consequently, they allowed themselves to remain permanently dominated, subordinated as the mental slaves of the white. This mental state of subservience, alienation and anomie, meekly accepting the inferiority status reproduced itself from generation to generation and hardened into Creole culture. Similarly, at the approach of independence in the 1960's, the Coloured who felt insecurely squeezed between the White at the top and the Asians and Blacks at the bottom of the social pyramid had no alternative but to pack up and emigrate when they felt betrayed by the White. In this respect, the Indians differed from the Coloured and the Creoles in totally rejecting white supremacy and in striking for their own Indianness and national independence at the earliest opportunity.

The Wretched of the Earth

By 1835, on the abolition of slavery, in a colonialist and racist **WIN-LOSE** situation and a totally unjust racist society, the Whites held the joker and all the cards thickly packed against their victims. The ex-slave owners came out always as the big winners as they had pocketed the jackpot of two million pounds of slave compensation from Britain. As usual, the big losers were the ex-slaves. Illiterate, absolutely helpless, exploited, leaderless, the ex-slaves, mostly of Mozambiquan and Malagassy origins, in a moment of frenzy like birds first let out of their cages, were driven away. They vanished from the cane fields and opted to live outside the plantations- according to official reports. The truth is that since they demanded high wages, they were literally kicked out from the plantations to make room for the more docile and less expensive Indentured labour.

"Le jour même où sonna leur liberté, ce jour là ils furent chassés de presque toutes les propriétés." (Remy Ollier)

It was a hard and painful decision to break away from society, determined by the ex-slave owners and planters. They knew that they had a price to pay before they could enjoy their new-won freedom. Their behaviour was determined more by emotion than by economic rationale. They had been so wounded by the atrocities of slavery that by all means they wanted to get away from the clutches of the white. Their overriding ambition was to enjoy their freedom to work or not to work as it pleased them, free from any legal or formal contract, indenture or any form of compulsion, particularly as they had little trust in the white planters. They preferred to scrounge for a living as unskilled and skilled manual workers, as market gardeners, small farmers, in and around Port Louis where they also worked as dockers, porters, servants and carters.

"In the streets of Port Louis, the slaves who are employed as scavengers are yoked together to carts and exhibit a very offensive and humiliating spectacle."

(Rt Hon. George Mullay to Sir Charles Coleville, No 56, 8th May 1829)

Others migrated as squatters into the coastal and the Black River areas as fishermen, subsistance farmers, small peasants and market gardeners, independent of the sugar estates. But they were soon driven away from all the land they had purchased, squatted upon or occupied either in Plains Wilhems, Port Louis or Black River. Abandoned by the Oligarchy and the British officials for having deserted the plantations, they slipped behind into a wandering, landless class, condemned to poverty, stagnation and marginalisation, in fact *an excluded community*. They were grilled into the vicious circle of poverty:- unemployment, lack of capital, lack of savings, victims of illiteracy, alcoholism, chronic diseases and epidemics of cholera, malaria, yellow fever, high infant mortality which decimated their population during the years of epidemics, 1840-56. Being physically strong, they did not shirk away from taking on hard physical labour as dockers, as masons. They were dimly aware of the difficulties ahead of them since they had turned their back on the plantations. But this was the price they had to pay for having abandoned agriculture in an essentially agricultural economy. Hence, they had cut themselves off from the opportunity to develop into a productive and land-owning class.

"They were not only fleeing from slavery's memories but from the inequalities that existed in a free society, as defined by planters. A process of marginalization of ex-slaves began after the 1840's which intensified over the years."

(Vijaya Teelock, Journal of Mauritian Studies. MGI.1990).

In a society, defined by the planters, plagued with colour and race discrimination, they were cruelly made aware of their black skin and their inferior status. Their unwitting neglect of the productive sector caused them to lose their economic grip and access to land ownership. Consequently, they slipped behind as casualties and victims of circumstances. Since birth, they were branded with deep inferiority complex that reduced them into comparative losers in a harshly competitive racialist society into which they were thrust at the receiving end or the so-called *dependency complex* of colonised peoples (Frantz Fanon).

White-Masked, Black Skinned

They were trapped under the white domination and were fast de-Africanised. Conditioned by white prejudices, they were told that Africa was the Dark Continent. The connecting link was brutally snapped. The pride in one's historical heritage was replaced by cultural dependence on western cultural domination, a situation which alienated them profoundly so that they were to lag behind in education as they could never command their master's English or French idioms. This led to a strong rejection of their African identity. They had no choice but to emulate the white man, his ideas, manners and prejudices as caricatures of *White masks, Black skins.* (Frantz Fanon).

This dependency mentality prevented them from assuming and developing their independent personality and individuality. They were always in the shadow of the white and the coloured. Working as domestic servants and orbiting around the white and Coloured bourgeoisie, they came to desire and envy westernisation as a way of life. They tried to emulate French manners, French music and songs, costumes which they assimilated into the Creole sub-culture. They went through a *whitening* process by assimilating table manners, the cleanliness, home furnishing and household habits of the White. This fostered an uncritically Euro-centric approach of utter dependence on the White and a total rejection of their Afro-Asianness.

Besides, the Catholic missionaries fuelled the flame of anti-Indian racism and the Blacks perceived the Malbars Coolies with the same contempt. The Church went about to denigrate the *Coolies as heathens, uncivilized, superstitious and filthy savages*, as if they were aliens freshly landed from an outer planet and who practised outlandish religion, the worshippers of elephant-headed and monkey-faced gods. And the Blacks swallowed the anti-Indian propaganda, line, hooks and bait: They followed rat-like and got drowned into deeper waters the tune of the White bagpipe player.

"Les Créoles ont été piéges par ce mariage parfait d'une certaine culture française et d'un certain catholicisme. Cela explique son retard sur le plan politique....L'église, depuis son origine à Maurice, est marquée par une certaine bourgeoisie occidentale surtout française.... Les descendants d'esclaves se laissèrent embarquer dans une entreprise de défense de la culture et de la langue française contre une soi-disante menace d'orientalisation."

(*La Situation des Créoles de L'île Maurice.* By L'Organisation Creole et Culture)

They figured themselves as being better-off than the newly enslaved Indians, permanently harassed, hunted down and jailed by Vagrancy Laws as once their ancestors, the maroons, had been. They thanked their stars on having escaped that unenviable fate.

Marriage Customs. Though they pathologically suppressed their African ancestry, they could not get away entirely from their African roots, instincts, psyche, genes and traditions which surfaced in their family customs. In their collective consciousness and according to past traditions, the Kreols retained part of the African custom of choosing their bride and changing partners freely, *nec pran amené*, without caring for parental consent, ceremony or loyalty to life-long conjugal obligations. Originally, according to the African customary law, the marriage had to be sanctioned and blessed by African chiefs after the offer of the appropriate dowry. But in the historical case of the Kreols, the dowry system had been dropped and no security was offered to the female concubines. In matters of sexuality, it became a permissive society into which the lonely Indians were lured into inter-mixing, during the early period of indentureship, 1835-46, owing to a chronic shortage of Indian female partners, caused by the gross disproportion of the sexes. This was to follow and to reproduce the pattern of inter-marrying with Creole women, earlier started under French administration in Ile de France.

The difference is that African marriage customs ensured that the African male could look after his polygamous wives and children spread all around him in the neighbouring huts. In the permissive, free Kreol society, it's a free choosing of partnership without much thought or obligation for the future. It's a response to an immediate mating instinct without the guarantee of life-long survival. It could also be a matter of mutual and temporary convenience without the social restraints of elders and other family members to stand watch over the couple. It's an entirely free agreement by mutual consent which could also end abruptly. This conjugal custom has also prevailed among the other Blacks in the Caribbeans.

In contrast, Indian marriage is an elaborate affair reaching back to millennia of culture, civilisation, religion and philosophy as examplified in the Ramayana. The *Kanyadan* is performed publicly around the sacred fire and the new couple steps into the *Grihasta Ashram* or conjugal life, with the blessings and approval of society. Henceforth, a new family, firmly nested in Indian culture and Vedic traditions, is created and it acts as a powerful nucleus which provides support to the children. The couple is riveted together inside the larger extended family and social network.

While the Indian labourers adhered to their customs, religion, traditions and valued their Indianness, the White-masked, Black - skinned Kreols had totally and unconditionally rejected their Afro-Asian-Malagassy identity. Having been *whitened* by contact with French culture, the Creoles regarded themselves as a step below the Coloured but superior to Black Africans and to the Asians. Yet there surfaced the vestiges of their African culture, buried deep inside their genes and their subconscious. Consequently, they felt more inclined to enjoy the immediate pleasures of life, without bothering for the morrow, as the sega goes *amuser Kréol.*

The Story of Alain

Take the typical story of Alain Soopaya, grand-son of Fernand Soopaya, a taxi owner and driver, Alain, inhabiting cité B, Beau Bassin, followed on his father's footsteps and at the early age of 18, he joined the CEAL as a caterpillar helper- driver. Shortly, he graduated into a machine operator and started earning big money. At 23, he migrated to Saudi Arabia as a heavy machine operator and earned fat money. On holidaying to Mauritius, he squandered his savings of Rs. 110,000 on renting a contract car, dining and wining in big restaurants. He went back to Saudi Arabia for another two years and back home once more, he threw away Rs 150,000 on lavish living within five months of holidaying and feasting with friends.

In 1987, he returned to join Rogers as fitter-petrole-mechanic on the ship platforms for 23 months, then shifted to Adam on Ville de Mahébourg ship and moved to a variety of highly paid jobs at international companies, here and abroad- in Madagascar, Diego Suarez, earning huge sums of money. Then he took a long holiday to Madagascar, Seychelles and Bangkok where he spent all his money on expensive restaurants and travels. After another spell at other companies, he took another holiday which he spent travelling as a tourist in a contract car and spending extravagantly with friends in bars and restaurants. Now, nearing his fifties, when he has been six months without a job, without money to pay rent for his house, or to procure his habitual Black label and expensive cigarettes and food, he came to realise that he had frittered away his fortune by pursuing his Creole penchant. He wished he had preserved his more frugal Indian instinct from his father's side. He regrets he had not emulated his six Indo-Mauritian friends who had worked by his side as common labourers at Saudi Arabia, earning a quarter his wages and who have all purchased a plot of land and a house on it.

At the same time, this basic African *happy-go-lucky* attitude, externalised in the big hearty resonant African laughter, has spared the Creoles from stress, hypertension and diabetes which normally plague the Europeans and Indians. In one thing, they were truly living up to the Vedic mantra which said that there are a hundred cures for a disease but there is one cure for a hundred diseases- and that is laughter.

"L'ancien esclave d'Afrique ou de Madagascar avait le don du sourire. Toute la paresse du Sud était dans sa voix, toutes les chansons aussi. Il a su apprendre aux autres à rire son grand rire de gorge, à chanter à pleins poumons, son folklore lointain et transpose, à danser ses ségas bachiques."

(Regis Fanchette, *Charmes de la Vie Créole*, Seve magazine)

The General Population and the Indo-Mauritians

Forming part of the wider Christian network of General Population since 1861, they valued the White as cultural models and the Coloured as supposedly their half-brothers but who kept them at arms' length. Similarly, they embraced the race prejudices of the leading members of the G.P. They tended to regard the Indentured labourers, living a rigorous life of vegetarianism, sacrifice, waking up at three in the morning, toiling in the fields, as belonging to an inferior, uncivilised and an alien race. The Blacks put on a negative label on what were really positive and winning attributes of the Indians which they derided as being: *"money-hungry, niggardly, stingy, cunning, energetic, resourceful, miserly, ambitious, avaricious, crafty, clannish"* (Ravi Dev, 2000).

In their turn, the Indians, aware of the value of their culture and religion, had worked out their own personal evaluation of the African and the European. While they believed in hard work and the philosophy of self-upliftment and self-reliance, they saw no objection to the White man's evaluation of the *African stereotype as being constitutionally lazy, indolent, pleasure-loving, violent, lacking assuidity and regularity and seeking immediate satisfaction.*

In A.Macmillan's *Mauritius Illustrated*, the Oligarch, Sir Henri Leclezio, described the Afro-Malagassy Creoles as the inferior class given to a variety of odd jobs like wood cutters, cooks, carpenters, masons, cane cutters, carters. Hence, they were condemned to remain an impoverished, insecure class from which no elite or bourgeois class could possibly emerge.

According to prof. Hubert Gerbeau, the two myths of Blackness and the hereditary laziness of the slave and of his descendants has prompted the arrival of the Indian indentured labourers who have consequently submerged the Blacks.

(Hubert Gerbeau Conference on Slavery. MGI Feb. 1985)

Ravi Dev holds that the Caribbean Indian had come to re-formulate the caste system into which he had incorporated all castes into the unitary *jati* and accordingly the African had been slotted into the non-status of the outcaste. In Guyana, the Blacks define the Caribbean as an African nation and the Indians were expected to assimilate the Creole culture. In political terms, it means that the Africans would go to any length to back up their legitimacy in retaining government jobs to which they felt entitled and from which Indians are excluded as the out-groups. In Mauritius, this obsession to evaluate one's group performance against the rival ethnic groups has fuelled the debate on the relative deprivation of the Creoles. Instead of facing up to the white and revolting against injustice, exploitation, colonialism and racism, the Indians tended to look inward, submit to suffering, sacrifices and self-punishment, resorted to wife beating, alcoholism, depression and suicide.

Enslaved by westernisation and enmeshed in the ideology of the Catholic Church, the slaves and the Creoles sought escape from daily stress and poverty in the physical pleasures of life. The Oligarchy could always escape from their social, political and moral responsibility towards the Creoles by cleverly diverting the conflict of class antagonism into a convenient anti-Indian hostility and race war. Now, instead of revolting against the wealthy racist minority in order to throw the yoke of oppression off their shoulders, the underdogs have gladly *collaborated with their very oppressors in the exercise of class exploitation, against their own interests*. They could never get together to fight a common cause against their oppressors. Quite the contrary, they would let down anybody who dared take up arms on their own behalf, just as they betrayed Sir Seewoosagur Ramgoolam who had dedicated all his life in combatting the evils of poverty, ignorance, ill-health and exploitation and in the establishement of the Welfare State. Instinctively, they rallied to the call of the exploiting White and the Catholic Church in its racialist opposition to the Indo-Mauritians in the march towards independence.

"Autre fait à retenir c'est que les esclaves des Mascareignes originaires de tant de régions d'Afrique et de Madagascar se méfiaient l'un l'autre et ne pensaient jamais à se soulever contre l'oppresseur. Ce sentiment de méfiance pour son prochain est un phénomene qui a été transmis de génération en génération et l'on retrouve de nos jours ce manque de cohésion, de fraternité, voire cet esprit d'entreaide si essentielle pour l'évolution socio-économique des groupes d'individus dans toutes les sociétés."

(Benjamin Moutou. Conference on Slavery in S-W Indian Ocean. MGI. Feb. 1985)

What follows is that from time to time, the Blacks have diverted their explosion of anger away from the white culprits in order to externalise it as racialised attacks on the suppressed Indian communities, the eternal scapegoats. Such eruption of anti-Indian violence has taken place quite frequently in the Caribbean islands where Indians are daily under Black racist attacks. This anti-Indian sentiment had been politically nurtured and exploited by the Oligarchy, the PMSD and the MMM. We have had a taste of anti-Indian ethnic violence around 1965 to 67, ahead of the pre-independence elections and in the February 1999 Kreol riot against State institutions.

The multi-ethnic composition of the society is recognized in the **Mauritian constitution** which broadly lumps the Mauritian population of varied African, Asian, European origins into two broad categories- the *General Population* and the Indo-Mauritians. The Mauritian constitution had therefore legalised the political creation of the GP under one ethnic umbrella. The idea was to create a balanced multi-cultural society in which social and political harmony is ensured by a system of checks and balances, including the *Best Loser System* designed to give adequate representation to each ethnic group. In this context, the General Population comprises all the Christian communities- the Whites, the Coloured, the Afro-Creoles and the Sino-Mauritians. The second category is made up of the Indo-Mauritians, comprising People of Indian Origins, Hindus and Moslems, both sharing a broad Indian culture and common past history

The label General Population distinguishes the Afro-Kreols, descendants of slaves from the Indo-Mauritians, descendants of Indentured labourers. Consequently, the Euro-centric Afro-Creoles, belonging to the common General Population, naturally envied the White as icons of Frenchness, French language and culture. But the great contradiction lies in the fact that while the Kreols share the label of General Population with the Whites, in practice the *power relationship* has boiled down into a predominantly master-servant-relationship. The ethnic reality is that the Whites clearly demarcate themselves from the Kreols whom they keep at arms' length. There is no social mixing. To the white, according to Sir Henri Leclesio, the leader of the Oligarchs, the Black Kreols only constitute a vast reservoir of cheap menail jobs. The huge economic, social and cultural gaps separating the White minority from the Kreols are exarcebated by traditional colour, race prejudices, dating to the days of slavery and after.

(Suzanne Chazan Gullig, *Journal of Mauritian Studies*. Vol. 2 No 1, MGI.2003)

Being a Kreol

In the Caribbean islands, the Christian and Euro-centric urban-dwelling Blacks took to western education and better jobs while the Indians held back in the plantations and avoided the denominational schools run by Christian organisations. But in Mauritius, it was the French-speaking Coloured bourgeoisie which took to education and white-collar jobs. The Blacks did not show any great inclination in the matter of education, either. They hovered on the fringe of society. They could not entirely get away from their African propensity to care only for the moment which prompted them to pick up from the White some of the wasteful aristocratic habits of fast spending, lavish living, Saturday night fever, sometimes ending in an orgy. This spending and showing off propensity is most apparent during festive occasions like weddings, pic nics, week-ends, pay day, Easter, Christmas, and New Year occasions followed by long spells of eating, drinking, dancing and merry-making.

Accordingly, they showed a pronounced fondness for luxury, for a life of *jhalsa*, enjoyment, music, sega dancing and festivity and modern fashion. Their overriding interests centred on the pleasure of the moment. They spent their income lavishly on eating, drinking and feasting with friends in a bid to seek immediate satisfaction, regardless of tomorrow. Nothing could be more important than spending lavishly on food and drinks, dress and shoes to show off particularly during wedding occasions, *to mette to l'armoire* as the saying goes. This trend also flared up among the factory girls and women who vied with one another in wearing the latest fashion. During the boom years almost every adult member of the Creole family could work and earn, yet few ever bothered to save for a rainy day. Many thought that the sunny day would last for ever.

Where have gone the high wages, bonuses and compensations enjoyed by the former dockers and the Ilois? In the long run, they have remained a wasteful and spending community, ever dependent on the dole and on State generosity. Without the sacrifice, the saving, the hard work, the long-term planning, the accumulated capital required for social mobility, the Blacks got caught up in the vicious circle of high consumption, indebtedness, dependence and poverty. It is not surprising that they have hardly been visible in trade, commerce, industry, in business, in the professions and in landed property. Their propensity to spend as quickly as they earned has resulted in little savings, in their failure to buy property which could be used as collateral to raise loans for investments. This could also explain the absence of an indegenous Creole entrepreneurial and professional class. They seemed to have accepted the culture of poverty and dependence on white employers and on welfare state hand-outs as the best options.

According to Dr Espelencia Baptiste, Haiti, the decline of the Mauritian Ti Kreols, the left-overs of slavery, can be partly explained by the *phenomenon of class reproduction* or the way they are stratified, trapped and slotted into the working class. In turn, this is a product of their failure in education which itself is a consequence of the alienation of their children from the educational system. The school system has been producing a high rate of failures and drop-outs, particularly among Kreol children from deprived areas of the *cités*, in the notorious ZEP schools. While educational *opportunity* has been open to all through free education, the real problem is one of *access* to the benefits of education. It appears that the Kreol children have difficulties in mastering the two foreign languages, English and French. The Kreol children do not have access to these languages at home where they speak only Kreol. Despite the interests of the parents in their academic success, the children get bored and alienated in class. Hence, the children fall behind. Besides, many Kreol children have generally been the targets of racial discrimination in the schools by teachers who have low academic expectations from such pupils whom they sometimes insult as Kreol Mozambique, the worst form of abuse imaginable!

Yet all children, irrespective of race, colour, class or sex have the potential to succeed as demonstrated in the author's book, *How Your Child Can Be Winner*. Dr Baptiste believes that slavery has nothing to do with a child's academic failure, since slavery is well behind us as it occurred 300 years ago. What matters is the motivation and support a child receives at home as there are countless examples of children of Kreol dockers, of masons, of fishermen who have made it to the top in education through parental support and hard work.

(Interview of Espelencia Baptiste, PH.D, Port Louis, August 2004).

Undeterred by the criticism, the Indians stuck to their frugal habits and their family life values. They had submitted themselves voluntarily to the discipline of indentured labour economy based on contracts, a regime of negotiations, leading to bargaining and the growth of the class of small holders and the ultimate prospects of social mobility. The Blacks had opted for a short-term working class culture providing little scope for social mobility and which lies at the root of their marginalisation, also decried as *Malaise Créole*.

The joint family became the nucleus of mutual support. In the villages, family members used to work co-operatively in order to keep the wolf from the door, to save to buy a plot of land, to build a better house and improve their economic conditions somewhere in a neighbouring village, away from the grips of the White planters. In contrast, conditioned by their past experience as slaves who had been forced to do unpleasant work, the Blacks did not show the same concern to secure a plot of land and build a house thereon. In general, Indians were prepared to impose self-restraint on their personal desires, plan their lives sometimes encompassing three generations ahead, including building a house, educating their children, marrying them and attending to their needs.

The Creoles did not have such priorities. Above everything alse, they valued their freedom and resented having to work for others which they considered as *evil* and something to be avoided at all costs. The Creole workers are notorious for absenteeism, *lundi cordonnier*, and for their inability to stick for long to a job. This is how Bourdieu is proved right when he talks of the reproduction of poverty and *class reproduction*:-

There is little scope for upward social mobility when generations after generations follow the same manual occupations, either as masons, carpenters or dockers. Consequently, they do not think as individuals caring for long-term progress, eager to compete with one another as do the Sino-Mauritians who want to keep up with the Joneses, that is, the rival clans. Kreols do not believe in postponing immediate satisfaction as an investment in long-term rewards. Left-overs of slavery, they had assimilated the lavish spending habit of the Whites, *vive kuma Blan*, forgetting that the Whites had got land, slave and indentured labour for nothing.

Lawlessness. As the domestic servants of the white, they had also observed how the racist masters had shown no compunction to punish, humiliate, whip or abuse the slaves and how the lawless despots got away with breaking all civilised rules.

"Cette punition n'est qu'un badinage si on la compare à la rigueur avec laquelle sont souvent traités les Noirs d'habitation. Car je dirai à la honte de certains hommes, il en est qui poussent la barbarie jusqu'à faire donner à leurs malheureux esclaves cent coups de fouet et même plus. Après ce cruel traitement, ils font frotter les fesses ensanglantés de leurs nègres avec un mélange de piment, de sel et de vinaigre.". (Grégoire Avine)

Picking up the lawless habits of their white role models, many of the Ti Kreols tended to adopt violence and the rule breaking habit, drinking, gossiping, gambling, big spending and entertaining friends. Deviations in sex, in moral lapses, family life were regarded as normal behaviour so long as they could get a kick out of it. The problem of poverty and indebtedness spawns a series of *other social ills*- namely delinquency, drug abuse, alcoholism, prostitution, broken homes, neglected children and petty offences which are quite rampant in many agglomerations, particularly the cites, lying in the outskirts of certain urban centres. Fortunately, there has been a recent movement to whip up Kreol consciousness in order to address these social issues.

Indians are often accused of being too emotionally attached to their family values. Marriages are mostly arranged and monitored by parents and celebrated as an important event in one's life. Within the Asian family, the parents or the elder brothers and sisters tend to sacrifice in order to invest in the education and welfare of the junior members. It fosters a sense of social responsibility and solidarity which promotes social mobility. In return, the children tend to respect and trust the authority and expereince of the well-meaning elders. In its turn, this fosters personal discipline. It lubricates the social system and maintians peace and harmony. Such social discipline is rarely seen within the Kreol family.

There is more permissiveness among the Kreols who choose their own partners without parental consent and consequently do not have the same social or moral responsibility in their married life, a factor which leads to frequent broken homes, change of partners, large families, neglected and street children. The Kreol youth do not brook parental interference in their enjoyment of a free life and they have no kinship solidarity, no strong family ethos which otherwise bind the Asians solidly to their homes.

(Thomas Hylland Eriksen, *Journal of Mauritian Studies*, MGI, Vol. 1 No 2, 1988)

Those Left Behind

At last, the inevitable had to happen. The ground had been prepared for the growth of Mauritian nationalism, spearheaded by Dev Virahsawmy and his advocacy of the Kreol language, encouraged by the Marxist-revolutionry MMM in its heady days in the 1970's under Siven Chinien's songs which blended the Indian with the sega. By the 1980's, the MMM abandoned its Marxist ideology to embrace economic liberalism. In the 1980's and 90's, Mauritius had emerged as a semi-industrialised country, marked by rapid economic development. Coincidentally, the dawning of Kreol consciousness, the search for the Kreol identity, the feeling of having been excluded and left out in the cold in the race for economic and social progress had sent a wave of malaise and protest among the Ti Kreols. In 1993, Rev. Cerveaux coined the phrase *malaise creole* to indicate the state of social exclusion. It led to a spate of soul searching and of new self-evaluation.

From it came the feeling that the Kreols had better take their distance from the Euro-centric Catholic Church, the White and the Coloured which had manipulated them as puppets and which had used colour hierarchy as the yardstick for entry into upward class mobility. After all, they discovered that the Church, dominated by the White and the Coloured, had consistently let them down. The myth built around Père Laval, brought by the Oligarchy to assuage the ex-slaves was exploded as it was realised that he had done nothing to enhance their civil or political rights but had rather acted meekly as an instrument to domesticate them to suit the white masters.

"Les anciens maîtres trouvèrent dans l'église une alliée inavouée pour rétablir une autoritée éffritée."
(Chan Low, 1999)

In 1985, the new Kreol back-to-Africa- consciousness rang in the music and songs of Kaya, inspired by Black American and Caribbean awareness, the phenomenon of Seggae, Rasta and Rastafarianism. The new Kreol movement carried a psychological flavour when it prompted a self-recognition awareness, a self-acceptance, a rejection of the unconditional Euro-centric approach, colour prejudices, servility to the Whites and the racial labels of the past. It went beyond the *sega engagé* type, dating back to the militant days, towards a search into one's Afro-Asian roots which were reflected in their songs and music, borrowing both from African and Indian costumes, tunes, instruments and traditions. Thus, we had Kaya singing: *"Pa laont ki mo pe dire mo ene batar"*. Renald Collet of the Racinn Seggae sang of the *"Racine mélanzé, Ras mélanze, kiltir mélanzé, la mizik mélanze"* while Ras Natty Baby sang of *Mo pep ti esklav, mo ène ti Mozambik, mo sévé crépi"*. The upwardly educated Creoles of mixed Indian, Black and

European descent, though lost to the Indian diaspora, are now increasingly reconciled to the reality of their mixed descent and tend to drop off their rabid anti-Indian posture.

But racial tensions simmer under the surface. Since the 1970's, in a bid to rally the Creole electorate and in its policy leading to a cummulative anti-Hindu build-up, the MMM had been pointing fingers at the Hindu State bourgeoise. The Hindus were blamed for the scanty presence of the Kreols among the bureaucratic, professional and business classes. This accusation flared up in the February 1999 racial riots against symbols of the state authorities in Port Louis. Few have bothered to identify the mechanism by which the traditional elites have reproduced themselves in power over the last three hundred years at the expense of pushing the Ti Kreols deep into the vicious circle of poverty.

"Dans les années 1950 et 1960, pendant que les familles créoles s'adonnaient joyeusement a des libations alcooliques et autres, dans les baitkas, dans les madrassas, des missionaires hindous et musulmans prêchaient à leurs co-religionnaires les devoirs de parents, d'éducateurs, auprès de leurs enfants. Ils leur prêchaient sans relache les vertus de l'épargne, du travail bien fait, la necessite de gagner son pain a la sueur de son front, le sens de dignite qui commande à un homme et a sa famille de sortir au plus vite de l'assistant. Les avons-nous entendus réclamer une quelconque compensation pour la coolitude subie depuis 1840?

Au sortir de la Seconde Guerre mondiale, les masses hidoues et musulmanes et meme chinoises n'étaient pas forcement mieux lotis que les créoles. Les champs de cannes ne leur étaient pas réservés ni les collèges privés car ils savaient alors ne pas pouvoir compter sur les collèges confessionnels qui leur étaient pratiquement fermés. C'est quand même pas l'Etat qui fait qu'il y a aujourd'hui plethore de médecins, d'avocats, d'ingénieurs non-chrétiens et peu de professionnels creoles. Et pouvons et devons nous poser la question de savoir ce que font ces rares professionnels créoles pour leur communauté tandis que tant d'universitaires non-chrétiens doivent leur éducation à la générosité d'un oncle plus fortuné. L'esprit de

partage, le sens de la solidarite mutuelle, familiale ou autre, seraient-ils devenus soudainement des valeurs non-chrétiennes?"
(Yvan Martial, Business Magazine.1 July 2003)

The Kreol Language

Earlier, we have seen how the slaves and their descendants had been made easy targets of assimilation. In that unequal society, erected on slavery, colonialism and racism, they hardly suspected that the more they assimilated western culture, the more they would have to trail way behind the French-speaking bourgeoisie. Finally, they had to invent their own weapons to fight their oppressors. Since they could not fight back openly they put up a strong underground resistance. They hit back by using the very weapon of the bourgeoisie and driving its sharp edge right into them. They asserted themselves through the new idioms which they invented out of the remnants of old eighteenth century French mixed with African linguistic strucutres, including Bantu and Swahili, into what was to constitute the very essence of Mauritian Kreol. The Kreol language carries within it everything to do with Creolism, including its folk lores, its popular religion, reminiscent of Malagassy and African beliefs and practices, the Kreol way of living, its music and songs, its *sirandanes* or riddles and folklores. We can still hear the rhythm of the sega resounding with its African and Malagassy beats, with the drums, the ravanne, the maravanne and the dance, *O la hé la la hé*! echoing around the bonfire.

Their historic achievement had been to develop a new Kreol identity through the Kreol language and folk culture. They put up a linguistic and cultural resistance against white onslaught, bolstered by the government-the judiciary and the Catholic Church which had all unconditionally supported and justified slavery, now internationally condemned as a crime against humanity. The Kreol language gave them the weapon to push back White domination which pressed like strings round their necks. The Kreols were overpowered with the weight of western culture, the French language, the Catholic Church, colonial administration, capitalism, racism, property ownership, legislation, technology and, above all, race prejudices- against which they had only one weapon- the Creole language, their badge, their identity.

Once liberated, the slaves were clean forgotten and cheated of their rights. They did not benefit from any compensation whatsoever- no money, no land, no job training or job opportunities or economic plan were offered them. Since that time they had been left as paupers.

"The negro population have been thrown exclusively on their own resources, a circumstance so unhappy with regard to their social progress and development."

(Gladstone to William Gomm, 14 May, 1846)

Having been dis-africanised, the Blacks thought they had *whitened* themselves with the Euro-centric brush and were genuine partners in the General Population and were therefore a step ahead of the children of the Coolies, still caught knee deep in agriculture. But the Indians had not given up and had walked out of the plantation boundaries to set up their own villages and to strike out for their cultural-social-religious-economic-and political independence.

Yet, the instruments of torture had left deep scars into the minds and hearts of the Afro-Creoles who still have to struggle hard to purge themselves of the stigma of past racial humiliation.

Inter and Intra Ethnic Relations

To sum up, the social landscape has somewhat changed from the days of Albert Pitot's social classification. The White is still the dominating force in the economy, in Mauritius, in South Africa, in the Caribbeans, in the west. In Mauritius, they are closely followed by the Chinese who have excelled in business, trading and the professions. The Chinese are known to keep hermetically close to themselves and networking with the Chinese diaspora in Asia and SEA. Next in importance are the Gujarati Muslims who have traditionally excelled in commerce, just as they have done in Reunion Island, in South Africa, in Europe. They have pulled the other Bhojpuri-speaking Muslims into petty trade and commerce.

Generally, the Hindus have shied away from trade and business, except for a handful of Gujarati, Sindhi and Marwari families who are among the leading traders in the country. Starting as Indentured labourers, the Hindus have focused on education and they boast of a substantial proportion of professionals, sub-professionals, civil servants, teachers and policemen, apart from agricultural workers and small planters.

Unfortunately, *the Indian children had to pay for the sins of their fathers*. The diaspora could not get away from the devastation caused by the social, linguistic, geographical and political divisions which had marked the social and political history of mainland India. The weakness of the mother country had been its *lack of a strong political and religious power structure at the centre, held together by a collective patriotic and nationalist consciousness*. It only required a handful of organized invaders to overrun Bharat and subjugate its people for nearly a millennium. Similarly, in the former colonies, after enjoying a honeymoon of political power, the Indians had relapsed into the comfort zone coma and had started fragmenting themselves into conflicting linguistic and sub-ethnic splinter groups to the delight of their traditional enemy. The white minority pounced on the occasion by cleverly aligning the Kreols, the Mullatos, other sub-ethnic Indian segments to wrench political power away from the majority Indians. It had been so easy to *convert a ruling majority into a conglomeration of conflicting sub-ethnic minorities. This has been a replay of the history of medieval India*. Through their inability to stick together as a majority community, the Hindus keep on losing power in Mauritius, in the Caribbeans and elsewhere.

Caste divisions also crop up from time to time though intra-ethnic relations and inter-marriage, inter-caste marriages are on the increase. The impact of assimilation, adaptation and westernisation, in the form of Creolisation, and the intra-ethnic and linguistic divisions, has encouraged a lot of inter-marriages and mixing between Hindus and the Creole community, their consequent Creolisation and loss of political power .as the majority community. The intra-sub-ethnic divisions have been skillfully exploited by Berenger who has focused his politics, known as scientific communalism, on further splintering the majority community into linguistic minorities.

Elsewhere, the Tamil diaspora predominates in South Africa, Malaysia, Sri Lanka and parts of Europe. While in Malaysia and Sri Lanka they have largely kept the language as medium of expression, in South Africa, due to four decades of absence of close contact with India and the aggressive evangelical education pursued in Apartheid schools, English has largely replaced Tamil and conversion has been widespread.

The relations between Indians and the Blacks have always been antagonistic and polarised in Guyana, Trinidad, and equally polarised between the Indians and the indigenous Fijians. Indians do not form the majority in these countries. At first, they had neglected education which had enabled the Blacks to monopolise jobs in government, the army and police so that they could always undermine Indians have not been able to hold political power for long in the Caribbeans.

In Mauritius. Historically, the Ti Kreols are situated at the bottom of the social scale and have formed the bulk of the working class, skilled, semi-skilled and manual workers, though a high proportion of their children are now educated. Descendants of Indian artisans and of African slaves, the Ti Kreols are able craftsmen, workers, capable of handling arduous jobs, requiring physical stamina. In this capacity, they play a crucial role in economic development. The general perception is that the Berenger administration is predominantly pro-Kreol. This stems from Kreol political subordination to the white, under the Catholic Church influence, and particularly to his MMM party. It explains why the administration is so keen to reward them with the spoils of offices and job distribution both in government and private sectors. It harks back to the colonial days when the White, under the influence of government and the Church, selected the Coloured as their preferred employees. The mass exodus of the

Coloured has opened the floodgate for Kreol entry into the private sector. The general sentiment of the Indians, Hindus and Muslims alike, flared up in the recent by-election in the North and the defeat of the MSM-MMM candidate, is one of widespread frustration at being discriminated against and being relegated to poverty under the Oligarchy's control.

Recognizing their Indianness

In his book, Mauriciens, Enfants de Mille Races, 2004, Jean Claude de L'Estrac, former Minister of External Affairs and current director of L'Express, reveals that the Mullatos are predominantly of mixed Indian and White origins, particularly of the petits blancs.

"*C'est ce métissage entre Blancs et Indiens qui a donné naissance à un groupe distinct- les gens de couleur- à l'intérieur de la population des Libres. Ainsi, l'ossature de la population métisse, " les gens de couleur", est formé par le métissage franco-indien*".

He argues that the eurasian blood predominated over the combined Afro-Malagassy-franco mixtures.

"*Ce qui a donné un métissage unique dans les colonies françaises, et peut-etre dans le monde, à prédominance nettement indienne*". Citing Milbert, he adds that the Indian predominance stemmed from the superior brand of the Indian women, " *d'une haute intelligence et d'une figure agréable*".

It appears that both the Mullatos and the Kreols are getting back to their Indianness and are recognizing their past mistakes. They are shaking off the dust of prejudices and taboos enforced during three centuries of colonial history under White domination. They are re-discovering the great Asian cultural and civilizational heritage. By emulating the White blindly, the Kreols and Mullatos had followed their ways which had driven them to such predicament and confusion. Afro-Asian Kreols and Mullatos, join hands with the PIOs. Soak up values from Indian culture and civilization which is also your heritage.

Draw new inspiration, vitality and dynamism from a whole intellectual world waiting to be discovered concerning :- Afro-Asian art, music, theatre, dance, literature, history, anthropology, geography, arts, sciences, natural sciences, natural medicine, philosophy.

Remember that assimilation is not a one way euro-centric traffic, you can also assimilate some of the positive and dynamic values of Indian culture. Afro-Creoles and Mullatos of Indian descent, wake up, throw away your colonial yoke and claim your PIO identity and privileges!

"Ramnath Jeetah helped me to settle down within the Hindu community, and this has helped me to discover certain values such as sharing, solidarity and how to plan one's life."

(Eloi Louis in *The Biography of Shri Ramnath Jeetah* by Joseph Willy Maunick 2001).

Long Live King Creole !

Historically, the ideal Creole leader has been the earlier president of the Labour Party, Emmanuel Anquetil, a simple, dedicated, visionary leader who identified himself with the needs of the downtrodden men and who tried to uplift them by organizing collective class conscious political and trade union.actions against the dominating Oligarchy.

On his death, in 1946, Guy Rozemont became the new Labour president. He was an equally dedicated trade unionist who allied with Dr S.Ramgoolam in a grand Creole-Indian working class alliance against the Oligarchy in a move to push forward with democracy, socialism, human rights, social progress, redistribution of wealth and the Welfare State. As the populist leader of the dockers, he lived their life, drank excessively and spent his time with friends which ultimately left a bad personal influence on the Creoles, thus reinforcing their spending, pleasure-loving and drinking habits.

His death in 1956 left a void in Creole leadership which was filled on the Oligarchy's side by Gaetan Duval, the dashing, charismatic, self-indulgent young Creole lawyer who mobilised the Catholic Church, the reactionary press, Le Cerneen and Le Mauricien, and the Creole voters in a grand alliance of the minority groups against the pro-independence Indian majority. Duval succeeded to Jules Koenig, a White lawyer, as leader of the Oligarchy's party, the PMSD. Like Rozemont, the populist Gaetan surrounded himself with a cohort of cronies, riotous drinking and feasting daily. But he went much further and carried the Creole vices to its limits by living extravagantly, spending lavishly in a carefree, lawless, flamboyant style, using violence and Fascist methods to whip up anti-Indian racial feelings. The climax came in the November 1963 meeting at Champ de Mars, Port Louis, when he incited racial violence and hatred and led the anti-Indian chorus:-

Malbars nou pa oulé
Enveloppe nou pas oulé

Duval reminded the naïve Creoles of their lost African king, somewhat in the style of the corrupt African life presidents and of the anti-Indian atrocities perpetrated under Burnham dictatorship in Guyana. For over a decade, the Indo-Mauritians were terrorised under Duval and his gang which climaxed in the bloody Muslim/Creoles riot in Port Louis, end 1967- beginning 1968. In a bid to perpetuate White supremacy, the anointed King Creole rallied the White, the Coloured and the urban Creoles under the PMSD banner against the majority Indians on the pretext of defending French heritage, against the threat of Indianisation and Indian hegemony about which the Creoles had nothing to do. The Indian threat never materialised as subsequently, the Oligarchy was to flag another white leader, Paul Berenger, to fragment the majority community and to head a new coalition of minority groups under cover of the post-independence nationalist ideology of Creolisation. In terms of leadership style, Duval had personified many of the negative Creole characteristics, namely:- a love of riotous living, riotous feasting, reckless spending, wasting public and municipal funds on friends and favourites, dependence on the white and on the Catholic Church, lawlessness and promiscuous living. The over-all effect was that he had set up a very bad moral example on his vast Creole following.

In contrast, there arose a new class-based party, the MMM, led by another dashing revolutionary, Paul Berenger, who dreamt to replace both the established class-based Labour Party and the declining PMSD. The Creoles had found another leader of an entirely different brand, cold, calculating and disciplined. Starting as a Marxist, in 1970, he tried to capture power by revolutionary means through an endless series of wild cat, insurrectionary strikes that grounded the economy to a halt before finally deviating into an ultra-liberal, pro-Oligarchy and adopted many of Labour's methods he had once condemned.

Set against the historic Labour Party, Berenger has used his Marxist style party structure in his single-minded pursuit of political power on a long, tortuous road, marked by political purges, opportunism, contradictions and inconsistencies before he achieved the impossible feat of attaining power by outwitting the inexperienced, self-indulgent Labour leader in 2000 in an electoral alliance with Sir Anerood Jugnauth's MSM. Berenger has poised as the ideal Creole leader, epitomising their envy of the Oligarchy, rallying the Catholic Church, the split Indian minority voters under his central authoritarian leadership.

10
A STRONGER INDIA, A STRONGER DIASPORA

IN CONCLUSION, we shall tie up the loose ends from the previous chapters and chart out a passage forward. *Voices of the Indian Diaspora* has been designed for you and is destined to carry your message round the world and shape the destiny of succeeding generations. This is a work of some substance, of universal appeal, a work of reference. It has not come about by chance but as the result of a deep commitment, of research, of hard and slow thinking over innumerable issues facing all of us. It stretches the great Indian vision far and wide and reaches out into the next 50 years.

Voices of the Diaspora is also your story, your statement to the world. It highlights our universally acknowledged undying core values. It also recogizes and exposes our past mistakes to enable us to move forward clear-headedly. It grapples with the social, cultural, economic, sociological and political concerns of New India and of overseas Indians. It celebrates the coming of age of New India, its ethos, its identity and the cultural, economic, political and professional contributions of a new breed of visionaries.

Getting There Together!

THE WORLD is now looking at New India, the emerging superpower, alongside the US, China and Europe. Half of the $48 bn. investments pouring into China comes from Chinese expatriates as compared to India with only $4 bn FDI's. The contributions of NRIs to the growth of the Indian economy are yet to happen. India must open itself to shed its third world mentality, its red tapism and other self-imposed barriers to development in order to raise the quality of its products and its brand name to meet world standards with the collaboration of NRIs'/PIOs' investments, ideas, technology and experience. In their turn, the NRIs must come out from hiding and step forward to answer the call of the motherland.

According to a recent study made by Gordon Sachs, by 2050, China's economy will hit the $ 55 trillion mark, followed by USA, $33 trillion and India $28 trillion. India must raise its self-image in the world media. Propelled by the NRIs and PIOs and Indian entrepreneurs, the sub-continent will have to brace itself to play an increasingly global role.

Just as overseas Chinese have contributed enormously to the transformation of China into a developed country through the adoption of western culture, civilization, education, technology, industry, manufacturing, trading skills acquired on the ground in the west, in SEA, in the Pacific countries, including massive flow of investments and the creation of new job opportunities- the same process is slowly happening to India thanks to the contributions of NRI/PIO communities. The only difference is that China had the wisdom to recognize and woo the overseas Chinese decades earlier and has thus leap-frogged during the intervening years. India will have to do its best to catch up with wasted opportunities and invite and involve the overseas Indians in its economic development.

It is expected that the 22 million overseas Indians in the far-flung 160 countries, speaking different languages, professing different religions and grounded in different cultures, will be playing an increasing role *in the branding of new India* in many fields- cultural, economic, educational, social, political. In this endeavour, the Minister of Overseas Indians Affairs, Mr Jagdish Tytler has called upon the diaspora to work together for India's growth in *tourism, education, infrastructure, health care, financial services and the service sector.* (Brussels Conference, 4th Oct. 2004).

But this can only happen in an open, competitive, global, knowledge-based society, buttressed by more liberal economic reforms, infra-structural facilities, the right motivation and positive signals from Bharat. Usually, entrepreneurs, those rare birds who create wealth, employment and export opportunities and who are risk-takers, shy away from doing business with countries which apply unnecessary deterrents, namely red tape, bureaucratic hurdles, disabling legislation, harking back to inspector Raj.

With its vast yearly output of scientists, doctors, engineers, professionals, India is now an intellectual power-house. But this should not be just a matter of sheer numbers. *The quality of its education must reach world class standards and be made accessible to every Indian child.*

Earlier, we have discussed the many issues facing the diaspora spread across a diversity of geographies and communities, coping with adverse cultural--socio-economic- and -political circumstances. *The need for a better understanding of the diaspora* and its relations with India is being keenly felt and it forms the central message of this book. Writers, academicians, media people, politicians, professionals, entrepreneurs must join hands to promote a wider diaspora awareness. We should pay tribute to the pioneers like Mahatma Gandhi, Manilal Doctor and a whole host of writers and researchers, from different universities in India, the West, the Caribbeans, Indian Ocean, Africa and who have contributed to the field of diaspora studies. Learning from the lessons of diaspora studies can only be beneficial to everybody, particularly in fostering global awareness, multi-disciplinary knowledge, in strengthening inter-ethnic and intra-ethnic relationships and the unity of the diaspora as a global force for good.

Networking

Equally important is the need to establish more intensive networking at all levels within the diaspora, particularly an *intra-diaspora business and marketing networking*, backed by the spread of knowledge and information by various channels, including the media, the setting up of *chairs of Diaspora Studies* in India and abroad. Apart from highlighting our strengths and weaknesses, they will help to identify, inspire, and provide successful role models to the Indian communities and foster confidence-building. Among the hundreds of successful NRIs, we may single out people like Karan Billimoria who left India with nothing to emerge as the CEO of Cobra Beers in the UK, noted for his inspirational and charismatic leadership and his deep faith in Indian moral values.

Media Power

The dialogue, through various channels, media, movies, publications, Information Technology, between mainland India and overseas Indians, will be mutually beneficial. In this role, the Indian media, press and television as well as overseas media will have to voice the interests of the diaspora and of its relationships with India. As India emerges into the super-power status, the Indian media, flanked by a network of correspondents, recruited both from India and possibly from inside the diaspora, will have to brace itself to play a proactive global role. The communications media will have to be multi-polar, covering a broad spectrum of global news and offering wider perspectives, improve the depth and quality of their range, content and technology so as to reach a wider global audience, somehow the way Bollywood is hot on the heels of Hollywood.

Living Our Values

India and the diaspora will need to pick up the Vedic strands to weave together the fabrics of the great Indian identity, culture and civilization that once illuminated the path of men since the beginnings of times. Our great cultural values, nested in the Vedas, contain within themselves the seeds of all the greatest thoughts ever conceived and reformulated by other civilizations and religions. They showed mankind:-

*the path of righteousness and justice (*dharma*),
*freedom, human brotherhood, (*vasudeva kutumbukam*),
*the unity of creation, (everything is God-pervaded, men, animals, plants, nature, the cosmos, the unity of the soul with the SuperSoul),
*respect of others, including of the animal and natural kingdoms, of the cosmos, the environment)
*non-violence (*ahimsa parmo dharma*, social harmony and co-existence, self-restraint, controlling one's emotions, the virtue of sharing and give-and take)
*tolerance, (the basis of democracy), moderation (the Middle Way),
*truthfulness (lead me from untruth to truth, truth always triumphs, Truth is God- Gandhi),
*love, compassion, kindness, generosity, promoting the welfare of others (*Om sarve bhavantu sukhi naha*, May all be happy, may all be healthy),
*a passion for knowledge, for learning, research, wisdom, and excellence.
*self-reliance (lift yourself by yourself, the Gita),
*the path of action, the path of devotion, the path of knowledge (the Gita),
*a life of goodness according to the dharma (message of the epics, Mbht, Ramayana),
*our sense of duty and respect to others, the elders, to society, to our family,
*work ethics (wealth creation by hard and honest labour, entrepreneurship).
* so that we can enjoy peace, beauty, goodness, contentment and happiness (*satyam, shivam, sundaram, ananda, shantih*, let there be peace everywhere, peace in the cosmos)

These cultural profiles constitute some of the core moral values which guide us on the path of righteousness, honesty, dharma or the virtuous path or good conduct. They build in us all the noble qualities, (the aryan Vedic culture) that nurture our personality growth and character building, based on self-discipline, the fighting spirit, endurance, determination, the sacrifice, the hard work, briefly the soul force that finally leads us to achieve our goal in life. It involves personal commitment, constant self-renewal, innovation, creativity and problem-solving. It equips us with the capacity to change and adapt to different circumstances. It sustains the process of growth, of change, of permanent evolution for the successful execution of one's strategy.

By adhering to these rules which blend the material with the spiritual, which define our beliefs, norms, attitudes, behaviours and expectations, we realise our vision and enjoy the four ends of life, from Dharma (right action), Artha (enjoyment of wealth and power), Kama (race propagation) to the attainment of Moksha- salvation- a life of supreme fulfillment and realization.

These winning values enfold within themselves the criteria which make for leadership, risk-taking, competitiveness, decisiveness, perseverance, success, sharing, ambition, commitment, team work, co-operation which are the success factors essential to any individual, including the student, the professional, the business entrepreneur and of the political leader.

No individual or society can ever dream of making headway in life and attain his vision if he does not follow the virtuous path. This is what gives balance to a person's life, when he performs his social duties, blending the physical, the material and the spiritual in perfect harmony. Briefly, our essential Indian identity grounded on the great Vedic culture maps out the direction to our future happiness. Dharma protects those who protect dharma and therefore, let us always stick to the path of dharma, righteousness.

No religion or philosophical or spiritual system has explored the deep reaches of the mind and of the soul than Hinduism and Buddhism. By pursuing spiritual knowledge and yogic discipline further, they take us to various stages of consciousness, super-consciousness and the attainment of enlightenment or moksha, or unity with the Godhead as illustrated by the lives of saints, yogis, spiritual masters and great swamis. This path is open to any ordinary human being who dedicates himself to the spiritual path can himself become a great soul.

The great Indian cultural and civilizational heritage, enriched by inputs, adjustments and renewal from NRIs and PIOs remain the cementing bond and the springboard of our collective strength. The Indian diaspora, drawing deep from the perennial moral values flowing from the Indus Valley Civilization, the Vedic, Buddhist, Vedantic and Islamic sources have been at the heart of our success. Since times immemorial, India had championed the spread of Indian culture across Asia, China, Japan, Korea, South East Asia as well as in west Asia. Today, Bollywood movies and entertainment are the carriers of Hindi, Indian culture, music, songs and traditional ethos- across the Middle East, Central Asia, UK, US, Canada and countries populated by overseas Indians. Inspired by the humanistic, universalistic Indian philosophy which emphasized the moral values:- of sharing, family solidarity, tolerance, moderation, forgiveness, hard work, sacrifice, peace, freedom, individual enterprise, self-reliance- *Indian culture had long endowed the world with the intellectual framework of democracy, liberalism, enterprise, human rights* and which explain the status of India as the largest democracy.

These precious cultural and moral values which have shaped the Asian moral consciousness have been as determining as the Anglo-Saxon Protestant ethics. Throughout the Asians' stay abroad, these cultural values have inspired them with the strength, the resilience, the fighting spirit and the vision to strive for a better life in the face of adverse circumstances. These values have flowered among the NRIs and PIOs across the world. They are the harbingers of a new era of expanded trade and of wider international relationships spanning across 110 countries plagued by de-stabilising terrorism.

A Stronger India

A Stronger India. Building upon the diplomatic ties set up by the Non-Aligned foreign policy of Nehru, and embedded in the Peninsula's geo-political and historic cultural influences, multi-cultural, secular, democratic and visionary India can tie up with the wide range of friendly nations and establish closer cultural, commercial, economic and diplomatic exchanges with those countries. The birthplace of Buddhism, India can well establish closer political, commercial and spiritual ties with the Buddhist diaspora of the world, in China, Japan, Korea, and other countries of South East Asia.

Similarly, having the second largest Muslim population in the world, India should not be shy to take its place among the Muslim countries of the world, particularly among the Gulf and Middle East, the South East Asian countries and engage in closer commercial and economic relations with the Muslim diaspora. Taking a leaf from the NRIs in the Gulf Countries, the Peninsula can network its vast potential and attract investments and resources of these countries and emerge as a stronger nation.

Historically, NRIs students have contributed to the political emancipation of India, to its economic growth. They have provided the key inputs in Information and communication technology, in the Green Revolution. Breaking out from its historic isolation and its protectionist shells, India has been opening up to the calls of a global society, in ICT, in manufacturing and commerce. Ignored until the 1980's, the NRIs/PIOs are now prized as India's *unofficial ambassadors*.

Our entrepreneurs, proud of their roots, organized within their respective Chambers of Commerce in the US, in Europe, in the Caribbeans, in Africa, and elsewhere are quite familiar with the commercial, financial, marketing, political and technological opportunities of their 160 host countries. They should stand brokers to help India do business with these countries. They must be lured to invest in the key sectors of the expanding Indian economy, help build trade networks and sell the new Indian brand name world-wide.

In the political fields, the path of the diaspora has been strewn with a *number of thorns*. Indians have had to put up with numerous restrictive immigration laws imposed by former colonial powers and the host countries. In countries where Indians have been in minority, namely:- South Africa, Uganda, Fiji, Trinidad, Guyana, Malaysia and in Europe, Indians have had to cope with problems of security, human rights abuses, residual racism, cultural racism, violence, social, economic, political disabilities, marked, as in apartheid South Africa or the plantation colonies-by a battery of anti-Indian legislation. Indians have been victims of violence and intolerance based solely on racial motivations. Unfortunately, most of these boycotts had stemmed from the Motherland's own fault. Previously, it placed itself in a position of weakness due to its own self-inflicted wounds. But in the wake of the economic reforms and globalisation, nuclear India has tried to re-invent a new India brand name, away from its past negative image. This poses a great challenge to the people and government of India to live up to its emerging reputation, flagged by its new breed of talented individuals, academicians, professionals, scientists, business-entrepreneurs and media people.

A Stronger Diaspora

In this context, Saudi Arabia has taken a right step forward in offering naturalization to one million NRIs, particularly professionals who have stayed over ten years in the country. It is expected that other Gulf countries will offer similar packages to the Indian expatriates. Similarly, we welcome the recent move made by the state government of Andra Pradesh in negotiating the emigration of 500 Andra farmers-who had otherwise been hit by drought, indebtedness and suicide- to settle and work on farmland in Kenya on a co-operative basis. Indian authorities might step in to negotiate further deals to re-settle the co-operative farmers hungry for land overseas in neighbouring countries like Mozambique, Tanzania, Uganda, Zaire etc.

Wherever they have gone, the PIOs have been dogged by the acute problem of insecurity unless they assimilate the host country's culture and religion and forfeit their ethnic identity and cultural values. Lip service is paid to their democratic rights, rights to their language, their culture and religion. This is an urgent problem calling for serious reflection and action by all those concerned with the survival of the diaspora. Nevertheless, it is extremely important for overseas Indians, men and women, wherever they may be, to stay united, strengthen their intra- and inter-ethnic affiliations, close their ranks, come out into the open, make their voices heard by getting involved in social and political affairs. They should not remain inward-looking, parochial but open out to the global world. That is, they should go out and excel in many fields, without limiting themselves just to their daily economic and professional activities.

In the wake of the PBD, it is expected that India will synergize the vast potential of businesspeople, journalists, writers, women, students, scientists, professionals, politicians, sportsmen within India and the diaspora. It might go a long way to strengthen India itself and overseas Indians if frequent international conventions are held in a bid to bring them together on special occasions to tackle critical issues. Remember that a strong India can bind the diaspora with intangible ties of pride, honour and confidence.

Besides, we, in the diaspora, would be proud to see Incredible India forging ahead as a tourist destination, equipped with:- modern infrastructure, dotted with a number of modern airports and free-ports, beach and hill resorts, offering an unforgettable panorama of Indian historical and cultural heritage, diverse sports attractions, healthcare, a safe haven for investments, and as the best place for learning and living.

India should learn from the maritime history of the western nations, particularly, England, France, Portugal and the Netherlands. It should also scrutinise the success story of maritime Mauritius, once called the star and the key of the Indian ocean under French rule, under Mahe de Labourdonnais , 1735 onward. The French had the vision to turn the Island into a strategic maritime and commercial centre in the Indian Ocean, now transformed into a quality tourist destination, much frequented by Europeans. After all, Labourdonnais employed Indian workers from the Malabar and Coromandel coast to build the harbour, the road and infrastructure of Port Louis, particularly the vessels, serviced by Indian sailors, known as Lascars. Ships sailed out from the Island to India, the Moluccas, the Philippines, Indonesia, Muscat,

Zanzibar, China, South America to trade and bring Indian textile commodities. Using Mauritius as a naval base, the French made the Indian Ocean a war theatre to harass British shipping.

It is high time for nuclear, peninsular and geopolitical India to overcome, once for all, its residual prejudices against crossing the *kalapani* and all the myth about caste purity in order to align itself as a knowledge-based and technology-driven country and emerge as a potential maritime power in the Indian Ocean.

This is perhaps where NRIs and PIOs can be partners in building the New India. It would encourage our affluent westernised NRIs' children who have no contact with India except through Bollywood movies to visit, cherish and contribute to their mother country. This is precisely where schemes like the PIO Cards, chairs of Diaspora studies and the invitations to join in the *Discover Your Roots Package*, sight-seeing, visiting of historic and tourist attractions in Bihar appears most welcoming, under the above logistic conditions. In the wake of the Bihar experience, it is hoped that other states, namely Andra Pradesh, Maharashtra, Punjab and Tamil Nadu could offer similar packages to the disapora, eager to reconnect with their heritage and possibly make some contributions to enhance life in their ancestral villages.

India will have to unfold itself as a hospitable, welcoming tourist paradise, capable of matching competitive tourist destinations, offering the best to the visitors who can go back home to vaunt the many wonders of Incredible India. It's also part of a global image-building exercise in which its tourist agencies will have to do everything it can to enhance its service industry.

All the above goes to prove that India and the diaspora are umbilically tied by a common destiny and which keeps strengthening each other. A strong India is indeed a strong diaspora, and a strong diaspora makes for a strong India.

APPENDIX

A. THE INDIAN MEDIA AND THE DIASPORA

IF IN the past India had suffered from a bad international press, filled with anti-Indian racial and colonial prejudices, and which focused on the disasters, poverty and overpopulation, it appears that attitudes towards new India have been changing in the wake of the India Shining campaign. This is largely reflected in the quality of the Indian emigrants. Under colonial days, the indentured immigrants were forced to escape from famines, from droughts, from poverty and depression to seek new homes in the plantation colonies where they had to overcome enormous sufferings, humiliation, exploitation and human rights abuses. Finally, their endurance paid off and they were generally able, despite difficult circumstances, to earn a better livelihood than they could ever have made it back home, in India. In contrast, the recent free passenger emigrants from independent India migrating to western countries have been of a better breed. The NRI community in the west has been drawn from educated people, professionals for the most part and many have done very well abroad in their professions, in education or in business.

Consequently, the impact of the talented and educated NRIs has been to change the image of India overseas from what it had earlier been under the indentured system. This goes to show that a strong, educated, developing India produces a strong diaspora which further helps to enhance the international credibility of India and of Overseas Indians.

The indentured Immigrants formed a labour emigration resembling somehow to the army of semi-skilled Gulf NRIs, working on contract labour. But everywhere accompanying the labour Immigrants, have been an army of Indian traders, entrepreneurs and businessmen, from among whom have emerged a class of highly successful entrepreneurs and professionals. The descendants of the Indentured immigrants have struggled hard to educate their children in order to shift from agriculture to step into the professions, into the services, into trade and into industry, apart from politics. Therefore, the colonial image of a poor, backward, over-populated India and of the Indian immigrants has had to change correspondingly through the progress achieved by Indians in education, in trade, industry and the professions.

The result is that a new India brand name, as an awakening giant, in the trails of China, is shaping up and projecting India as an emerging super-power. Nuclear India, democratic India and an economically strong India steadily pursuing the path of economic reforms, making gigantic strides in education, in health, in infrastructure, in technology, in urbanisation, as well as the attendant problems and issues, are some of the concerns which are being reported in the press. The massive brand building publicity around India Shining had no doubt been widely reported internationally and had given India new credentials and a new image that had lured new foreign investors.

Similarly, the film industry, spearheaded by Bollywood, by television, by great advances in advertising, in publishing, in fashion industry, in commerce and industry have helped to export a new dynamic image of India abroad. India is fast changing and these changes are being reflected both in the Indian media and foreign media.

For a moment, just imagine the world without the contributions of India and its diaspora. The world would have been the poorer without its deep spirituality and rich cultural and civilizational heritage. .

Nowadays, India's great contributions in the fields of I. C.T and education are propelling the knowledge-based economy, with India leading the way in the BPO sector. Accordingly, GOPIO Mauritius is pressing ahead with the setting up of a central PIO University, based in India, with campuses abroad, manned by Indian and diaspora personnel for the benefit of disadvantaged PIO children who cannot gain access to expensive western universities.

I shall now focus on the relationships between the Indian media and the diaspora.

Remember that much depends on media people like you, in your different capacities, here and abroad, to further contribute in forging a fresh image of an emerging New India. Taking advantage of the liberalisation of the press from its past dependence on the state, the availability of free radio and television channels, the booming communication industry fuelled by the internet, the e-mail, mobile phones, information circulates more freely and the repressed people can voice their grievances more easily. But still, in the majority, the key international media, particularly in the west, has been controlled by a handful of Jewish families. As a result, they have ensured that the Jews, particularly Israel, always enjoy a good press. Indian media barons must emulate the example of the successful Jewish media magnates, in building a strong global media network in order to expand their influence throughout the world.

So why not position yourself, your organs and the Indian brand image to articulate the ambitions and expectations of a forward-looking, new refulgent India and the diverse concerns of the far-flung diaspora? Overseas Indians must follow the early examples set by Mahatma Gandhi in South Africa when he set up a press in order to ventilate the Indian opinion. So, the message is clear. Get hold of the media power into your own hands. Don't ever let it slip into the hands of your enemies. We must strive to be seen and heard through owning and managing a vociferous press in our host countries. We must train a body of world class reporters and journalists writers and publishers who are bold enough to dig for the truth and go deep into the issues concerning the diaspora. It means that we have to get into and control the printing, publishing, advertising and information industry. Then the network of Indian and overseas Indian journalists can frequently meet in conclaves of this sort to discuss common topics and issues facing the Indian media. We have to seize on human rights issues and use the media to express ourselves freely and fearlessly if we wish to keep the media our of the hands of our traditional racist enemies who may vilify us and paint us black in their news media

Here's your opportunity to be the architect, the pioneer, the visionary and the voices of a worthwhile creative future, that is also articulated in my book, entitled *Voices of the Indian Diaspora.* This book should be an indispensable resource for media people like you, interested in developing a closer understanding of the diaspora and of its relations with India. I believe that through your kind co-operation, this book which provides a body of useful information and provokes serious thinking on issues affecting us, you can contribute to make it achieve its goal of spreading a new global diaspora awareness and thus shape the destiny of generations to come.

I strongly believe that the Indian media should continue to glorify and share our universally acknowledged cultural and civilizational heritage. It should encompass the social, cultural, economic, sociological and political concerns of New India and of overseas Indians. And let the world take note, we should celebrate the coming of age of New India, its ethos, its identity and the economic and business contributions of high achievers and successful visionaries, both in India and abroad.

The Indian media have been emerging from the shadows of the initial period of colonial hibernation, subordination and political sycophancy to grow sufficiently independent, mature, and vociferous and to respond creatively to the diverse expectations of India's ever-expanding educated population and new middle class. The media has now come of age. It reflects the advances in Information and Communications Technology, in economic development, in health. The Indian media is sufficiently broad and diverse and is fast developing s to reflect the diversity of interests of its public.

Fuelled by a larger reading public, an increasing middle class, an expanding economy, a thriving advertising industry, and emboldened by democratic autonomy and the principles of human rights and, firmly embedded in freedom of speech, the Indian media is now grappling with a host of issues which were formerly thrust under the carpet. It brings out into the public glare cases of corruption, of human rights abuses, of crime and violence and the aspirations of the common men for a better life. In the past, under the state monopoly of broadcasting, the nationalised Indian media was an instrument of state propaganda which generally condoned the excesses of the Licensing Raj, the abuses of a mindless bureaucracy and rampant corruption. But, in the wake of privatization, liberalisation, economic development and globalisation, the media has now grown more courageous in advocating a better society governed by the democratic principles of the Rule of Law, of transparency, corporate governance, social justice, free enterprise and economic progress.

One of its functions should be to clear away the remaining road blocks on the path of economic development. It should help to open up new privatization opportunities to local and overseas businessmen and make India an attractive investment and tourist destination. India should brace itself to respond effectively to the challenges of global competition.

In other words, the Indian media should emerge from a period of past splendid isolation and exclusion to come out into the open, to assume the new role of an emerging super-power and measure up to world standards.

The glare of globalisation is now beaming over the sub-continent. And in this global context, during its first PBD, India has hailed its diaspora as its *unofficial ambassadors* abroad. This means that the mistakes of the past must be recognized and corrected. The climate of suspicion and misunderstandings that once alienated the NRIs and PIOs from the corrupt Bureaucratic Raj is slowly giving way to one of understanding and co-operation, based on transparency and corporate governance that should form the brand image of new India.

This means that, apart from the annual PBD celebrations, India should continually keep in touch with the diaspora, its expectations and its potential. The Indian media cannot pay lip service to this new responsibility. They must be firmly committed to developing a broad diaspora awareness, based on research on the ground. And, in their turn, the geographically diverse diaspora must follow the happenings and development of New India so that together, they can work shoulder to shoulder at different levels, under the Ministry of Overseas Indians Affairs and the over-arching GOPIO to move ahead in gigantic strides.

In achieving this objective, media people like you, in your different capacities, here and abroad, who are now contributing to forging a fresh image of an emerging New India must update your understanding of Overseas Indians. If you network with Overseas Indians spread in the Atlantic, Asia-Pacific and Indian Ocean regions, grounded in diverse cultures and civilizations, you are extending your arms right across the globe and embracing a global news network.

In the GOPIO Business Conference held in Brussels in October last, it was realised that Indians knew little about Europe, its cultures, civilizations, traditions, economic and political systems, business and marketing opportunities and much less about the European Union and the functioning of the European Parliament. Similarly, the Europeans have inherited out-dated prejudices and misunderstandings about India from western media and which could be cleared through a better system of news and information exchanges. To achieve this aim, the Overseas Indians in Europe or in Mauritius who are educated on European culture and civilization, fluent in English, French and Indian languages, can be called upon to act as reporters and agents of communication between India and Europe. They can fulfil the functions of interpreters, mediators and the unofficial ambassadors of India abroad.

You will have to increase your visibility among the diaspora countries and acquire knowledge and news on the ground, perhaps through the agency of a chain of local diasporic news reporters. Mahatma Gandhi made the Indian voice heard through his newspaper in Natal. One of the most important contributions of his disciple in Mauritius, manilal Doctor was to found a newspaper called the Hindusthani, 15th March 1909 with the motto: Equality of individuals! Fraternity of men! Equality of Races!In Mauritius, APCA, an Indian news agency, has recently set up a local newspaper called LE MATINAL. Such an exercise can be reproduced in various other countries populated by Overseas Indians, namely in South Africa, Malaysia, the Caribbeans, Fiji, the UK.and the USA. Recently, NDTV has given an excellent report based on the Islands called Island Ryhthms and which bring out the mix of cultures and civilizations and which show how Indian traditions have been transformed through contact with other cultures. Such frequent reporting on the ground will go a long way to foster interest and understanding in the diaspora and provide an unending flow of creative experiences and new ideas for the future.

The people in the diaspora, particularly the youth, brought up in western cultures and civilization, modern education and new technology, tend to be critical, rational, materialistic and pragmatic. They have been brought up in advanced, fast changing and dynamic societies. They are put off by traditional, stagnant, rural-based societies, grounded in medieval social customs and superstitions. They cannot be wooed by emotional appeals alone. They are more quality conscious, corporate and cosmopolitan in their daily attitudes to life. They are less tolerant of the myths and theologies that once overshadowed the Hindu religion. Nothing less than the dissolution of the Licensing Raj, the corrupt bureaucracy, coupled with advances in education, health, infrastructure, technology and the advent of fast-track economic development will succeed to win over their heart and mind.

So why not position yourself, your organs and the Indian brand image to articulate the ambitions and expectations of a forward-looking, new refulgent India and which projects the image of an optimistic, self-confident, forward-looking country?.

The Indian media should continue to glorify and share our universally acknowledged cultural and civilizational heritage. They should also encompass the social, cultural, economic, sociological and political concerns of New India and of overseas Indians. And let the world take note, the media should celebrate the coming of age of New India, its ethos, its identity and the economic and business contributions of successful achievers and visionaries

However, if Bollywood, the Indian television, advertising, fashion and entertainment industry have been pushing headway, they have a long way to grow to match up with some of the world's dominant media like Hollywood, the fashion industry in the west, the British press, the French press, the BBC, the CNN. Nevertheless, the Indian media are racing ahead and some of their television channels like NDTV, Zee T.V, and some newspapers and magazines are fast catching up and are showing signs of emerging into the front line of world media.

We would like to see the Indian media enlarging its scope to encompass the affairs and concerns of the Overseas Indians. We need to share and consolidate our common values as well as keep both the Indian public and the geographically diverse diaspora better informed and in touch with one another. Better communications and reporting would ensure that both Indians and the diaspora would get to know and understand one another better, through stronger networking, closer relationships, backed by a flow of exchanges, communications, commerce and ideas. Buttressed by a chain of advertisers and entrepreneurs, the Indian media will have to send their reporters to report on happenings concerning the diaspora in the countries populated by them.

The conclusion is that, in a bid to project the brand image of new India, and to compete with western media, the Indian media will have to break its tradition of parochialism. It has to go out or build a network of reporters to report on the diaspora, not once during the annual PBD, but all the time in a spirit of partnership and exchange with their re-united brothers and sisters from overseas.

B. NRIs/PIOs- WHO ARE WE?

BOTH, THE PIOs or Persons of Indian Origin and the NRI's or Non-Resident Indians are expatriate or Overseas Indians. The only difference is historical. The PIOs emigrated earlier while the NRIs are late arrivals.

Historically, the earlier batches of PIOs started flowing from India since the beginnings to settle in neighbouring countries, like Malaysia, Sri Lanka, Burma. Many of them went under contract labour, known as the kangani system, to work in the rubber plantations of Malaysia.

Indian Slaves

SINCE THE 1720's, under French colonial system, Indians were either kidnapped or sold out by other Indian traders from Chandranagore and Mahé and the Malabar Coast, French posts, to be used as slaves in the Mascarene islands of Mauritius and Reunion. Since they were slaves, they had absolutely no rights or freedom, they were forcibly converted into Christianity. Being mainly of male sex, they had to mix with the Black slaves women to produce the later Kreol population. The Indian slaves were employed as esclaves a talents, or artisans, the builders of roads, public buildings, harbour, and the early urban infrastructure of Port Louis. Their children, being of mixed Indian and African or Malagassy blood became skilled Kreol artisans. Other Indians were employed as labourers in the plantations while the third batch, including Indian girls and women were the domestic servants. It's mainly from among the Indian female members, many of whom were known as *doudous*, or kept girls and women, that the mixed white and Indian children were born, known as Coloured or Mullatos.

Indian Convicts

THE THIRD movement of Indian immigrants concerned the small batches of male Indian convicts who were sent to Mauritius and to Singapore since the early 1815, under British colonisation. These were chained, bearded people who sweated under the hard sun as hewers of stone and road builders. The public roads of Mauritius linking Port Louis to the north and the south, or the roads in Singapore bear the imprint of the labour and sweat of those Indian convicts. Once more, they had to mix with local population and in Mauritius it was with Black slave women to produce successive Kreol generations, bearing Indian blood and vestiges of Indian culture and civilization. Similarly, in Singapore, the Indian convicts, the early male Indian immigrants intermarried with Malay or Chinese women to produce mixed Indian Singaporeans. It is sad that no monument had ever been erected, no celebration and no tribute is ever paid to the contributions, sacrifices of those convicts labourers and who did so much to lay down the infrastructure of the colonies. Anyway, this goes to say that in large respect, Indian blood and Indian culture and civilization run into the veins of practically every Black Kreol or Mullatto. Once more, under French and British colonisation, these people were forcibly Christianised and alienated from their Indian roots, then treated as being of inferior quality. Indians, known as Malbars in the Mascarenes, were considered as heathens, barbarian.

Our Cousins, the Kreols - our Stolen Identity

THERE IS hardly any sign left of pure Kreol or Kreol of pure African or Malagassy blood so much has the inter-racial intermingling taken place as is borne by the dark brownish complexion and straight hair of the descendants of mixed Indian and African slaves. This Creolisation or intermixing process is still taking place and is an integral part of Mauritian society. This proves that our cousins, the Kreols, distantly related to us, can historically lay claim to being people of Indian origins, just as the Anglo-Indians, many of whom had migrated overseas, to Australia and other destinations after the independence of India. It is also true, as had occurred in French colonial plantations that the converted Indians had merged into the Kreol population.

Under French colonisation, forced assimilation into the Christian and French culture and civilization in the French colonies of Reunion, Guadeloupe, Martinique and Ile de France, descendants of Indians had been stolen of their Indian identity and of their Indian civilizational heritage. Once they were converted, they fell completely under the swoop of the all-powerful Catholic Church. As Indo-Christians, they were forcibly alienated from their past Indian heritage. The women gave up their saris, their tika, their mangalsutras and all signs and symbols of their past Indianness. Politically, they started aligning themselves under the umbrage of the Oligarchy and the Catholic Church against the majority Hindus.

The process of conversion has enlarged itself on a global scale. It now forms part of the wider clash between two opposing proselytizing forces, Islam versus Christianity. The Hindus, wherever they may be, in India, in South Africa, in the Mascarenes, in the Caribbeans are the easy targets of conversion. Hindus are caught up under the cross-fire of the clash of civilizations, in the struggle for demographic, military and political control between two proselytising religions. The Hindus, because of their tolerance, their liberalism happen to be the easy targets of proselytization. The evangelicals have been pouring in unending streams on a mass scale. Funded by American and Australian churches, they come knocking at our door steps, pulling away members of our families, our relatives and causing conflicts, tensions and demographic and political turbulence.

In a bid to protect Confucianism and Buddhism from outside attacks and preserve the basic Chinese or Japanese civilization, China, Japan, Singapore had put a brake on the activities of the evangelicals. Strangely enough, the enemies of Hinduism are given every liberty to create havoc in our democratic countries with the result that the Hindu majorities are now being converted into minorities. Under the Creolisation and indigenization process which moves inexorably like a steam roller, the mass of the Hindus are being flattened and moulded into Christianity. Numerically strengthened through the policy of conversion, the Oligarchy, our old enemy, is bold enough to send its political tentacles through proxy to seize power back, both economic and political, through the backdoor. Recently, aided by a Hindu majority community fragmented into splintered minorities, this loss of political power has taken place under our very eyes in Mauritius. You will agree with me that this is an urgent issue which strikes directly at the roots of our security and our political base. It concerns the future of Indian culture, civilization, Hinduism. It has wider economic, social, political implications. We expect GOPIO and the Ministry of Overseas Indian Affairs and all Hindu organizations to address this issue urgently and take necessary measures in the wake of what China, Singapore and Japan have done. Otherwise there would be no more PIOs and NRIs left in the world.

Indentured Immigrants

It was after the abolition of slavery that the successive waves of Indian immigration, numbering half a million, were transported overseas, first in larger numbers to Mauritius as from 1834, then to other plantation colonies, including Trinidad, Tobago, Guyana, Fiji, Surinam, South Africa. To know more about the story of:- their harsh conditions of labour, the exploitation they went through, the low wages, sometimes withheld, the severe Labour legislation, deprivation of their income through the double cut system, the enforcement of the Pass laws by which thousands of labourers were clapped into Vagrant Depots, I shall refer you to my book, VOICES OF THE DIASPORA. See chapter three, entitled Across the Seven Seas and in Chapter five, entitled The Indian Immigrants.

It is very important that we should all acquaint ourselves with their history. We need to study Indian immigration not in isolation as it occurred in our own country and thereby develop a frog-in-the well approach to our own past. This is where a knowledge of Diapora Studies comes in as a helpful tool to enable us to grasp the wider reality and to look at Indian immigration, that is, the NRIs and PIOs, globally in all their vast economic, cultural, civilizational, political implications. We need to compare and contrast their conditions, their struggles, their contributions and achievements under diverse geographical circumstances so that we can draw important lessons of history. We have to understand the tactics and policies used by the Oligarchy so that we do not repeat the mistakes of the past and lose political power as has happened to Indians in Guyana, Trinidad, Fiji and recently in Mauritius. If you want to understand about yourself, your past and about your strengths and how to overcome your weaknesses, I invite you to refer to Voices of the Diaspora.

Despite all the torments, prejudices, ill-treatment, the Indian Immigrants and their descendants showed tremendous resilience and survival capacity thanks to the inherent qualities of their culture, civilization and religion. In other words, they were saved by their very Indianness. Not only have they survived, preserved their languages, culture, civilization and religion, the PIOs, that is, the very descendants of the Indentured immigrants, have overcome their initial difficulties and made remarkable headway in the fields of education, professions, trade, industry, politics. A large proportion of the children of the PIOs have been educated abroad and have consequently twice migrated to western countries where they have had access to larger incomes and wider professional and business opportunities. More than 100,00 of the Suranamese Indians have migrated to the Netherlands while above 300,000 Guyanese Indians have migrated to the US. In the 1970's, about 75,000 Gujarati Indians from Uganda had migrated to the UK where they have done fairly well in retail business, while their children have moved to higher professions and larger businesses.

But they are not the only ones. Accompanying the early Indentured labourers overseas as free immigrants or free passengers were the Indian traders, jewelers from Gujarat, later joined by Marwari and Sindhi traders. Their descendants have made more progress still in education, the professions and in business. From their different bases, whether in Mauritius, the Caribbeans, South Africa, Zambia, Dubai, Saudi Arabia, the trading PIOs have been the most successful overseas Indians. For the most part, their descendants, mainly educated in western universities, have twice migrated from the former colonies to re-settle in Australia, Canada, the UK and the US where they have access to higher incomes and to more opportunities in education, in the professions and in business. The general trend has been to migrate twice from India to the former colonies and from there towards western countries.

The NRIs

SINCE THE END of the Second World War, the Non Resident Indians, generally drawn from among the best educated Indians who have benefited from subsidised higher education in independent India, have migrated to western countries. The Silicon Valley Millionaires, the IT professionals, the businessmen have done very well in the US, the UK, Canada, Australia and are reckoned to be among the highest earners. These are the high achievers, the successful overseas Indians. Similarly, there is another group of Gulf NRIs who have done extremely well in the professions and in business

Being the first generation of Indians overseas, the NRIs tend to bear close relations with India while their western educated children, dubbed the ABCD, American Born and Confused Dersi, tend to be less attached to India and more assimilated into the host countries. The challenge facing the NRIs is how to bring their children, the PIOs, into the mainstream of Indian cultural and civilizational heritage. One of the reasons is that the attraction to the west stems from the economic and military power of the west as compared to the past image of India as being a poor, underdeveloped and over-populated country. But things have been changing fast. New India has been shining and it is fast moving in the direction of evolving into a developed country by the year 2020. The challenge for the NRIs is to contribute in investments, technology and in knowledge in order to make India strong both economically and politically in order to evolve as a pole of attraction for its children overseas.

Relations with India

GENERALLY SPEAKING the first generation of overseas Indians, whether it concerned the early Indentured Immigrants or the NRIs, feel strong attachment to India. Wherever they have gone, they have tried to stay close to one another to form new communities of overseas Indians. Their primary aim has been to. preserve their languages, their culture, their traditions and their Indianness. Their secret ambition is to work hard, study hard, educate their children, make enough money than retire back home to India. A certain percentage of the migrants realise this aim but when they find that their children have been more assimilated to their new host countries, they prefer to stay back.

Historically, their relations with India have been stormy. The old, feudal, casteist India held strange notions of the overseas Indians as being almost outcastes and foreigners to India. The close emotional and language bonds started to wear out. Due to the absence of understanding of the circumstances in which first the NRI and PIOs live, there has been a general lack of interest, lack of knowledge, study and research in the NRIs and PIOs. Consequently, a widening gap of misunderstanding and suspicion has been growing between resident and overseas Indians.

Resident Indians have looked down upon the PIOs, whether in Trinidad, In Fiji, in Malaysia, in South Africa, Uganda and elsewhere as of little importance and relevance to them. The East Indians or Indo-Trinidadians have tried to make a brave attempt to preserve the Indian songs in a new multi-cultural setting, called the Chutney music, mixed music, sometimes blending with Calypso or Afro-Creole rhythms. To these, they have creatively added a local carnival flavour. Yet the Indian response has been negative. Indo-Trinidadians have been flatly rejected by native Indians who jeered at them and told them that you can't even speak our language. In other words, you are none of us! Indians have still been hugging to a past third world, casteist, mentality by which they weaken themselves by self-inflicted wounds. They show intolerance of overseas Indians, contrary to the great universal precepts of vedic tolerance and world brotherhood. They go on committing cultural and geo-political suicide by disclaiming their own distant cousins overseas who are only adding to their strength and global influence. This attitude has to change and is changing under the impact of the successful NRIs who are fast becoming the models and the envy of the ambitious Indian youth who are eager to break through traditional geographical barriers and to shine globally. Once a member of the family in the village or the town is settled abroad and is doing well, it tends to pull other go-getting members in a dynamic process of migration. Hopefully, in the wake of further liberalisation and privatization, more Indian corporations will expand abroad, more trade will develop carrying behind more Indian expatriates. This will prompt more Indian exports so that we can expect to see closer relations between mainland India and overseas Indians.

We have to emulate the successful example of mainland China. Firstly, it has facilitated mainland Chinese to emigrate and secondly it has welcomed Overseas Chinese, given them recognition and encouraged them to come back, invest and develop China with new technology and expertise and open up wider market opportunities. China has offered them extensive legal, infrastructural and economic facilities within very short notice. In the case of NRIs and PIOs who had shown interest in trading or investing in India, the Indian response has been negative. At first, it had closed down the gate to overseas investments on overseas Indian entrepreneurs who were willing to risk their capital, create employment, new expertise, new marketing opportunities and new technology as well as wider export possibilities.

There are many stories of how prospective overseas investors have been rebuffed by short-sighted Indian politicians and bureaucrats, still held back by the self-wounding Licensing Raj. Instead of attracting and facilitating the investors, they have generally thrown cold water on the projects and imposed all sorts of stupid bureaucratic obstacles in a bid to drive them away, thus killing at birth the hens that lay the golden eggs.

This is where closer networking as well as literature on Diaspora Studies and intensive media campaigning come in as a useful tool to bridge the gap and bring all the diverse NRI/PIOs communities closer to the motherland and the motherland closer to her overseas children.

Who Are We?

THE CENTRAL question is who are we? On the surface, it looks as if all NRIs and PIOs are overseas Indians. But the long period of colonialism and western domination has resulted in the alienation of a large number of PIOs and NRIs who have fallen under western influence and who have lost touch with Indian culture, civilization and religion. It boils down to a question of identity. Overseas Indians tend to regard themselves as belonging to distinct sub-ethnic identity groups, either as Punjabis, Sikhs, Sindhis, Biharis, Tamils, Telegus, Marathis and not as Hindus or Indians. Sometimes there is little interaction, give-and –take or solidarity among the different groups. The division is further compounded by ancestral and regional differences. The confusion about their identity is stretched so far that the sub-ethnic groups ignorantly claim that they are Tamils or Telegus and do not identify themselves as Hindus. They do not know about their extended identity, that they are Indians, but also Tamils, Hindus as well as Indo-Mauritians or Indo-South Africans.

The blame for the fragmentation must be shared by all. At the beginning, all the Hindus who had suffered under the plantations and under the exploiting White joined their efforts in order to win independence and to throw the white out of power. But once seated in power, the Hindus started discriminating among themselves. Certain sections of the privileged caste started to grab the nominations, appointments, offices and rewards from the state and jealously excluded the other Hindu bothers and sisters, belonging to other castes or language groups.

The division and fragmentation began to deepen. This is marked by almost every cultural or religious organisations, local, international or even global. If you scrutinise their membership, you will see that they tend to be monopolised by a few members belonging to the same caste or family relationships, to the exclusion of the out-groups. As the other sub-ethnic groups are rebuffed and excluded from the mainstream Hindu organisations, they tend to drift apart and club together to form distinct and parallel sub-ethnic organisations, thus further deepening the fragmentation of Hindu society on caste and linguistic lines.

Clearly, this identity confusion plays into the hands of politicians and particularly our old enemy who keeps on practising the policy of scientific communalism to divide us further from one another. This is quite apart from the problems of further divisions into different castes and sub-castes within the sub-ethnic groups. The Hindus fail to see themselves in their multiple identities, first as an Indian, secondly as a Mauritian, Trinidadian, South African or whatever, thirdly as a Hindu, regardless of the linguistic differences, fourthly as a Caribbean- all joining in a perfect sangam.

The fragmentation of Hindu society has put the geographically diverse NRIs/PIOs communities at tremendous political, economic and cultural disadvantages vis-a-vis other ethnic groups within their host countries. In a democratic set-up where political power is won on the basis of demographic strength, Indians who continue to regard themselves as belonging to distinct linguistic, regional or caste minorities and fail to see the larger picture, become their own worst enemies within the intense ethnic competition for power. It is unfortunate that the nature of democratic representation tends to deepen the rifts within the Hindu community.

In the competitive game for power, people with political ambitions will not hesitate to exploit the caste, linguistic and regional differences in order to win votes against one another. They easily play into the hands of the traditional enemies of the Hindus, the minority of white colonialists, who had always exercised power through the policy of divide and rule. This is how the Oligarchy has scanned all our weaknesses and has developed the winning strategy of scientific communalism by which they profit from splintering the majority Hindus into conflicting sub-ethnic minority groups. This is where fragmentation into sub-ethnic identity has become our worst enemy. It explains why, despite their numbers, the PIOs have lost political power in Guyana, Trinidad, Fiji and recently in Mauritius.

Another issue stems from the problem of adaptation to change and modernity It is a fact that the Indentured Indians had originally been drawn from rural background in India. They had been conditioned by their past agricultural, rural, static traditions. They had no Indian models of adaptation to modernity or to urbanisation. They have failed to evolve naturally in order to adapt to the challenges of a competitive, dynamic, rational, legal western environment. As simple agricultural people, they felt left behind in the racc for economic and political progress in an urban setting, marked by sophisticated international trade, industry, banking, modern management, a complex legal system. They could not adapt properly to the demands of the democratic political traditions of the west.. All these complexities have left them quite baffled. Emerging from a rural, peasant, agricultural environment, they find it hard to cope with urban western civilization and with all the complex demands of modern civilization. Their first defense mechanism had been to fold themselves up inside their closed traditional socicty. This is where they fcel like losing grips on themselves when they have to face rival ethnic groups, drawn from the west. They feel their self-confidence oozing out and they crumble down before the more aggressive White racist colonialist exploiters, more accustomed to the intricacies of modern life.

It further complicates the problem both of identity confusion and of role confusion. Within that fast-changing panorama, they confuse modernisation with westernisation. The disunity within the ranks of the Hindus stands in sharp contrast with the unity and solidarity within the ranks of the Jews, the White races, the Chinese, the Japanese, the Koreans and the Arabs. This is where Indians, particularly Hindus differ from the Japanese, the Chinese, the Singaporeans and Koreans who have self-confidence and are firmly embedded in in their culture and civilization which they consider to be the best and far superior to western civilization. The Chinese culture becomes a cementing bond. It keeps them closely united and builds strong ties of ethnic solidarity.

In contrast, Indians have yet to learn from the Jews who are known to be a tightly- knit community. They have to learn from the white who preserve their hegemony by sticking closely together through the bonds of culture, language, civilization, racism, religion. The Moslems have learned to adapt the spirit of unity from their enemies, the Jews. Thanks to the influence of the oil-rich Gulf countries, the rise of Islamic expansionism, fundamentalism, terrorism, the Arab influence has spread like a new imperialism. They are pushing forward for the establishment of Islamic states and the ideology of world Islamic brotherhood. Similarly, the Chinese value their Chineseness as constituting the main cause of their success and as being far superior to western culture which they see riddled with numerous weaknesses.

This continuing fragmentation of Hindu society has been happening at a time when the Indian Muslims have been drifting away from their Indian roots, claiming to be loyal to Pakistan or to Arab countries. Influenced by the global Islamic movement, funded by Gulf countries, wearing the signs, symbols, Arab dress and identifying themselves with the Middle East, learning Arabic in preference to Urdu, the Indian Muslims seek their identity in a global Islamic brotherhood in a bid to oppose western influences.

Originally, the Immigrants, the Jahajis, comprising Hindus and Muslims, all fared the same fate in the plantations. They had to struggle together and they shared the same broad-based Indian cultural and civilizational values. But since the late 1970's, in the wake of the rise of Islamic fundamentalism, the Islamic opposition to the west and the long and bloody Palestinian struggle against Israel have helped to solidify their distinct Islamic identity oriented towards the Arab world.

Conclusion

THE LESSON from the above is that overseas Indians should re-discover their Indianness, go back to their roots, draw inspiration from the struggles and contributions of their Immigrant forefathers. They should take a fresh look at themselves through the diasporic mirror and develop closer ties with mainland India. They should take pride in their broader, global diasporic identity. The emerging diaspora awareness may foster a new spirit of mutual tolerance and solidarity among the different components of Indian society for the good of one and all. Hopefully, this will enable them to see the larger picture, the wider opportunities opening up, the networking and the global awareness that will sustain them against a challenging, competitive environment.

C. TRACING OUR ROOTS

THE HISTORY of Indian immigration does not date to the landing of our Immigrant ancestors into the plantation colonies or the shores of South East Asia. What they carried with them was the proud legacy of an ancient culture and civilization dating back to millennia before Christianity or Islam and that's where their history began- in pre-historic times. So, if we are engaged to track their early roots, we have to plunge deep into history and capture the essence of their early spirit and civilization as these evolved along the river banks, mountain flanks and impenetrable jungles.

Apart from the physical ruins of the Indus Valley Civilization in the Mohenjodaro and Harappa regions, there is another intangible civilization that is still with us. It is everywhere alive in us and around us. This is what gives our life a meaning, a depth and a vision. It informs our prayers, our ceremonies, our customs, our daily life, our dress, our food, our music, our melody, our thoughts, our identity, our very Indianness. Sometimes, it manifests itself in the rocky temples of Mahabalipuram, south of Madras, in the temple of Madurai, in the ruins of Nalanda, in the Buddhist temples of Sanchi and countless impressive Buddhist monuments spanning across China, Japan, Korea, South East Asia. And anywhere you turn across the whole spiritual landscape of Asia, even extending across the desert of the Middle East, in Iraq, you will meet the intangible spirit of Indian culture and civilization. The spirit of Indian culture and civilization is also inscribed in the cave paintings of Ajanta, the temple sculpture of Ellora, Elephanta Caves, Batu Caves in Kuala Lumpur. It is there in Ayodhya, in Mathura and has descended down into the chants of countless bards and saint poets, from Kabir to Dyneswar, Tiruvelluvar, Guru Nanak to Ramakrishnan, Vivekanand, Swami Dayanand. While the very message and spirit are unbeatable in their profundity and meaning, unfortunately they have been kept sealed and made inaccessible to the rest of the non-Asian world. They have not been packaged, structured, institutionalised, broadcast, marketed and communicated to the world the way the two proselytising faiths, Christianity and Islam, have done. In other words, Indians have been shy about their religion and philosophy.

Today, at the PBD, when we gather to celebrate the third meeting of the diaspora, somewhere deep inside our mind, hearts and soul, it is the very spirit of this civilization that we are proudly celebrating. Our faith lay hidden deep inside our heart and soul. It looks somehow how the devotee, Sri Hanuman, bared his chest to show the picture of Lord Rama and Sita seated inside. This is the root cause of our very being. It should now be reinvigorated and presented to a world sick with the clashes of religious intolerance, fundamentalism and religious imperialism.

This is also the story of how our immigrant forefathers left the shores of India in difficult circumstances and at different times to disperse into different parts of the world, into the Indian Ocean, Asia Pacific and Atlantic regions. They knew that so long as their motherland lay bleeding at the hands of the imperialists, the Moghuls and the British, so long as colonialism and its sequel- exploitation, misery, famines, unemployment, poverty, despair and desolation stalked the ancestral land, there was little hope left. So, forced by circumstances, they felt they had to seek new pastures and new horizons in the fond hope of making some fortune and return home to their villages to build better homes for their children and grand children.

But they did not leave India empty-handed. They carried with them and implanted overseas a slice of the heart, the mind and the soul of their mother country. That was the baggage of Indian culture and civilization which has long survived them. They have added a set of new rhythms, new idioms, a touch of oriental wisdom, fresh colours, spicy flavours and some originality and variety to enrich the world's cultural heritage.

From their adventures have sprung up successive generations of PIOs who have struggled hard, sacrificed, suffered and contributed to do honour to their motherland and their countries of adoption. Though they met with hostility, incomprehension, intolerance and ridicule from their racist oppressors, yet they felt their mind fortified with the epic example of Lord Ram enduring his fourteen years' exile in the jungle. And they bowed down to the Almighty as they humbly sat down cross-legged to draw solace in the melody and philosophy of the Ramayana verses, flowing like the sparkling Ganges gushing out from the Himalayas towards the Indian Ocean. They harked to the eternal words of Lord Krishna on the Battlefield of Kurukshetra exhorting Arjuna to arise and defend the dharma against the oppressors. Emboldened by the eternal spirit of Indian culture and civilization which they passed on to successive generations, their combative spirit and their commitment to Indianness lives on in the mind of the NRIs and PIOs gathered here to celebrate the PBD.

Today, we stand in awed silence to pay tribute to the spirit of those soldiers of the Hindu dharma who dared to cross the seven seas, facing the unknown but determined to hold their heads high, to improve the lives of their families and their descendants. They succeeded largely due to their indomitable spirit to struggle, to strive, to work hard and to live an honest life, to save and sacrifice and never to yield according to the traditions of Indian culture.

This is to say that our spiritual roots had far preceded the arrival of those physically frail and battered Jahajis who landed fatigued, aged at the Immigration depots in Port Louis, Port of Spain or Suva. Our real roots were enriched by the Indian spiritual and civilizational legacy embedded in the ancient days of Vedic India reverberating in the Sanskrit verses created somewhere along the Ganges, by the flanks of the Himalayas, into the forest deep. There, the divine wisdom flashed into the third eyes of those sages who, meditating under the pipal trees, composed the eternal Vedic hymns to guide faltering mankind on the early path to divinity. From these sacred verses were born the essence of Indian philosophy, including the idioms, the arts, the music, the dancing steps, the chants, the prayers, the sciences and the deep thoughts and wisdom that were to guide humanity on their first steps towards civilized life. That was it -the Vedic light of knowledge and wisdom.

Truly, the most ancient book known to men were the Vedas, the book of knowledge and divine wisdom, the mother of all religions, sparkling with unsurpassed philosophy.

Millennia after, these same ancient values stood by our Immigrant forefathers as they grappled with the onslaught of westernisation and evangelism that came hot on the trails of colonialism and racism, backed by western military, political and technological might. The invisible soft power of Indian culture and civilization had formed the common bonds of Indian legacy, the trade marks of their Indianness, that had spread into the far corners of the world on the steps of the labour immigrants. In response to the hard power of the west, the Immigrant labourers countered with the soft spiritual power that Mahatma Gandhi was to use as Satyagraha to topple the might British Empire.

Long before their landing, the distant lands of the earth had resounded with the sciences, the mathematics, knowledge, wisdom, the economy, cultures and civilizations of the East. So, our forefathers landed with the spirit of spiritual conquerors to reclaim and spread the glory of their ancient culture. This is the challenge which we, as their inheritors, following in their footsteps, should really undertake, that is, to reconquer the world peacefully for the triumph of Indian culture and civilization. We owe it to the efforts and sacrifices of our immigrant ancestors.

The Physical Roots

ON THE PHYSICAL side, we may invoke historical and cultural instances dating back somewhere to 5th Century B.C to show how Indian immigrants had long traded with and settled in various corners of Asia, in Java, Sumatra, Borneo, Cambodia, Malaysia peninsula. Everywhere they had gone, the ancient Indians had also spread their language, religion, customs, political system, social system, culture and civilization, as witnessed by temple architecture across SEA.

The second wave of immigration was marked by the kangani system of contract labour to Burma, Ceylon, Nepal, Malaysia and other SEA countries. In 1819, Indian soldiers settled in Singapore, followed by the merchants in 1824.

Since 1721, the third batch of immigrants were the Indian slaves who were kidnapped and looted from the French naval bases in Chandanagore, in Bengal, in Mahe, Pondicherry, along the Coromandel and Malabar coast brought as slaves to Mauritius and Reunion island. Further historical researches need to be made into the archives of these places and all the intricacies concerning the evolution of the Indian slaves should be raked. These were the talented people who built the harbour, the roads, pubic buildings and who passed on their crafts and skills to their Creole children, born of their Black slave wives. This goes to prove one point, that the Creoles of Mauritius and Reunion have also inherited Indian blood and as such are entitled to lay claim to their Indianness.

Fourthly, since 1816, more than 1500 Indian convicts were despatched to work in construction and road building works in Mauritius. Other Indian convicts drawn mainly from Punjab and Madras, were sent to do the same road building works, the canals, harbour, sea walls, jetties and lay the network of infrastructure of Singapore. This is the time when we should pay tribute to the blood and sweat of those bearded, exploited men who erected the foundation of civilized living in those colonies and for whom no tribute, no monument has been erected.

But the largest wave of Indian immigration, 1.5 million, followed in the wake of the abolition of slavery, from 1834 to 1920. . The first experiment was carried out in Mauritius which, indeed, received the largest proportion of Indian Immigrants, nearing 500,000 or 70% of the population. In majority they came from the rural areas of the Gangetic plains, from Uttar Pradesh, Bihar, from the Madras Presidency, from Andra Pradesh and a sprinkling came from Bombay presidency to Mauritius.

From 1842 to 1872, the number of Immigrants to the plantation colonies stood as follows:-

Mauritius	351,401
British Guina	79,691
Trinidad	42,519

Other West Indian islands 7,021
Natal 6,448
Reunion and French colonies 31,346
(Ly Tio Fane, *Lured Away*, MGI, 1984).

Henceforth, the story of the 1.5 million Indian immigration can be illustrated as follows:-
In 1653-the first batch of Indian immigrants were sold as slaves in the Dutch Cape Colony
1860- Indian Immigrants poured into Natal, forming 10% Coolies from Bihar, UP, 50% Tamils, 10% Telegus and 20% free Gujarati traders. – From 1873- 1916, 40,000 Indians immigrants were brought to Surinam, populated by 40% Creoles, 40% Indians and 20% Javanese. Later, on independence, 180,000 Indians migrated to the Netherlands, leaving only 160,000 back in Surinam.
453,063 poured into Reunion Island.
143,934 into Trinidad
238,979. into Guyana
60,000 into Fiji

Another breakdown of the places of recruitment of the Emigrants for the period 1842-70, mainly from North West India would be as follows:

		Bengal				NW
	Orissa	Western	Central	Eastern	Bihar	Provinces
British Guyana	719	14,028	2,166	238	24,681	25,551
Mauritius	3,116	33,131	8,951	1,118	108,156	47,286
Trinidad	378	8,396	1,305	176	11,278	16,027
Jamaica	147	3,214	341	106	4,496	4,654
Natal	2	216	24	356	370	-
Réunion	19	1,667	171	29	4,027	4,469

(G.B, Parliamentary Papers, 1874.XI-VII. As cited in V. Teelock's book, *Mauritian History 2001*)

The first batch of coolies were drawn from the Dhangars or Hill Coolies from Chota Nagpur consisting mainly of the Santals, Mundas, and Oraons who had lost their employment as a result of the closing of their clothes factories to make way for British textile industry and export to India. This trend was to force massive unemployment in India driving whole villages from the north and South into unemployment and poverty and forced emigration.

The emigrants had drifted from their villages and the neighbouring districts of the Twenty Four Parganasover to the ports and the towns where the unemployed were looking for job opportunities. The recruiters drew their cohort mainly from the north-western districts of Bihar,and

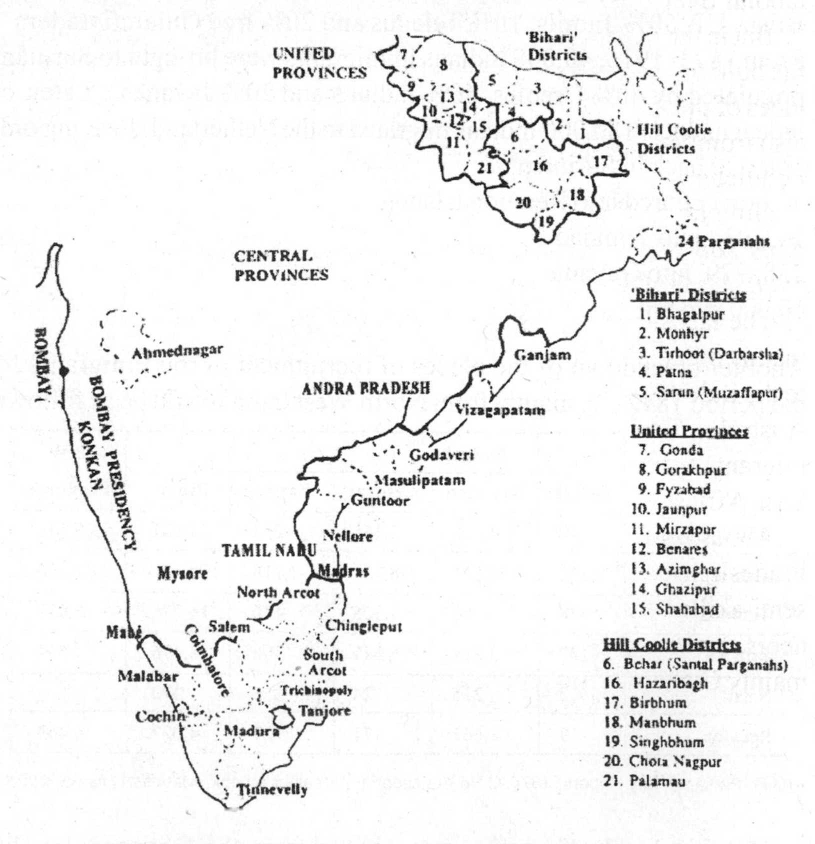

Map showing areas of recruitement of indentured labour in India

from Benares, mainly the districts of Arrah, Midnapur, Burdwan, and Cuttack, Azamgarh, Gorakpur, Muzaffaarpur, Champaran, Shahabad, patna and Gaya. Districts. Many were driven by the severe famine in the 1840's.

In the South, in Madras, the recruiters raked the districts of Tanjore, Trichnopoly, South Arcotand the Telegu districts of Vizagapatnam, Ganjam and Rajahmundry for the poor, landless, people overburdened with debts and taxes.

(Hugh Tinker. A New System of Slavery. The Export of Indian laboiur overseas 1830- 1020.OUP. 1974)

But in the French colonies of Reunion Island, Guadeloupe, Martinique, the bulk of the emigrants were drawn from the French-controlled provinces of the South, 90% consisting of the 14 Tamil, and Telegu districts, also from Kerala, and Mysore,. The immigration depots were located in Pondicherry and Karikal.

(Juliette Smeralda-Amon. *La Question de L'immigration indienne dans son Environnement Socio-Economique Martiniquais. 1848-1900.* L'Harmattan. 1996).

The last successive waves of NRIs, since World War II, consisting mainly of individuals, professionals, engineers, technocrats who migrated to the industrial countries of the west, including Britain, the US, Canada, Australia. To these highly educated migrants must be added the twice migrants from Mauritius, Guyana, Trinidad, Fiji, Suriname, South and East Africa.

About 3.5 million Indians, mainly from South India, Kerala and Andra Pradesh, have also migrated to the Gulf countries, performing largely semi-akilled and skilled labour, with a sprinkling of professionals, engineers, architects, doctors, accountants, technocrats and businessmen, mainly Gujaratis, Punjabis and Sindhis.

D. SOME POEMS BY ANAND MULLOO

From *Dust of Time*, 1970.

Unfinished Journey

Sometimes the road across was shady
Sprinkled with greenery
Honeyed with love
Sometimes hard, hilly
Sometimes scorching
The burden pressed hard
The load was shared.
Though fatigued, sickened
The traveller, undefeated,
Sometimes pushed,
Sometimes paused,
On his
Unfinished
Journey…

The Vagabond

I roam the streets
Scenting liquors and cigars.
On terminus, at street end,
I note the giddy drama of life,
The merry-go-round.
Palms stretched, eyes hollow,
Breasts heaving, hips wriggling
Sagging, aging, without protest,
Pursuers of dream, children of darkness,
Household tyrants
And disguised dictators
Feasting on others' wants
Deaf to their groans
Riding high on caste and colour
Crawling, and clutching, labelling and rotting
In their narrow mental prisons.

Kolicatta

Left the grey mist hovering over Howrah bridge
Disguising Hoogli and old Kolicatta
Pin pointed with porters,
Crammed with passengers and luggages
Passengers here, passengers there,
cPouring from all over the peninsula
Lounging in waiting rooms,
Squatting on platforms,
Treading on toes,
Cracking nuts, peeling bananas,
Chewing betels, puffing beedis,
Biting chappatis, sipping hot tea,
Stealing glances, hiding blushes,
Dreaming of parted friends,
The holy Ganges,
Of nawabs of old
Selling Bongodesh to out-bidders,
Of tigers flayed,
Of carpets shipped
To adorn alien homes.
Turbaned men, saried women
Girls in veil, gipsies in jewellery,
Bubbling brides, bored businessmen,
Bewildered tribesmen,
Groaning beggars, orphaned refugees,
Waiting for the whistle, the clanking chains
Frantic rushes, excited voices, hurried kisses, tears.
The heavy wheels rattle on railroads.

Land of Indra

Land of my forbears
Roots of my roots
Sources of man's consciousness
To you, I pour libation.

The meditations of Vedic sages;
Love all, serve all
Echo in my soul
For the glory of Mankind

The verses of the Gita
Man's tottering steps guide
In this battle-field of life
This Kurukshetra eternal.

No rituals, no praises,
Ram, I long to be,
Ram, the righteous
Ram, the perfect.

Here's Ram riding across
The rocks of Mahabalipuram
Siva, the Supreme Yogi,
Kailash temple upholds
Buddha meditating in Ajanta
Dayanand in the Himalaya
Gandhi in the hearts of Harijans.

Land of Indra
Light this animal world
This universe torn by men's egoes,
Teach us how to be Man.
Forsake us not
To this chaotic wilderness
Our age restore to Vedic purity
Indra, Mother of Mankind

The Black Princess

The black princess of Ajanta
Weaves a starry flower
Round her fingers.
Below her breasts,
Her diamond necklace
Sparkles in the cave.
Her bent head,
Nose and lips
Glow in the eternity
Of youthful beauty.

Wardha

An old weather-beaten Maratha porter
Moustache drooping, khaki-clad
My luggage piled on his head
Like Hanuman flying with the hill.

A cold morning, biting..
I climbed into a cycle rickshaw
It bumped and jerked and creaked
On the dusty stony road.

The rickshawalla, barefoot, red-turbaned,
Pedalled, panted, pedalled, panted,
Gasped huge mouthfuls of cold air.
The wheels rumbled and jingled.
My heart felt sick
At the human beast pulling me.

Day break.
Dust, noise.
Huts, dark, filthy, bare.
Roads and twisted lanes
Narrow, un-swept, winding.
Sluices and dunghills,, flies and stench,
Men sweeping hotels and verandahs.

Along the station, famished folks
Dust-soilewd, haggard, bony
Crawled on floor, lay on their backs
Asking for alma in feeble tone.

From the station bench,
A starving, girl, diseased skin,
Weak, blind with hunger,
Death pale, tottered,

Lurched, in a supreme effort, to the post
In the agony of slow death.
Buddha and Gandhi fasting.

Along the rail road,
Tribals cooked in dirty pots,
Turning over chappatis.
Palms stretched;
A coin dropped in the pot.

From a tent burst forth.
A lovely gipsy girl.
Hurriedly, pulled out my sketch book
To pencil her rare beauty.
She flung at me with knife in hand.

At Wardha railway junction,
Central India, I took a tonga
To reach Sevagram where Gandhi
Once experimented with Truth,
With humanity.

REFERENCES

Allen, Richard. *Indian Immigrants and the Restructuring of the Mauritian Sugar Industry. 1848- 1910* in Journal of Mauritian Studies. MGI. Vol0000. I Series I.2000.

Amon, Smwlrada Juliette. *La Question de L'Immigration Indienne dans son Environnement Socio Economique 1848- 1900*. L'Harmattan. Paris. France. 1996.

Appasawmy, Selva. *The Hidden Priest. Ewdard Charles Clifford of Chudleigh 1803-1843*. 2003.

Atmaram, Pandit. *Truth At Last*. 1949.

Author of Padima. *A Transport Voyage to Mauritius*. 1831.

Barnwell, P.J. *Visits and Dispatches*. (1598-1948) 1948.

Baumann, Martin. *The Hindu Diasporas in Europe and an Analysis of Key Diasporic Patterns*.

Beaton. Rev. *Creoles and Coolies*.

Bee, Helen. *The Growing Child*. Longman. N.Y 1999.

Bedel, Maurice. *Tropiques Noirs*.

Benoit, Gaetan. *The Afro-Mauritians*. MGI Press. 1985.

Bissoondoyal, Basdeo. *Life in Greater India*. Bharatiya Vidya Bhawan. 1984.

Bissoondoyal, Uttam. *Indians Overseas*. The Mauritian Experience. MGI Press.1984.

Bissoondoyal,U & Servansingh. *Slavery in South West Indian Ocean*. MGI Press. 1989.

Bowen, George Ferguson, Sir. *Thirty years of Colonial Government*. Longman. 1889.

Boyden. J& UNESCO. *Families*. Gala Book Ltd, London.1993

Brah, Avtar. *Cartographies of Diaspora*. Routeledge.London.1996

The Brennen Memorandum. 1845.

Britter, Alfred. *A Commentary on Facts: Being a Survey of the Principal Issues raised by the Recent Unrest on the Sugar Estates of*

Mauritius. Port Louis. 1937.

Brown, Percy. *Indian Architecture.Buddhist and Hindu Periods.* Taraporewala & Sons & Co. Bombay. 1971.

Bundhoo, S. *Goodlands & Her Neighbours*. 1989.

Buxani, Ram. *Taking the High Road*, Motivate Publishing, Dubai 2003.

Carter, Mariner, *Lakskmi's Legacy*. E.O.I. 1994.

Carter Mariner, *Colouring the Rainbow. Mauritian Society in the Making*. CRIOS. 1998.

Carter, M & Deerpalsing, S. *Living and Workinng Conditions Under Indenture.*Vol. I-III MGI

Carter, M & Torabally, Khal. *Coolitude. An Anthology of the Indian Labour Diaspora.* Wimbledon Publishing Co. London. 2002.

Cole, Lowry, Sir. *Memoirs of Sir Lowry Cole*. 1934.

Coombes, North, M.D. *Struggles in the Cane Fields. Small Cane Growers and Millers 1921- 37* in Journal of Mauritian Studies. Vol. 2. MGI. 1987.

Coombes, North, *Studies in the Political Economy of Mauritius*. MGI Press. 2000.

Coward, Harold & Botting , Heather. *The Hindu Diaspora in Western Canada*.

Daneck Marguerite. *Indian Sculpture. Masterpieces of Khmer and Chem Art*. Hamlyn Publishing Group Led. 1970.

Das Guruchan. *India Unbound*. Penguin Books. 2000.

De Challaye. A. *Maurice sur L'Immigration des Indiens*. 1844.

De l'Estrac, JeanClaude, *Mauriciens Enfants de Mille Races*, 2004.

Denmark, Marguerite. *Indian Sculpture.*

D'Epinay. *Notice Biographique Sur Adrien D'Epinay*. Imprimerie du Cernéen. 1840.

Dev, Ravi. *Racist Crimes Against Indians. Hindus in the Caribbean*, from his address at the symposium, The Civil Disorders of January 12, 1998.Georgetown, Guyana. 1998.

Dubey, Ajay. *Indian Diaspora. Global Identity*. Kalinga Publications, Delhi. 2003.

DCDM. *Patterns & Trends in the Feminisation of Poverty in Mauritius*. Sept. 2001

De Plevitz, Loretta. *Restless Energy. Adolphe de Plevitz*. MGI Press. 1987.

Emigrant. *Indian Emigration*. 1924.

Fanchette, Regis. *Charmes de La Vie Creole* in Seve Magazine

Ferguson, Ted. *A White Man's Country. An Exercise in Canadian Prejudice.* Doubleday Canada Ltd. Toronto. 1975.

Fokeer, A.F. *Sir William Newton & His Times*. Gen. Printing & Stationery. 1917.

GOPIO. PIO's *The Emerging Diaspora*. ICCR Conference. New Delhi. Jan. 2003.

GOPIO. *Entrepreneurs Global network For Socio-Economic Upliftment*. VI Asian Conference. Putrajaya. Malaysia. Aug. 2003.

GOPIO. *Empowering PIOs for Socio-economic Development*. New Delhi. Jan. 2004.

GOPIO. *Reach Out Globally Act Locally*. 2nd Asian Conference Papers. Melaka Malaysia. Aug. 1995.

Goordyal, Ranjit. *Lectures on Social and Economic History of Mauritius*. University of Mauritius. May. 1975.

Gordon, Hamilton, Sir. *Mauritius Records of Private and Public Life, (1871-74)*. 1894.

Moutou B., *Etapes et Sequelles de L'Esclavage à L'Ile Mauric et à L'Ile Rodrigues*. MGI. Feb. 1985.

Hazareesingh, K. *A History of Indians in Mauritius 1950.*

Hazareesingh, K. Ed. *Indian Centenary Book*, MGI, 1976.

Hennessey, James Pope. *Verandah*.

Hitie, Evenor.. *Histoire de Maurice*. 1897.

Hooper. *Report of Uunrest in Sugar Estates*. 1937.

Indian Express, Pune. Jan. 8.2003.

India Today. Special Issue on *The Global Indian Doing Us Proud*. Jan.11, 2003.

Jagatsingh, Kher. *Petals of Dust*. Port Louis. 1981

Jain, Prakash. *Indians in South Africa*. Kalinga. Delhi. 1999

Jain, Ravindra. *Overseas Indians in Malaysia and the Caribbeans*:

Comparative Notes. JNU.

Jumeer, Musleem,. *Towards a New Conceptual Framework for Slavery in Mauritius*. MGI. 1985.

Kalla, A. C. *The Gujarati Merchants in Mauritius*. 1850-1900. in Journal of Mauritian Studies. Vol. 2 No 1. 1987.

Kumar, Sudarshan. Ed. *Pioneers of Prosperity*. Baleswar Agarwal. New Delhi. 2000.

Lady. *Recollections of the Mauritius* by a Lady. 1830.

Le Code Noir ou Recueil de Règlements. Mars. 1685.

Lingayah, Sam. *Mauritian Immigrants in Britain*. Mauritians' Welfare Association. Kimberley. London. 1987.

Macmillan, Alistair. *L'Isle de France*. 1914.

Macmillan, A. *Mauritius Illustrated*. 1914.

Mangru, Basdeo. *Indians in Guyana*. Adams Press. Chicago. Illinois. 2000.

Mannick, A.R. *Mauritians in London*. Dodo Books. Sussex. UK. 1987.

Meighoo, Kirk. A. *Trinidad sans renier le passé nous sommes tournés vers l'avenir*. Interview in Week end.23 May 2004.

Moore, Jill. *Community Values in Multi-Cultural Mauritius*. A View from Britain. In Journal of Mauritian Studies. Vol. 1 No 1. 1986.

Motwani, K.Jagat. *America and India in a Give & Take Relationship*. Center for Asian, African and Caribbean Studies.New York. 2003.

Mulloo,Anand. *Interview of Prof. Joseph Harris*, Howard University, Washington. D.C in Femmes des Iles. June 1985.

Mulloo, A. *Our Struggle*. Visionbooks, N.D. 1982.

Mulloo, A. *Marathi Settlements in Mauritius*. Quad. 1991.

Nagapen, Amedee. *Le Catholicisme des Esclaves à Maurice* in Journal of Mauritian Studies. MGI. 1985.

Naipaul, V.S. *The Overcrowded Baracoon*. Penguin Books. UK. 1972.

Nandan, Satiendra Nath. *Lines Across Black Waters*. Academy press. 1997.

Paramananda, Swami. *Prayer*. sgas@intnet.mu. 2003.

Paratian, Rajendra. *La République de L'Ile Maurice. Dans le sillage de la délocalisation*. L'Harmattan. Paris. France. 1994.

Petition of the Old Immigrants of Mauritius presented on 6th June 1871.

Pike, Nicholas. *Sub-Tropical Rambles*. 1873.

Pinco, Ly Tio Fane. Feb. *International Seminar on Slavery in South West Indian Ocean*. MGI.

Ly Tio Fane. *In the Grips of the Eagle. Mathew Flinders at Ile de France.1803-1810*. MGI. 1988.

Lured Away. History of Cane Workers. MGI Press. 1984.

Isle de France 1715-1746, MGI. 1993.

Pitot, Albert. *Isle de France. Esquisses Historiques.*

Prosper, J. G. *L'Africanité Mauricienne à Travers Les Lettres du Térroir*. MGI.Feb. 1985.

Protector of Immigrants's *Annual Reports*, 1859-65.

Ramgoolam, Sir Seewoosagur, *Speeches* in Legislative Council.

Ramhota, Pavi. *A Research Project on Petty Traders in a Village Market* in Journal of Mauritian Studies.Vol.4 No 2. MGI. 1993.

Raya, N. Unpublished Research and doctoral thesis. *Poverty and Social Exclusion*. The Creole Community in Mauritius. Open University London. 2004.

Rennards. T. M. Stipendiary Magistrates- *Observations*. Black River. 1865-68.

Roland Benjamin. *Art and Architecture of India.*

Roy, J.N. *Mauritius in Transition*. 1960.

Roy, J.N.*Whither Indo-Mauritians?* 1937.

Rouillard, Guy. *Histoire des Domaines Sucriers de l'île Maurice.* Les Pailles. Mauritius. 1979.

Sawant, Ankush. Ed. India and South Africa. *A Fresh Start.* Kalinga. N.D. 1994.

Seecharan, Clem. *India and the Shaping of the Indo-Guyanese Imagination*. 1890-1920.University of Warwick. UK. 1993.

Sharma, D.S. *A Primer of Hinduism*. 1981.

Singh, Kunwar Maharaj *Report on Mauritius* Mitra Sept 1925.

Singhvi, L. *Towards Global Togertheness*. N.D.2002.

Singhvi.L. *Report of the High Level Committee on the Indian Diaspora.*

St Pierre, Bernardin de. *Voyage to Ile de France*. 1769.

Subramanil. *Altering Imagination*. Suva. Fiji. 1995.

Swettenham, Sir Frank, O'Malley & Woodcock. *Royal Commission of Inquiry*. 1910.

Teelock, Vijaya. *Decolonising Sugar; The Rise and Fall of Small Planters in Mauritius*. 1998.

Teelock, Vijaya. *Bitter Sugar and Sugar Slavery in 19th Century Mauritius*. MGI. 1998.

Teelock, Vijaya & Alpers, Edward. *History, Memory & Identity*. University of Mauritius. 2001.

Tinker, Hugh. *A New System of Slavery*. Oxford University Press. 1974.

Vanmeerkeck, E. *Jean Lebrun*. La Sentinelle. 1865

Varma, M. *Indian Immigrants and Their Descendants in Mauritius*. 1973.

Virahsawmy, Raj. *La Petite Production Agricole. Romantisme ou Réalité*. In Journal of Mauritian Studies. No 5.MGI. June 1980.

Virahsawmy, Raj. *Characteristics of Island Economies*. Seminar papers. University of Mauritius. Ed. 1977.

Werbner Pnina & Modood Tariq. *Debating Cultural Hybridity*. Post colonial Encounters. Sed Books. London. 2000.

Wertheim, W. F. *The Rising Waves of Emancipation. From Counterpoint Towards Revolution*. Annual Meeting of the British Sociological Association. University of York. U.K. 14 April 1972.

NEWSPAPERS

Indian

The Asian Age.N.D. www.asianage.com. 10 & 11 Jan. 2003.

Hindustan Times.N.D. www. hindustantimes.com. 9, 11 Jan. 2003.

Mid Day N.D. 13 Jan. 2003.

The Hindu. N.D. 10 Jan. 2003.

Jeeroburkhan, Jooneed. Interview. *Il n'y a pas mille façons: il faut reprendre l'état en main*. Mauritius Times. 6 May 2004.

The Economic Times. N.D. 12 Jan, .& 2 Feb. 2003.

The Economic Times. Mumbai, Boundless Bharat. The Emerging Global Power. 28 Jan. 2003.

Economist: Born in India, at home in UK. Lord Meghanath Desai.

The Indian Express. Jan. 10,2003.

Nandy Ashis. *Hinduism Versus Hindutva. The Inevitability of a Confrontation*. Times of India. 18 Feb. 1991.

The Times of India.N.D 11, 12 Jan. 2003.

Interview. C.K. Prahalad. *World- Class India*. Times of India. N.D. Jan. 15, 2003.

The Times of India . Pune.

Local

Burrun. B. *De Lucknow à L'île Maurice. Dabydeen Reetoo*. Week-End 20, Aug, 10 Sept 1995.

Notice *Biographique sur Adrien D'Epinay*. Imprimerie du Cernéen. 1840.

Manilall Doctor. L'Express. 27.Jan. 1974.

Gerbeau, Hubert. *Maurice-Reunion: du 18e au 20e Siècle*. L'express. 8 May 1980.

Maurice-Reunion: *Du 18e Au 20e Siècle*. L'express. 8 May 1980.

L'Homme, L'Eoville. L'Express. 4 August 1896.

Maurel, F. L. L'Express. 21 July, 1896.

Mauritius Mitra. 14th Sept. 1925.

Meighoo, Kirk, Dr. *A Trinidad sans renier le passé, nous sommes tournés vers l'avenir*. Week-End 23 May 2004.

Neerohoo, Prakash. *Manilal Doctor à L'Ile Maurice* in Le Militant. 2 Oct. 1975.

Noel, Karl Dr. *L'esclavage à l'Isle de France*, 1715-1810. Review by Philippe Rey. L'Express. 6.Aug.1991.

Raynal, Gaetan. Gandhi à Maurice. Le Cernéen.26 Oct. 1968.

MAGAZINES AND JOURNALS

Business Magazine. Yvan Martial. *A L'écoute de la Société Mauricienne*. 25 June. 2003.

India Today. Special issue- *How to Build an Indian Century*. March 29. 2004.

Femmes des Iles. Jan. 1985.

Jeeroobarkhan, Jooneed. (Interview) *.Il faut reprendre L'état en mains. L'Oligarchie s'est renforcée*. Mauritius Times. 30 April 2004.

Journal of Mauritian Studies. Vol. 1. No 2 MGI. 1988.

La Revue Rétrospectives de L'Ile Maurice.Vol. 4 No 3. 1953.

Martial, Yvan. In Business Magazine.1st Jult 2003.

Seshadri, H.V. *The Mother Wakes up Again*. The Hindu.

We! Isis International No 45. July 2004.

PAPERS PRESENTED

Anenden Nursimloo. A.D. *A Sense of Kind and a Sense of Difference and the Notion of Identity in a Plural Society*. Int. Conference. MGI. 1984.

Alpers,E. Prof. Univ. of California. *Caribbean Perspectives on Post-Emancipation Mauritius*. MGI. 23-26 June 1999.

Arya, Ratna Deo, Capt., Mumbai. *Achievement of Arya Samaj in Education and Religion*. On the 125th celebration of Arya Samaj in Mauritius.

Asaratnam. S. Univ. of New England, Australia. *The Evolution of Malaysian Indian Society*. Int. Conf. on Indian Labour Immigration. MGI. Oct. 1984.

Bana Surendra. *A Historiography of the Indentured Indians in Natal*. Review and Prospects. Int. Conference on Labour Immigration in Mauritius. Oct. 1984.

Basri, Ghazali. Malaysia. *Religious and Communal Harmony*. A

Way Forward. 1st International Interfaith Conference. IBN SINA Academic Research Centre. Quatre Bornes. 25-26 August 2004.

Coombes-North.M.D. University of Natal. Struggles in the Canefields. Small Cane Growers, Millers and Colonial State in Mauritius, 1921-27. Journal of Mauritian Studies. Vol.2 No 1.1987.

Coombes-North. *From Slavery to Indenture. Forced labour in the Political Economy of Mauritius*, 1834-1867. Int. Conference. MGI. 1984.

Dubey, Ajay. *Indian Diaspora in the Francophone Africa.*

Eisenholr Patrick *Language ideology & Imaginations of Indianness in Mauritius*. Dissertation Proposal. Univ. of Chicago. 3 June 1997.

Fok Cheung, Mark. *Paper on Les Cantonnais de l'Ile Maurice.* MGI.

Fraser, Bashabi (Mrs). Edinburgh University *Multicultural Voices in Beyond Borders*. Regional Voices in the Market Place.

3 International Writers' Conference. Mauritian Writers' Association.Issue No 4. August 2004.

Gayan-Nursimooloo.Surya. *A Brief Analysis of the Strategy of Small Planters in Mauritius.*

Goordyal, Ranjit. *Social and Economic History of Mauritius.* Lectures. University of Mauritius.1975.

Gayan Nursimooloo. Surya. *A Brief Analysis of the Strategy of Small Planters in Mauritius*. Journal of Mauritian Studies. MGI.

Gundara, Jagdish. Inst. of Edn, Univ. of London. Whither inclusive Nehruvian State: *The Global, the National and Knowledge in the Indian Ocean Region*. MGI. 8-12 Dec. 1998.

Gupt, Bharat. *What is Ethnic?* 6/17/2003. Http:/ indiastar.com.Guptl.html.

Haraksingh, Kusha. Univ. of the West Indies. *Culture, Religion and Resistance among Indians in the Caribbean*. Conference on Indian Labour Migration. MGI Oct. 1984.

Holass. D. Miss. *Health and Sanitation in Post-Emancipation Mauritius*. MGI. June 1999.

Jahangeer, Amina. *Ethnicity: A Comparative Study.* Seminar on

The Concept of Mauritian Studies. MGI. Aug. 29, 1994.

Jayaram. N. Occasional Paper No 1. Bangalore University. *TheStudy of Indian Diaspora. A Multidisciplinary Agenda*. 1998. http:/www.uohyd.ernet.in/sss/cinddiaspora/occasional1.html

Jha. J.C. Patna University. *An Indian National Panchayat* of *Trinidad*, 1899. MGI. Oct. 1984.

Kalla. A.C. *The Gujarati Merchants in Mauritius*. 1850-1900. Journal of Mtian Studies. 1987.

Kelly, John. *Coolie as a Labour Commodity*. MGI. 1985.

Kin, Tsan Man, Joseph. *L'Heritage Hakka à Maurice*. MGI.

Lee Raymond M & Rajoo R. Univ. of Malaysia. *Sanskritization and Indian Ethnicity in Malaysia*. Modern Indian Studies. Cambridge Univ. Press. 1987.

Low Chan. J.C. *Roots, Rasta and Riots*. MGI. June 1999.

Ly Tio Fane Pineo, Huguette. *Patterns of Chinese Immigration: areas for Research*. MGI. Aug. 1994.

Manrakhan. J. University of Mauritius. Examination of Certain *Aspects of Slavery-Indenture Continum of Mauritius*. Int.Conference. MGI. Oct. 1984.

Miles, F.S.W. Northeastern Univ,.Massachusetts. *Mauritian Decolonization in Comparative Perspective*: The Anglo-French Dimension. MGI, Dec. 1998.

Mohamed, Noriah. Prof. Malaysia. *The Story of five Pandawas. The Javanese and Malay Perspectives*. 3rd International Writers' Conference. Mauritian Writers' Association. August 2004.

Moss, R. Dr. Univ. of Mauritius. Julia Blackburn's "*The Book of Colour: A Search for Identity in 19th Century Mauritius*". MGI. 23-26 June 1999.

Narang, Harish.JNU. *Globalization, Diaspora and Cultural Identity.*

Naz, Virgile, Sir. *Conference sur L'immigration Indienne à la Chambre d'Agriculture*. 18 Nov. 1891.

Organisation Créole et Culture. *La Situation des Créoles de L'Ile Maurice.*

Ramparsad Sheila. Centre for Caribbebean Studies. Univ. of

Warwick, UK. 1998. Copjh@csv,warwick.ac.uk.

Ray Manas. *Bollywood Down Under. Fiji Indian Cultural History and Popular Assertion.*

Riggs, Fred. Diasporas and Ethnic Nations. *Causes and Consequences of Globalization.* Conference of the International Studies Association in Los Angeles, March 16,2000. httpwebsites.soc.hawaii.edu.fred:dinglehtml.

Shamsul, A.B & Hussin Supyan. Institute of the Malay World & Civilization. *One Civilization* in Mauritian Writers' Association Magazine. No 4 August 2004.

Tinkcr, Hugh. *Continuity Beteeen Slavery and Indenture?* Int. Conf. on Indian Labour Immigration. MGI. Oct. 1984.

Vayid, Mohamad. *Unipolar World* in Mauritian Writers' Association Magazine. Issue No 4. August 2004. Vertovec, Steven. Uni. of Oxford. *Transnational social formations- Towards conceptual cross-fertilisation.* (Paper presented at Workshop on Trannational Migration: Comparative Perspectives, Prince to University 30 June. 2001.

Vertovec, S. *Three meanings of diaspora, exemplified among South Asian religions.* Diaspora. 7 Feb.,1999.

Virahsawmy, Raj. *A Form of Liberation. From the Camp to the Village.* Journal of Mauritian.

INDEX